The Visual Encyclopedia of
# NAUTICAL TERMS
# UNDER SAIL

**Principal Advisers**

George P. B. Naish, late Honorary Secretary, The Society for Nautical Research, Greenwich, England

Alan Villiers, Master of the ship *Joseph Conrad*, 1934–36, the *Mayflower* replica, 1956–57, and others

Basil W. Bathe, Assistant Keeper in charge of Water Transport Collections, Science Museum, London, England

Derek Howse, Head of Navigation and Astronomy, National Maritime Museum, Greenwich, England

W. J. Tuck, Lt Cdr RN (Retd)

Alec A. Purves (maritime flags and signals)

**Contributors**

Lt Cdr Peter C. Whitlock, RN, Commanding Officer, HMS *Victory*, Portsmouth, England

Martin Lee BA (Open), Master Mariner (Square Rig Endorsement), Trinity House Pilot, England

Commander W. E. May, RN, former Deputy Director, National Maritime Museum, Greenwich, England

Alan Stimson, Deputy Head of Navigation and Astronomy, National Maritime Museum, Greenwich, England

Anita McConnell, Science Museum, London, England

**U.S. Advisers**

Robert H. Burgess, Curator of Publications, Mariners Museum, Newport News, Virginia

Captain Fred K. Klebingat, Associate Maritime Historian, San Francisco Maritime Museum and B. P. Bishop Museum, Honolulu

Dr John Lyman, Contributor, 'Mariner's Mirror' and 'American Neptune' (North Carolina)

# The Visual Encyclopedia of
# NAUTICAL TERMS
# UNDER SAIL

*Crown Publishers Inc.*
*New York*

Published in the USA in 1978 by Crown Publishers
Inc. New York

Created, designed and produced by
Trewin Copplestone Publishing Ltd., London

© Trewin Copplestone Publishing Ltd. 1978

First published 1978 in Great Britain as
*The Country Life Book of Nautical Terms Under Sail*

Library of Congress Cataloging in Publication Data

Bathe, Basil W.
THE VISUAL ENCYCLOPEDIA OF NAUTICAL
TERMS UNDER SAIL

1. NAVAL ART AND SCIENCE –
DICTIONARIES. I. Villiers, Alan John, 1903 –
Joint Author. II. Title. V23.B32 623.82′2′03

ISBN 0–517–53317–0 77–28560

Colour origination by Positive Plus, London
Phototypesetting and reproduction by
Tradespools Limited, Frome, Somerset, England

Printed in Italy by New Interlitho Spa, Milan

This visual encyclopedia of nautical terms under sail is divided into
twenty main sections. Each of these (with the exception of Sections 1
and 2, which are concerned with basic nautical terms) opens with an
introductory essay setting the subject in perspective.

Every section is divided into sub-sections each of which, for the most
part, falls across two facing pages. Sub-sections are given their
appropriate reference numbers; for example, the second sub-section
of Section 4 is numbered **04.02.**

The terms within each sub-section are usually listed in alphabetical
groups, but Sections 15 to 19, which deal with navigation and related
subjects, are not listed alphabetically. The terms in these sections
require a more systematic listing so as to provide a basic conceptual
understanding of the subject matter. The reader is therefore advised,
when consulting a term in these sections, to read the entire sub-section
in which that term is contained.

Terms used within a definition that are cross-referred to another
definition are shown in small capital letters, thus: BUNTLINE

When the definition of the term is to be found in a different
sub-section, the term is followed by the other sub-section number in
parentheses, thus: BUNTLINE **(04.09)**

If the definition of the term appears in the same sub-section, no
reference number is given.

The alphabetical index at the end of the book lists all the terms,
accompanied by the number of the sub-section in which they are to
be found.

# Contents

"But he, being a man well experienced in the navigation of those seas, bid us all prepare against a storm . . . Finding it was likely to overblow, we took in our sprit-sail, and stood by to hand the fore-sail; but making foul weather, we looked the guns were all fast, and handed the mizen. The ship lay very broad off, so we thought it better spooning before the sea, than trying or hulling. We reeft the fore-sail and set him, we hauled after the fore-sheet; the helm was hard a weather. The ship wore bravely. We belayed the fore-down haul; but the sail was split, and we hauled down the yard, and got the sail into the ship, and unbound all the things clear of it. It was a very fierce storm; the sea broke strange and dangerous. We hauled off upon the lanyard of the whipstaff, and helped the man at helm. We would not get down our top-mast, but let all stand, because she scudded before the sea very well, and we knew that the top-mast being aloft, the ship was the wholesomer, and made better way through the sea, seeing we had sea-room. When the storm was over, we set fore-sail and main-sail, and brought the ship to: then we set the mizen, main-top-sail, and the fore-top-sail. Our course was east-north-east, the wind was at south-west. We got the starboard tacks aboard, we cast off our weather-braces and lifts; we set in the lee-braces, and hauled forward by the weather-bowlings, and hauled them tight, and belayed them, and hauled over the mizen tack to windward, and kept her full and by as near as she would lie."

from *A Voyage to Brobdingnag* by Captain Lemuel Gulliver (1727)

# Acknowledgments

The Publishers gratefully acknowledge permission to reproduce illustrations from the following sources:

Mrs A. Bromley-Martin, 11.02. *The Ashley Book of Knots* © Clifford W. Ashley 1944, 05.13. *HMS Victory, Restoration, Rebuilding and Repair,* A. Bugler (HMSO), 03.09 *tl*, 03.11 *br*, 03.12 *tl*, 04.06 *l*, 04.08 *l*, 05.01, 05.02 *bl*, 06.01 *br*, 06.03 *tl*, 10.03 *br*, 12.13 *tl*. Jonathan Eastland (Ajax News Photos) pages 1, 3, 7, 8; 03.03 *tr*, 03.10, 03.14 *t*, *br*, 03.15 *t*, *br*, 03.17 *l*, 04.01, 04.02 *r*, 04.03 *r*, 04.04 *tr*, 04.05 *tl*, *br*, 04.06 *tr*, 04.09 *r*, 04.12 *tl*, *br*, 12.10 *bl*, 15.12 *br*, 17.05 *br*, 18.02 *bl*. Mary Evans Picture Library, 10.03 *bl*, 10.06 *tr*. Mansell Collection, 03.11 *tr*, 07.01 *bl*, *br*, 10.03 *tr*, 10.06 *br*, 14.02, 14.03 *tr*, 18.02 *tl*, 18.03 *tl*. Meteorological Office (Crown Copyright), 17.05 *l*, *tr*. Museum of London, 09.02 *b*, 09.03 *l*, *br*. National Maritime Museum, page 4; 03.09 *bl*, 03.11 *l*, 03.12 *tr*, 03.15 *l*, 05.02 *tl*, 07.01 *tr*, 07.02 *tl*, 09.02 *c*, 09.03 *tr*, 10.01, 10.02 *l*, *br*, 10.03 *tl*, *cl*, 10.04, 10.05 *r*, 10.06 *l*, 10.07, 10.09 *r*, 11.03 *l*, 12.01 *bl*, 12.02 *r*, 12.04 *bl*, 14.04 *l*, 15.04, 15.05, 17.04 *l*, 18.01 *l*, 18.04 *l*, 18.05, 18.06, 19.01 19.02, 19.03 *bl*, *r*, 19.04 *bl*, *r*, 19.05, 19.06. Radio Times Hulton Picture Library, 02.02 *l*, 02.03 *tr*, 02.04 *tl*, 07.01 *tr*, 14.01 *r*, 14.03 *l*, *br*, 14.04 *br*, 18.03 *bl*, 20.03 *br*. Royal National Lifeboat Institution, 09.01 *l*. Alan Villiers, 02.04 *br*, 04.11 *br*, 05.07, 11.01.

Details from the *Encyclopédie Méthodique* are reproduced from a copy courteously loaned by the Royal Institution of Naval Architects.

Special artwork for this book was drawn by: Gordon Davies, John Gardiner, Len Huxter, Gerald Rose, Mike Strickland, Jane Tamblyn, Bill Ward, Brian Watson.

# Foreword

## by *Basil Greenhill* CMG BA FSA FRHists
### *Director, National Maritime Museum, Greenwich*

There has long been a need for a simple illustrated guide to the old sea terms which are rapidly vanishing beyond the horizon of living memory. The compilation of a full, formal and definitive dictionary of the old language of the sailing ship would be a huge task, needing the combined and co-ordinated services of many scholars. Some progress has in fact been made in several different countries in this direction, but such a dictionary, when it is produced, will be mainly for the specialist historian. What is also needed is an informal and reliable guide to the old sea terms which were a living part of our language until the final demise of the merchant sailing ship in the years between the two world wars, so that the modern layman and woman can easily and readily comprehend something of the ancient and fascinating technology involved with these vessels.

The old sea language was the language of men largely isolated from the normal life of the great majority of their fellows. The evolution of their involved and complex terminology cut them off yet further, and indeed it tended to alienate them from landsmen, who found much of what sailors had to say quite incomprehensible. Many of them applied their everyday terms to things ashore. To take a very simple instance, an 86-year-old master mariner friend of mine who spent forty years at sea in sailing ships, still quite unselfconsciously refers to the boot of my car as the stern locker. A hundred years ago this kind of usage was quite common.

A dictionary of sea terms must be accurate within reasonable bounds of human error, but the language of the sailing ship was a living language right down to its last days and, moreover, the language developed in many different ways in different localities. Terminology acceptable in vessels belonging to one coastal community was not necessarily entirely acceptable in vessels hailing from ports only a few miles away. It is indeed perhaps best that the job of compiling a simple dictionary should not be done academically, but by people who actually depended for their livings on the mutually comprehensible, sensitive and exact use of professional terms. The best and most reliable kind of dictionary is one prepared by men who used the terms themselves when the technology was still alive.

The greater part of this dictionary has been prepared by such men. Martin Lee, Trinity House Pilot, holds a Master Mariner's Certificate of Competence with the now very rare square-rig endorsement, gained in service in the Finnish four-masted barque *Pamir* on her last passages as a merchant sailing vessel in the early 1950s. Alan Villiers, for twenty-five years a Trustee of the National Maritime Museum, is one of the two or three most experienced living merchant sailing ship seamen whose mother tongue is English. Alan Stimson, Deputy Head of Navigation and Astronomy at the National Maritime Museum, was a merchant ship's officer for years before he became a student of the history of science. Edward May, a former Deputy Director of the national Maritime Museum, joined a Royal Navy in 1912 in which the memory of sail was still strong, and which in many ways was closer to the Navy of the mid-nineteenth century than to the Navy of today. Derek Howse, Head of Navigation and Astronomy at the National Maritime Museum, also had a distinguished naval career before he became an historian.

What these and the other distinguished contributors, experts in their fields, have compiled is a thoroughly workmanlike publication which is attractively presented with apt illustrations, not all of them solemn. Allowing for the variations in usage, terminology and dialect to which I have already referred, this is a very useful compendium of terms. You do not have to agree that every definition is perfect. In fact, I have rather enjoyed spotting a few things I think I could have done better myself; within limits, for the reasons I have given, everyone can define their own technical terms and make their own dictionary. Yet I think that everyone concerned in any way with the maritime aspects of human history, or simply interested in that vast subject, will be well advised to have it on their shelves. Is it, after all, so inconceivable that sail in some form may return to the world's sea lanes, should the cost of fuel rise to heights at which it becomes potentially profitable to utilize the wind again in some measure? Should this happen, it would be most interesting to see to what extent the old terms come to be used and adapted to completely different circumstances. And to some extent the old sea language is still alive among sailing people and modern professional seafarers. Although a degree of simplification, formalization and adaptation has taken place to meet greatly changed requirements, many of the terms defined here will be familiar to those who sail for pleasure or follow the profession of seafaring today. They, in particular, may enjoy the examination and discussion of terms no longer in use.

# The Ship – Basic Terms

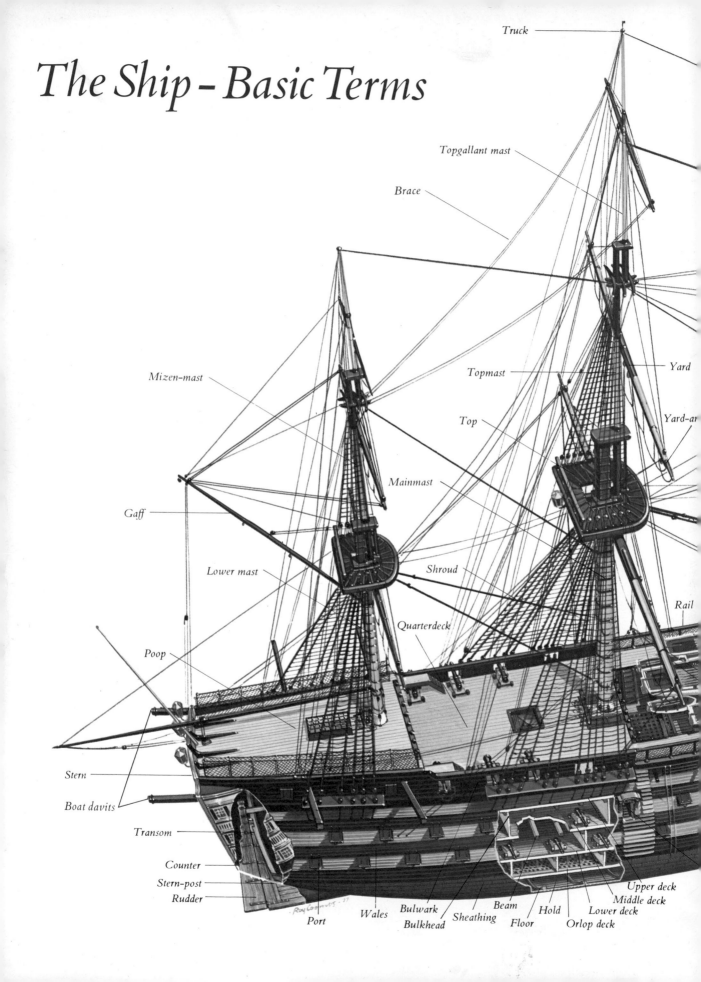

Truck

Topgallant mast

Brace

Mizen-mast

Topmast

Yard

Top

Yard-ar

Mainmast

Gaff

Lower mast

Shroud

Rail

Quarterdeck

Poop

Stern

Boat davits

Transom

Counter

Stern-post

Rudder

Port

Wales

Bulwark

Bulkhead

Sheathing

Beam

Floor

Hold

Upper deck

Middle deck

Lower deck

Orlop deck

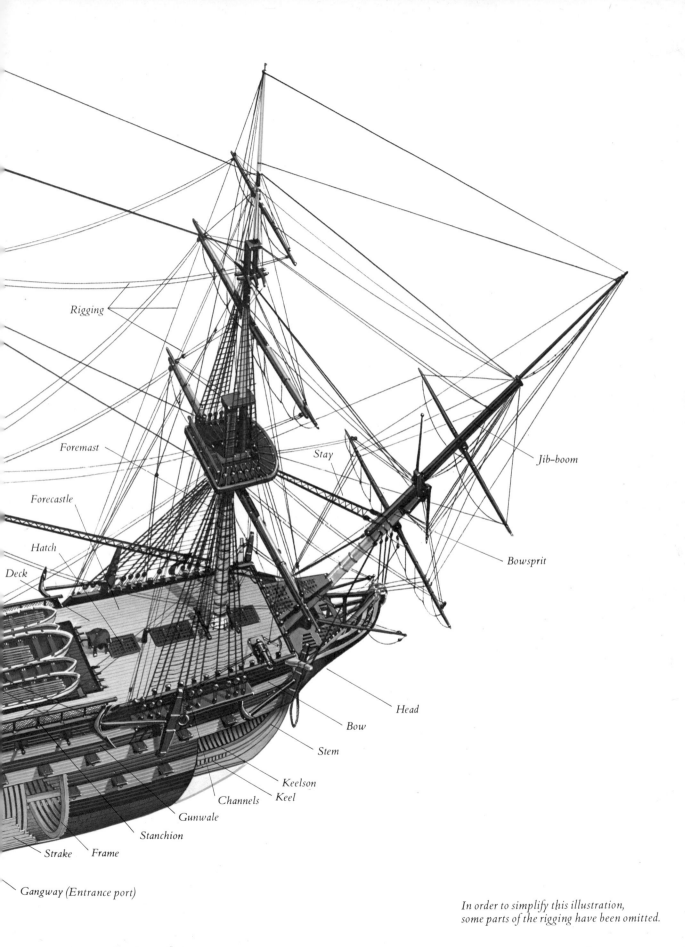

Rigging

Foremast

Forecastle

Hatch

Deck

Stay

Jib-boom

Bowsprit

Head

Bow

Stem

Keelson

Channels        Keel

Gunwale

Stanchion

Strake      Frame

Gangway (Entrance port)

*In order to simplify this illustration,
some parts of the rigging have been omitted.*

# The Ship – Basic Terms

**Aft.** Behind or near the stern of a vessel.

**Beam.** One of a number of thick strong timbers stretching across the ship from side to side, supporting deck and sides and firmly connected to the frames by strong knees. Beams of large ships can be in several pieces. They are generally higher in the middle than at the ends, to allow water to flow off the decks more easily. The longest beam is the midship beam, which is mounted across the widest frame, the MIDSHIP FRAME (03.05).

**Bow.** The forward part of a ship's side, from the point where the planks curve inwards to where they meet at the stem.

**Bowsprit.** Large spar projecting over the stem and carrying sail forward, in order to govern the fore part of the ship and counteract the force of the sails extending aft. The bowsprit is also the principal support of the foremast, since the stays holding that mast are secured to the middle of it.

**Bulkhead.** Vertical partition between two decks of a ship, running either lengthwise or across, forming and separating different compartments.

**Bulwark.** Planking round the edge of the upper deck which stops the sea washing over the decks and prevents members of the crew being swept overboard in high seas.

**Channels,** or **chain-wales.** Broad thick planks projecting horizontally from the side of a ship, used to spread the shrouds and thus provide better support for the masts. The upper ends of the CHAINS (04.08) pass through notches on the outer edges of the channels.

**Counter.** Arched section curving upwards and aft from the WING TRANSOM (03.08) and BUTTOCK (03.01) to the bottom of the stern above.

**Deck.** Planked floor running the length of a ship or only part of it, connecting the sides and covering in the various compartments and holds.

**Floor.** The bottom of a vessel. All that part of the bottom extending horizontally on either side of the keel, and on which the vessel would rest if aground.

**Fore.** In the forward part of a vessel; towards the stem.

**Forecastle.** The forward part of the upper deck, extending from the BEAK-HEAD (03.07) to the foremast or to just aft of the foremast. In merchant ships, the seamen's quarters.

**Foremast.** The forward mast in a vessel with two or more masts.

**Frame.** One of the curved transverse members of a ship's structure, branching outwards and upwards from the keel, determining the shape and strength of the whole, and providing the framework for the ship's planking. Also called a *rib* or *timber*. Each frame comprises several pieces: *floor timber, futtocks* and *top timber*. To give solidity to the frame, it is made up of two parallel sets of pieces, staggered so that the joints do not coincide. Frames set at right angles to the keel are called *square-timbers*; those set at oblique angles are *cant-timbers*. The foremost of the bow frames are called *knuckle-timbers*; at the stern, the aftermost frames are the *fashion pieces*.

**Gaff.** Spar to which the head of a four-sided fore-and-aft sail is attached. One end often has a jaw which fits round the mast.

**Gangway.** Entrance at ship's side, and the bridge leading to that entrance from the shore. Also, any narrow passageway or thoroughfare on board ship.

**Gunwale,** or **gunnel.** Uppermost strake, or run of planking, or a ship's side. In modern usage, also the upper edge of the bulwarks.

**Halyard,** or **halliard.** Rope or tackle used to hoist or lower a sail, yard or gaff.

**Hatch,** or **hatchway.** Rectangular opening in the deck of a ship, providing access from one deck to another, or to the hold.

**Head.** The front or fore part of a vessel, including the bows on each side. The FIGURE-HEAD (03.07) is also often called the head.

**Hold.** Internal cavity of a ship, between lower deck and floor, where cargo, stores and ballast are kept.

**Hull.** The body of a vessel, excluding masts, sails and rigging.

**Jib-boom.** Spar extending the bowsprit and taking a forward stay and the foot of the forward JIB (04.11).

**Keel.** Principal length of timber in a ship, running fore and aft. It is usually the first component laid on the blocks in shipbuilding, and generally comprises several sections SCARFED (03.03) together, bolted and clinched from above. The keel supports and unites the whole structure, and with the attached frames shapes the ship's bottom and holds it together.

**Keelson.** Internal keel mounted over the FLOOR-TIMBERS (03.15) and immediately above the main keel, providing additional structural strengthening.

**Knee.** Angled piece of timber, generally used to connect the beams of a ship with her sides or frames. The vertical member of a knee sometimes forms an oblique angle fore or aft in order to accommodate a gun port or, occasionally, because knees of the right sort were scarce and the angle was governed by the shape of the knee.
Knees are said to be either *lodging* or *hanging*: the former are fixed horizontally in the ship's frame, with one arm bolted to the beam and the other crossing two or three timbers; the latter are fixed vertically.

**Lower deck.** Deck immediately above orlop deck.

**Lower mast.** Bottom part of the mast, erected upon the keel and carrying the other parts of the mast and the lowest sails.

**Mainmast.** Principal mast: chief mast in a two-masted vessel; centre mast in a three-masted vessel; second mast from forward in others.

**Mast.** Vertical or raked spar stepped (mounted) on a vessel's keel and carrying sails, yards, rigging and other gear. A mast can be made of one or more pieces of timber, or of tubular steel, and high masts consist of several masts one above the other.

**Mizen-mast.** Third mast from forward in a vessel with three or more masts.

**Orlop deck.** Lowest deck in a warship, laid over the beams of the hold; used for coiling cables and keeping sails and various stores.

**Poop.** Highest and aftmost deck of a ship.

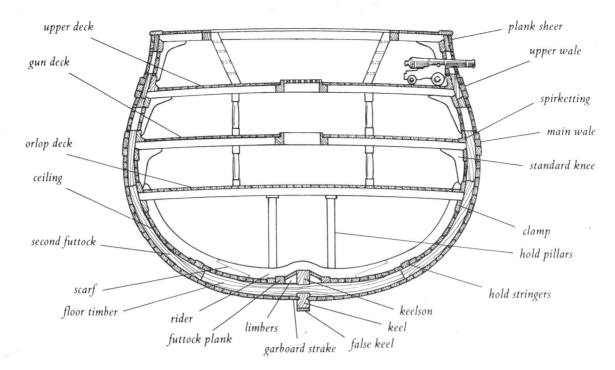

upper deck
gun deck
orlop deck
ceiling
second futtock
scarf
floor timber
rider
futtock plank
limbers
garboard strake
keel
false keel
keelson
hold stringers
hold pillars
clamp
standard knee
main wale
spirketting
upper wale
plank sheer

**Port.** In shipbuilding, an opening in the ship's side for access, loading, ventilation, light and so on.

**Quarterdeck.** That part of the upper deck from the mainmast to right aft or to the poop.

**Rail.** Upper edge of the bulwarks.

**Rigging.** General term for the ropes and wires of a vessel, including those which support the masts and yards (the *standing rigging*) and those used in working the sails (the *running rigging*).

**Rudder.** Hinged device at the stern of a vessel, by which she is steered.

**Sail.** Shaped expanse of fabric used to exploit the force of the wind in order to move a vessel. *Square sails* hang from yards across the line of the keel; *fore-and-aft sails* are set on gaffs or stays, along the line of the keel.

**Sheathing.** Covering, usually of copper, nailed over the outside of a ship's bottom below the WATER-LINE (02.02) to protect it against marine animals and fouling.

**Sheer.** The longitudinal curve of a ship's deck or sides.

**Shroud.** Rope or wire rigging supporting a mast laterally, running from the mast-head to the side of the ship.

**Side.** That part of the hull of a ship between stem and stern, delineated by the gunwale above and the lower edge of the main-wale or the WATER-LINE (02.02) below.

**Spar.** General term for a rounded length of timber, such as a yard, gaff or boom.

**Stanchion.** Small wooden or metal pillar supporting bulwarks, rails, AWNINGS (03.15) and so on. Also, an upright post supporting a deck beam or a bulkhead.

**Stay.** Rope that sustains a mast in a fore-and-aft direction.

**Stem.** Upright component uniting the sides of a vessel at the fore end, rising from the keel, with the bowsprit resting on its upper end. The fore ends of the ship's planking are let into the stem.

**Stern.** The rear end of a vessel.

**Stern-post.** Vertical component mounted on the after end of the keel, terminating the hull and holding the rudder.

**Strake,** or **streak.** Continuous range of planking running fore and aft along a ship's side.

**Top.** Platform across the head of a lower mast. It rests on the CROSS-TREES (04.03) and TRESTLE-TREES (04.03), and helps spread the upper rigging.

**Topgallant mast.** Mast mounted above the topmast; third part of a complete mast. In wooden ships, it is a POLE-MAST (04.01).

**Topmast.** Mast mounted above the lower mast; second part of a complete mast.

**Transom.** One of the beams fastened across the stern-post, strengthening the stern and giving it shape. The *deck transom* holds the ends of the lower-deck planking; above it is the highest transom, the *wing transom*. The curve described by the transoms as they narrow in and down towards the keel is called the *flight* of the transoms.

**Truck.** Circular piece of wood at the top of a mast, often with SHEAVES (05.01) mounted in it for flag halyards.

**Upper deck.** Highest uninterrupted deck.

**Waist.** That part of the ship between quarterdeck and forecastle.

**Wales.** A number of strong planks extending the entire length of a ship's side at different heights, reinforcing the decks and forming the distinctive curves of the ship. The principal wales are the *main-wale* and the *channel-wale*.

**Yard.** Large spar mounted across a mast to carry sails. In a square-rigged ship, it is held in place by SLINGS (04.05) and LIFTS (04.09), and by a TRUSS (04.03) or PARREL (04.03); its angle can be changed with BRACES (04.09) to make the best of the wind. A yard mounted diagonally across a mast is a *lateen yard*.

**Yard-arm.** Outer part of a yard, between the LIFT (04.09) and the tip of the yard.

# General Terms

## Directions

**Abaft.** Further aft, or nearer the stern.

**Abeam.** Running at right angles to the longitudinal line of a vessel.

**Aboard.** Into or within a ship; ALONGSIDE.

**Abreast.** Side by side, parallel to; said of two or more ships which are lying with their sides parallel to each other and their heads equally advanced. Within the ship, abreast means on a line with a beam across the ship, or by the side of any object aboard.

**Afore.** Old term for FORWARD or forward of.

**After.** Relating to that part of a ship which lies in or towards the stern.

**After part.** That part of a vessel or of an area or object on board closer to the stern.

**Aftmost.** Nearest the stern.

**Ahead.** In front of the ship, in the direction towards which her stem is directed.

**Aloft.** Up in the tops, at the mast-heads or anywhere about the higher yards and rigging.

**Alongside.** Side by side; or joined to a ship, wharf or jetty and lying parallel to it.

**Aloof.** At a distance. Old term meaning to WINDWARD.

**Alow.** Below.

**Alow and aloft.** At deck level and above deck level.

**Amidships.** The middle of the ship, either along her length or across her breadth.

**A-port.** Towards the PORT side of a vessel.

**Ashore.** On the shore or land. A ship is ashore when she has run AGROUND (20.01).

**Astern.** Behind the ship.

**Athwart.** Across. In navigation, across the line of a ship's course.

**Athwartships.** Reaching across the ship, from one side to the other.

**Before.** Closer to the forward part of a vessel.

**Below.** Beneath the upper decks.

**Bound.** Said of a vessel leaving port: *outward bound* when leaving the home port; *homeward bound* when heading back. Also used when specifying a destination, as in 'London-bound', 'Frisco-bound' and so on.

*HMS* Triton, *with her yards a-box. Painted in 1797 by Nicholas Pocock*

**Fathom.** Nautical measure equalling six feet (1.828 metres).

**Fore and aft line.** Imaginary line drawn between stem and stern, along the keel.

**Forward.** Relating to that part of a ship which lies in or towards the bows and stem.

**Headmost.** Said of a ship which is furthest ahead of a line or fleet.

**Inboard.** Any part of a ship or end of a fixed piece of equipment that is nearer to the fore-and-aft centre-line.

**Larboard.** Left-hand side of a ship, looking forward. Now supplanted by the term PORT.

**Lay alongside.** To range a ship by the side of another.

**Lee.** That side of a vessel sheltered from the wind, opposite to that from which the wind is blowing. More loosely, any place out of or away from the wind.

**Lee side.** The side facing away from the wind and sheltered from it.

**Leeward.** Away from the wind; on the side sheltered from the wind.

**Midship.** At the middle of the ship – viewed either transversely or longitudinally.

**Midships.** Contraction of AMIDSHIPS.

**Outboard.** In a direction away from the central fore-and-aft line. The outside of a vessel's hull. Also said of anything attached to or projecting outward from the vessel's side.

**Outward bound.** Said of a ship putting to sea from her home port. More generally, said of any ship putting to sea.

**Overboard.** Over the sides of a ship or boat and outside it, in the water.

**Port.** Left-hand side of a ship, looking forward.

**Starboard.** Right-hand side of a ship, looking forward.

**Sternmost.** Said of a ship which is furthest astern of a line or fleet.

**Thwart hawse.** Ahead of another vessel and across her fore-and-aft line.

**Thwartships.** Contraction of ATHWARTSHIPS.

**Weather bow.** Bow on the WINDWARD side of a vessel.

**Weather shore.** The shore lying to WINDWARD of a ship.

**Windward.** Towards the wind; the side from which the wind is blowing.

# Ships and their Gear

*A Derelict*

**Apparel.** Equipment and fittings of a ship that are removable – such as sails, rigging, awnings, anchors and boats.

**Barnacle.** Marine crustacean which attaches itself to ships' bottoms, thus increasing the drag of the hull.

**Bottom.** The bed of a body of water. Also, that part of a ship which is under water when the ship is laden.

**Broadside.** Side of a vessel above the WATER-LINE, as distinguished from her bow or stern. Also, the simultaneous firing of all guns on one side of a warship.

**Cappanus.** Type of sea-worm which adheres to ships' bottoms and attacks them.

**Coffin ships.** Ships which through serious defects or overloading were unseaworthy. Term became obsolete after safety measures were enforced by legislation.

**Cordage.** Collective term for ropes and lines.

**Derelict.** Vessel abandoned at sea by her master and crew, without hope of recovery.

**Foot.** Lower end (of a mast) or lower edge (of a sail).

**Furniture.** The equipment of a ship, such as sails, masts, rigging, anchors, derricks, winches and boats; but not consumable stores, such as fuel or provisions.

**Gear.** Collective term for the ropes, blocks or tackle of a particular spar or sail. More generally, fittings, implements, tools and so on.

**Glory hole.** Space into which miscellaneous gear or even litter and sweepings from the deck are pushed out of sight.

**Irish pendant.** Derogatory nickname for a loose end of rope or twine left hanging and blowing free in the wind. Also, a frayed flag or ensign.

**Kippage.** Old term for the equipment – or equipage – of a ship, which included the personnel aboard her.

**Knuckle.** Sharp angle in a wooden member of a ship's frame. Also, the outer edge of a sharp bend in a jetty or pier-head.

**Rate.** Classification of old sailing warships, in accordance with the number of guns carried. First-rate ships carried 100 or more guns; second-rate 84 or 90 to 100; third-rate 70 or 80 to 84 or 90; fourth-rate 50 or 60 to 70 or 80; fifth-rate 32 to 50 or 60; and sixth-rate less than 32 guns.

**Rig.** The distinctive arrangement of a vessel's masts, spars and sails.

**Sea acorn.** BARNACLE.

**Slug,** or **slugg.** Term used in the seventeenth century for a slow sailing ship.

**Staunch.** Said of a vessel that is well built, sturdy and free of leaks.

**Taunt.** High or tall. Masts are said to be taunt when they are extraordinarily high.

**Taut.** Extended or stretched out; usually applied to a rope or sail.

**Tom,** or **tomm** (vb). To support, or shore up.

**Tommed up.** Supported, shored up.

**Tonnage.** Measure of the the weight of a vessel or of her cargo-carrying capacity.

**Top hamper.** Equipment above the main deck, including upper rigging, spars, tackle and top sails, and all gear aloft.

**Topsides.** That part of a ship's sides above the WATER-LINE or above the upper deck. Colloquially, the term means 'on deck'.

**Tree.** Generally, a wooden beam used as part of a vessel's fittings, as in CHESS-TREES (03.15).

**Water-line.** Horizontal line marked by the surface of the water along the side of a vessel afloat. Its height will vary with the loading.

**Well found.** Well equipped and well supplied with food, stores, grog, spare sails and all other necessities.

**Wooden walls.** Term for sailing warships, which were considered the outer barrier defending England from attack.

*First-Rate Ship*

# Sailing Vessels and their Characteristics

**Abroad.** Said of a flag when hoisted or of the sails of a ship when raised or extended.

**Adrift.** At the mercy of sea and weather; unmoored and not under control.

**Afloat.** Said of a vessel when it is borne on the water. Generally, said of anything floating on the surface.

**All-a-taut.** Said of a ship when she is fully rigged and everything is in place.

**Amain.** At once, suddenly.

**Bring up.** To come to a standstill, by letting go an anchor, by fouling an obstacle or the sea bottom, or by throwing the ship ABACK (12.11), quickly taking way off her.

**By the head.** Said of a ship when her head is lower in the water than her stern.

**By the stern.** Said of a ship when her stern is lower in the water than her head.

**Canting.** The act of turning something over.

**Capsize.** To overturn, so that the vessel's keel is above water and her masts under the surface.

**Cast away.** Said of a ship that has been purposely wrecked, or of a ship-wrecked person.

**Chafe** (vb). To rub or fret the surface of a rope, mast or yard.

**Clear.** Variously applied to weather, coasts, cordage, navigation, and so on. The weather is clear when it is fair and open; a coast is clear when it is free of obstructions or dangers; cables are clear when they are untangled and ready for use.

**Ditch.** Slang term for the sea. Also, to throw overboard.

**Draw.** A vessel is said to draw a given depth of water in order to float. Sails are said to draw when they are steady and well filled with wind.

**Even keel.** Said of a vessel when her keel is horizontal and she DRAWS the same DRAUGHT (03.01) of water both forward and aft.

**Fast.** Said of anything made secure, attached or fixed. To *make fast* is to secure.

*By the head*

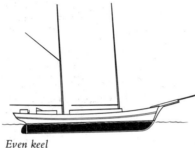

*Even keel*

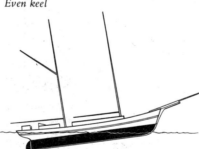

*By the stern*

**Foul.** Unfavourable, entangled, contrary. Thus, a foul wind is one against the direction of a ship's course; a ship's bottom is foul when it is covered with seaweed or barnacles; a harbour or coast is foul when it is rocky, full of shallows or dangerous in other ways; cables are foul when they are twisted round each other; a ship runs foul of another when it entangles itself in the other's rigging.

**Full due.** Expression indicating permanency or finality.

**Galled.** The state of a mast, yard or rope chafed by friction. The most vulnerable spots are often covered with canvas or other materials to protect against galling.

**Go by the board.** Said of a piece of equipment that breaks away from the deck and goes overboard, particularly of a mast that breaks off near the deck.

**Headway.** A vessel's forward movement through the water.

**Hogging.** The result of stress on a vessel's hull causing it to droop fore and aft, while the middle arches.

**Home.** The situation of an object, either when it makes its full effect, or when it is properly lodged in a secure place. In the first sense, sails are hauled home when their clews (lower corners) are extended right down to the yard-arm underneath. In the second sense, goods are home when they are safely and compactly stored in the hold; the anchor comes home when it is freed from the ground and hauled in to the ship.

**House** (vb). To make secure. Said particularly of lowering an upper mast and securing it to the lower mast in anticipation of bad weather; of bringing an anchor hard up to the HAWSE PIPE (03.07); or of running a gun back and securing it.

**Jammed.** Squeezed or wedged tight so that it is immovable; said of RUNNING RIGGING (04.09), items of cargo, and so on.

**Jettison.** To throw goods or equipment overboard in order to lighten a ship in danger of foundering due to heavy seas or any other emergency.

**Kelter.** Good condition, all in order.

**Launch** (vb). To set a newly built vessel in motion down the LAUNCHING WAYS (03.04) and into the water.

**Leak.** Split or breach in the deck, side or bottom of a ship which lets water into the hull. When a leak starts, the vessel is said to have *sprung a leak.*

**List.** Tilt of a vessel to one side or the other.

**Loom** (vb). To appear indistinct and unnaturally large when seen through fog or mist.

**Main.** Principal. Thus, mainmast, mainsail, mainhold, mainland, and so on. Also, the open sea or ocean.

**Open.** Exposed to the wind and sea, with little or no shelter for shipping. Also used of a distant object to which there is unobstructed passage or view.

**Overset** (vb). To turn upside-down; to CAPSIZE.

**Pay** (vb). To daub or cover the surface of any body in order to protect it against wind, weather or water. Materials used for the purpose include tar, pitch, tallow, sulphur, resin and turpentine.

**Sailing.** Using sail as a means of propulsion. Also said of a vessel leaving a point of departure.

**Salvage.** Recovery of a vessel from danger, or of a vessel or her contents from under water. Also, the proportion of the value of a ship or cargo paid on their recovery, based on the extent of the danger and the amount of labour expended.

**Scupper** (vb). To SCUTTLE.

**Scuttle** (vb). To purposely sink a vessel by opening its side or bottom to let in the sea.

**Ship** (vb). To embark a person or to put or receive something aboard ship. Also, to fix something in its place.

**Shipbreach.** SHIPWRECK.

**Shipwreck.** Destruction of a vessel at sea or along a coast.

**Sink** (vb). To drop beneath the surface of the sea or below the horizon; to go to the bottom of the sea; to inflict damage to that effect.

**Split.** The condition of a sail torn apart by a storm or by any uneven strain across its surface. When applied

to a ship, the state of being stranded and BILGED (03.10) on a rock or shore.

**Spring a leak.** To develop a leak.

**Sprung.** Said of a wooden mast or spar which is split or warped out of shape, or of a curved plank in the hull which has broken loose and is projecting outwards beyond the curve of the hull.

**Stability.** The property of a vessel by which she maintains an upright position or returns to that position after heeling over.

**Stable equilibrium.** State of a vessel when she is highly stable and returns to an upright position after heeling over.

**Sternway.** A vessel's movement astern through the water.

**Stove in.** Broken by external force. A boat, cask or barrel is said to be stove in if any plank or stave has been smashed from outside.

**Trim.** Difference between the draughts of a vessel forward and aft, determined by the degree to which she is deeper in the water at the head or at the stern. When applied to sails and yards, the trim is the general arrangement and adjustment calculated to make the most of the wind.

**Turn turtle.** To capsize, to overturn in the water.

**Unstable equilibrium.** State of a vessel which is insufficiently stable and is in danger of capsizing when heeled over.

**Upright.** The condition of a ship when her sides incline neither to right nor to left and are equidistant from the surface of the water.

**Water-borne.** Carried by water; afloat. Particularly said of a vessel which has just left DRY-DOCK (20.02) or which has been refloated after GROUNDING (20.01).

**Waveson.** Cargo or stores left floating on the surface after a vessel has been sunk or wrecked.

**Way.** A vessel's motion through the water.

**Weep** (vb). To leak very slowly.

**Wet.** Said of a vessel that is prone to ship water too readily.

**Wreck.** Vessel damaged by weather, stranding or other causes to such an extent that she is no longer SEAWORTHY (12.01) and is a total loss.

**Wring.** To distort and strain through excessive stress.

*The* Cromdale *wrecked at the Lizard, May 1913*

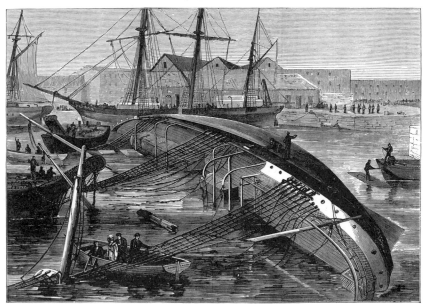

*The iron clipper* Eastminster *capsized in London docks, 1878*

# Sailors' Words

**Before the mast.** Expression used to describe an ordinary seaman or rating. Derived from the past practice of accommodating common sailors in the forecastle while officers were accommodated aft. Thus a common seaman was one who had 'sailed before the mast'.

**Black Book of the Admiralty.** Folio of ancient Admiralty laws and statutes, dating from the thirteenth century to Tudor times.

**Clap on.** To increase power, by adding to the number of purchases used or by using more men. Also, to set more sail.

**Davy Jones.** Legendary demon who takes possession of all men drowned at sea, reputed by some to have been a Welshman who became storekeeper of the underwater realm. Otherwise said to derive from 'Duffy Jonah', duffy being an old Negro word for ghost.

**Davy Jones's Locker.** Davy Jones's domain at the bottom of the sea; the ultimate destination of drowned men and foundered ships.

**Deck passage.** Voyage on deck when no other accommodation is available; undertaken by pilgrims or refugees, or for short voyages.

**Filibuster.** Buccaneer, adventurer. Derives from Dutch *vrijbuiter* – 'freebooter' – an illicit trader or smuggler.

**Hail** (vb). To salute and call to a ship from a distance, either at sea or in port, generally with the help of a megaphone.

**Handsomely.** Slowly and with care; particularly when handling ropes under strain.

**Heave.** To pull strongly on a rope or cable, or to raise an anchor. Also, the rise and fall of the waves.

**Jonah,** or **Jonas.** Someone whose presence on board is thought to bring ill fortune to a ship. Derived from the biblical story of the prophet Jonah.

**Landlubber.** Contemptuous name for a landsman. Also used in a derogatory sense for an inefficient or useless sailor.

**Maiden voyage.** First voyage made

*Jack outwitting Davy Jones*

by a ship after she has undergone all her trials and has been put into regular service.

**Piracy.** Unlawful and forcible wresting of a vessel, her appurtenances or her cargo from the possession of her owners.

**Pompey.** Seamen's nickname for Portsmouth, British naval base on the English Channel. May have derived from the local fire brigade, known as the Pompiers.

**Rally in.** To haul in rapidly.

**Regatta.** Race meeting of yachts and boats. Derived from the traditional Venetian gondola race, still held annually.

**R.N.** Royal Navy.

**R.N.L.I.** Royal National Life-boat Institution.

**R.N.R.** Royal Navy Reserve.

**Roundly.** Smartly and swiftly.

**Salt.** Landsman's name for a sailor. Old term for an old experienced sailor.

**Sea.** A single wave, or waves collectively; a swell; or the direction and condition of the waves or swell in relation to ship or shore. Conditions are regulated by *fetch*, or the distance the waves travel. A *long fetch* produces a *long sea*, where there is a long distance between each wave; while a *short fetch* produces a *short sea*.

**Shipwright.** One skilled in building and repairing ships.

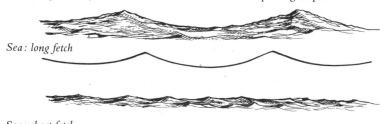

*Sea: long fetch*

*Sea: short fetch*

**Shipyard.** Place, alongside a stretch of water, where ships are built and repaired.

**Slew** (vb). To turn something on its own axis; to swing a boom round.

**Stand by.** To be ready.

**Stave off.** To thrust a boat or a floating object away from a jetty or a ship's side with a spar, boat-hook or similar implement.

**Strike** (vb). To lower or let down a flag, sail, yard or topmast; also applied to lowering the colours as a token of surrender to an enemy. In navigation, to run ashore, or touch bottom when passing over a bank or shallow.

**Swamp** (vb). To cause a vessel to become hopelessly awash with water, though not necessarily enough to sink her.

**Take charge.** When said of an object, to break loose and get out of control.

**Unship.** To remove something from the place in which it was fixed.

**Voyage**. A sea-journey from one port to another. In one sense, a merchant ship's voyage begins on arrival at the loading port and ends twenty-four hours after safely mooring at the discharging port. In another, a crew's voyage consists of a round trip from the home port.

**Working up.** Bringing a vessel to peak efficiency after she has been laid up for repair or REFIT (20.01).

# Building a Ship - Keel to Bulwarks

The design and trade skills that were necessary to create the functional yet gracious form of a ship's hull can be readily appreciated. When considering the heyday of the sailing vessel, there is nevertheless an important aspect that greatly affected design and construction for centuries and yet still resulted in a structure that was a delight to behold. This factor, which applied to all vessels of any size right into the nineteenth century, was the very necessary one of being able to defend the ship and her cargo. The hull had to be secure not only against the ravages of the sea but also against would-be enemies. These two needs were usually incompatible.

The factors that had to be considered by the constructor, in designing the hull, and the builders, in implementing that design, were sea-keeping qualities, forward movement through the water and carrying capacity on a stable platform for both cargo and armament. Shock and stress on the structure resulting from sea action and the firing of guns could be quite tremendous and warranted much careful thought. Consider the building of a 100-gun First Rate ship-of-the-line in the eighteenth century and it gives an idea of the immense construction tasks that faced a work force which was without the mobile crane, tubular scaffolding or electric power. Some 2,000 to 2,500 oak trees were needed to transform a sheer-line drawing into a ship, and they had to be transported to the building site by horse or ox-drawn timber drag over roads which were often little more than tracks. This timber then had to be seasoned by being placed clear of the ground to allow good air circulation and roofed over to protect it from the elements.

These First Rate ships were built principally of oak because it was the best and most plentiful hardwood growing in England and North America within reach of the seaports. But despite the phrase of David Garrick, 'Heart of oak are our ships, jolly tars are our men', oak was not the best shipbuilding material. Teak was appreciated as being the best wood, but what a transportation task! Producing the oak in the right place was a monumental enough undertaking. Oak is prone to heart decay if unventilated, and soon attracts fungal decay and wood-boring insects. Designers did try and contain this decay problem by allowing for ventilation gaps in the inner skin of a ship where possible to allow air to circulate around the frame (ribs) of the structure. Gouging out grooves in the timber to assist the air-flow, called 'snail creeping', was also performed occasionally. An idea of the extent of the decay problem can be gathered from the fact that Britain lost 357 ships during the Napoleonic wars

before taking into account the effects of enemy action — and this was the tally of ships that just beached, foundered and fell apart. 'Those far distant, storm beaten ships, upon which the Grand Army (of Napoleon) never looked, but which stood forever between it and the dominion of the world', to quote Admiral Mayhan, took a tremendous beating from the stress of weather and fungal decay. That Napoleonic war lasted twenty-two years. Admiral Collingwood remarked in a letter in 1803, while he was on blockade duties, that there was 'but a thin sheet of copper between us and eternity', indicating that his ship's hull had rotted away leaving practically nothing but the sheathing.

The master builder who designed these ships and the sawyers and shipwrights who constructed them ingeniously made allowance for the stress to which the whole hull was subjected by the sea. The massive beams which ran athwartships, carrying the decks and holding the frame together, are a good illustration. These beams, some 14 inches square in a large ship, were not in one piece but had a scarf (tapered joint) in the middle of the length of the beam. At this joint the timber was held together by the use of three or four wrought-iron fastenings, in between each of which were little coax pieces or shock pins some 2 inches in diameter and 3 inches long and usually made of lignum vitae (a very hard timber) to take shock and prevent the fastenings from sheering.

The fastenings used in building the ship in the seventeenth and early part of the eighteenth century were generally of wrought iron, with wooden tree-nails or trunnels, but problems arose with this method of fastening after an experiment by the British Admiralty in 1761. This experiment concerned the protection of ships' hulls. Great damage was done to the hull by the teredo worm, which infested the water in warm latitudes, and by the gribble worm in temperate latitudes. Both worms bore into the hull of the ship. Protection was given to some extent by sheathing the hull with pine below the water-line and renewing it at a subsequent refit – hopefully before the worm had reached the oak planking of the hull. The successful experiment of 1761 substituted a series of small copper sheets for the pine sheathing to deter the worm and increase the speed of the vessel by discouraging marine growth. This however led to a new problem – the copper reacted when in contact with the head of a wrought-iron fastening and it became necessary to substitute copper fastenings for wrought-iron ones below the water-line. This was a massive undertaking, and resulted in a sharp rise in the price of copper. A ship-of-the-line needed something in the order of 17 tons of copper to make 4,000 sheets, and 30 hundredweight of copper nails to fasten the sheathing alone.

Picture the scene when building a ship-of-the-line in the mid-eighteenth century. Construction was in a dry dock because of the size and weight of the hull. The timber came from many countries in the south of England and some even from the continent of Europe because English oak stocks were being exhausted. Baltic oak in particular was thought to be more resistant to salt water than English oak and tended therefore to be used below the water-line. A Royal Dockyard would have some 2,000 men employed on a six-day week. Shipwrights, caulkers, oakum boys, joiners, carpenters, scavel men, pitch heaters, sawyers and labourers were engaged on or associated with hull work. Nearly one-third of this force would be shipwrights. Wages were around three shillings a day plus an overtime allowance – these were quite good wages at that time. The keel, a 20-inch-square piece of English elm about 150 feet long, made from six or seven trunks, would first be laid on the blocks. The keelson, dead-wood and frames would soon follow. Timber would be bent to the required shape by placing a length so that it extended over a pit in which a fire was then lit. Water would be poured onto the timber and weights applied until the wood bent to the required curve. This work would be done in a steam kiln today.

The hull was all the better for being allowed to stand 'in frame' for some time, for this enabled the decay, soon apparent in unseasoned timbers, to be seen and rectified. The ship at this stage would look something like the skeleton of an upturned whale. Frames were placed very close together to give adequate strength, and the horizontal planking would then be fitted as inner and outer skins to the structure. Beams were held in place by a hanging knee in the vertical plane and a lodging knee in the horizontal plane. These knees were grown to shape and came from the stubby oak trees with great sweeping limbs that were found in parklands and known generally as 'compass oaks', since their limbs extended through all points of the compass. The grown shape was necessary for strength. By the early 1800s these knees were in short supply, and in consequence a change became necessary. The hanging and lodging knee method of securing a beam at the ship's side gave way to the use of a chock on the underside of the beam where it joined the ship's side, and this received extra support from an iron diagonal shape known as an iron knee, fitted on either side of the beam at each end.

Another evolution during this period, which although not a major one certainly altered the lines of a ship for the onlooker, concerned the stern. During the eighteenth century the sterns of ships of war had beautiful open galleries or walk-ways, but towards the end of the century sterns closed in with sash windows became the acceptable design. Even so, much thought went into beauty of design and a tremendous amount of correspondence on stern windows was exchanged between the Navy Board and the Royal Dockyards before a functional elegance was achieved.

The early part of the nineteenth century saw the gradual disappearance of the elaborate basket-work beak head under the bowsprit; in its place came the the much more practical round bow designed by Robert Sepping. This was now almost the end of the era of the beautiful wooden wall. These great ships, which had a maximum speed of probably 6 knots (the frigate might make 11 knots, which was the mach one of the day), were now changing. Composite construction – timber cladding on an iron frame – was now the acceptable design. The last major warship action under sail was the Battle of Navarino in October 1827 when a combined British-French-Russian fleet defeated a Turco-Egyptian fleet during the Greek War of independence. There was still one short span of the graceful sailing ship era left to come, marked by the slender fast hull of the clipper carrying tea, grain and wool on the romantic Australia and China runs. Armament no longer had to be taken into account for a merchant vessel.

From this time onwards, the steam age rapidly altered the hull. The boilers had to be accommodated, along with the funnel and the associated paddle-boxes or screw. The interim stage of steam as a secondary means of propulsion did not last long. The expression 'up funnel and down screw' was of quite short duration. The 'iron clad' and the 'Dreadnought' were soon to be the way of the world at sea.

The shipwright working on the hull of a ship with his adze also had to change with the times. The thirteen miles of watertight seams for one ship's hull were no longer needed, nor the 3,000 feet of spar timber required to make masts and yards.

The shipwright now deals less with wood than with metal, but the names associated with parts of a ship's hull from the great age of sail still live on. The lower-deck gun-ports of a ship-of-the-line, so close to the water that most of the time at sea the guns were run in and the lower gun ports closed tight shut, lashed and caulked, have disappeared. The eyes, the hawse, the forecastle, the quarterdeck and so on, these names survive and are understood by those who go down to the sea in ships and pursue their business in great waters.

PETER WHITLOCK

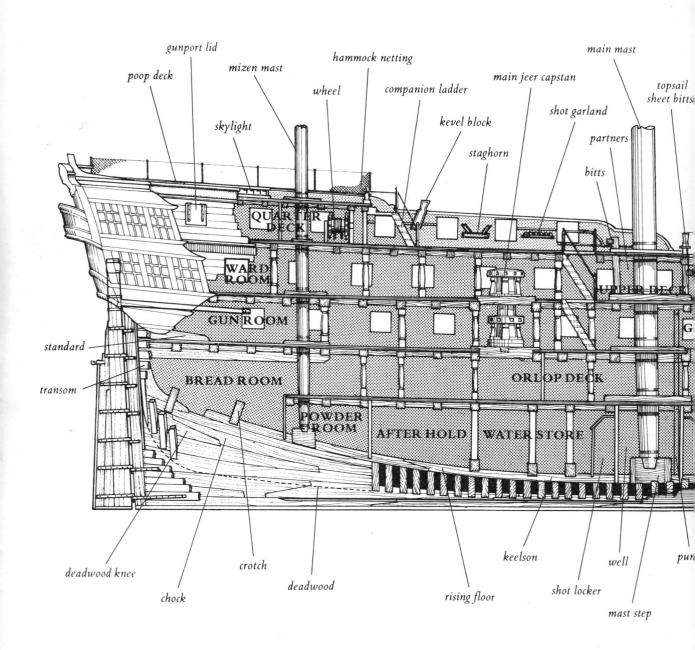

gunport lid

poop deck

mizen mast

hammock netting

wheel

skylight

companion ladder

kevel block

staghorn

main jeer capstan

shot garland

main mast

topsail
sheet bitts

partners

bitts

QUARTER DECK

WARD ROOM

GUN ROOM

standard

transom

BREAD ROOM

UPPER DECK

ORLOP DECK

POWDER ROOM

AFTER HOLD

WATER STORE

G

deadwood knee

chock

crotch

deadwood

rising floor

keelson

shot locker

well

mast step

pur

**Cross-section of a Representative Ship**

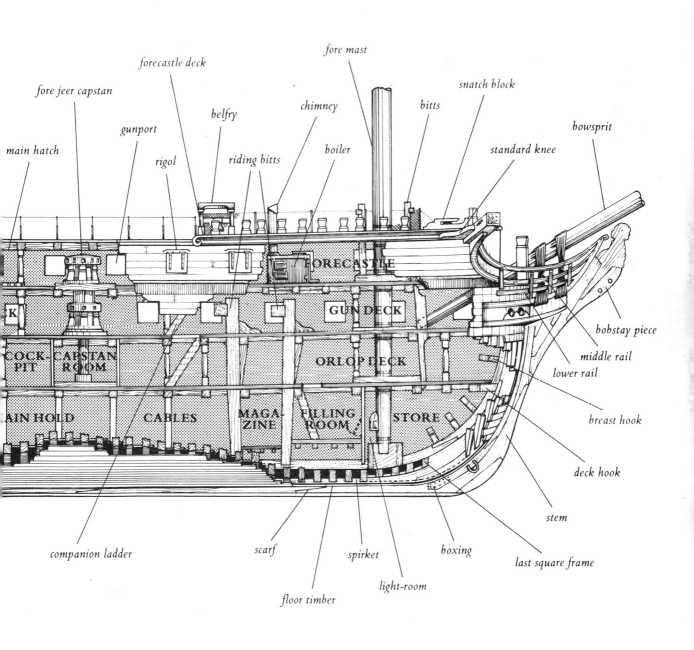

fore mast

forecastle deck

fore jeer capstan

snatch block

belfry

chimney

bitts

gunport

bowsprit

boiler

standard knee

rigol

riding bitts

main hatch

FORECASTLE

GUN DECK

K

bobstay piece

COCK-
PIT

CAPSTAN
ROOM

ORLOP DECK

middle rail

lower rail

AIN HOLD

CABLES

MAGA-
ZINE

FILLING
ROOM

STORE

breast hook

deck hook

companion ladder

scarf

spirket

boxing

stem

last square frame

light-room

floor timber

# Planning and Models

**Bluff bowed.** Said of vessels with broad and clumsy bows, that push through the water rather than cut through it.

**Boatswain's pride.** Slight forward inclination of a ship's mast.

**Breadth.** The measurement of a ship's width.

**Breadth line.** Line drawn fore and aft along the upper ends of the TOP-TIMBERS (03.05).

**Broken-backed.** State of a ship structurally so weakened, through age, accident or strain, that both ends droop.

**Build.** The particular form or construction of a vessel which distinguishes her from others of a different class, construction or nation. For instance, a ship can be frigate-built, CARVEL-BUILT (03.03), English-built, and so on.

**Builders' old measurement.** Method adopted in Britain in 1773, by which the tonnage rating of a vessel was calculated. The formula was:

$$\frac{\text{length} - 3/5 \text{ breadth} \times (\text{breadth} \times \frac{1}{2} \text{ breadth}}{94}$$

**Buttock.** The convex part of a ship under the stern.

**Buttock lines.** In ship design, longitudinal sections of the hull parallel to the keel and taken at uniform intervals from it.

**Camber.** The transverse arching of a ship's deck, which is higher in the middle than at the sides so that water will flow off.

**Capacity plan.** Plan of a vessel showing the capacities of its holds, tanks and other cargo-carrying spaces.

**Cargo plan.** Vertical or horizontal diagram of a vessel's cargo spaces emphasizing its holds, tanks, bunkers and containers.

**Clean lines.** Said of a vessel which has a fine ENTRANCE (03.07) into the water and attractive lines in her design.

**Clipper bow.** Term for a bow which curves forward above the water-line.

**Clipper built.** Said of any vessel with a concave bow, fine lines and raked masts.

**Close-lined.** Said of a vessel or its holds when the internal planking is so close to the sides that there is no air space.

**Cod's head and mackerel tail.** Said of a vessel with bluff bows and a narrow, tapered stern.

**Cutting-down line.** Curved line forming the upper side of the FLOOR TIMBERS (03.05) amidships and continuing to the stem and stern over the DEAD-WOOD (03.06), representing the curve on which the keelson lies.

**Dead flat.** Point marking the MIDSHIP FRAME (03.05) which effectively divides the fore half of the ship from the after half.

**Dead rise.** Line on the body plan showing the angle that the MIDSHIP FRAME (03.05) makes with the horizontal plane of the keel. It is expressed by the number of inches rising above the base line at half breadth.

**Dead-work.** Old name for the part of a ship which is above water when she is laden. See also FREEBOARD.

**Displacement.** Amount of water displaced by a vessel, which can be expressed either as weight (of the vessel) or as volume (of the immersed portion of the vessel).

**Draught.** Depth of water needed to float a particular ship, measured from bottom of keel to WATER-LINE (02.02).

**Draught marks.** Figures cut into the stem and stern posts and picked out in paint, used to determine a vessel's DRAUGHT and adjust her trim.

**Fair curve.** In delineating ships, a winding line whose shape varies according to the part of the vessel it is meant to describe. The curve is not answerable to any of the figures of conic section, although it occasionally partakes of them all.

**Fairing.** Correcting a vessel's plans before building begins.

**Fall home, or falling home.** See TUMBLE HOME.

**Fall out.** Said of a vessel's sides when they slope upwards and outwards.

**Fine lines.** Describes a vessel with a fine ENTRANCE (03.07) and narrow beam.

**Freeboard.** Distance between the upper deck and the water-line.

**Half breadth plan.** Plan from a vessel's centre line to one of its sides, detailing bow, buttock and water lines at various draughts.

**Heeling experiment.** Operation which entails deliberately causing a vessel to HEEL (12.06) over in order to check her ability to right herself.

**Hogging strain.** The strain which causes a vessel to droop stem and stern and so break her back.

**Inclination of ship.** Angle of a vessel's LIST (02.03) from the vertical.

**Initial stability.** The ability of a vessel, when in a vertical position, to resist forces which would cause her to HEEL OVER (12.06).

**Level lines.** Lines drawn parallel to the keel, delineating horizontal sections of a ship.

**Light draught.** Condition of a vessel which is carrying no cargo and has minimum DRAUGHT.

**Load draught.** Distance from the bottom of the keel to the water-line at a particular load.

**Longitudinal stress.** Any form of strain that is liable to distort the longitudinal shape of a vessel or any longitudinal member in its construction.

**Main breadth.** The greatest distance between any two opposite frames in the hull of a vessel.

**Mean draught.** Figure reached by dividing the sum of the forward and after draughts of a vessel by two.

**Midship bend.** MIDSHIP SECTION.

**Midship body.** That thwartship section of a vessel's hull which is more or less constant in shape and dimensions.

**Midship section.** The broadest part of the hull, formed by the MIDSHIP FRAME (03.05) and adjoining frames of the same breadth.

**Mould.** Thin, flexible piece of timber used by shipwrights as a pattern for the frames and other curved pieces. The *bend-mould* determines the convexity of the timbers; the *hollow-mould*, their outer concavity, where they curve in and down towards the keel, particularly at the ends of the ship. The form given the timbers by this pattern is called their *bevelling*.

**Moulded depth.** Vertical depth of a vessel measured between two imaginary parallel planes passing through the uppermost deck beams at the vessel's sides and through the keel.

**Moulding.** The correct shaping of a vessel's frames and timbers when the vessel is being built.

**Mould loft.** Covered area in a shipyard where the MOULDS for the various parts of a vessel are prepared.

**Profile draughts.** Two SHEER PLANS giving schematic profiles of the ship: one details the vessel's layout, the other the layout of her fittings.

**Proportional lengths.** The correct lengths of masts and spars in relation to a vessel's dimensions.

**Rake.** The projection of a ship, at stem or stern, beyond the ends of the keel; also, the inclination of the masts forward or aft from the perpendicular.

**Reserve buoyancy.** The buoyancy that keeps a vessel's watertight deck above the level of the load water-line (see LOAD LINES 07.01).

**Ribband lines.** The fore-and-aft sections of a vessel which lie at an angle to the keel.

**Rising line.** See DEAD RISE.

**Round ribbed.** Describes a vessel with a curved TUMBLE HOME.

**Sheer plan.** Drawing showing the layout of a vessel's fore-and-aft, thwartship, horizontal and vertical sections.

**Swim.** The overhanging portion at bow or stern which, the more the ship is loaded, increases her water-line and hence her buoyancy.

**Thames measurement.** Method of measuring a yacht based on her THAMES TONNAGE.

**Thames tonnage.** Method of calculating the tonnage of a yacht by the formula

$$\frac{B^2(L-B)}{188}$$

where B is the beam and L the length in feet.

**Tipping centre.** The point along the fore-and-aft centre-line at which the ship will tip if her TRIM (02.03) be altered.

**Tons burden.** The burden or tonnage of a ship is that weight which is required to bring the ship down from the *light water-line* to the *load water-line* (see LOAD LINES 07.01). This will depend on the volume of the timber and other materials of which the ship is constructed. Tons burden may be found by calculating the number of cubic feet multiplied by 74 and divided by 2,240 to give the tonnage.

**Tons per inch.** That number of tons which, when loaded into a vessel, increases its DRAUGHT by one inch.

**Topside line.** Sheer line drawn along the upper edge of the gunwale.

**Tread.** The length of the keel.

**Tumble home.** Inward slope of a ship's sides as they rise from the broadest point to the upper deck.

**Underwater body.** That portion of the hull which is below the water-line at a given DRAUGHT.

**Volume of displacement.** Cubic measurement expressing the amount of water displaced by the ship.

**Wall-sided.** Said of a ship whose sides are vertical, rather than inward-curving.

**Waterplane.** Theoretical horizontal section through a ship's hull at the water-line, representing her outline at a given DRAUGHT.

**Wetted surface.** That external part of a vessel's hull which is beneath the water when she is afloat.

**Whaleback.** Term used to describe a ship whose deck has a steep CAMBER.

*Profile draughts*

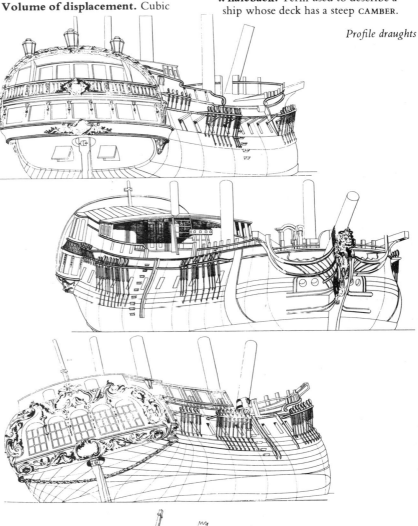

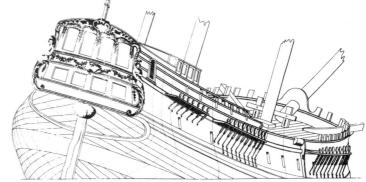

# Materials

**Barnacle paint.** Early type of anti-fouling paint used to discourage the growth of weeds and barnacles.

**Batten.** Thin piece of wood used for various purposes. Battens in the form of long narrow laths are nailed over tarpaulin edges at the sides of a hatch to keep water out in a storm..

**Baulk.** Heavy beam used in the building of wooden vessels, extending from side to side of the vessel and supporting the deck planks.

**Blare.** Mixture of tar and animal hair used for CAULKING (03.03) deck planks and seams.

**Bolt.** Iron or copper pin used in ship-building, either to fasten several members of a ship's frame solidly together, or to fix any movable object for a particular purpose. The first kind have flattened small round heads and are secured by placing a washer over the end and driving a flat iron wedge (a *forelock*) through a narrow hole in the bolt. Other bolts have either large round heads or eyes, with or without attached rings. *Rag bolts* do not go right through the components and, since they are barbed, are self-securing. *Fender bolts*, used to protect the planks of a ship from chafing, have large round protruding heads.

**Compass timber.** Wood that is naturally curved or bent, and can therefore be used for various parts of a ship's construction.

**Deck nail.** Six-inch iron or copper nail used to secure the deck planking to the beams beneath.

**Forelock.** Small, flat metal wedge driven through a hole in the end of a bolt or shackle pin to fix it firmly in place and prevent its drawing out.

**Grown spar.** Spar made in one piece, from a single tree.

**Hook bolt.** Bolt with a hooked head, used for various attachments.

**Oakum.** Substance made from old ropes unravelled, loosened and picked apart. Principally used in caulking seams, planks and so on.

**Ochre.** Type of red chalk once used by shipwrights for marking timber.

**Pitch.** Dark resinous substance distilled from tar, and used in caulking seams.

**Pledget.** Length of OAKUM used in caulking deck or plank seams.

**Rag bolt.** Bolt with jagged notches across its shank which prevent it drawing out of the timber.

**Ribbing nail.** Large copper or iron nail used for fixing RIBBANDS (03.05) to the frames of a vessel.

**Roove.** Small copper washer over which the nail ends in CLINKER-BUILT (03.19) vessels are flattened to make a firm fastening.

**Rosebur.** Another name for ROOVE.

**Scantling.** Any piece of timber of a particular standard square-section.

**Scupper nail.** Nail with a short shank and a large head.

**Shake.** Shipwrights' name for a crack or rent in timber caused by the sun or weather.

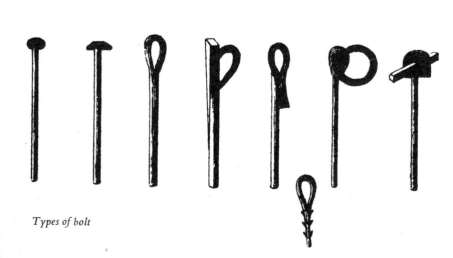

*Types of bolt*

**Shakes.** Shipwrights' term for unseasoned timber that is badly split and is unfit for use.

**Sheathing nail.** Cast nail of copper and tin alloy, used to fasten copper sheathing to the hull of a wooden vessel.

**Tar, or Stockholm tar.** Blackish liquid gum extracted from pine trees and used to coat the sides of ships and boats, and their rigging and yards, in order to protect them against the weather.

*Compass timber*

**Tarpaulin.** Canvas treated with tar or with other waterproofing materials; used to cover hatchways and in other places where protection against sea and weather is needed.

**Tarpaulin canvas.** Pliable strong coarse canvas, made from second-quality yarns and covered with tar or paint to render it waterproof.

**Timber.** Large piece of wood used in building a ship. More particularly, a frame or rib.

**Treenail.** Cylindrical wooden pin used to fix a ship's planks to its frames. Treenails usually measure one inch in diameter for 100 feet of the vessel's length. They swell with moisture when the ship is afloat, thus making a firm fitting.

**Wring bolt.** Bolt employed during construction of a wooden ship to bend a strake into position and hold it until it can be permanently fastened.

# Tools and Techniques

*Auger*

**Auger.** Tool used by a carpenter for boring holes.

*Caulking Iron*

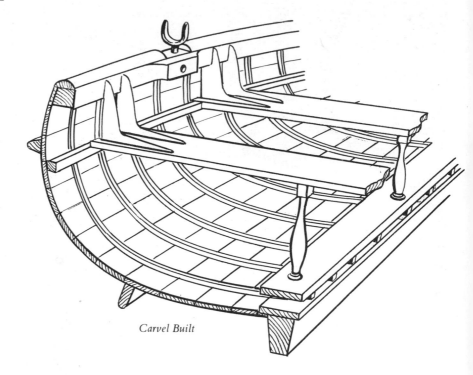

*Carvel Built*

**Caulking iron.** Chisel-shaped iron used for hammering OAKUM (03.02) into a ship's seams or between deck planks.

**Caulking mallet.** Wooden mallet with a short handle, wedge-shaped at the hammerhead, used to strike a CAULKING IRON or REEMING IRON.

**Chinsing iron.** Caulker's tool with a curved lower edge scored with a groove, used to force cotton or OAKUM (03.02) into seams in planking.

**Half breadth staff.** Wooden rod used for measuring a vessel's beams; marked in half lengths of beams.

**Mallet.** Small heavy wooden hammer, with its striking faces often ringed with iron, used on ships by caulkers, riggers, sailmakers and shipwrights. Also called a *beetle*.

**Maul.** Heavy wood or iron hammer.

**Overcast staff.** Scale or measure used by shipwrights to determine the difference between the curves of timbers at the ship's broadest points and those at stem and stern.

**Planking clamp.** Clamp which holds a plank to a frame until it is fastened.

**Pole-axe.** Old boarding weapon consisting of an axe-head backed by a curved spike and held by a short wooden handle. The spike was used to get a grip on the sides of a ship or on masts, and the axe-head to slash rigging and for use against the enemy.

**Reeming beetle.** Heaviest mallet used in CAULKING (03.03). It is fitted with soft steel rings at the striking faces and is used for opening up the seams so that OAKUM (03.02) or cotton can be driven into them.

**Reeming iron.** Iron chisel used to open up seams in the planking, usually used in conjunction with a REEMING BEETLE.

**Ripping iron.** Long-handled tool resembling a two-tined fork with the prongs bent at right angles. Used for tearing the wood and copper sheathing off a vessel's bottom.

*Maul*     *Mallet*

**Rising square.** Square which indicates the upward sweep of a vessel's lines at any given part of the vessel.

**Rooving iron.** Small tool, rather like a hollow punch, which holds a ROOVE (03.02) over a nail end for fastening.

**Wring staff.** Wooden spike used in the fixing of WRING BOLTS (03.02).

**Bearding.** The process of removing wood from a vessel's hull to modify or improve its lines.

**Bevel.** (vb). To hew a timber with the proper regular curve, according to a mould laid along one of its surfaces.

**Carvel built.** Said of vessels which are built with the planking running fore and aft but built edge to edge and not overlapping as in CLINKER-BUILT (03.17) boats. The hull of a carvel-built vessel is therefore smooth and flush. The word *carvel* is believed to have originated from *caravel*, an early type of shallow-draught, two to three masted vessel developed by the Portuguese.

**Caulk** (vb). To make the seams of a wooden ship's decks or sides water-tight by driving in OAKUM (03.02) or some other fibre, and covering it with hot melted pitch or resin.

**Chinse** (vb). To stop a seam or crack with OAKUM (03.02) as a temporary expedient when CAULKING is not immediately possible.

*Shipwrights*

**Close butt.** Said of a joint in a vessel's timbers so well made that CAULKING is unnecessary.

**Coaking.** Method of joining spars, yards or timbers by SCARFING a projection on the end of one piece into a corresponding recess in the end of the other.

**Dub** (vb). To finish off a timber or a spar by smoothing it.

**Dumb fastening.** Temporary fastening holding a plank or a strake in position until it is permanently fastened.

**Fair** (vb). To adjust a member or unit of a vessel's construction to its correct shape or dimensions.

**Fair in place.** To FAIR an item without moving it from its place.

**Fay** (vb). To fit any two pieces of wood together so that they form a close join. A plank is said to fay to the timbers when it bears or lies closely along all the timbers.

**Hook and butt.** Joint made in a vessel's planking or timbers by SCARFING.

**Horsing.** Caulking the seams in a vessel's sides.

**Let in.** To fix a suitably shaped part of one piece of timber into a corresponding cavity in another.

**Rabbet.** Deep groove or channel cut in a piece of timber to receive the edge of a plank.

**Reconcile** (vb). To join a vessel's timbers in such a manner that the curve of the hull is smooth and unbroken.

**Ribband carvel.** Method of construction which is CARVEL BUILT but with battens running fore and aft over the seams inside the hull.

**Rip** (vb). To pull the old caulking out of a seam before re-caulking.

**Rollers.** Cylindrical timbers placed under boats in dockyards or under heavy loads in order to facilitate moving them.

**Scarf** (vb). Method of joining the ends of two pieces of timber, by tapering or bevelling them so that they overlap without increasing thickness at the joint. When two pieces are butted together and another piece is fastened across the joint, this is called *scarfing the timbers*.

**Staunching.** Process of filling a boat or any wooden container with water so that the wood swells, thereby closing the seams.

**Stop** (vb). To plug a leak in a seam or joint.

**Strap.** Plate secured across a joint in wood or metal to give it added strength.

**Syphering.** Lapping one bevelled edge of a plank over another in such a manner that both make a plain surface at the join.

# Framing

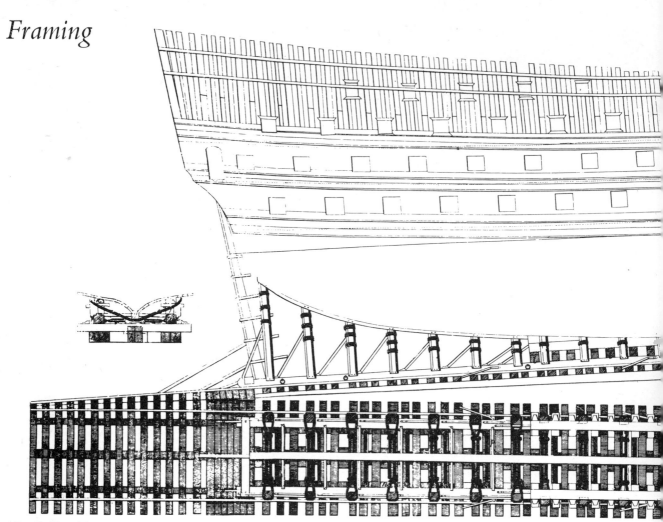

*Detail of launching ways*

**Bilgeway.** Fundamental part of the CRADLE supporting the ship until its launching: a lengthwise timber running under the ship's BILGE (03.10).

**Bolt strake.** Plank of a vessel's hull to which the beams were bolted.

**Building-slip.** Inclined structure on which a ship is built.

**Camber keel.** Keel that is of greater depth at bow and stern than in the middle.

**Cradle.** Framework which supports a ship while she is being built or while she is otherwise out of the water.

**Crotch.** Angled timber mounted on the end of the keel, where the hull narrows. Also, the name of a forked wooden or metal support for a boom or spar.

**Dagger.** Piece of timber used to support the SHORES holding a vessel on the BILGEWAY.

**Dagger plank.** Piece of timber joining SHORES and stepping up pieces in a vessel's launching CRADLE.

**False keel.** Second keel fitted underneath a vessel's principal keel in order to protect it should the vessel run aground.

**Heel.** Junction of the after end of the keel and the lower end of the stern-post.

**Heel knee.** Timber connecting the keel to the stern-post.

**Hog frame.** Strong fore-and-aft frame meant to prevent the vessel from HOGGING (02.03).

**Keel staple.** Iron or copper staple which fastens the FALSE KEEL and the keel together.

**Launching ways.** Heavy timbers over which the CRADLE slides when a vessel is launched.

**Rockered.** Describes a keel which increases in depth as it sweeps aft. Yacht keels are built thus to give them greater stability.

**Shore.** Prop or large stanchion fixed under a ship's sides or bottom, to support her while she is on the stocks or aground.

**Skeg.** Wooden knee connecting keel and stern-post and strengthening the joint between them.

**Spur.** Timber prop between BILGE (03.10) of vessel under construction and BILGEWAY.

**Stocks.** Structure on which the ship and her launching CRADLE are built. The stocks slope down in the direction of launching.

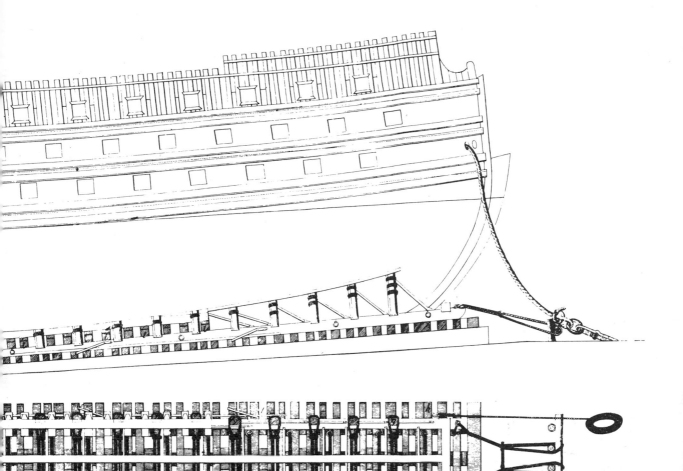

*Building-slip and stocks*

# Framing

**Cant-frames.** The frames at each end of the vessel. They are canted, set at an oblique angle, rather than set at right angles to the keel. The upper ends of those at the bows incline towards the stem, those in the after part incline towards the stern-post.

**Cross pawl.** Heavy baulk of timber used to temporarily hold the frames of a wooden vessel in position while it was being built.

**Cross timber.** That part of the frame of a wooden ship which crosses the keel at right angles with its centre fixed upon it; a FLOOR-TIMBER.

**Ekeing.** Piece of timber used to lengthen a supporting beam or timber. Hence the expression 'to eke out'.

**Floor head.** Upper extremity of a FLOOR-TIMBER.

**Floor hollow.** Concave curve formed by the upper edge of a FLOOR-TIMBER.

*Futtocks and timbers of a man-of-war*

**Floor-timber, or floor.** Lowest section of a frame, placed immediately across the keel (between it and the keelson). The bottom of the ship is formed upon the floor-timbers.

**Futtock.** One of the middle sections making up a frame, between the FLOOR-TIMBER and TOP-TIMBER. 'Futtock' is probably a corruption of 'foot-hook', referring to the 'foot' of the timber and the shape of the piece.

**Futtock timbers.** Middle sections between the upper and lower FUTTOCKS of a frame.

**Half beam.** Beam cut to allow for a HATCHWAY (01.01).

**Half floor.** Timber extending from the keel to the bottom of the second FUTTOCK.

**Half timber.** Short FUTTOCK used in vessels where the bottom is not flat but rounded or angled.

**Joggled timber.** Frame shaped in such a way that each attached strake slopes outwards, giving the planking the appearance of being CLINKER-BUILT (03.17), though the planks do not overlap.

**Knuckle-timbers.** The foremost CANT-FRAMES, in the ship's bows.

**Long timber, or long top-timber.** Single timber among the CANT-FRAMES stretching from the DEAD-WOOD (03.06) to the head of the SECOND FUTTOCK and forming a floor.

**Midship beam.** Longest beam in a vessel's MIDSHIP BODY (03.01).

**Midship frame.** The broadest and largest frame of a ship.

**Navel futtock.** The lowest FUTTOCK in the MIDSHIP FRAME of a vessel.

**Rib.** Frame or timber.

**Ribbands.** Long, flexible strips of timber nailed across the outside of the frames from stem to stern-post while the ship is being built, to keep the frames in place.

**Rising floor.** The fore-and-aft upward sweep of a vessel's FLOOR TIMBERS.

**Rising wood.** Timber worked into the underside of a FLOOR-TIMBER and into the keel, which holds the keel firm.

**Room and space, or timber and room.** The distance between the moulding edges of two adjoining frames, which must always contain the breadth of two frames and sometimes two or three inches between them.

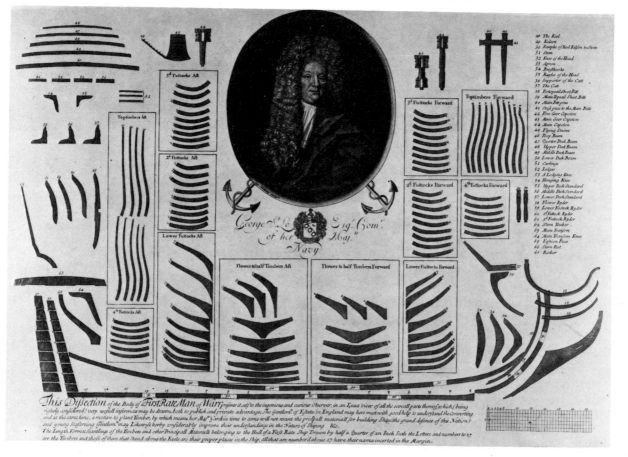

**Rung.** Lowest timber in a frame.

**Rung-head.** FLOOR HEAD.

**Second futtock.** The section of a frame second from the keel.

**Spirket.** Space between FLOOR-TIMBERS.

**Timber and room.** ROOM AND SPACE.

**Timber head.** Continuation of a frame above deck level, serving as a bitt for belaying ropes. Sometimes the head was carved as a decoration.

**Top-timber.** Topmost component of a frame, above the FUTTOCKS.

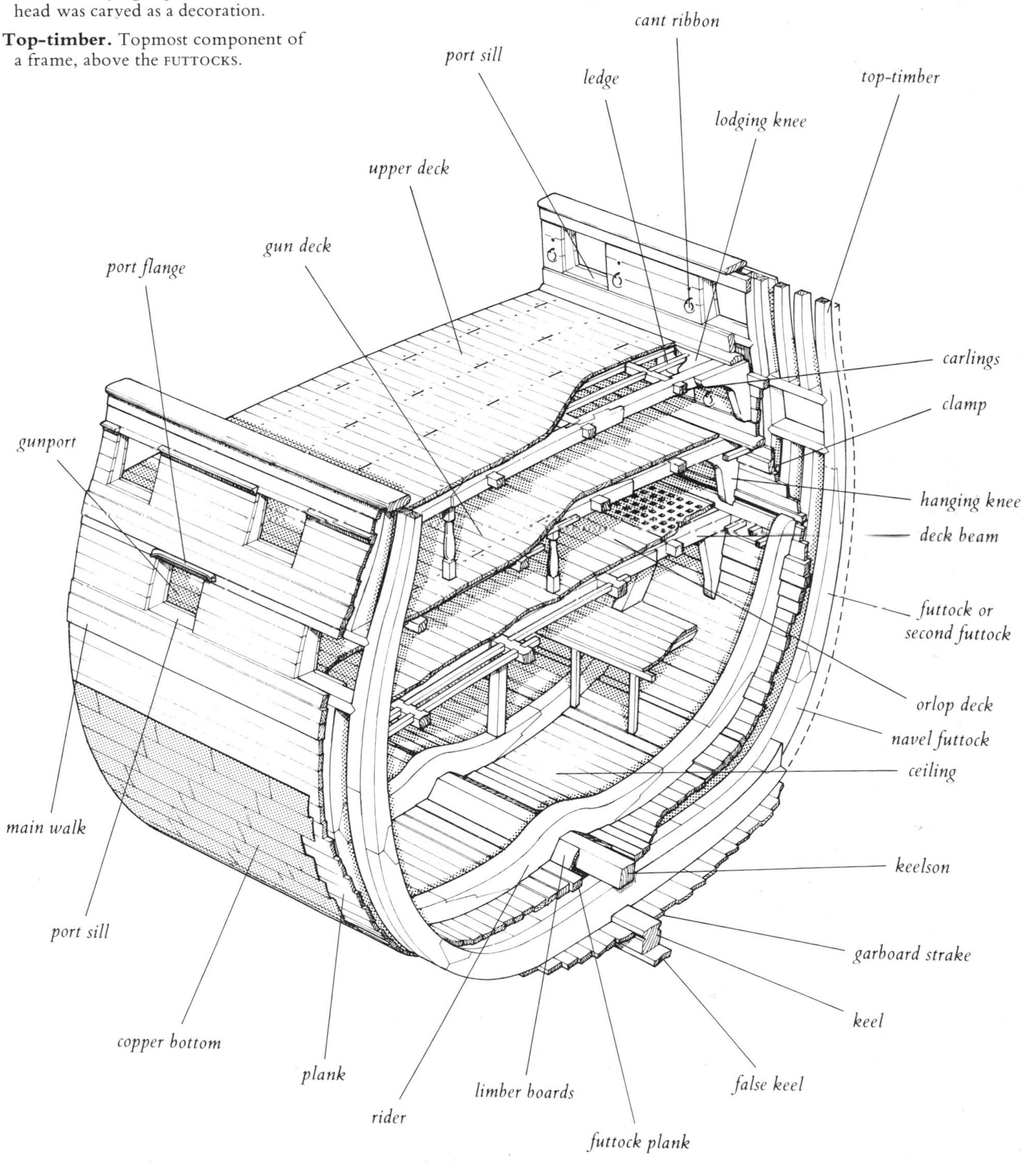

*cant ribbon*

*port sill*

*ledge*

*lodging knee*

*top-timber*

*upper deck*

*gun deck*

*port flange*

*carlings*

*clamp*

*gunport*

*hanging knee*

*deck beam*

*futtock or second futtock*

*orlop deck*

*navel futtock*

*ceiling*

*main walk*

*keelson*

*port sill*

*garboard strake*

*keel*

*copper bottom*

*false keel*

*plank*

*rider*

*limber boards*

*futtock plank*

# Framing

**Beam Knee.** Heavy right-angled piece of timber connecting a beam to the vessel's frame.

**Breech.** External angle of a knee timber.

**Clamp.** Thick horizontal plank supporting the ends of beams. The clamps run close under each deck along the ship's side from stem to stern.

**Dagger knees.** Knees fitted to a vessel's timbers at an angle and not vertically.

**Dagger piece.** Any piece of timber in a vessel's frame which is fixed at an angle.

**Hanging bracket.** Bracket fixed with its horizontal part at the bottom.

**Hanging knee.** Vertical knee with its horizontal arm fixed to the underside of the deck planking or the underside of a beam.

**Knee timber.** Another name for a wooden knee or right-angled bracket.

**Lodging knee.** Strong right-angled bracket of wood fixed horizontally to a vessel's structure, one arm bolted or nailed to a beam and the other fixed across the timbers of the side. Lodging knees are vital in that they contribute very greatly to a vessel's strength.

**Sleeper.** Knee connecting a transom to the ship's after timbers.

**Standard knee.** Large angled piece of timber with one arm bolted horizontally to a beam and the other to the ship's side, for the purpose of strengthening the sides against any sudden or violent shock.

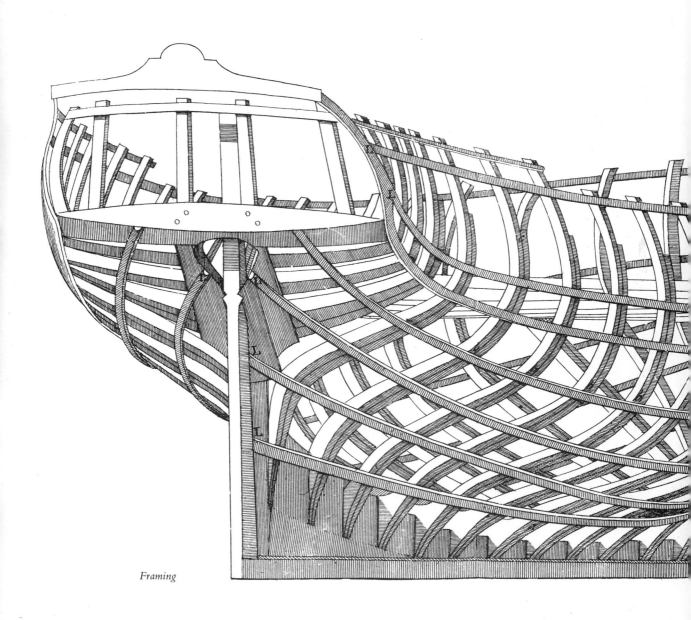

*Framing*

**Deck beam.** Thwartship timber forming part of a vessel's framework and supporting the deck planking.

**Dousing chocks.** Thwartship timbers in the bows extending to the KNIGHT HEADS (03.07).

**Hold beam.** Deck beam over a hold. Also, another name for a HATCH BEAM (03.14).

**Hold pillars.** Supports between floor and beams in a vessel's hold, which support the deck and strengthen the ship against transverse strains.

**Hold stringers.** Fore-and-aft strengthening timbers along the sides of a vessel's hold.

**Pad.** Curved timber seated on top of a beam to give the required angle or shape.

**Pillars.** Carved or turned vertical columns of wood supporting the decks and beams of a vessel and also sustaining the vessel's framework on the vertical plane.

**Rough tree rail.** Timber secured to the top of a vessel's frames and forming the upper bulwarks.

**Shelf,** or **shelf piece.** Stout fore-and-aft timber fastened to the inside of a vessel's frames as a support for the deck beams.

**Stringers.** Timbers running fore and aft across the insides of a ship's frames to strengthen the structure and provide support for the decks.

**Transverse member.** Structural assemblage composed of a thwartship beam with the frames, floors and pillars connected to it.

# Bilges and Limbers

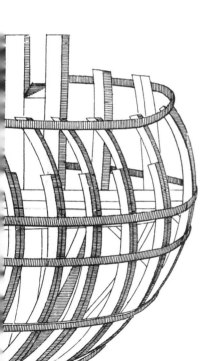

**Bearers.** Thwartship timbers just above the keelson of a vessel and in the STERN SHEETS (09.02) of a boat.

**Bilge boards.** Coverings over a vessel's BILGES to stop the cargo being damaged by bilge water; also to prevent rubbish from falling into the bilges and stopping bilge water reaching the bilge PUMP (12.13).

**Bilge planks.** Planks used either outside or inside the BILGES to reinforce them.

**Bilges.** Cavities between the ship's sides and the keel where water tends to collect.

**Ceiling.** The internal planking of a ship.

**Dead-wood.** Blocks of timber attached to the keel fore and aft, where the hull is narrow and the angle of the timbers at its most acute. The dead-wood extends from the stemson and stern-post, and forms a solid upwards extension of the keel to which the timbers can be fastened.

**False keelson.** Second keelson fitted above the principal keelson.

**Futtock plank.** First CEILING plank next to the keelson.

**Housing** (of bowsprit). That inboard part of a vessel's bows which holds the bowsprit.

**Limber boards.** Short planks laid as covers for the LIMBERS, and forming part of the lining of a ship's floor alongside the keelson. They can be removed when the limbers need cleaning.

**Limber-holes.** Apertures cut through the lower parts of the FLOOR-TIMBERS (03.05), either side of the keelson, allowing water to drain into the LIMBERS and thence to the pump WELL (03.13).

**Limbers.** Channels running fore and aft either side of the keelson, through which water drains off to the pump WELL (03.13).

**Limber strake.** The strake adjacent to the keelson.

**Mast step.** Wood or steel fitting which takes the heel of a mast. Mounted on the keelson, it is in the form of a strong framework or socket into which the squared-off heel fits.

**Rider.** Additional, interior, frame mounted inside a ship's hold along a main frame and bolted to it in order to strengthen the ship's structure. It too has its own FLOOR-TIMBER (03.05), FUTTOCKS (03.05) and, occasionally, TOP-TIMBER (03.05).

**Side keelsons.** Fore-and-aft timbers, one on each side of the keelson, which provide additional longitudinal strength.

# Head

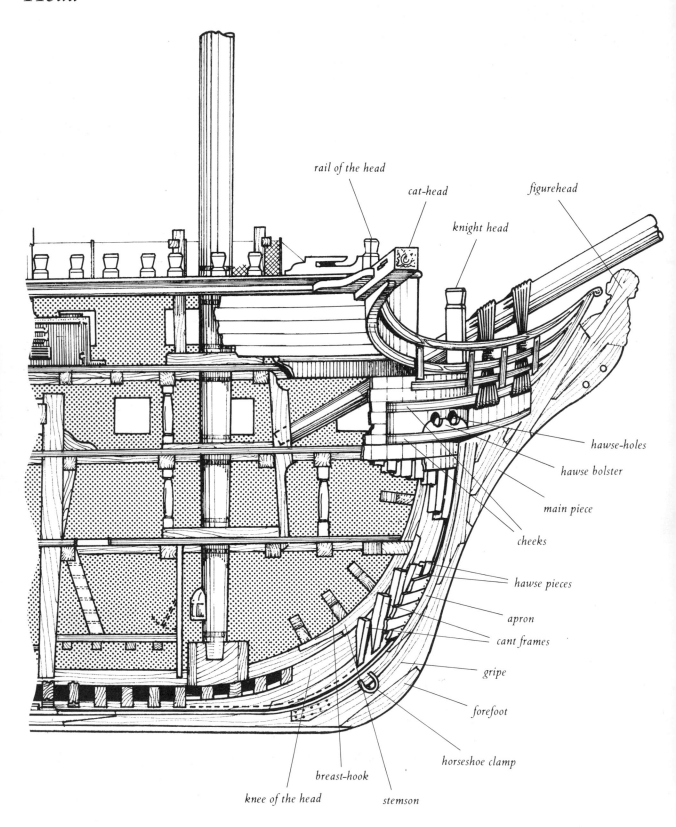

rail of the head

cat-head

figurehead

knight head

hawse-holes

hawse bolster

main piece

cheeks

hawse pieces

apron

cant frames

gripe

forefoot

horseshoe clamp

breast-hook

knee of the head

stemson

**Apron.** Curved timber of uniform thickness, fixed behind the lower section of the stem immediately above the leading end of the keel.

**Beak-head.** The ship's head forward of the forecastle, forming a small deck built over the stem. In ancient warships it formed a strong, pointed projection, a 'break'.

**Billet head.** Ornamentation at the bows of a vessel not fitted with a figure-head.

**Blind buckler.** Large wooden plug used to seal a HAWSE HOLE when the cable has been removed.

**Bobstay piece.** That part of the KNEE OF THE HEAD to which the BOBSTAY (04.08) is secured.

**Breast-hooks.** Thick curved pieces of timber, or horizontal knees, bolted across the inside of the stem, strengthening the fore part of the ship and holding bows and sides together.

**Breastwork.** Balustrade running across the fore ends of quarterdeck and poop. Also, the balustrades enclosing the forecastle fore and aft.

**Bucklers.** Large wooden plugs which fitted into the HAWSE HOLES to prevent the sea washing in. Unlike BLIND BUCKLERS, they were shaped to accommodate the anchor cable.

**Cat-head.** One of the two short beams projecting over the bows on each side of the bowsprit. The sheaves in its end take the CAT (06.02) tackle, with which the anchor can be hove up to the cat-head clear of the bow.

**Cheeks.** Large upward-curving knee pieces between the KNEE OF THE HEAD and the bows on either side.

**Clump cat-head.** Short wooden beam projecting from a vessel near the bow. The anchor is suspended from it when the cable has been unshackled and used for mooring the vessel to a buoy.

**Cutwater.** KNEE OF THE HEAD.

**Deck hook.** Timber framework in the bows of a vessel reinforcing the bow and supporting the fore end of the deck.

**Entrance.** Name frequently given to the foremost underwater part of a ship.

**Eyes.** Those parts of a ship near the HAWSE-HOLES, at the forward end.

**Face piece.** Timber fastened to the KNEE OF THE HEAD to shape and thicken it.

**False stem.** Shaped cutwater fixed with iron or copper clamps to a vessel's stem to give the bows symmetry.

**Fiddle head.** Decorative moulding on a vessel's bow, shaped rather like the scroll-work on a violin.

**Figure-head.** Carved figure, often human or animal, fixed on the stem just beneath the bowsprit.

**Flange bows.** Flared bows.

**Flare.** Curve of a vessel's bows upward and outward.

**Forefoot.** Timber curving upwards from the leading end of the keel to the lower end of the stem and forming part of both.

**Fore-hooks.** BREAST-HOOKS.

**Fore rake.** All that part of a vessel which rakes beyond the fore end of the keel.

**Gripe.** Curved outer surface joining keel and KNEE OF THE HEAD, forming the front of the FOREFOOT.

**Harpings.** The forward parts of the wales; the exceptionally strong planking forming the bows.

**Hawse block.** Large wooden plug shaped to fit the HAWSE HOLE and prevent sea washing in when the vessel was in heavy seas.

**Hawse bolster.** Heavy planking above and below the HAWSE HOLE to protect against the hard wear these areas suffer.

**Hawse-holes.** Cylindrical holes cut through the bows of a ship on each side of the stem, through which the anchor cables pass.

**Hawse hook.** A BREAST HOOK which is fitted above the upper deck.

**Hawse pieces.** The foremost timbers of a ship, whose lower ends rest on the KNUCKLE-TIMBERS (03.05), the foremost CANT-FRAMES (03.05). They are usually parallel to the stem.

**Hawse pipe.** The pipe up which the cable runs from the anchor to the CAPSTAN (06.03) or WINDLASS (06.03).

**Hawse timber.** Heavy vertical timber in a vessel's bows in which the HAWSE HOLES are cut.

**Head board.** Foremost bulkhead within a vessel.

**Hard knee,** or **cheek knee.** Knee fitted edgeways to the cutwater and stem to strengthen the former.

**Head timber.** Timber supporting the gratings in the fore part of a vessel.

**Horseshoe clamp.** Iron clamp between the lower part of the stem and the DEAD-WOOD (03.07).

**Ice beam.** Heavy beam of timber protecting a vessel's bows from ice.

**Independent piece.** Tapered projection beneath a vessel's bowsprit.

**Knee of the head.** Foremost part of the stem, forming a curved leading edge wider at the top, to part the water as the ship advances. It supports the FIGURE-HEAD, and is itself secured to the bows by strong horizontal knees called the *cheeks of the head*. Also called the *cutwater*.

**Knight heads,** or **bollard timbers.** Two heavy baulks of timber, one on each side of the stem and rising above it to support the bowsprit, which is fixed between them. In ancient ships the knight heads were carved to resemble human heads, hence the name.

**Loof.** After part of a ship's bow; that part of her side where the planks begin to curve in towards the stem.

**Main piece.** Piece of timber let into the stem and shaped to take the BOBSTAY PIECE.

**Prow.** Old name for the pointed stem, or beak, of a ship.

**Rail of the head.** Curved piece of timber extending from the bow to the continuation of the stem, supporting the KNEE OF THE HEAD.

**Ram.** Bronze or iron-shod stem or projecting FOREFOOT on ancient warships, used for ramming enemy vessels.

**Ram bow.** Bow of a vessel equipped with a RAM.

**Scroll,** or **scroll head.** Ornamental moulding at the stem of a ship in place of a FIGURE-HEAD.

**Stem head.** Upper end of the STEM POST.

**Stem knee.** Strong angled timber, of structural importance, which connects the stem to the keel.

**Stem piece.** Wedge-shaped timber inserted on either side between STEM POST and KNIGHT-HEADS to provide for the width of the bowsprit and give additional support to it.

**Stem post.** Strong timber forming the foremost part of the ship's frame, rising from the keel. In large ships it is usually a composite post made up of several pieces of wood scarfed together.

**Stemson.** Curved timber aft of the APRON (03.07), reinforcing the latter's SCARF (03.03). In large ships it consists of two pieces.

**Supporters.** Knee timbers placed under the CAT HEADS for their support and security.

# Stern

**Balcony.** Another name for the ornate stern GALLERY of vessels of the sixteenth to eighteenth centuries.

**Counter stays.** Timbers supporting a projecting stern.

**Ekeing.** Moulding or carving on a QUARTER-GALLERY.

**Escutcheon.** The place in the middle of a ship's stern where her name and port of registry are inscribed.

**False stern-post.** Additional timber clamped or bolted to the stern-post to reinforce it.

**Fashion pieces.** The aftermost frames of a ship, which delimit its breadth and set the shape of the stern. They run between the stern-post and the ends of the WING TRANSOM.

**Gallery.** Balcony projecting from the stern or quarter of an old man-of-war or large merchantman. The partition behind it, framing the cabin windows, is the *screen-bulkhead*, and the arched roof of the gallery is the *cove*.

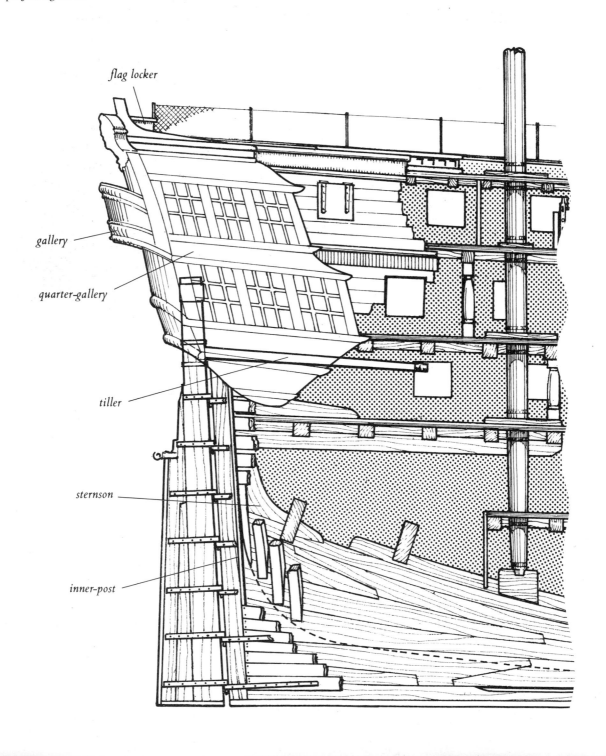

flag locker

gallery

quarter-gallery

tiller

sternson

inner-post

**Horn timber.** Strong timber extending aft and upwards from the keel and forming the main structural member of the counter.

**Inner-post.** Length of timber mounted along the fore side of the stern-post, strengthening the stern and holding the transoms.

**Overhang.** That part of a vessel's stern projecting aft beyond the rudder head.

**Quarter.** That part of a ship's side between the main-chains (see CHAINS 04.08) and the stern.

**Quarter boards.** Boards erected around the poop and quarterdeck to prevent waves from breaking inboard when sailing with a following sea in bad weather.

**Quarter-gallery.** Small balcony on a ship's QUARTER, usually with doors leading to the stern-gallery.

**Quarter timber.** One of the frames of a vessel's quarter.

**Stern frame.** Timber frame composed of the stern-post, transom and FASHION PIECES. The basis of the whole stern.

**Stern knee.** The knee strengthening the joint at the heel of the INNER-POST.

**Stern port.** Opening at the stern which serves for ventilation, allows guns to be fired astern, or facilitates the loading of cargo.

**Sternson.** Curved timber joining keelson and INNER-POST.

**Stern walk.** Balcony constructed across the stern, level with one or more of the upper decks. Stern walks were abolished in 1797 but reintroduced in 1814.

**Taffrail.** Ornamental rail along the upper edge of the stern.

**Transom knee.** Curved timber or piece of iron which joins the ship's QUARTER to the transom. It is bolted to the transom and to the after timbers.

**Tuck.** That part of a ship where the ends of the bottom planks meet under the stern or counter. When this part forms a perpendicular or oblique plane rather than a curved surface, it is called a *square tuck*.

**Tuck rail.** Horizontal rail fixed to the upper edge of the WING TRANSOM, marking the lower edge of the counter.

**Wing transom.** Major transom bolted across the inside of the stern-post, resting on the head of the INNER-POST and forming the foundation of counter and stern.

# Rudder

**Balanced rudder.** Rudder in which the stock is placed some distance abaft the leading edge, so that water pressure on the forward area is balanced by pressure on the after area, thus decreasing the amount of power needed to turn the rudder.

**Gudgeon,** or **brace.** Metal clamp bolted to the stern-post. PINTLES on the back of the rudder fit into corresponding holes in the gudgeons, thus hinging the rudder to the stern-post.

**Helm.** Specifically, the TILLER, the lever controlling the rudder. In a wider sense, the apparatus by which a ship is steered, consisting of the rudder, tiller and STEERING WHEEL.

**Helm port.** Opening in the stern of a vessel housing the RUDDER STOCK and allowing it entry into the hull for connection to the HELM.

**Helm port transom.** Timber reinforcement of the HELM PORT.

**Jury rudder.** Temporary rudder rigged when a vessel's true rudder is carried away or smashed.

**Jury steering gear.** Temporary steering gear rigged when the vessel's proper steering gear is inoperable.

**King spoke.** Steering wheel spoke which, when in a vertical position, usually indicates that the helm is amidships. It is marked by a brass cap or by some form of decoration.

**Locking pintle.** Flanged PINTLE preventing the rudder from becoming accidentally unshipped.

**Pintle.** Vertical bolt at the back of the rudder which fits into a GUDGEON on the stern-post to form a hinge.

**Quadrant.** Fitting at the head of a RUDDER STOCK, in the shape of the sector of a circle, to which the STEERING CHAINS are attached.

**Rudder brace.** Horizontal metal bracket on the fore edge of a rudder, holding either a PINTLE or a GUDGEON. Also called a *rudder band*.

**Rudder breeching.** Short rope, one end made fast inboard, the other to the rudder, which takes some of the weight of the rudder from the GUDGEONS.

**Rudder chains.** Lightweight chains fastened to each side of the rudder and leading into the stern. They keep

*Steering wheel with tiller rope of HMS* Victory
*Jury steering gear*

the rudder from being lost if unshipped and also provide emergency connections if the main STEERING CHAINS part.

**Rudder coat.** Canvas housing fitted over the RUDDER STOCK where it emerges from the RUDDER TRUNK to prevent the sea entering.

**Rudder head.** The upper part of the RUDDER STOCK.

**Rudder hole.** Housing in the stern which accommodates the RUDDER HEAD.

**Rudder iron.** RUDDER BRACE.

**Rudder pendants.** Lengths of steel wire or rope by means of which the RUDDER CHAINS can be connected to the RUDDER TACKLES if necessary.

**Rudder port.** Housing above the HELM PORT through which the RUDDER STOCK passes into the vessel.

**Rudder post.** Vessel's stern-post when the rudder is hung on it.

**Rudder stock.** Stout vertical beam to which the blade of the rudder is fixed.

**Rudder stops.** Wood or metal projections, on the rudder or on the stern-post, which stop the rudder from turning more than approximately 40° to either side.

**Rudder tackles.** Tackles which can be connected to the RUDDER CHAINS and used to control a vessel's helm when the connections from rudder to steering wheel part.

**Rudder trunk.** Housing for the RUDDER STOCK, running from the HELM PORT to the deck, where the rudder QUADRANT or TILLER is mounted

**Shole.** Horizontal piece of timber fastened along the bottom of a rudder to reinforce it and to protect it if the vessel runs aground.

**Sole.** Piece of timber attached to the foot of a rudder to bring it into line with a FALSE KEEL (03.04).

**Spoke.** Hand-grip of a steering wheel. A brass-capped spoke is used to indicate when the helm is amidships.

**Steering chains.** Chains led from a barrel attached to the ship's STEERING WHEEL to the TILLER, for the purpose of steering the ship.

**Steering gear.** The mechanism of ropes or chains leading from the rudder or TILLER to the STEERING WHEEL on deck. Patent steering gear which did away with ropes and chains came into use during the nineteenth century.

**Steering wheel,** or **wheel.** Wheel, usually fixed to the quarterdeck, linked by rope, chain or gear to the rudder, by which the ship is steered. Sometimes termed *helm.*

**Tiller.** Wood or iron bar fitted in the head of the rudder, for the purpose of moving it from one side to the other in order to steer the ship.

**Tiller chain.** Chain linking the TILLER to a barrel on the ship's STEERING WHEEL.

**Tiller head.** That end of the TILLER farthest from the rudder.

**Tiller rope.** Rope connecting the TILLER HEAD to the barrel of the STEERING WHEEL. It is made of untarred rope or hide, and by its means the tiller is worked and the ship steered.

**Wheel.** STEERING WHEEL.

**Wheel chains.** STEERING CHAINS.

**Wheel ropes.** Ropes leading from the STEERING WHEEL to the TILLER for the purpose of controlling the rudder.

**Whipstaff.** Slender vertical lever with an EYE-BOLT (03.15) in its lower end that toggled onto the GOOSE-NECK (04.07) at the end of the TILLER. In ships with several decks, it allowed a helmsman on an upper deck to move the tiller below. It was in use from the fifteenth to the seventeenth centuries, but allowed only limited lateral movement of the tiller and was replaced at the beginning of the eighteenth century by the STEERING WHEEL.

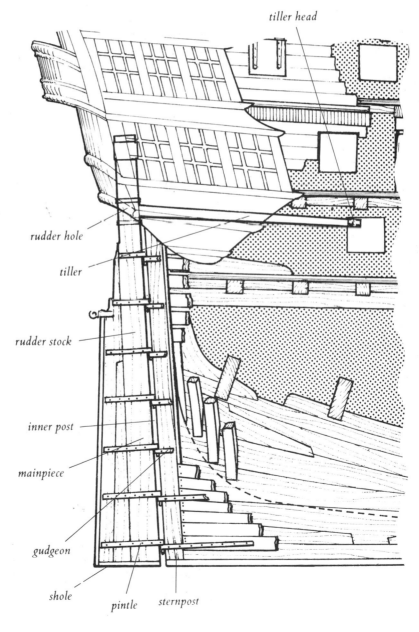

tiller head

rudder hole

tiller

rudder stock

inner post

mainpiece

gudgeon

shole

pintle   sternpost

# Planking and Sheathing

**Bends.** Another name for wales.

**Between wind and water.** That part of a ship's side which is just at the water-line.

**Bilge.** That part of a ship's bottom, curving in towards the keel, on which the ship would rest if aground. A ship fractured along the bilge is said to be *bilged*.

**Black strakes.** Range of planks in a ship's side immediately above the wales, painted with a mixture of tar and lamp-black (to preserve the wood and to contrast with the other, lighter, colours of the ship).

**Butt.** The end of a plank in the ship's side or bottom, where it adjoins the end of the next plank.

**Butt joint.** Joint in which the ends of two timbers are flush. The joint may be strengthened by a plate or timber fixed across it. When such a joint leaks due to a vessel's excessive labouring in heavy seas, the vessel is said to 'have sprung a butt'.

**Carvel joint.** Joint in which the two members are flush; a BUTT JOINT.

**Chine.** Upper edge of a deck WATER-WAY (03.11), projecting above deck level to make it easier to caulk the SPIRKETTING.

**Coat.** Canvas cover fixed over the junction of mast and deck, bowsprit and stem, or rudder and counter, to keep out water.

**Copper bottomed.** Describes vessels whose bottoms were sheathed in copper to protect them from teredo worm and prevent fouling. The method was used from the second half of the eighteenth century, and probably the last vessels protected in this way were the wooden light-vessels of Trinity House, which were sheathed with Muntz metal.

**Copper fastened.** Said of a vessel whose fastenings are made of corrosion-resistant copper rather than iron.

**Devil.** Name given to the deck seam immediately adjacent to a vessel's side.

**Drift piece.** Timber, either upright or curved in shape, connecting the PLANK SHEER to the gunwale.

**Fash.** Crooked or irregular seam in a vessel's planking.

**Fender bolt.** Bolt with a large head, which served as a FENDER (09.02) to protect a vessel's sides.

**Foot-waling.** CEILING.

**Fore hood.** Foremost plank in a strake.

**Garboard strake.** The first strake, or range of planks, laid along a vessel's bottom next to the keel. The edge of this plank is let into a groove or channel in the side of the keel, which is called the garboard-strake RABBET (03.03).

**Graving piece.** Wooden inset let into a rotten or holed plank.

**Hooding-ends.** Those ends of the planks which fit into the RABBETS (03.03) of the stem and stern-post.

**Jacket.** Additional timber fixed on the outside of a vessel's hull for protective purposes, such as defence against ice pressure.

**Landing strake.** Second strake down from the gunwale.

**Plank.** A strong board from one to four inches thick, often cut from oak, pine or fir.

**Plank sheer.** The uppermost plank running along the TOP-TIMBERS (03.05) of a vessel's frames.

**Seam.** Longitudinal joint between planks in a ship's decks or sides, filled with OAKUM (03.02) and covered with hot pitch.

**Shell.** External planking of a vessel.

**Shift of butts.** The fastening of a vessel's planking in such a manner that the BUTT JOINTS are staggered and are not vertically aligned.

**Skin.** Outside plates or timbers of a vessel.

**Spirketting.** The planks running between the WATER-WAYS (03.11) and the sills of the ports.

**Springing.** Loosening a plank in the hull of a vessel.

**Stealer.** Plank used to compensate for the tapering or widening of a ship's planking towards stem or stern-post. A method of losing or gaining a strake and so avoiding over-wide or over-thin plank ends.

**String.** Highest interior range of planks in a ship's side.

**Stuff.** Any composition of materials used to smear or PAY (02.03) the sides or bottom of a ship, including turpentine, varnish, tar, oils and various mixtures.

**Tight.** Watertight, without any leaks.

*Views of the planking of the Wasa during restoration*

# Decks and Compartments

*Gun deck of the Wasa (1628)*

**Accommodation.** General living space allocated to passengers and crew in a vessel for eating, sleeping and toilet purposes. The conditions and areas of accommodation varied enormously until legislation made a given allowance of space per person mandatory.

**After-hold.** That part of the hold which lies abaft the mainmast.

**Barricade, or baricado.** Strong wooden rail, supported by small pillars or stanchions, extending across the foremost part of the quarterdeck. In warships during battle it was hung with bedding or other materials as a protection against small shot.

**Bow locker.** General term for a small storeroom in the bows of a vessel, where working stores are kept.

**Break.** The point where the forecastle and the poop rise from the main deck.

**Carlings.** Short pieces of timber ranging fore and aft between beams, strengthening beams and deck.

**Companion ladder.** Ladder or steps leading from one deck to another; specifically, from the quarterdeck to the upper deck.

**Deck head.** The underside of the deck above one's head.

**Deep-waisted.** Said of a ship when forecastle and quarterdeck are

considerably higher than the upper deck.

**Flush-deck.** Continuous upper deck laid from stem to stern.

**Gutter bar.** Angle bar which forms the inboard side of the WATER-WAY at each side of the deck.

**Half deck.** Deck above the main deck which does not continue for the whole length of the vessel. Also, the name given to that part of the upper deck which contains accommodation for officers and apprentices; and, in the Royal Navy, the after part of the lower deck, used as officers' accommodation.

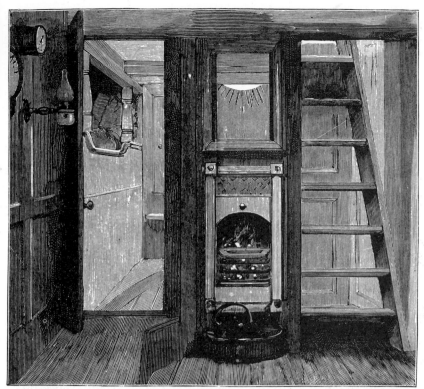

*A corner of the cabin*

*Mess table and stools on the lower deck of HMS* Victory

**Half poop.** Poop lower than the height of a man.

**Ledge.** Piece of timber installed between beams athwartships to provide additional support for the deck.

**Long waisted.** Describes a vessel which has a long waist, that is, an open deck between the poop and the forecastle.

**Main deck.** Principal deck of a vessel. In wooden warships which had three complete decks, the main deck was the one beneath the upper deck.

**Monkey poop.** Low poop deck.

**Moonsheered.** Said of a vessel which has a more than usual sheer forward and aft.

**No-man's land.** Space amidships between the after part of the *Belfry* and the fore part of a boat when it is stored on the BOOMS (03.13). It is used as storage for any blocks, ropes or tackle that might be needed on the forecastle. It derives its name from being neither on the starboard nor port side, and neither in the waist nor on the forecastle.

**Poop-royal.** Short deck or platform over the aftmost part of the poop in the largest French and Spanish men-of-war, and used as a cabin for masters and pilots. Called a *topgallant poop* in England.

**Sheer line.** Line of a vessel's main or upper deck where it meets the side.

**Standard.** Inverted knee mounted above the deck instead of beneath it, with the vertical arm pointing upwards.

**Superstructure.** Any permanent construction, such as a wheel-house or raised quarterdeck, built on the upper deck.

**Tonnage deck.** Deck forming the upper limit of the space measured to assess tonnage. It is the upper deck in a ship having only one or two decks; in others it is the second deck up.

**Upper-works.** Generally, all that part of a vessel above the water-line when she is properly balanced for a sea voyage.

**Water-way.** Gutter along the side of the deck, forming a channel for water to run off into the SCUPPERS (03.15).

# Decks and Compartments

**Between-decks.** The space contained between any two whole decks of a ship.

**Caboose.** Originally, a housing for the chimney of the cook's galley on a merchant ship. Later applied to the galley itself, or to any confined space.

**Coach.** Compartment near the stern of a large man-of-war, generally used as the captain's quarters.

**Cockpit.** In a man-of-war, a compartment under the lower gun-deck where the wounded were attended to by the surgeon during battle.

**Dead door.** Wooden shutter sealing off a square window in a vessel.

**Light-room.** Small compartment with double-glazed windows, close to the MAGAZINE in a man-of-war, where the gunner could fill powder cartridges.

**Magazine.** Storeroom on a man-of-war in which gunpowder and any form of explosive is kept. It is illuminated by light from the LIGHT ROOM nearby.

**Main hold.** Main cargo space, beneath the main hatch.

**Mess deck.** Deck on which the ship's company take their meals. This is a term used by the Royal Navy rather than the Merchant Navy, which uses the term *mess room*.

**Round-house.** Deck-house aft of the mainmast; also an old name for the poop.

**Steerage.** Accommodation forward of the main cabin, and inferior to cabin accommodation.

**Wheel house.** Construction built around the STEERING WHEEL (03.09) to protect the helmsman from the weather. It also contains the BINNACLE (19.06) and in time increased in size to hold other navigational equipment.

**Wing.** The area of a hold or BETWEEN DECKS nearest the sides.

*Captain Hardy's day cabin of HMS Victory*

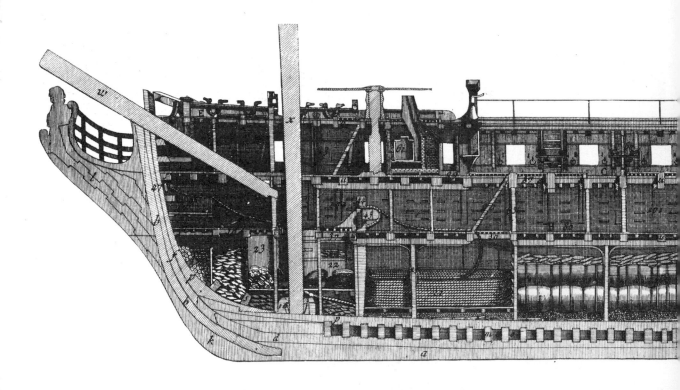

*Galley of the* Wasa

# Decks and Compartments

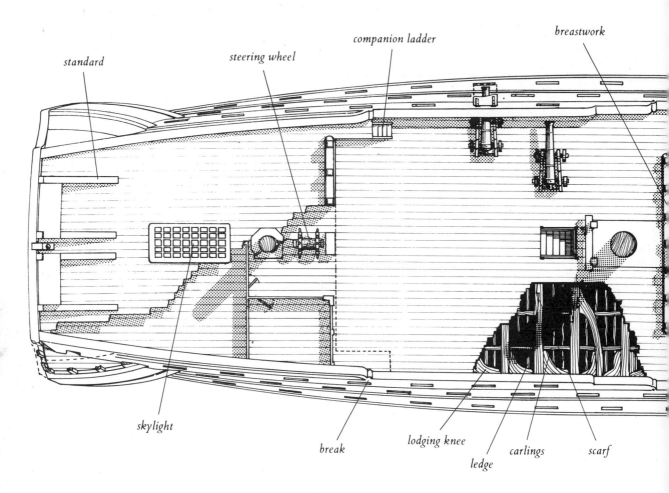

standard  steering wheel  companion ladder  breastwork

skylight

break  lodging knee  carlings  scarf  ledge

**Booms.** Deck space between mainmast and foremast where boats and spare masts and spars are kept.

**Cabin.** Compartment used as living quarters on a ship.

**Cable locker.** Compartment in the bows of a vessel where the anchor cable is stowed and its inboard end secured. When the anchor was being hoisted, one or two members of the crew were detailed to the cable locker to stow the cable as it came in.

**Cable tier.** Place on the lowest deck or in the hold where the cables are coiled up and stowed.

**Close quarters.** Strong wooden barriers erected across a ship's deck, from behind which the crew could fight off boarders.

**Cuddy.** Cabin in the fore part of a boat.

**Fore cabin.** Part of a vessel's passenger accommodation, second in importance to the SALOON.

**Fore-hold.** That part of the hold situated in the fore part of the ship, forward of the main hatchway.

**Gun-room.** Compartment at the after end of the lower gun-deck on a man-of-war, used by the gunner or as a mess for lower-rank officers.

**Heads.** The vessel's lavatory, which was formerly a grating over the bow or BEAK-HEAD (03.07).

**Lady's hole.** Small compartment for stores.

**Lazarette, or lazaretto.** Storeroom for ship's provisions, often in the after part of the hold. Also, a room used to quarantine any person with an infectious or contagious disease and to confine malefactors.

**Locker.** Generally, a cupboard or small lockable compartment. Lockers are used for stowing food, clothing or cleaning and other gear.

**Manger.** Small compartment across the lower deck between the HAWSE-HOLES (03.07). Its after part is formed by the *manger-board*, a bulkhead which stops any water coming in through the hawse-holes from flowing aft and reroutes it through the SCUPPERS (03.15).

**Mast-carlings.** Fore-and-aft timbers on the underside of the deck which help support the mast and strengthen the deck where it is pierced by the mast. They are also called *mast partners*.

**Mast trunk.** Sheath of wood or metal in which the mast of a small vessel is stepped.

**Partners.** Timber framework strengthening the deck where it is pierced by mast, capstan, pump or bowsprit.

**Powder room.** Storeroom in a man-of-war where gunpowder was kept

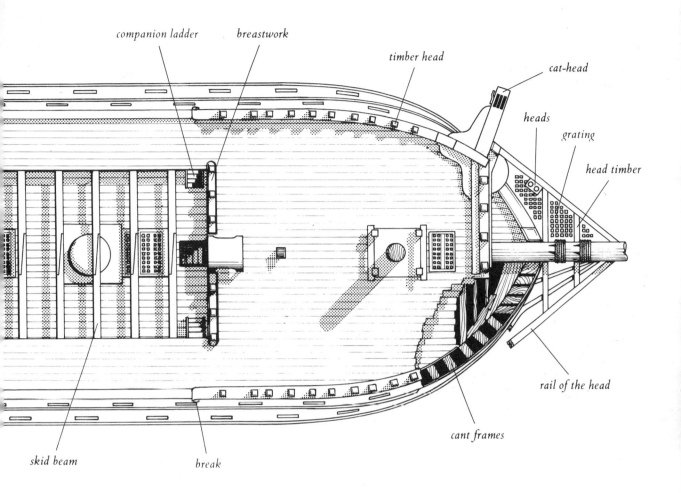

*companion ladder*  *breastwork*  *timber head*  *cat-head*  *heads*  *grating*  *head timber*  *rail of the head*  *cant frames*  *skid beam*  *break*

in bulk before being made up into charges. Also, where a cargo of explosives could be carried.

**Pump well.** Compartment in a vessel's hold into which the water flows and whence it is pumped out. The well is so constructed as to prevent the entrance of ballast and debris which could choke the pumps.

**Sail room.** Storeroom in which a vessel's sails are stowed.

**Saloon.** Main accommodation for passengers in a passenger-carrying vessel. Also, the officers' mess in a merchant ship.

**Screen bulkhead.** Upper-deck bulkhead closing off either end of midships accommodation.

**Sick bay,** or **sick berth.** Area or compartment used for the treatment of injury or illness.

**Slop room.** Place where spare clothing for the crew is kept.

**Spar deck.** Temporary deck constructed of spars seated on beams.

**Spurling pipe,** or **navel pipe.** Tube leading from the CABLE LOCKER to the cable deck or forecastle. The ship's cable passes through this pipe.

**Tabernacle.** Vertical casing forming three sides of a square around a mast, within which the mast is stepped and clamped. In small ships with a pivoted mast, the cheeks of the tabernacle extend above the deck and carry the pivot pin.

**Tireplate.** Iron plate fastened under the decking around the mast. It serves to prevent distortion of the deck planking when chocks or wedges are driven in around the mast.

**Ward robe.** Strongroom used to hold valuables captured from enemy ships. Sometimes, when empty, used as the lieutenants' mess room.

**Ward room.** Officers' general mess room, used in Royal Navy ships by lieutenants and higher ranks, excepting the commanding officer.

**Weather deck.** Any uncovered deck which is not protected from the weather or the sea.

**Well.** Enclosed space in the bottom of a ship containing the PUMPS (12.13) or their suction-pipes, and into which bilge-water runs to be drawn off. Also, in fishing vessels, a compartment filled with sea-water and used for keeping live fish.

**Well deck.** Any portion of an upper deck which is bounded fore and aft by bulkheads carrying a higher deck.

# Hatches and Ports

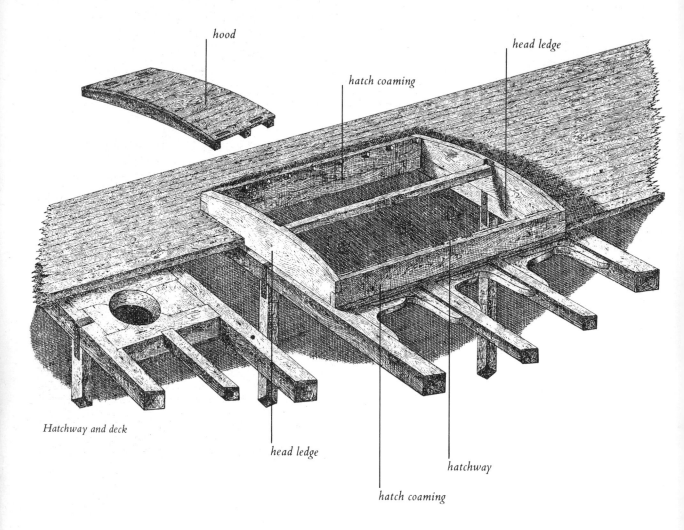

hood

head ledge

hatch coaming

Hatchway and deck

head ledge

hatchway

hatch coaming

**Accommodation ladder.** Light staircase with handrails or entering ropes, fitted at side of ship for convenient access to a suitable entrance.

**Booby hatch.** Small hatchway with a sliding cover, giving access to a locker or storeroom, or to the accommodation on board small craft.

**Catwalk.** Gangway without any form of handrail or hand rope.

**Coamings.** Raised borders round a ship's hatches which prevent water from running in.

**Companion.** Wooden hood over a cabin hatchway.

**Companion way.** Stairway or ladder leading from the deck to the accommodation below.

**Dead-light.** Wooden shutter fixed across a cabin window to keep out water during a storm.

**Entering ropes.** Two ropes hanging from the upper part of a ship's side, on either side of the ACCOMMODATION LADDER.

**Gallows bitts.** Vertical wooden structure in which spare yards, spars or timbers are stowed on deck.

**Gallows top.** Cross timbers at the top of the GALLOWS BITTS.

**Grating.** Open lattice-work covering for a hatch, providing light and ventilation. Gratings are covered with tarpaulin in bad weather.

**Gutter-ledge.** Cross-bar running fore and aft across the middle of a large hatch to support the covers.

**Half port.** Cover extending over half a gun port, with a cutaway section to accommodate the gun.

**Hatch bar.** Iron or steel bar, flat in section, locked across a hatch cover.

**Hatch beam.** Beam lying across a hatchway, which can be lifted out to permit loading and unloading of the hold. When replaced, it restores transverse beam strength.

**Hatch coaming.** Low wall of iron or wood which encloses the hatchway and holds the lugs to which the HATCH BARS are secured.

**Hatchway screens.** Canvas screens used around hatchways when loading or unloading bulk cargo such as coal or iron ore, which may be dirty or dusty. In wooden men-of-war, wooden hatchway screens were rigged as a precaution against fire and to mask the hands fetching gunpowder from the magazine.

**Head ledge.** Thwartship hatchway coaming.

**Hood.** Cover screening a hatch or COMPANION WAY from wind and weather.

**Light.** Aperture in a vessel's sides or deck which lets in light.

**Light port.** Glazed PORT HOLE or SCUTTLE.

**Locking bars.** Flat iron bars holding the canvas hatch covers over the hatches and which can be locked on lugs on the hatch COAMINGS.

**Main hatch.** A vessel's largest hatch.

**Port hole.** Circular window in a vessel's sides or deck housing. During heavy weather it can be sealed from the inside with a heavy, hinged cover known as a DEAD-LIGHT.

**Raft-port.** Square aperture in the end of a merchant ship or a naval transport, through which long timbers could be loaded.

**Scuttle.** Small hatchway or hole cut through a ship's side, deck or hatch-covering; usually fitted with a lid which can be firmly closed when necessary.

**Sea suction.** Submerged opening in a vessel's hull which allows sea water to be pumped in for sluicing and other purposes.

**Skylight.** Hinged, glazed window in the deck providing light and air below decks.

**Slab hatch covers.** A number of hatch planks fixed within a steel frame which can be lifted out by a crane or derrick.

*Port hole*

*Gun-port of the* Wasa

# Rails, Fixtures and Ornaments

**Awning.** Canopy of canvas extended over a deck for protection from sun or rain. It is supported by a number of stanchions and suspended by a CROW-FOOT (05.01).

**Backstay stool.** Short platform taking the lower ends of the BACKSTAYS (04.08).

**Badge.** Ornament placed on the outside of small ships very near the stern, containing either a window or its representation; usually decorated with marine figures, martial emblems, and so on.

**Cant ribbon.** Decorative moulding, gilded and/or brightly painted, running along a vessel's sides and canted up towards the stem and stern.

**Chess-tree.** One of two pieces of timber mounted vertically on each side of the ship, used to hold the CLEWS (04.12) of the mainsail to windward. The mainsail TACKS (04.09) run through holes in the tops of the chess-trees.

**Chevils.** Wooden projections serving as cleats for the TACKS (04.09) and SHEETS (04.09) of sails.

**Crank.** Iron brace supporting a lantern on the poop quarters.

**Drifts.** The breaks in the SHEER RAIL which end in a scroll, as at the quarterdeck, poop deck and forecastle.

**Eye-bolt.** Iron bolt driven into decks or ship sides, with an eye at one end to which ropes or TACKLES (05.05) can be fastened.

**Eyebrow.** RIGOL.

**False rail.** Length of timber added to a rail in order to strengthen it or as a facing.

**Fife rail.** Rack containing BELAYING PINS (10.07) for securing various ropes and FALLS (05.04). Fitted at a vessel's sides and on deck around the masts.

**Friezing,** or **frieze.** Painted decoration along the upper part of a ship's quarter, stern or bow.

**Grab rail.** Rail bolted round the deck house of a vessel for the safety of the crew in rough weather.

**Guard-irons.** Curved iron bars protecting ornamental figures on a ship's head or quarter.

**Guard rails.** Iron safety rails, or chain, rope or wire suspended from

*Ornamented stern of HMS* Prince

stanchions, along the side of a deck exposed to the sea.

**Hammock netting.** Rows of netting above the bulwarks of a man-of-war in which the crew's hammocks were stowed when the vessel was in action, providing cover against flying splinters and musket and pistol fire.

**Head netting.** Ornamental network decorating the bulkheads of the fore part of a wooden warship.

**Jack ladder.** Ladder with rope sides and wooden rungs.

**Jacob's ladder.** JACK LADDER going up a topgallant or royal mast, or running from a boat to a BOAT BOOM (09.03).

**Jumping ladder.** Rope ladder hanging from a vessel's side for the use of boats' crews.

**Kevel.** Large cleat fixed to the ship's side and used for belaying (tying off) large ropes.

**Kevel head.** Extension of a frame, projecting above a vessel's gunwale and functioning as a KEVEL for belaying large cables or ropes.

**Lightning conductor.** Strip of copper running from a mast-head to the sea, to discharge any atmospheric electrical charges.

**Loop holes.** Apertures cut in the bulkheads and other parts of a ship, through which small arms could be fired at a boarding enemy.

**Monkey rail.** Light rail fixed above the bulwarks of the quarterdeck.

**Munnions.** The ornamental mouldings between the windows in a ship's stern.

**Newel.** Post which holds the ends of the rails going from the fore end of the poop or the after end of the forecastle to the gangway entrance.

**Pin rack.** RACK holding BELAYING PINS (10.07), usually fixed inside the bulwarks or around the bottom of a mast.

**Pin rail.** Longer form of PIN RACK fitted to a vessel's side.

**Port flange.** RIGOL.

**Portlast.** Another name for the gunwale of a vessel.

**Port sash.** Window frame in the upper half of a square port.

**Port sill.** Sill of a square port.

**Preventer bolts.** Bolts holding the lower edges of the PREVENTER PLATES.

**Preventer plates.** Iron plates bolted onto the CHAINS (04.08) and to the planks below. Their function is to prevent the vessel's seams opening when subjected to the strain of the shrouds as the vessel pitches and rolls.

**Quarter-cloths.** Lengths of painted canvas fastened along the side of the quarterdeck to keep out sea spray.

**Quarter-netting.** Rope net-work extended along the rails on the upper part of a ship's QUARTER (03.08). Hammocks were often stowed there.

**Quarter-rails.** Narrow planks running along the side of the quarter-deck and forming a safety fence.

**Quick-work.** In shipbuilding, that part of a ship's side above the upper deck; it does not need to be built to the same standard as other parts and can therefore be installed relatively quickly.

**Rack.** Frame of wood or iron holding BELAYING PINS (10.07) or leads for ropes, such as blocks or single sheaves.

**Riding bitts.** Two short, strong posts of iron or wood in the fore part of a vessel used for turning up the cable.

**Rigol.** Curved moulding or ledge fitted above a PORT HOLE (03.14) or SCUTTLE (03.14) to prevent any water running down the ship's side from entering the opening. Also called *eyebrow*, *port flange* or *spurnwater*.

**Rime.** Rung of a ladder.

**Rounds.** Wooden rungs of a JACOB'S LADDER or JACK LADDER.

**Samson post.** In small craft, a single BITT (06.03), placed amidships just forward of the mast, to which a cable can be made fast.

**Scupper.** Lead-lined channel cut through a ship's side or WATER-WAY (03.11) in order to carry water off the deck into the sea.

**Scupper hose.** Short length of canvas or leather piping which carries the water from the SCUPPERS clear of the vessel's side.

**Scupper leather.** Piece of shaped leather at the SCUPPER outlet forming a valve to prevent the re-entry of sea water.

**Scupper lip.** Flange projecting from a SCUPPER outlet to throw water clear of the vessel's sides.

**Scupper shoot.** Short semi-circular conduit which ejects SCUPPER water clear of the vessel's sides.

**Scuttle butt.** Lidded cask in which fresh water was kept for daily use.

**Shark's mouth.** Narrow dip made in an AWNING when it is stretched over some part of the rigging.

**Sheer rail.** Lowest continuous line of planking in a vessel's bulwarks.

**Side ladder.** Rope ladder suspended over a ship's side for access to and from boats.

**Skid beam.** Beam supporting a deck upon which boats are stowed.

**Span shackle.** Heavy steel or iron bolt fitted below the forecastle deck and equipped with a strong socket in which the CAT DAVIT (06.02) was seated.

**Spurnwater.** RIGOL.

**Stage.** Platform hung over a ship's side or in a hold for hands to work from.

**Stern-ladders.** Rope ladders suspended on each side of the stern for access to boats or for other purposes.

**Waist cloth.** Canvas sheet used to cover the hammocks stored in the HAMMOCK NETTING in the waist of a ship.

**Waist pipe.** Strengthened or reinforced opening in the midships bulwarks through which the hawser passes when the ship is moored at a quay.

**Wash port.** SCUPPER.

*Pin rack*

*Rails of the* Wasa *seen during restoration*

# Iron-Ship Terms

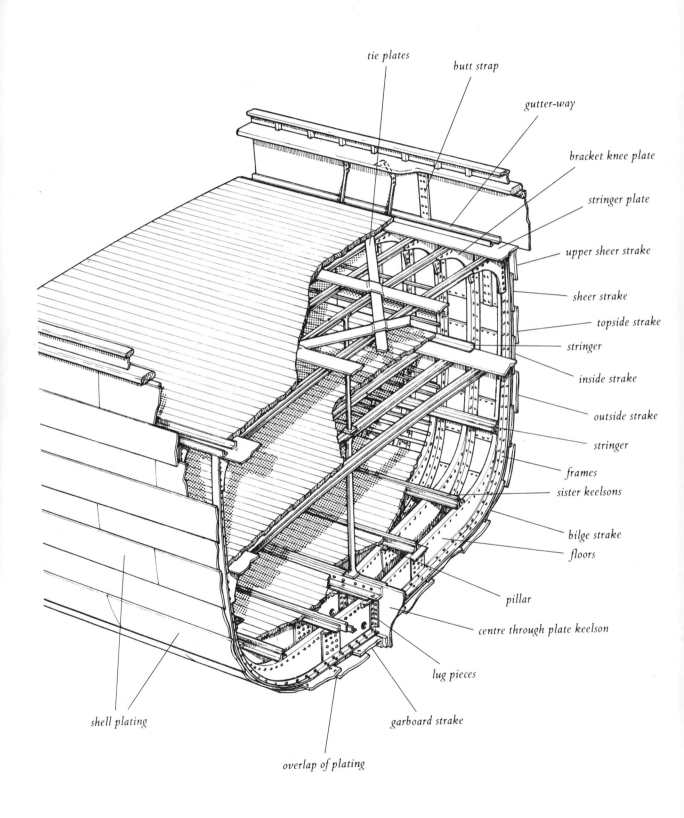

tie plates

butt strap

gutter-way

bracket knee plate

stringer plate

upper sheer strake

sheer strake

topside strake

stringer

inside strake

outside strake

stringer

frames

sister keelsons

bilge strake

floors

pillar

centre through plate keelson

lug pieces

garboard strake

overlap of plating

shell plating

**Angle-bar.** Rolled iron or steel bar having an L-shaped cross-section. The flanges may be equal or unequal in width.

**Angle stringer.** Longitudinal member made up of angle-bars, sometimes strengthened by a bulb bar, usually fitted midway between the deck and the bilge.

**Bar keel.** Keel composed of flat iron bars, joined together longitudinally by overlapping, to which the flanges of the GARBOARD STRAKE are riveted.

**Bending slab.** Large, cast-iron perforated plate about six inches thick. Iron pegs, known as *dogs*, are placed in the holes to form the pattern of the shape of a particular frame. The red-hot frame is brought from the furnace to the bending slab and, by using MAULS (03.03) and SQUEEGEES (03.17), worked against the dogs until it reaches the correct form.

**Bilge keels.** External fins made up of plates and angle-bars, or of an angle-bar alone, riveted to the hull at right angles, at the turn of the bilge, and extending some distance over the midship length. The bilge keels reduce roll and give additional longitudinal strength to the hull.

**Bilge strake.** Continuous horizontal range of plating at the turn of the bilge, extending from end to end of the vessel.

**Bosom piece.** Short length of angle-bar fitted inside the angle of another angle bar for strength, or inside the angles of two other angle-bars to join them.

**Box beam.** Strong form of beam made up of four long plates riveted together by means of angle-bars so as to form a box section.

**Box keelson.** Keelson formed with a foundation plate, side plates and a top plate, united in box form by riveting to angle-bars. The foundation plate was riveted to the top of the FLOORS at the centre-line.

**Bracket knee plate.** Flat plate, usually triangular in shape, used at the juncture of a FRAME and beam to unite and strengthen the connection.

**Breast plate.** Horizontal plate that joins the side plating at the stem.

**Bulb plate.** Iron or steel plate with one edge worked up into a bulb.

**Bulkhead stringer.** Plate-stringer set on gussets and connected by angle-bars to a bulkhead as a stiffener.

**Butt strap.** Metal strap covering the butt joint between adjoining plates;

it was riveted to each plate and so gave strength to the joint.

**Centre through plate keelson.** Continuous girder along the centre-line of a vessel, made up from a vertical plate with an angle-bar riveted to each side and to the FLOORS.

**Chain riveting.** See DOUBLE RIVETING.

**Channel bar.** Rolled iron or steel bar having a U-section.

**Clinker plating.** Method of plating in which the STRAKES (03.17) overlap each other.

**Cross strap.** An extra horizontal strengthening plate fitted on the top of the FLOORS and over the keelson plate.

**Crutch.** Triangular plate fitted horizontally in the stern to connect the ends of stringers and other longitudinal members.

**Deck plating.** Flat iron plating laid on the deck beams to provide a deck.

**Docking keel.** Alternative name for a BILGE KEEL.

**Double angle iron.** Form of girder made by riveting together two angle-bars; also known as *back to back bar*.

**Double plate keelson.** Form of keelson made up of a vertical longitudinal plate with angle-bars riveted on each side at top and bottom.

**Double riveting.** Rivets placed two abreast in close parallel lines.

**Doubling plate.** Strake of plating fitted over the SHELL PLATING (03.17) where extra strength is required.

**Dove-tail plate.** Shaped plate used at the connection of the keel with the stem and stern-post.

**Drifting.** Using a punch with a tapered end and parallel shaft to bring holes in two plates into alignment. The practice was condemned, since it forced and tore the plates and enlarged the holes.

**Flat plate keel.** Shaped horizontal plate, strengthened with angle-bars, which forms a keel outside the bottom SHELL PLATING.

**Floors.** Vertical plates in the vessel's bottom, extending from bilge to bilge, to which the frames are connected.

**Flush plating.** Method of plating in which the plates are fitted edge to edge and the joints secured with BUTT STRAPS.

**Frames.** Iron and steel sections extending upwards from the floor and forming the transverse ribs of a vessel.

**Garboard strake.** The line of longitudinal plating fitted next to and on each side of the keel.

**Girder.** In a ship, a section made up of iron or steel plates and angle-bars usually employed longitudinally under the sides of a deck or along the centre-line.

**Gusset plate.** Flat shaped plate placed horizontally, often at the junction of plates or angle-bars, for connection and strength.

**Gutter-way.** Channel formed between the gunwale and gutter-angle plate on the upper deck.

**Hollow iron keel.** Keel formed by bending an iron plate to shape and not by fabrication from plates and angle-bars.

**Hollow plate stern-post.** In early iron shipbuilding practice, the stern-post was sometimes formed by bending a plate to the required form.

**Hook.** Triangular plate fitted at the fore end of a vessel for connecting the ends of the STRINGERS (03.17) and strengthening the stem.

**Horseshoe plate.** Plate in the form of a horseshoe fitted under the counter, round the RUDDER STOCK (03.09).

**I bar.** Iron or steel bar having an I-shaped cross section.

**In and out plating.** Method of plating in which the edges of alternate STRAKES (03.17) overlap or are overlapped by the adjoining strakes.

**Inner bottom.** Plating laid on top of the FLOORS; or the upper plating of a double bottom.

**Inside strake.** Plate in direct contact with a FRAME.

**Intercostal keelson.** Keelson formed by a range of vertical plates fitted between the FLOORS. The lower edges of the plates are connected to the bottom plates by angle-bars.

**Intercostal plate.** Short plate fitted vertically between the FLOORS to form an INTERCOSTAL KEELSON or horizontally between the FRAMES to form an intercostal STRINGER (03.17).

**Joggling.** The operation of shaping the edges and seams of plates or the flanges of a FRAME, so that the plates and frames fit closely together.

**Keel plate.** One of a number of horizontal plates which together form a FLAT PLATE KEEL.

**Lap joint.** Joint formed by overlapping the edges of adjoining plates.

**Lining piece.** Strip of plate used as a filling piece, often inserted between plates and frames to avoid the necessity of JOGGLING (03.16).

**Lug pieces.** Short pieces of angle-bar used for uniting and strengthening various components of the ship's structure.

**Main sheer strake.** Range of longitudinal plating fitted along the line of the main deck.

**Outside strake.** Line of plating fitted over two inside STRAKES. The longitudinal edges of outside strakes overlap and are riveted to the longitudinal edges of the inside strakes.

**Overlap of plating.** That part of a STRAKE of plating covering part of another strake.

**Panting.** Inward and outward vibrating motion of the FRAMES and plates of a vessel.

**Partners.** System of angle-bar, bulb-plate and plates fitted for support and strength on and between the deck beams round masts and under capstans and windlasses.

**Pillar.** Vertical iron or steel bar fitted to support a deck or super-structure.

**Plate.** Iron or steel rolled to an equal thickness.

**Reverse frame.** Angle-bar riveted to the inboard edge of a FRAME (03.16) so that its flange goes in the opposite direction to that of the outboard flange of the frame.

**Rivet.** Small iron or steel bar with a head at one end. Another head is formed on the other end by hammering when the rivet is in place. Rivets are designated by the shape of the head; that is, conical, counter-sunk, panhead or snaphead.

**Sheer strake.** Line of side plating on a level with a deck above the main deck.

**Shell lugs.** Short angles fitted between the outside plating and the deck STRINGER PLATES.

**Shell plating.** The plates covering the outside of the hull of a vessel.

**Side bar keel.** Keel made of two side plates, between which the keelson plate is fitted.

**Single frame.** FRAME (03.16) formed from a single angle-bar.

**Sister keelsons.** Keelsons fitted along the inside of the bilges on each side.

**Solid bar stern-post.** Stern-post forged in one piece.

**Squeegee.** Cam-headed implement used for shaping frames on the BENDING SLAB (03.16).

**Stern-post.** Heavy iron or steel forging or casting extending from the after end of the keel upward to the upper or poop deck.

**Strake.** Continuous range of side plating extending from bow to stern of a vessel.

**Stringer.** Longitudinal member of a ship's structure, running fore and aft across the frames.

**Stringer plate.** Line of plates placed flat on the ends of deck beams to which they are riveted. Also, a range of interior horizontal plates in the vessel's side.

**T bar.** Iron or steel bar having a T-shaped cross-section.

**Thin plate keel.** Keel made up of an assemblage of plates laid side by side. The butts of the several layers are shifted (see SHIFT OF BUTTS, 03.10).

**Tie plates.** Narrow plates riveted onto the beams alongside hatchways on various decks to strengthen and bind the beams and to form a strong girder with the HATCH COAMINGS (03.14).

**Topside strake.** Line of side plating fitted immediately above the MAIN SHEER STRAKE.

**Transom plate.** Flat transverse plate fitted into the FRAME (03.16) at the extreme after end of a vessel.

**Treble riveting.** Rivets placed three abreast in close parallel lines.

**Upper sheer strake.** Line of continuous side plating fitted immediately above the TOPSIDE STRAKE.

**Wash plates.** Plates fitted vertically between the floors about half-way between the middle-line and the bilge to check the wash of water in the bilges when the vessel rolls.

**Web frame.** Extra-strong frame, composed of plates and bars, fitted between every fifth and sixth frame.

**Z bar.** Iron or steel bar with a Z-shaped cross-section.

**Z frame.** Frame made up of two angle-bars riveted together, with their angles reversed. This type of frame was used particularly for composite-built ships. Also known as a REVERSE FRAME.

**Zigzag riveting.** Rivets placed in parallel rows but alternately spaced; that is, not abreast.

# Yacht and Dinghy Terms

**Centre board.** Another name for a DROP KEEL.

**Cheese cutter.** Form of DROP KEEL for small craft.

**Clinker built.** Said of boats where the planks run fore and aft but with the lower edge of one plank overlapping the edge of the plank below.

**Diagonal built.** Said of boats with planks fitted edge to edge as in CARVEL-BUILT (03.03) boats but set at an angle of forty-five degrees to the keel. Naval sailing launches and pinnaces were diagonally built in two thicknesses, the inner thickness having the gunwale ends of the planks sloping aft and the outer thickness the gunwale ends sloping forward.

**Drop keel.** Iron plate housed in a wooden frame over a slot in the bottom of a boat and raised and lowered by a wire pendant rove on a drum fitted with pawl and ratchet gear, worked by a handle. When tacking, the drop keel is lowered to prevent the boat making LEEWAY (12.05).

**Landing.** The overlap of the strakes or planks in a vessel's sides.

**Lands.** Planking overlaps in a CLINKER-BUILT boat.

**Lee board.** Heavy iron-bound tapered board pivoted by its forward edge to the side of a flat-bottomed vessel. It is lowered by a chain to serve as a DROP KEEL when the vessel is TACKING (12.08) and thus reduce LEEWAY (12.05).

**Mussel bow.** Type of yacht with bows that are cut away to form a shallow shape rather like that of a mussel shell.

**Sewn boat.** Boat built of two thicknesses of Honduras mahogany. The inner thickness of 5/32 inch is secured at right angles to the keel; the outer thickness of $\frac{1}{4}$ inch is fixed to the frames longitudinally. These two thicknesses, together with the timbers and floors, are sewn together with annealed copper wire.

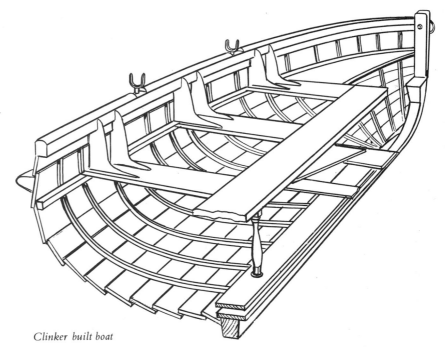

*Clinker built boat*

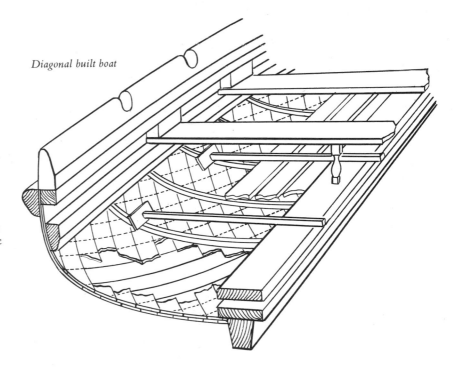

*Diagonal built boat*

# Masts, Spars, Sails & Rigging

I am writing here of ocean-going square-rigged ships propelled wholly by sail – acres of it, spread hostage to the wind high aloft on giant masts usually built up in immensely strong sections of steel, iron or the best of mammoth trees, the principal masts often reaching towards the limit of 200 feet (keel to truck) and strong and stoutly rigged enough to come through any storm, even hurricanes. The great principle in all rigging was that the masts and yards, being the basis, should survive any ferocity of sea and wind, but sails could usually be replaced as often as necessary. Masts and spars stood up and stayed there: canvas could blow away.

All big sailing ships had considerable stores of sails, a minimum of two whole suits and plenty of old Trade Winds patched spares as well. For those happily more or less constant winds blowing in the ocean's tropical zones, old, patched-up sails suited very well. The Trades could be fresh or even strong, but they were normally constant. They did not charge about the sea, shifting viciously or violently as the mood might take them, nor did they roar round the Earth in wild, cyclonic movements and shifts which had to be guarded against day and night. Not at all, for they were the friendly winds of the sea.

In any consideration of the square-riggers' 'machinery', the masts come first. They obviously began as single flawless great trimmed trees (as in Arab dhows) and, as trees grew so high and no higher, masts had to have extensions to enable them to carry more sail, whether the sail was set from or between yards (lesser trees) set up aloft or, as in schooners, fore and aft abaft the masts. The dhow-type was content with the one huge lateen sail set from one lateen yard on the main (often the only) mast, though the larger dhows in the Indian Ocean trades (mainly date-carriers from the head of the Persian Gulf peddling their wares along the monsoonal coast of East Africa as far down as Zanzibar, and carrying back mangrove poles cut from Rufiji swamps) always had two. Obviously, the more masts, the more sail could be set, and these dhows (Arab and Indian or Somali) sailed very well; so well, indeed, that having developed a thousand years or so ago, and being well suited to their monsoonal trade, they survived in the northern Indian Ocean right through the centuries – simple, adequate, good sailing vessels.

What more could be wanted? It was the Europeans and Americans who built up masts in sections, adding more and more yards until some of their huge full-rigged ships looked like somewhat bare forests wired for sound. Masts were for carrying sail to catch the wind. Spars (or yards) were added across them – some hoisting, some fixed – to catch more wind and so drive the ships more efficiently. Such ships were called square-riggers and were instantly identifiable, for many other large ships carried only fore-and-aft sails set between a fixed boom (lower spar) and hoisting gaff, both always abaft the mast. The latter type, the schooners, were in time rigged with four, five, six and even seven masts, each mast carrying two sails only, both set between a lower boom and hoisting gaff. This type lent itself to simplified mechanization and was very economical with manpower, especially in such areas as the tropics of the Pacific, the monsoonal zones of the Indian Ocean and the Trade Winds of the Atlantic.

In all these areas, schooners large and small prospered for a very long time. They might be slow (in comparison to those set with square sails, which caught much more wind with greater impact), but they were economical and reasonably efficient, which made them almost ideal for cargoes such as big lumber in the shape of felled and trimmed trees from Californian, North-West American and British Columbian forests. One remembers scores of these huge, fat schooners and the occasional barquentine coming into Melbourne, Sydney, Auckland or Wellington, during the First World War and for some years afterwards, almost awash beneath the enormous timber stacks which formed their cargoes. Square-riggers were not at all suitable for carrying huge timber stacks, especially on deck, for their decks and all their rigging were essentially working places. The big fore-and-after was a very different proposition, with minimal sail, set abaft her masts out of the way of her deck cargo, easy to get at and to work, especially if there were a big donkey-boiler and winch by the break of the forecastle head. Such a boiler, and some half-dozen men, brought many an enormous stack of sawn timber from Puget Sound and the State of Washington into the parts of Australia and New Zealand. I remember gazing with astonishment at them as a boy, but I sought to join none.

No. It was square-rig for me, the *real* thing: barques, full-riggers, the Cape Horn men who took on the sea world. The square-riggers could show (and use) a real spread of canvas, stretched high aloft on yards hoisted on topmasts and topgallant masts, these last built up on huge steel lower masts – solid, seaworthy, built to use gales, not Trade Winds wanderers, flying-fish chasers. I was biased, perhaps; but the wind sang so powerfully in those huge square-rigged masts, while it offered nothing but a few gentle sighs as it slipped through the sparse staying of a schooner's masts – even if there were six of them. Some of the low-gutted, over-filled things might as well have been motor-ships. There had to be real masts, spars, sails and rigging for me! That symmetrical, orderly, properly developed sweep of controllable square sail was the inspiration of the artist whether he be poet (such as Masefield), composer (such as Percy Grainger), etcher (such as Arthur Briscoe), great Grain–Race winner (such as Captain Ruben de Cloux) or conqueror of Cape Horn (such as Captain Robert Hilgendorff of the Laeisz Line).

The ordered maze of masts, yards and rigging grew and was developed for the really tough sailing routes, such as that round Cape Horn. The development was slow at first, perhaps originally confined to the finer weather zones of the world where the seasonal winds – later known as Trade Winds, monsoons and so on – were gradually exploited by men, men who in time learnt to harvest the earth and to trade by sea with the fruits of that harvest. Indeed, it was a marvellous system, this system of winds and oceans, of rivers and ports and harbours, of trees for shipbuilding and flax for sails, of hemp and manila fibre and coir for cordage and for ropes. And how remarkable was the courageous ability of the seamen!

So, slowly, the ship grew, growing from rafts of floating logs, hollowed-out tree-trunks. At first the tree-trunk formed the whole boat, then it slowly developed into the keel of a built-up ship. Eventually came the ships which gave stowage for people, water, stores and cargo, slipping with them through the seas on countless passages, carried on the winds, the seasonal winds of the tropical zones. As understanding of winds and seas and the grasp of the science of sailing grew, the ships were steadily improved, their voyages lengthened, and the seas and the lands great and small of this Earth were slowly sailed to, opened up, and developed.

In all this the prime agents were the sail and man's ingenuity and courage.

ALAN VILLIERS

*The Norwegian sail training square rigger*
Statsraad Lehmkuhl

# Types of Mast

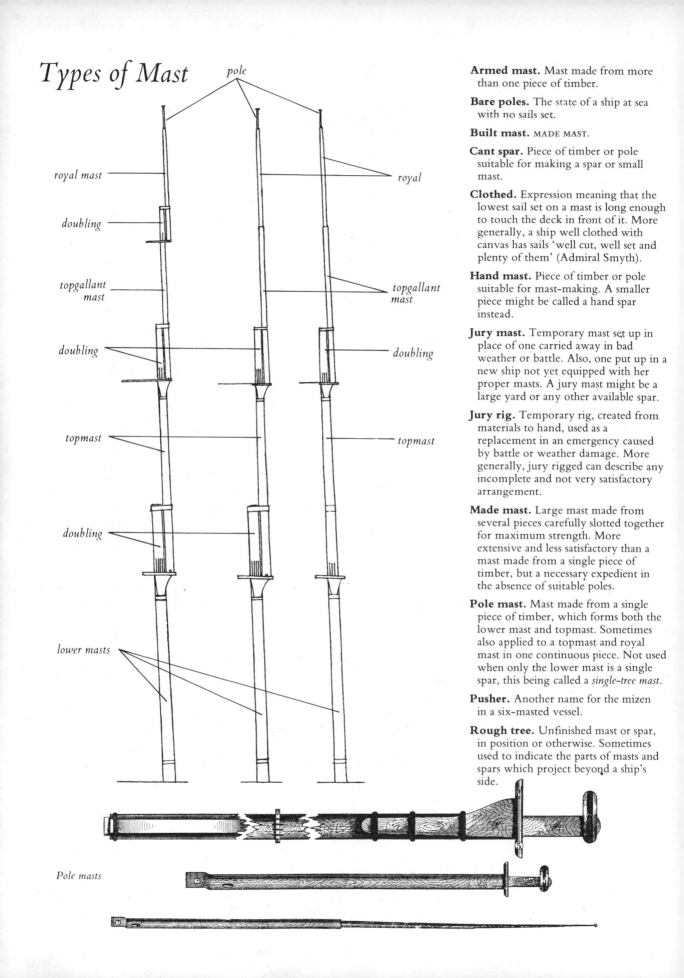

pole

royal mast

doubling

topgallant
mast

doubling

topmast

doubling

lower masts

royal

topgallant
mast

doubling

topmast

Pole masts

**Armed mast.** Mast made from more than one piece of timber.

**Bare poles.** The state of a ship at sea with no sails set.

**Built mast.** MADE MAST.

**Cant spar.** Piece of timber or pole suitable for making a spar or small mast.

**Clothed.** Expression meaning that the lowest sail set on a mast is long enough to touch the deck in front of it. More generally, a ship well clothed with canvas has sails 'well cut, well set and plenty of them' (Admiral Smyth).

**Hand mast.** Piece of timber or pole suitable for mast-making. A smaller piece might be called a hand spar instead.

**Jury mast.** Temporary mast set up in place of one carried away in bad weather or battle. Also, one put up in a new ship not yet equipped with her proper masts. A jury mast might be a large yard or any other available spar.

**Jury rig.** Temporary rig, created from materials to hand, used as a replacement in an emergency caused by battle or weather damage. More generally, jury rigged can describe any incomplete and not very satisfactory arrangement.

**Made mast.** Large mast made from several pieces carefully slotted together for maximum strength. More extensive and less satisfactory than a mast made from a single piece of timber, but a necessary expedient in the absence of suitable poles.

**Pole mast.** Mast made from a single piece of timber, which forms both the lower mast and topmast. Sometimes also applied to a topmast and royal mast in one continuous piece. Not used when only the lower mast is a single spar, this being called a *single-tree mast*.

**Pusher.** Another name for the mizen in a six-masted vessel.

**Rough tree.** Unfinished mast or spar, in position or otherwise. Sometimes used to indicate the parts of masts and spars which project beyond a ship's side.

*The masts of the* Peking

**Spencer mast.** Auxiliary light mast, placed immediately behind the mainmast or fore lower mast, to which a fore-and-aft sail called a SPENCER (04.11) was attached by HOOPS (04.04).

**Stump mast.** Lower mast rigged on its own, with no tops and with no mast above it.

**Stump topgallant mast.** Topgallant mast with no royal mast above it.

**Telescopic topmast.** Topmast which can be withdrawn into the lower mast by means of an arrangement of SHEAVES (05.01) and wires. Used on canal and river vessels which have to pass under low bridges.

**Tripod mast.** Three-legged mast. The extra rigidity of this arrangement eliminates the need for shrouds and much of the rest of the standing rigging.

**Trysail mast.** Spar or auxiliary mast rigged immediately abaft the foremast or mainmast to take the trysail.

**Wrung.** Term used to describe a mast bent or strained out of its natural position by badly set up rigging.

# Mast Fittings and Parts

**Acorn.** Small shaped piece of wood, fixed above the mast-head to take the *wind vane.*

**An-end.** Position of any yard rigged perpendicularly. For example, a topmast is an-end when hoisted and fixed in place. Term also applied to any rope coiled down and/or clear for running.

**Body hoops.** Metal hoops which hold the parts of a MADE MAST (04.01). together.

**Bolsters.** Rounded pieces of hardwood on top of TRESTLE-TREES (04.03). preventing the rigging from chafing on their sharp edges.

**Cap.** Two-holed fitting which holds an upper mast in one hole against the top of a lower mast which fits in the other hole.

**Capshore,** or **cap-shore.** Supporting spar between the CAP and the TRESTLE-TREE (04.03).

**Chafing board.** Piece of wood positioned to prevent chafing.

**Chafing gear.** Wide variety of protective coverings designed to prevent unnecessary wear on a vessel's spars and rigging.

**Chafing mat.** Portable mat of woven rope or yarn used to prevent a rope from chafing against a spar or plank.

**Cheeks.** Flat timbers or iron plates bolted either side of the mast and projecting forward to form a bracket to support the HEEL of an upper mast.

**Dolphin.** Strap of plaited cordage placed round a yard or its PUDDENING as a support.

**Doublings.** Section of overlap between the top of the lower mast and the bottom of the upper one. Also, the space between the TRESTLE-TREES (04.03) and the CAP.

**Fid.** Square-section pin of wood or iron, with a shoulder at one end, inserted through a hole in the heel of the topmost into the TRESTLE-TREES (04.03). The topmast is then said to be fidded or fixed in place.

**Filler,** or **filling.** Filling piece in a MADE MAST (04.01).

**Fish,** or **fish piece.** Long, convex piece of wood, designed to reinforce a damaged mast or spar. Usually fastened in pairs on both sides of the damaged section. To splint a mast in this way is to fish it.

**Fish front.** Strengthening slab in a MADE MAST (04.01).

**Futtock hoop,** or **futtock band,** or **spider band.** Iron band round lower mast, having a number of eye-bolts to take the lower ends of the topmast FUTTOCK SHROUDS (04.08).

**Futtock plate.** Iron plate fitted with DEAD-EYES (05.01), placed at the edge of the lower top. The FUTTOCK SHROUDS (04.08) are attached to the lower edge of the plate, the dead-eyes of the topmast rigging to the upper edge.

**Heel.** The lower end of a topmast. The heel of a lower mast rests in a step, but that of a topmast stands on a FID.

**Horseshoe rack.** Rack curved in the shape of a horseshoe, placed abaft a mast to take blocks acting as FAIRLEADS (05.03) for the running rigging.

**Hounds.** Projections on either side of the head of an upper mast or the head of a small mast, supporting the TRESTLE-TREES (04.03). Similar in functions to the CHEEKS of a lower mast.

**Hounds band.** Metal band round the upper part of a mast to which the shrouds are attached.

**Mast bands.** Metal bands round a mast, fitted with lugs to take blocks.

**Mast coat.** Conical canvas cover fitted round a mast where it emerges through the deck, to prevent water penetrating below.

**Mast-head.** Upper part of a mast, above the rigging.

**Masting sheers.** Pair of SHEER-LEGS (07.01) mounted on shore or on a sheer hulk, used as a crane to hoist a mast and lower it into place on a ship.

**Preventer fid.** Additional bar of wood or iron put through a mast about two feet above the FID (04.02) hole as an insurance against the fid breaking.

**Puddening,** or **pudding.** Band of plaited cordage, tapering towards the outer edges, placed around a yard in order to keep it in place in case of damage.

**Rubbing paunch.** Piece of wood running down the front of a mast, or

covering the hoops of a MADE MAST (04.01), to prevent damage to yards during hoisting or lowering.

**Scotchman.** Piece of stiff hide, or a wooden batten or similar protection, placed over standing rigging to prevent chafing.

**Shroud hoop.** Metal band fitted with eyes through which the upper ends of shrouds are fastened.

**Side fishes,** or **fish sides,** or **aris pieces.** Side pieces of a MADE MAST (04.01).

*Spider*

**Spider.** Iron outrigger used to keep a block clear of the ship's side.

**Spider band,** or **spider iron.** Iron band round a lower mast near the deck fitted with sockets for BELAYING PINS (10.07).

**Spider hoop.** Metal band round the mast to secure the shackles of FUTTOCK SHROUDS (04.08). Also, another name for SPIDER BAND.

**Spindle.** Timber core of a MADE MAST (04.01).

**Spring** (vb). To crack a mast or yard.

**Spring.** Crack running obliquely through a yard or spar, making it unsafe to carry the normal amount of sail.

**Tongue,** or **tumbler.** Block of wood pivoted on a pin between the jaws of a gaff, designed to assist it to slide up and down more easily. The pivot enables the tongue to fit the angle of the raised gaff.

**Trucks,** or **top buttons,** or **buttons.** Circular wooden caps on upper mast-heads, usually fitted with sheaves for signal halyards. Also, spherical wooden beads (or bull's-eyes) threaded on the gaff jaw rope, making it easier to slide up and down. Similar bull's-eyes are also used as FAIRLEADS (05.03) to prevent rigging from jamming.

**Wrung.** Said of a mast or spar that has been badly strained or distorted.

*Main mast of the* Grace Harwar

# Tops, Cross-trees, Parrels and Trusses

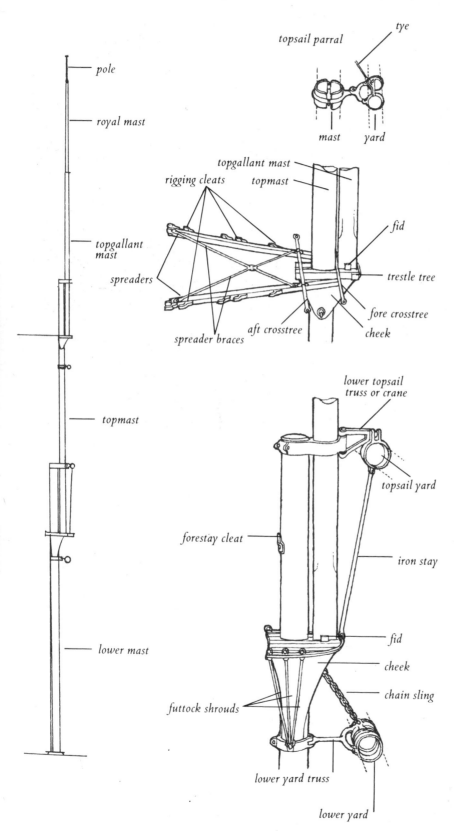

pole

royal mast

topgallant mast

topmast

lower mast

topsail parral

tye

mast    yard

topgallant mast

topmast

rigging cleats

spreaders

spreader braces

aft crosstree

fore crosstree

cheek

trestle tree

fid

lower topsail truss or crane

topsail yard

forestay cleat

iron stay

fid

cheek

chain sling

futtock shrouds

lower yard truss

lower yard

**Cross-trees.** Timbers laid across the upper end of a mast, supported by the CHEEKS (04.02) and TRESTLE-TREES (04.03). They carry the framework of the top and increase the span of the shrouds. Also, general description of the area where an upper mast is attached to a lower one.

**Grab ratline.** Line placed above rim of tops to assist men coming up the shrouds.

**Lubber's hole.** Space between the head of the lower mast and the inner edge of the top. An alternative route into the top to the futtock shrouds for the timid climber, and frowned on by seamen.

**Main top.** Platform at the head of the mainmast, resting on the CROSS-TREES. Serves both to spread the topmast shrouds and as the position from which the upper sails are controlled. In battle, a useful vantage point from which to discharge weapons.

**Nave line.** Small tackle rigged from the head of the mainmast and foremast and fastened to the middle of the PARREL, to keep it in place and directly parallel to the yard, particularly while hoisting or lowering.

**Parrel, or parral.** Rope or iron collar which attaches the centre of a yard to the mast and can slide up or down the mast as required. Also, the rope which fastens the jaws of a gaff to the mast.

**Parrel trucks.** Large wooden beads (or bull's-eyes) threaded onto the PARREL joining the jaws of the gaff. Their rolling action makes it easier to raise or lower the gaff.

**Rib and truck, or jaw parrels.** Alternating ribs and trucks threaded on a PARREL rope. The ribs are pieces of wood about a foot long with a smooth inner end resting against the mast; they serve to separate the PARREL TRUCKS.

**Rim, or brim.** Circular outer edge of a top.

**Round top.** Early tops were circular in plan view. The name stuck, despite the fact that, by the eighteenth century, tops had assumed a different shape.

**Spreaders.** Extensions bolted on each side of the CROSS-TREES to spread the topgallant and royal backstays (in a square-rigger) or the topmast backstay (in a schooner). Also, metal bars rigged out horizontally in small craft with sharp bows, to give more spread to the HEAD SHEET (04.09), on the same principle as WHISKERS (04.07).

**Top-lantern.** Large signal lantern in the after part of a top.

*Out on the yards of the* Joseph Conrad

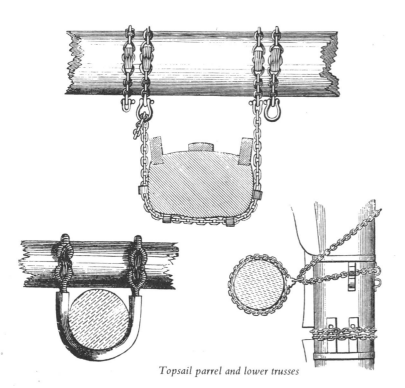

*Topsail parrel and lower trusses*

**Toprail.** Rail secured to STANCHIONS (01.01) along the after edge of the lower top.

**Top rim.** Circular sweep of the fore part of a top, covering the ends of the CROSS-TREES and TRESTLE-TREES to prevent the topsails from chafing on them.

**Trestle-trees.** Two strong pieces of timber placed fore and aft, resting on the CHEEKS (04.02) at the head of a mast. Those on the lower mast support the CROSS-TREES, top and topmast. Those on the topmast support the cross-trees and topgallant mast.

**Truss,** or **parrel of the lower yard.** Rope binding securing the lower yard to the mast. Generally replaced in later years by the metal GOOSE-NECK (04.07).

**Truss hoop,** or **clasp hoop.** Open-ended iron hoop to fit round a mast or spar. The two ends can be locked together with a wedge or key.

**Truss-parrel.** The part of a rope PARREL which goes round the yard.

# Yards and Yard Fittings

**Brace pendant.** Length of chain suspended from the yard-arm, to which a yard-arm brace block is attached.

**Bullwanger.** Short length of rope with an eye in the end, nailed to the back of a lower yard to prevent the EARING (04.13) slipping under the yard.

**Cross-jack,** or **crojack,** or **crossjack yard.** Lower yard on mizen mast or the sail it supports.

**End ring.** Metal band fitted at yard ends, to prevent them from splitting.

**Flemish horse.** Short extra FOOT-ROPE for men working at the outer end of the yard. Attached at the GOOSE-NECK (04.07) of the STUDDING-SAIL BOOM (04.07) and at the brace-block STROP (05.01).

**Foot-rope.** Rope stretched under the yards and jib-booms, for men to stand on while loosing or furling the sails. Also, the rope sewn to the lower edge of a sail.

**Hoops.** Bands of wood or iron placed round a spar to strengthen it. Also, rings which attach a sail to a spar or mast, and which enable the sail to slide up and down.

**Horse.** FOOT-ROPE running from the opposite quarter of a yard to near the end. Also, a rope attached to the foremast shrouds, with a DEAD-EYE (05.01) to take the spritsail sheet and keep it clear of the flukes of the ANCHOR (06.02).

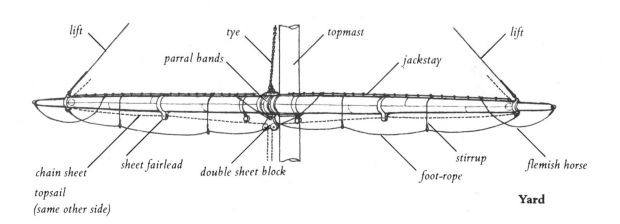

*lift*     *tye*     *topmast*     *lift*

*parral bands*     *jackstay*

*chain sheet*     *sheet fairlead*     *double sheet block*     *stirrup*     *flemish horse*

*topsail*
*(same other side)*     *foot-rope*

**Yard**

**Jackstay.** Rope, batten or iron bar fastened to the upper side of a yard or spar, to which the head of a square sail is attached.

**Jeers.** Tackles used for swaying (hoisting) or striking (lowering) the courses (foresail, mainsail and mizen); the equivalent of halyards for these sails.

**Lateen yard.** Long spar hoisted obliquely to the mast, the lower and usually shorter end in front of the mast, the higher and longer behind. Forms the leading edge of a LATEEN SAIL (04.11).

**Quarter of yard.** Distance between the middle (slings) and half-way point of a yard.

**Reefing jackstay,** or **jack line,** or **reef line.** Rope rove through the GROMMETS (05.09) of a REEF BAND (04.12). Used for reefing with a toggle on the JACKSTAY.

**Rolling chock,** or **rolling cleat,** or **parrel cleat.** Piece of wood fastened to the middle of an upper yard, half encircling it, secured by a PARREL (04.03) to steady the yard.

**Saddle.** Notched chock of wood fixed to one spar, forming a rest for another. An example is the saddle used to support the HEEL (04.02) of the jib-boom on the bowsprit.

**Sliding gunter.** Light upper mast fitted behind the mast to carry royals, skysails and the like.

**Sling** (vb). To pass a chain round the yards as a safeguard against possible damage. Generally, to pass a rope round an object in order to lift it with a tackle.

**Sling.** Rope or chain support for a non-lowering yard. Also, the middle area of the yard to which the sling is attached.

**Snorter,** or **snotter.** Small rope or strap on the end of a light yard, to which halyards or TOPPING LIFTS (04.07) are attached.

**Snotter.** Loop of rope or metal passing round the mast of a SPRIT rig and supporting the lower end of the sprit against it. Generally, any loop used to prevent slipping. The other usage of snotter is more properly rendered as SNORTER.

**Sprit.** Diagonally placed boom supporting a four-cornered fore-and-aft sail. Also, spar or spars keeping the SHEERS (01.01) of a sheer hulk at the right angle.

*Aloft in Italian sail trainer* Amerigo Vespucci, *1974*

**Stirrups.** Short ropes nailed to a yard, supporting the FOOT-ROPE, which is led through eyes in their lower ends.

**Top chain.** Additional chain sling used on warships to take the weight of the yards, as a precaution against the normal supports being shot away.

**Yard-arm iron.** Metal fitment on the end of a yard, with rings to take STUDDING-SAIL BOOMS (04.07).

**Yard rope.** Rope used for hoisting or lowering those yards which are usually left in position. The equivalent rope for a lowering yard is a halyard.

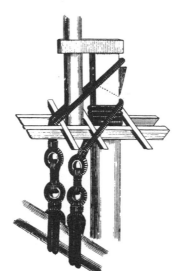

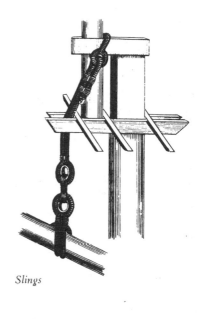

*Slings*

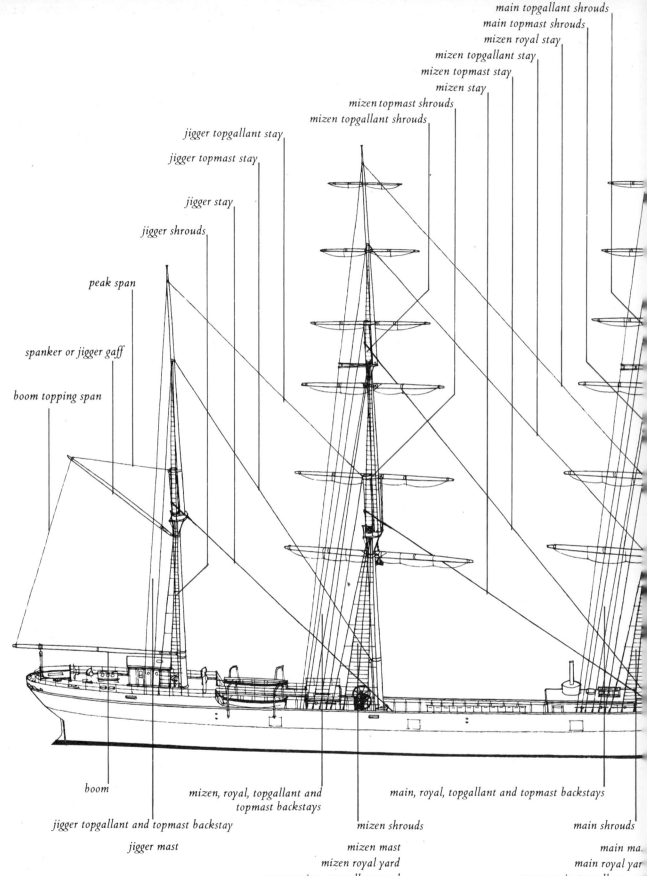

main topgallant shrouds
main topmast shrouds
mizen royal stay
mizen topgallant stay
mizen topmast stay
mizen stay
mizen topmast shrouds
mizen topgallant shrouds

jigger topgallant stay

jigger topmast stay

jigger stay

jigger shrouds

peak span

spanker or jigger gaff

boom topping span

mizen, royal, topgallant and
topmast backstays

main, royal, topgallant and topmast backstays

boom

jigger topgallant and topmast backstay

mizen shrouds

main shrouds

jigger mast

mizen mast

main ma.

mizen royal yard

main royal yar

upper mizen topgallant yard

upper main topgallant yar

lower mizen topgallant yard

lower main topgallant yar

upper mizen topsail yard

upper main topsail yar

lower mizen topsail yard

lower main topsail yar

mizen yard

main yar

**Four-Masted Barque**

# Masts and Spars of a Representative Ship

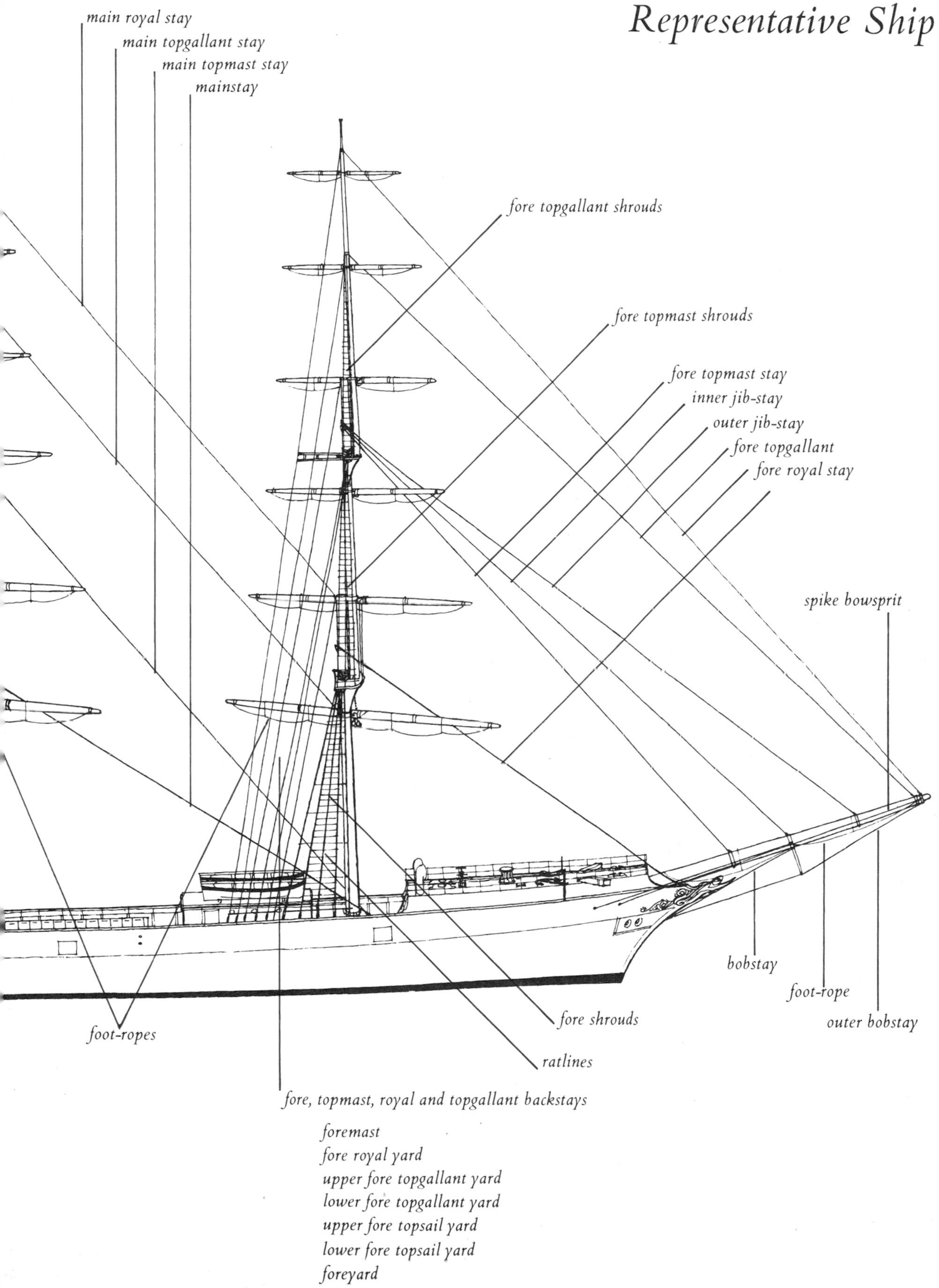

main royal stay

main topgallant stay

main topmast stay

mainstay

fore topgallant shrouds

fore topmast shrouds

fore topmast stay

inner jib-stay

outer jib-stay

fore topgallant

fore royal stay

spike bowsprit

bobstay

foot-rope

outer bobstay

foot-ropes

fore shrouds

ratlines

fore, topmast, royal and topgallant backstays

foremast

fore royal yard

upper fore topgallant yard

lower fore topgallant yard

upper fore topsail yard

lower fore topsail yard

foreyard

# Bowsprit, Jib-boom and their Fittings

**Bowsprit cap,** or **crance,** or **crance iron.** Iron fitting at the tip of the bowsprit, with a hoop or ring to take the jib-boom.

**Bowsprit collars.** Metal bands fitted round the bowsprit to prevent the wood from splitting.

**Crance iron.** See BOWSPRIT CAP.

**Crupper chain.** Short length of chain securing the heel of the jib-boom to the bowsprit head.

**Dolphin striker.** Short wood or metal spar pointing downwards from the end of the bowsprit, spreading the MARTINGALES (04.08), and counteracting the upward pull on the jib-boom end.

**Gammoning.** Tautened rope or chain lashing, staying the bowsprit to the KNEE OF THE HEAD. It serves to hold the bowsprit down against the upward pull of the forestay.

**Heel chain.** Short length of chain that secures the heel of the topmast to the lower mast-head.

**Heel rope.** Rope passed through the heel of a spar in order to haul it into position. In particular, the rope used for hauling out the jib-boom or STUDDING-SAIL BOOM (04.07), or, in the case of some small craft, the bowsprit.

**Jackstaff.** Flagpole, usually on the BOWSPRIT CAP, from which the jack (bow flag) is flown.

**Jib iron.** Iron hoop encircling the jib-boom and able to travel freely along it. The jib iron takes the lower foremost corner of the jib.

**Pillow.** Block of timber supporting inner end of bowsprit.

**Spike bowsprit.** Bowsprit formed of a single spar.

**Steeving.** The angle of a bowsprit from the horizontal.

*Gammoning of the bowsprit of HMS* Victory

*Bowsprit of training schooner* Captain Scott

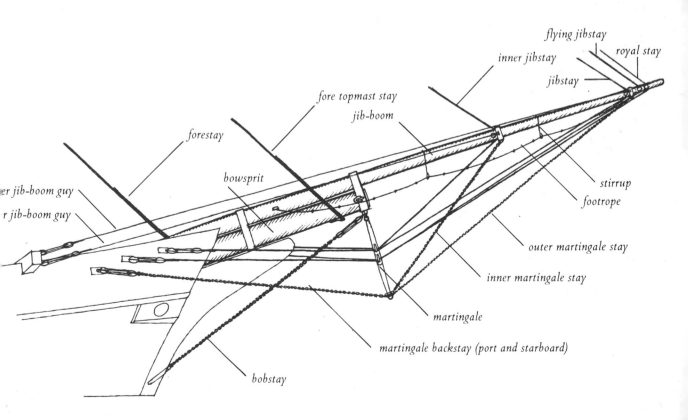

flying jibstay

royal stay

inner jibstay

jibstay

fore topmast stay

jib-boom

forestay

stirrup

footrope

bowsprit

er jib-boom guy

r jib-boom guy

outer martingale stay

inner martingale stay

martingale

martingale backstay (port and starboard)

bobstay

# Booms, Gaffs and their Fittings

**Bentinck boom.** Boom stretching the foot of the foresail, used on some smaller square-rigged merchantmen. The boom, which ran from CLEW (04.12) to clew of the sail, pivoted on its centre. The device made it possible to adjust the sail quickly and easily when going about, thus saving labour.

**Boom.** Spar used to stretch out the foot of a sail.

**Boom cradle.** Fitting on deck into which a boom is lowered and which keeps it in place.

**Boom crutch.** Fitting upon which the booms of small fore-and-aft rigged craft are rested when in harbour.

**Boom guy, or lazy guy.** Rope or tackle used to steady the SPANKER BOOM when running free.

**Boom iron, or withe.** Iron band at the yard-arm with a fitting through which the STUDDING-SAIL BOOM runs in and out, and which holds down the heel of the boom when rigged out.

**Boomkin, or bumkin, or bumpkin.** Short boom, projecting at either side of the bow, used to extend the lower windward corner of the foresail. This is done by passing the TACK (04.09) through a large block at the end of the boom. Also, a similar short boom rigged on the quarter of a ship to take one of the main brace blocks.

**Boom stays.** Fittings which secure the heel of a boom to its mast and retain it in its correct position.

**Bumpkin.** Small boom or outrigger over the stern of a boat, usually to extend the mizen.

**Clip.** Alternative name for the THROAT of a gaff or boom.

**Club.** Spar set at the foot of any triangular sail, such as a jib.

**Fancy line.** Line running through a block at the jaws of a gaff and acting as a DOWNHAUL (04.09). Also, line used for cross-hauling the lee TOPPING LIFT.

**Goose-neck.** Form of universal joint used for attaching a swinging boom to a mast, to the ship's side and so on.

**Guess warp boom, or guest warp boom.** Boom swung out from the side of a ship to provide a temporary mooring for small boats, tenders and so on.

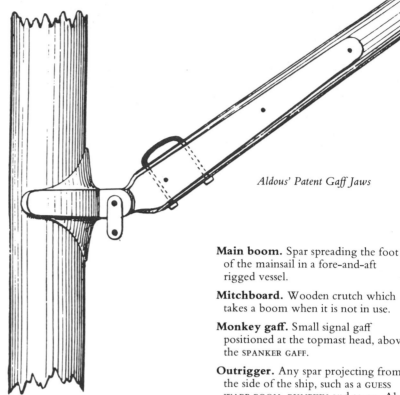

*Aldous' Patent Gaff Jaws*

**Horns.** Points of the jaws of a boom. Also the outer ends of CROSS-TREES (04.03).

**Jaw.** Pronged inner end of a gaff or a boom, shaped to fit onto a mast.

**Jaw rope.** Rope attached across the jaw of a gaff in order to hold it to the mast. Usually rove through bull's-eyes—freely revolving wooden beads designed to reduce friction between jaw rope and mast.

**Jib guys.** Ropes which stay down the jib-boom against the pressure of its sail and other strains.

**Jumper guys.** Ropes which stay down the ends of the bowsprit WHISKERS.

**Lower boom.** Originally, studding-sail boom rigged out from the yard-arm in light winds. Later a GUESS WARP BOOM.

**Main boom.** Spar spreading the foot of the mainsail in a fore-and-aft rigged vessel.

**Mitchboard.** Wooden crutch which takes a boom when it is not in use.

**Monkey gaff.** Small signal gaff positioned at the topmast head, above the SPANKER GAFF.

**Outrigger.** Any spar projecting from the side of the ship, such as a GUESS WARP BOOM, BUMPKIN and so on. Also, small spar used in tops and CROSS-TREES (04.03) to spread the BACKSTAYS (04.08).

**Quarter iron.** Hinged fitment holding the heel of a STUDDING-SAIL BOOM fixed about two-thirds of the way along the yard from the yard-arm.

**Snaffle.** Metal fitting on a boom or yard which takes the pin of the GOOSE-NECK by which a boom is suspended and swivelled.

**Spanker boom.** Boom of the fore-and-aft mizen sail.

**Spanker gaff.** Standing or running gaff to which the spanker is attached.

**Spinnaker boom.** Long light boom for extending the foot of the SPINNAKER (04.14). It swings out on the side opposite to the main or fore boom.

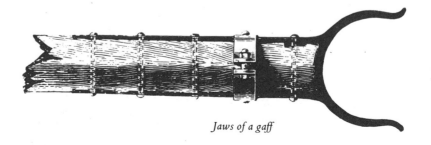

*Jaws of a gaff*

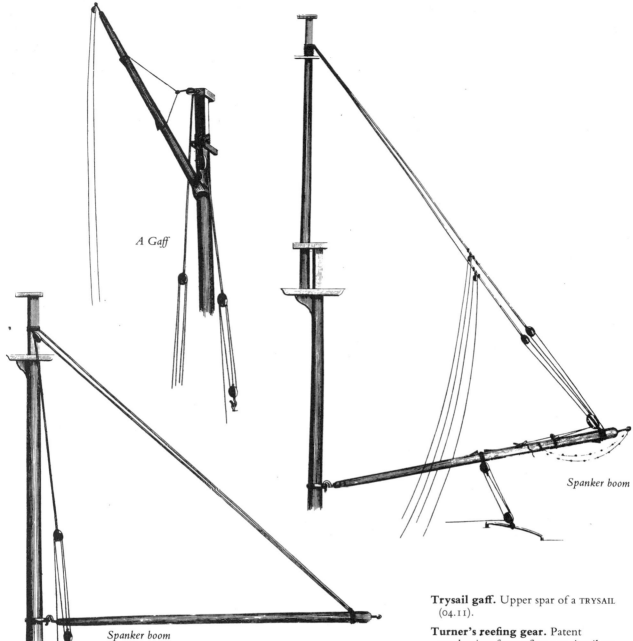

*A Gaff*

*Spanker boom*

*Spanker boom*

**Spritsail gaff.** Yard rigged beneath the bowsprit to carry a spritsail.

**Studding-sail booms,** or **stunsail booms.** Spars rigged out from the yards, upon which the studding sails are set.

**Throat.** The end of a gaff, widened and hollowed to fit the mast. The other end is called the *peak*.

**Throat bolts.** Eye-bolts in the throat of a gaff and in the lower part of a top which hold the THROAT HALYARDS (04.09).

**Throat brails.** Ropes attached to the gaff and going out to the LEECH (04.12) of a fore-and-aft sail, used for gathering the sail into the gaff as well as the mast.

**Throat downhaul.** Rope for hauling down the THROAT of a gaff.

**Topping lifts.** Ropes or tackle supporting the head of a spar, DAVIT (06.02) or DERRICK (07.01). In particular, the ropes running from mast-head to yard-arm, used to raise, lower or square the latter.

**Trucks.** Large spherical wooden beads, threaded onto a rope to reduce friction. When fitted to a gaff JAW ROPE, for example, the rolling action of the trucks makes it easier to hoist the gaff into position.

**Trysail gaff.** Upper spar of a TRYSAIL (04.11).

**Turner's reefing gear.** Patent mechanism for reefing a mainsail set on a boom, restricted almost entirely to yachts. The sail is rolled down by rotating the boom. The gear is designed to be operated single-handed.

**Vane.** Wind-direction indicator or weather cock usually fitted at the top of a mast.

**Whisker booms,** or **whiskers.** Wood or iron spars which project from the CAT-HEADS (03.07) on either side of the bow, in order to spread the rigging of the jib-boom and keep it clear of the anchor gear. Also, light spars with jaws at one end to go round the mast, and a spike at the other to take the CLEW (04.12) of a sail. In smaller vessels, these were used to hold the clew of a sail out to the side.

# Standing Rigging

*Ratlines*

**Back rope.** Rope or chain for staying the DOLPHIN STINKER (04.06).

**Backstays.** Ropes which support the mast against the forward thrust of the sails. They stretch from the mast-heads back to either side of the ship, or to the channels.

**Bentinck shrouds.** Extra shrouds to support the mast as the ship rolls. They extend from the weather FUTTOCK SHROUDS to the lee channels. Obsolete by the later nineteenth century.

**Black down** (vb). To tar rigging in order to preserve it.

**Bobstay.** Rope or chain leading from the end of the bowsprit to the stem, holding the bowsprit down against the strain of the foremast stays.

**Bowsprit shrouds.** Ropes or chains leading from the end of the bowsprit to the sides of the bow, giving it lateral support.

**Breast backstay.** BACKSTAY running down through an OUTRIGGER (04.07) from the head of an upper mast to the channels, supporting the upper mast from windward.

**Burton pendant, or burton.** Rope with an EYE in the upper end which goes over the topmast head, and with a tackle attached to the other end, used for lifting heavy weights. The fish-tackle burton or fish-tackle pendant is used in particular for lifting anchors over the bows when no anchor crane or DAVIT (06.02) is fitted. In this case, it is attached to the fore topmast head. The term can also describe the tackles used for setting up the shrouds.

**Catch ratline.** Specially strengthened RATLINE (04.08) interspersed regularly with the ordinary ratline.

**Cat-harpins, or cat-harpings, or catharpins.** Ropes under the tops bracing in the lower end of the FUTTOCK SHROUDS, making more room to brace the yards round, and keeping the futtock shrouds taut.

**Cat-harpin swifter.** Foremost shroud of the futtock rigging, never confined by the CAT-HARPINS.

**Chains.** Strengthened areas of a sailing ship's hull to which the shrouds are attached. The shrouds are led over projecting ledges, the channels or chain-wales, which serve to spread them. Below the channels are fixed the chain-plates, metal bars to which the shrouds are secured by a system of DEAD-EYES (05.01) and screws. The fore chains were the usual place from which the leadsman took his soundings. The chains were also used for the natural functions of the crew when bad weather made the HEADS (03.13) untenable.

**Collar.** EYE in the end or bight of a shroud or stay looped over the mast-head. Also, rope formed into an eye with a DEAD-EYE (05.01) inside.

**Cutter-stay fashion.** Method of setting up (tautening) lower rigging resembling that used in cutters. Each LANYARD is knotted at one end, then rove through the upper and lower DEAD-EYES (05.01).

**Eye.** Loop of a shroud or stay to go over a mast. Also, any closed loop formed at the end of a rope.

**Fore cat-harpins.** The CAT-HARPINS of the foremast shrouds.

**Futtock shrouds.** Originally, short lengths of rope or chain supporting the top of a lower mast. They ran from the FUTTOCK PLATES (04.02) on the side of the top downwards and inwards to a FUTTOCK HOOP (04.02) around the lower mast, or alternatively to staves in the lower shrouds immediately under the top. Later they were replaced by metal bars.

**Futtock staff/stave.** Short piece of wood or metal attached to the upper part of the shrouds, to which the CAT-HARPINS are secured.

**Gob line, or gob rope, or martingale backrope, or stay.** Rope or chain, one of a pair running from the end of the DOLPHIN STRIKER (04.06) back to the sides of the bows. Serves to stay the jib-boom and the flying jib-boom against the forward and upward pull to which they are subjected.

**Jumper stay.** General name for any stay set up in heavy weather to prevent a yard jumping out of place.

**Ladies' ladder.** Description of shrouds in which the RATLINES are set too close together.

**Lanyard, or laniard, or lanierd.** In general, any short piece of line fastened to an object to secure it or to act as a handle. More particularly, the short lengths of line securing shrouds and stays.

**Main rigging.** Rigging of mainmast. Term sometimes restricted to the shrouds of that mast.

**Martingale.** Rope or chain passing down from the jib-boom end to the DOLPHIN STRIKER (04.06), staying the jib-boom against the upward pull of the jib and jib-stay. Also, alternative name for the dolphin striker.

**Monkey chains.** Small ledges outboard abaft the main channel on either side of the vessel, which hold the royal and topgallant BACKSTAYS.

**Preventer.** Any rope used as an additional security for another. A preventer backstay, for example, supplements a backstay.

**Ratlines, or ratlings.** Horizontal lines running across the shrouds at short intervals, forming a series of rope rungs.

**Rattle down the shrouds.** To fit RATLINES to the shrouds, using a series of CLOVE HITCHES (05.10).

**Set up.** To take up the slack in standing rigging: the shrouds, stays and BACK-STAYS which secure the masts.

**Sheer batten, or sheerpole, or stretcher.** Wooden or iron bar lashed horizontally across the shrouds, just above the DEAD-EYES (05.01) to prevent twisting. Usually fitted with BELAYING PINS (10.07).

**Shifting backstay.** Extra BACKSTAY used with a great press of sail and capable of being shifted from one side of a ship to the other as required.

**Shroud plate.** Iron plate on a vessel's side holding the DEAD-EYES (05.01) to which the lower ends of the shrouds are secured. Also, an iron hoop, with projecting rings, at the lower mast-head, which takes the lower dead-eyes of the FUTTOCK SHROUDS.

**Span.** Small line with its middle attached to a stay, and blocks or THIMBLES (05.03) fitted at the free ends to act as FAIRLEADS (05.03) for other

ropes. More generally, any rope fastened at both ends, so that a block and tackle can be attached to the m middle.

**Span shackle.** Eye-bolt with shackle attached, fastened to the deck and used to lash spars or boats in place.

**Spring stay.** Additional rope running above a stay acting as a substitute in case of damage. Also, a synonym for TRIATIC STAY.

**Standing rigging.** Fixed rigging used to support the masts.

**Swifters.** The aftermost shrouds on fore and main masts, the last of all the shrouds to be set up.

**Topmast backstays.** Ropes supporting the topmast from the back, set up between the topmast CROSS-TREES (04.03) and the ship's bulwarks. There are between one and three to the side, depending on the size of the ship.

**Topmast stay.** Rope or wire supporting the topmast from the front. An eye at the top is put round the topmast head while the bottom end is attached to the bowsprit (for the fore mast) or the deck (for main and mizen masts).

**Triatic stay.** Horizontal stay running between the mast CAPS (04.02).

**Tye.** Length of thick rope or chain by which a yard is hoisted. Attached at one end to a topsail or topgallant yard, rove through a sheave at the mast-head, and led down to the halyard. Often considered together with the halyard under the latter's name.

**Unrig** (vb). To dismantle a ship's standing and running rigging.

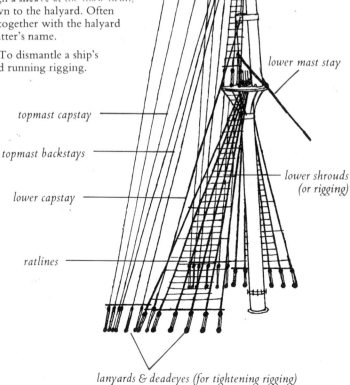

royal stay

royal backstay

topgallant stay

topgallant backstay

topgallant shrouds (or rigging)

topmast stay

topmast shrouds (or rigging)

lower mast stay

topmast capstay

topmast backstays

lower capstay

lower shrouds (or rigging)

ratlines

*lanyards & deadeyes (for tightening rigging)*

# Running Rigging

**Belly halyard.** Additional halyard rove through a block at the middle of a gaff to give support.

**Blackwall ratline.** RATLINE (04.08) seized to the foremost shroud of the rigging, in order to confine running gear.

**Bowline.** Line attached to the LEECH ROPE of a square sail, and leading forward. It is used to hold the weather side of a CLOSE-HAULED (12.11) sail forward and steady, enabling the ship to sail as close to the wind as possible.

**Bowline bridle.** Span, or short length of wire or rope, fastened to the LEECH ROPE of a square sail and to which the bowline is attached.

**Bowline cringle.** EYE (05.12) worked into the LEECH ROPE of a square sail to take the BOWLINE BRIDLE.

**Brace.** Rope or wire attached by a block or pendant to a yard-arm, used to adjust the yard in a horizontal plane.

**Brails.** Ropes used to gather in a fore-and-aft sail. They run from various points on the outermost LEECH (04.12) of the sail down to the deck, via leading blocks on the MAST BANDS (04.02).

**Breast gaskets,** or **bunt gaskets.** The GASKETS in the middle of the yard.

**Buntline.** Rope attached to the foot-rope of a topsail, passing up in front of the sail to a block on the yard. Used to pull the bottom of the sail up and spill the wind out of it.

**Chafing cheeks.** Old name for sheaves used instead of blocks on the yard-arms of lightly rigged vessels.

**Clew-garnets,** or **clue-garnets.** Tackles attached to the CLEWS (04.12) of a COURSE (04.11) and running up towards the centre of the yard. Used to pull the clews up and inwards when furling of 'goose-winging' a sail.

**Clew-line,** or **clue-line.** Rope equivalent to a CLEW-GARNET on any other square sail except a COURSE (04.10), but otherwise identical in form and function.

**Clothe** (vb). To rig a ship with running rigging and sails.

**Deck sheet.** Sheet controlling the foot of a studding sail. It is led directly

to the deck, and can be used to bring the sail in if the DOWNHAUL is carried away.

**Downhaul.** Rope used to haul down a jib or staysail. It is attached to the upper corner of the sail and passes down through the loops which fasten the sail to its stay.

**Fore bowline.** Rope leading from the LEECH (04.12) of the foresail to the deck.

**Fore halyard.** Rope used to hoist the foresail.

**Fore sheet.** Rope which controls and retains the lower corner (clew) of the foresail.

**Furling line.** Any line used to bind a sail to the mast when furled. Normally, this will be a GASKET.

**Gasket.** Short line, attached to the yard, used to secure a furled sail. When not in use kept coiled lying in front of the sail.

**Head sheets.** The sheets of sails set before the foremast, especially of jib and staysails.

**Inner turns.** Those turns of the EARING (04.12) lashing the upper corners of a square sail to the yard-arm which are inside the LIFT and closer to the corner of the sail, as opposed to the OUTER TURNS (05.12) which are outside the lift, right out on the yard-arm.

**Jib downhaul.** Rope which pulls the jibsail down the JIB-STAY.

**Jib halyard.** Rope used for hoisting the jib.

**Jib outhaul.** Rope for pulling out the back of a jib.

**Jib sheet.** Rope used to control and retain the after lower corner (clew) of the jib.

**Jib-stay.** Foremast stay on which the jib is set.

**Leech line.** Halyard fastened to the LEECH (04.12). It passes up in front of the sail to blocks under the top, then down again. Used to gather the sail up to the yard for furling or other operations.

**Leech rope.** Vertical section of the BOLT-ROPE (04.12), usually sewn to the LEECH (04.12) of the sail.

**Lifts.** Ropes running from the mast-head to the yard-arms. Used to square or alter the vertical angle of the yards.

**Long gasket.** Type of GASKET normally used at sea. In port, however, the shorter harbour gasket is used, which gives a smarter appearance to the furled sails.

**Luff hooks.** Halyard fitted with a hook at each end, leading from the LEECH (04.12) of a mainsail or foresail to an oak block on the ship's side. Used to lift the sail during FURLING (12.12) or reefing operations.

**Main halyard.** Rope used for hoisting the mainsail.

**Main tack.** Rope holding the weather CLEW (04.12) of the mainsail.

**Martnet.** Another name for the LEECH LINE of a sail.

**Passaree,** or **pazaree,** or **passarado.** Rope used to haul out the CLEW (04.12) of a studding sail along a lower. STUDDING-SAIL BOOM (04.07), so as to spread it fully when sailing before the wind.

**Peak downhaul.** Rope rove through a block at the after end of a gaff to haul it down.

**Peak halyard.** PURCHASE (05.04), usually made up of several blocks, by which the peak, or outer end of the gaff, is hoisted.

**Peak purchase.** PURCHASE (05.04) fitted to standing peak halyards to sway the peak up taut. Formerly used on cutters.

**Peak tye.** Wire or chain leading from the lower mast-head to the peak of a standing gaff to support it.

**Preventer brace.** Additional BRACE rigged as a second line of defence in case a brace breaks or is shot away.

**Reef earing.** Short lines used to reef the head of the sail to the yard-arm.

**Reefing halyards.** Ropes used in various forms of patent roller-reefing gear to rotate the yard and thereby reef the sail.

**Reef line.** Any line improvised to reef a sail in an emergency.

**Reef pendant.** In a fore-and-aft sail with a boom this is a line to the after LEECH (04.12) of the sail, going through a sheave in the boom, and attached to a tackle. It is used to pull the leech of the sail down to the boom to reef it. Also used to describe a REEF TACKLE on a lower yard.

**Reef points.** Short lengths of line attached to the sails in order to tie the reefed part of the sail to the yard.

**Reef tackle.** Tackle used to haul the reef band up and taut, thus allowing the sail to be reefed. It is attached to the leech of the sail, just below the reef band, and to the yard-arms, passing then to the centre of the yard and thence by another block to the deck.

**Robands,** or **rope-bands,** or **rovings,** or **robbens.** Small lengths of line passed through the eyelet holes at the head of a sail to attach it to the yard or or jackstay.

**Running rigging.** Moving rigging used for raising, lowering or adjusting yards and sails.

**Sheet.** Rope or chain attached to one or both of the CLEWS (04.12) of sails to extend them or hold them in place. It is taken aft, unlike the TACK, which goes forward.

**Slab lines.** Ropes passed from foot to head of a square sail, used to gather up the sail for furling. They pass

through blocks on the yard behind the sail, to the middle of the yard and down to the deck.

**Spilling line.** An alternative to a BUNTLINE. It too goes down to the foot of the sail, but continues up on the after side instead of ending there. Used in spilling the wind from the sail before FURLING (12.12).

**Tack.** Lower forward corner of a fore-and-aft sail. In square-rigged ships, the rope controlling the weather lower corner of a CLOSE-HAULED (12.11) course or staysail. Also, the rope used to haul out the CLEW (04.12) of a studding sail to the boom end.

**Tackling.** Running rigging and sails of a vessel.

**Throat halyard.** Rope or tackle used to hoist the inboard end of a gaff and its part of the sail.

**Top rope.** Rope used to hoist and lower a topmast or topgallant mast. Attached to the CAP (04.02) of the lower mast.

**Topsail sheet.** Rope extending and holding down the bottom corners of a topsail, and led aft.

**Vangs.** Ropes leading from the end of a gaff down and out to the ship's sides, steadying the gaff when under sail and keeping it amidships when no sails are set.

*Three-masted gaff schooner*

# Types of Sail

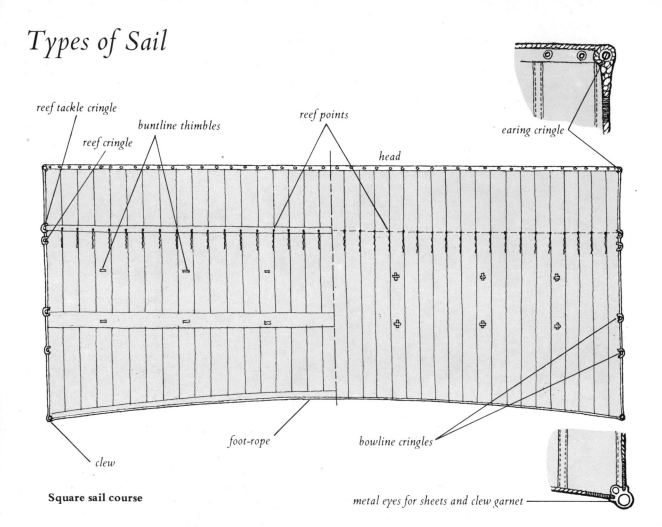

*reef tackle cringle*

*reef cringle*

*buntline thimbles*

*reef points*

*head*

*earing cringle*

*foot-rope*

*bowline cringles*

*clew*

**Square sail course**

*metal eyes for sheets and clew garnet*

**After sails.** Those sails on the after masts and on the stays running aft from the mainmast.

**Bentinck.** Triangular or narrow-footed COURSE with the foot extended by a boom. In either case the bottom of the sail or boom pivots about its centre, making it particularly easy to go about.

**Big topsail.** Type of square topsail carried on yachts rigged with a square yard above a gaff mainsail.

**Boom square sail.** Square sail that can be set on the lower foremast of a schooner or the lower mast of a cutter.

**Courses.** The sails attached to the lower yards: the foresail, mainsail and mizen. Sometimes the staysails on the lower masts are included.

**Double topsail.** Two narrow sails, without REEFS (04.12), taking the place of a single topsail. In rough weather, it is easier to FURL (12.12) one of these than to REEF (12.12) a full topsail. The yard of the lower sail is attached to the lower mast cap.

**Fore course.** The foresail, the principal and lowest sail on the foremast.

**Gaff topsail.** Light triangular or quadrilateral HEAD-SAIL (04.11) with its lower end on the gaff of the lower sail, and the upper extended on a small gaff which hoists to the topmast.

**Jimmy green,** or **jamie green.** Four-sided fore-and-aft sail set under the bowsprit and jib-boom by clippers in *light airs*. The upper side is attached to a rope running from the end of the jib-boom to the CAT-HEAD (03.07), the lower end stretched down to the tip of the DOLPHIN STRIKER (04.06).

**Jolly jumpers.** Collective name for sails set above the MOONSAILS. For use in *light airs*.

**Loose footed.** Describes a fore-and-aft sail the foot of which is not attached to a boom.

**Main course.** The mainsail, the principal and lowest sail on the main-mast.

**Middle topsail.** Additional square topsail, curved sharply outwards from the foot to the middle, used in some schooners, cutters and sloops. In use, it was set at the heel of the topmast.

**Moonsail,** or **moonraker.** Fine-weather sails set above the skysails.

**Plain sail.** Sail normally carried in ordinary weather, not including studding sails, skysails and other fairweather sails.

**Riding sail.** Triangular sail set on the mainmast of a stationary fishing vessel to keep its head to the wind and lessen rolling. Still used in trawlers.

**Skyscraper.** Triangular sail set above the skysail (a square sail here would be a MOONSAIL). A similar sail set above the moonsail is described as a *star-grazer*.

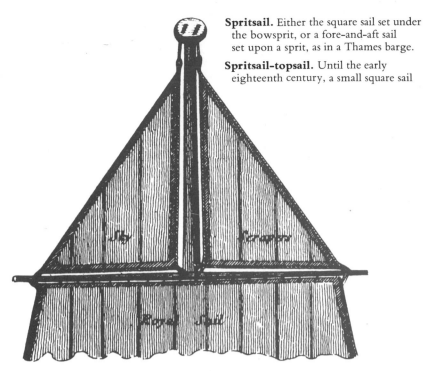

**Spritsail.** Either the square sail set under the bowsprit, or a fore-and-aft sail set upon a sprit, as in a Thames barge.

**Spritsail-topsail.** Until the early eighteenth century, a small square sail set on a small vertical mast stepped in a top at the outer end of the bowsprit. Later, the term was applied to a second square sail, additional to the spritsail, set under the jib-boom.

**Square sail.** Generally, any four-cornered sail set on a yard athwart-ships. More specifically, a square sail set upon the fore yard of a schooner, cutter or sloop, when running before the wind.

**Steering sail.** Sometimes used as a synonym for studding sail.

**Storm sails.** Set of sails made in a smaller size and with stronger canvas than normal, for use in rough weather.

**Suit of sails.** Complete set of sails used in a given state of the weather. Most sailing ships would have one suit of sails for fine weather, one for moderate conditions and a suit of storm sails for bad weather.

**Water sail,** or **save all.** Small fair-weather sail, sometimes set under the lower studding sail or driver boom.

*Mainsail, crojack, spanker and two staysails on the* Parma

# Fore-and-Aft Sails

**Angulated sail,** or **mitred sail.**
Triangular sail in which the cloth runs
a different way at the top than at the
bottom, meeting in a mitred join. This
arrangement saves on canvas and
spreads the strain of the sheet better
than that of a conventionally made sail.

**Battened sail.** Sail fitted with
horizontal battens or splines of wood,
to keep the sail taut and to assist in
gathering in sail in a squall. Usually
fitted as the mainsail of small yachts
and sailing canoes, particularly in the
East, but not often used in larger
vessels.

**Boom foresail.** Triangular foresail, such
as a JIB, whose foot is extended by a
boom.

**Double clewed jib,** or **quadrilateral
jib.** Jib with two sets of sheets, used
as a combination of JIB and flying jib
by some racing craft. One set of sheets
is taken right aft.

**Driver.** Generally, synonym for the
gaff mizen sail, or SPANKER. Originally
used to describe a square sail set as a
sort of studding sail on the outer end of
the gaff mizen.

**Head sails.** General name for all
sails set on the bowsprit, jib-boom and
flying jib-boom.

**Jackyard topsail,** or **jackyarder,** or
**lug topsail.** Square-cut sail set above
a gaff sail. Its head is attached to a
short yard set at an angle across and
on one side of the mast, like a lug-sail.

**Jib.** Triangular sail set on a stay before
the foremast, extending from the jib-
boom or bowsprit.

**Jib headed.** General name for all
triangular sails not set on LATEEN YARDS
(04.04), including staysails and Bermuda
sails as well as JIBS.

**Jib of jibs.** A sixth and outermost JIB
sometimes set.

**Laced mainsail.** Fore-and-aft sail
attached to its mast by a continuous
lacing running spirally round the mast
and threaded through eyelet holes in
in the sail.

**Lateen sail.** Long triangular sail
attached by its foremost edge to a long
yard which is hoisted at an angle to
the mast. The typical sail of the
Mediterranean and the Indian Ocean,
though formerly used for the mizen

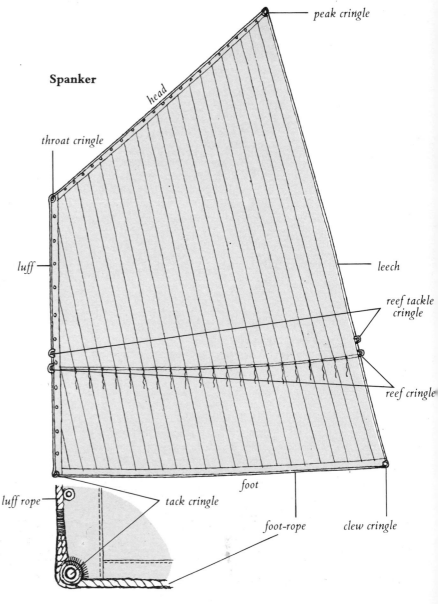

**Spanker**

peak cringle

head

throat cringle

luff

leech

reef tackle
cringle

reef cringle

foot

luff rope

tack cringle

foot-rope

clew cringle

on square-sailed ships elsewhere. A similar sail with the extreme foremost corner cut off to make it quadrilateral is also referred to as a lateen sail.

**Ring tail.** Type of studding sail set on the after end of the gaff mizen sail. The lower end of this sail is set to a ring-tail boom, extending beyond the mizen boom.

**Spanker.** Fore-end-aft sail with boom and gaff, set on the mizen mast.

**Spencer.** Gaff sail on any mast of a square-rigged ship except the mizen.

**Staysail.** Any triangular sail hoisted on a stay, except one before the foremast, which is a JIB.

**Trysail.** Sail of reduced size used by small craft in place of the mainsail during a storm. Alternatively, a fore-and-aft sail set on the mast of a square-rigged ship.

**Working foresail,** or **working jib.** Medium-sized JIB used in ordinary conditions, as opposed to a storm or balloon jib.

**Yankee jib topsail.** Racing jib topsail, the front edge of which extends from the bowsprit to the mast-head. Cut diagonally, it is attached to the TOP-MAST STAY (04.08).

*Three-masted gaff, schooner*
Bell Espoir II

# Parts of the Sail

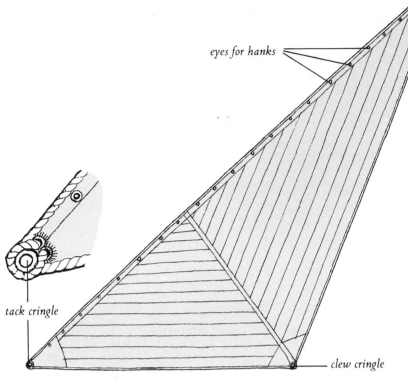

**After leech.** Aftermost or lee edge of a fore-and-aft sail.

**American grommet.** Brass eyelet fixed into a sail or any other piece of canvas.

**Bag reef.** Short reef taken in to prevent bagging, hence the fourth or lower reef of a sail.

**Band.** Strip of canvas stitched across a sail to strengthen the parts most in need of reinforcement.

**Belly band,** or **middle band.** Reinforcing band running horizontally across a square sail, half-way between the close reef and the foot. So named from the belly, or swell, of a sail.

**Bolt-rope.** Rope sewn all the way round the edge of a sail to prevent the canvas tearing.

**Bonnet.** Additional piece of canvas laced to the bottom of a sail in moderate weather to give it more area. By the later nineteenth century the term was restricted to the fore-and-aft sails of smaller craft.

**Bunt.** Middle part of a sail. When furling a sail, the bunt is the middle part tossed up onto the middle of the yard.

**Buntline cloth.** Additional strip of canvas sewn on the front of a sail to prevent chafing by the BUNTLINES (04.09).

**Clew,** or **clue.** Lower corner of a square sail. Also, the after lower corner of a fore-and-aft sail.

**Clinker pieces.** Small strengthening pieces at the corners of a gaff sail.

**Drabler.** Additional piece of canvas laced onto the lower edge of a BONNET.

**Earing.** Short length of rope used to lash the upper corners of a square sail to the yard-arm.

**Eyelet hole.** Reinforced hole in a sail, which takes short lengths of rope such as ROBANDS (04.09) or REEF POINTS (04.09).

**Flat seam.** Overlapping edges of two pieces of canvas sewn together.

**Glut.** Small piece of canvas sewn into the middle of a sail, near the head, with an eyelet in it to take a line.

**Goring.** Describes any sail, such as a topsail, that widens towards its foot.

The word 'gore' means a wedge-shaped piece of cloth, originally used by tailors to widen a garment.

**Goring cloth.** Wedge-shaped outer cloth of a topsail. Its sloping outer edge makes the sail wider at the foot than at the head.

**Harbour gaskets.** Special GASKETS (04.09) used in port to give a decorative appearance to furled sails. At sea, furled sails are fastened with long gaskets.

**Head.** The upper part of anything, in this case the sail, including its upper edge.

**Laskets.** Small lines, like hoops, sewn to BONNETS and DRABLERS in order to secure them to the sail above.

**Leech.** The side edges of a square sail. Also, the after edge of a fore-and-aft sail.

**Mast hoop.** Sliding ring of wood or metal which attaches the edge of a fore-and-aft sail to the mast.

**Mast lining.** Extra piece of canvas attached to the back of a topsail to protect it from wear against the mast.

**Monkey seam.** Extra-strong seam sewn down the centre of a sail during its manufacture. The selvages of the centre cloths are overlapped, stitched and TABLED.

**Naval line,** or **navel line.** Rope hanging from the mast-head passed round the truss supporting a yard to keep it up.

**Nock.** Forward upper end of a sail set on a boom.

**Peak,** or **peek.** Uppermost corner of a gaff sail.

**Pricking the sails.** Practice of sewing a middle seam between the two side seams joining two overlapping pieces of canvas. This was usually done when the sails were worn, though it would be done at the start with STORM SAILS (04.10), which needed the extra strength.

**Reef.** Area of a sail between the head and any of the REEF BANDS.

**Reef band.** Narrow band of canvas, sewn along the REEF-LINE (04.09), and pierced by eyelet holes for the REEF POINTS (04.09).

**Roach.** Curve of the edge of a sail, either inwards, as in the case of the centre of the foot of a SQUARE SAIL (04.10), or outwards, as in the luff of a jib.

**Round seam.** Seam joining the edges of two pieces of canvas without over-lapping them.

**Sailcloth.** Canvas made from flax or cotton of a quality suitable for sail-making.

**Sail clutch.** Iron band used as an alternative to a hoop to hold a sail to a mast.

**Sail cover.** Protective cover, usually made of canvas, placed over a furled sail.

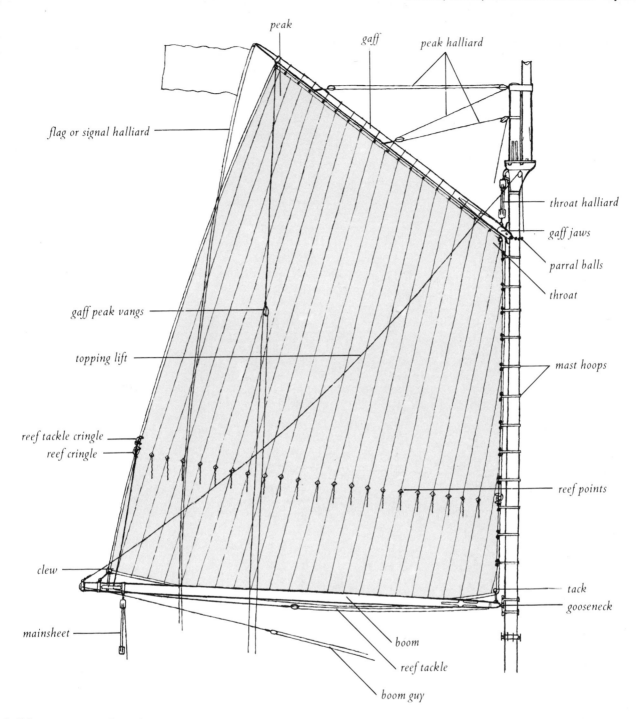

*peak*

*gaff*

*peak halliard*

*flag or signal halliard*

*throat halliard*

*gaff jaws*

*parral balls*

*throat*

*gaff peak vangs*

*topping lift*

*mast hoops*

*reef tackle cringle*

*reef cringle*

*reef points*

*clew*

*tack*

*gooseneck*

*mainsheet*

*boom*

*reef tackle*

*boom guy*

**Sail hoops.** Hoops of wood or metal attached to a sail and passing round the mast, enabling the sail to be raised or lowered.

**Side stitch.** Extra line of stitching on the seam of a sail giving additional strength.

**Slab.** Slack part of sail which hangs down when LEECH LINES (04.09) are hauled up.

**Spectacles,** or **spectacle clew,** or **spectacle iron,** or **clew iron.** Fitting consisting of three or four metal rings,

used at the CLEW (04.12) of a sail to take the BOLT-ROPES, sheets and other ropes.

**Stay holes.** Hole in the front edge of a staysail or jib to take the lacing or hanks by which the sail is fastened to the stay.

**Strain bands.** Bands of canvas reinforcing the belly of sails against strain.

**Table** (vb). To reinforce a sail's hem by turning the edge over on itself and sewing it down.

**Tabling.** Broad hem on the edge of a sail, to strengthen the part sewn to the BOLT-ROPE.

**Tan** (vb). To preserve sails by soaking them in an extract of oak bark. Later, other items were used in the preservative. The method produced the brownish-red sails typical of Thames barges and similar vessels.

**Top lining.** Lining on the after part of a sail to prevent chafing against the rim of the top.

**Wrinkle.** Crease in a sail, when it is set, or a small bulge in a furled sail.

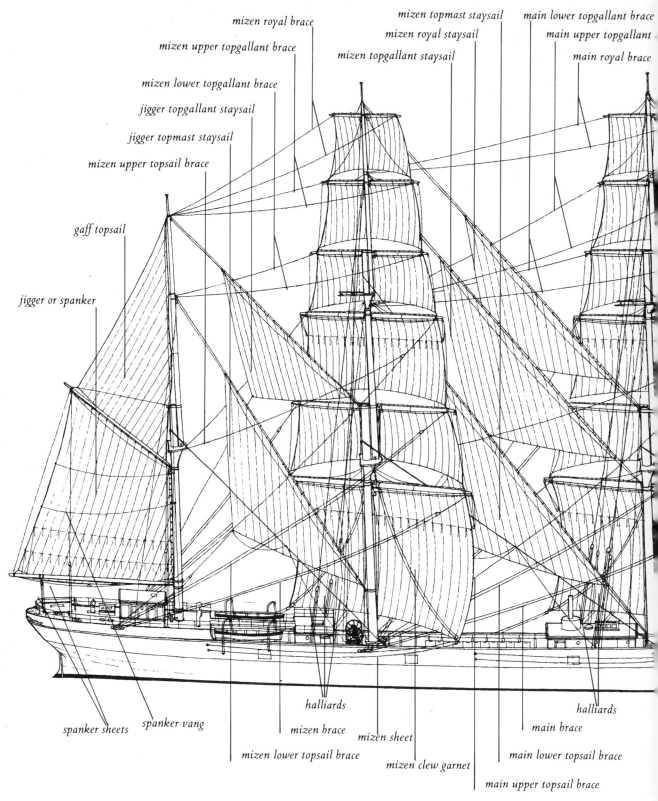

mizen royal brace

mizen topmast staysail

main lower topgallant brace

mizen upper topgallant brace

mizen royal staysail

main upper topgallant

mizen lower topgallant brace

mizen topgallant staysail

main royal brace

jigger topgallant staysail

jigger topmast staysail

mizen upper topsail brace

gaff topsail

jigger or spanker

spanker sheets    spanker vang

halliards    halliards

mizen brace    main brace

mizen sheet

mizen lower topsail brace    main lower topsail brace

mizen clew garnet

main upper topsail brace

mizen royal    main roy.

mizen upper topgallant    main upper topgalla

mizen lower topgallant    main lower topgalla

mizen lower topsail    main upper topsa

mizen upper topsail    main lower topsa

mizen course or cro'jack    main course or mainsa

**Four-Masted Barque**

# Sails of a Representative Ship

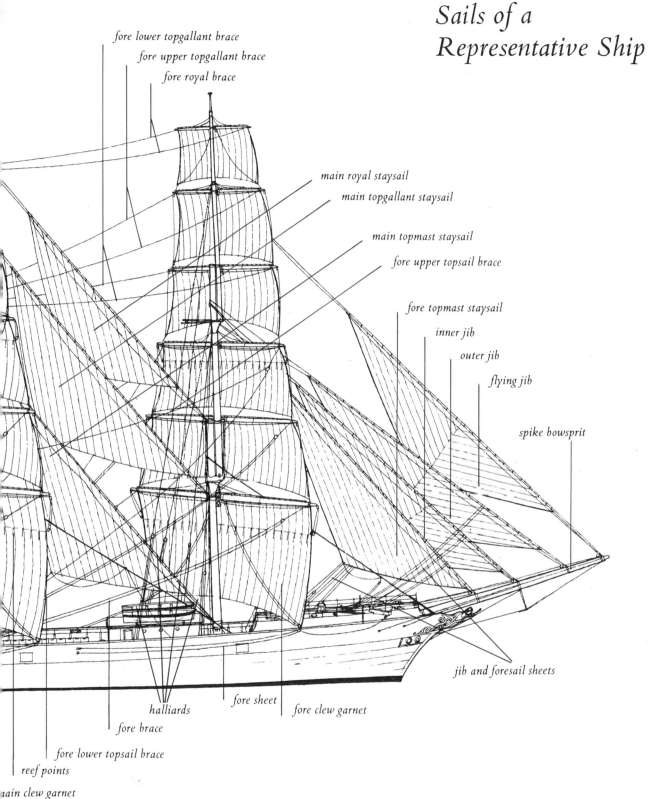

fore lower topgallant brace
fore upper topgallant brace
fore royal brace

main royal staysail
main topgallant staysail

main topmast staysail

fore upper topsail brace

fore topmast staysail

inner jib

outer jib

flying jib

spike bowsprit

jib and foresail sheets

halliards

fore sheet

fore clew garnet

fore brace

fore lower topsail brace

reef points

main clew garnet

sheet

fore royal
fore upper topgallant
fore lower topgallant
fore upper topsail
fore lower topsail
fore course or foresail

# Small-Craft Sails

**Balanced lug.** or **French lug.** Lug sail with the lower end attached to a boom. From a fifth to a sixth of the sail is in front of the mast. In TACKING (12.08), the front of the yard is dipped round the mast, but the boom stays the same side of the mast on either tack.

**Dipping lug.** Lug sail with the halyards attached to the yard about two-fifths from its forward end. The sail is moved from one side of the mast to the other by dipping the front end of the yard round the mast while TACKING (12.08).

**Leg of mutton sail,** or **shoulder of mutton sail.** Triangular sail with its fore end attached to the mast; basically the Bermuda rig.

**Lug,** or **lug sail.** Quadrilateral sail with the forward edge shorter than the after edge and the yard set obliquely to the mast.

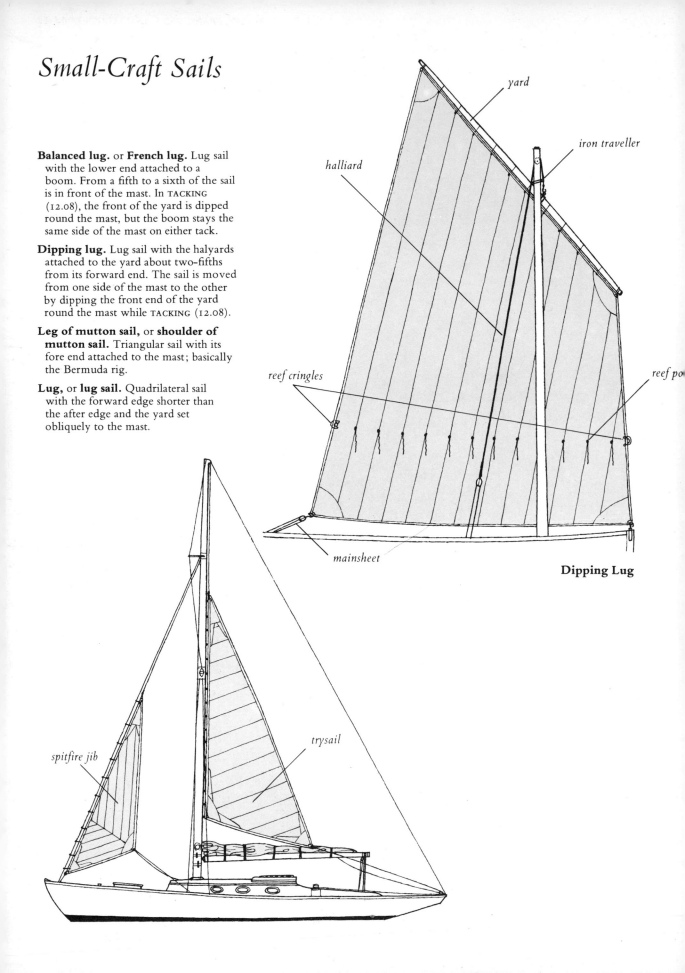

yard

iron traveller

halliard

reef cringles

reef po

mainsheet

**Dipping Lug**

spitfire jib

trysail

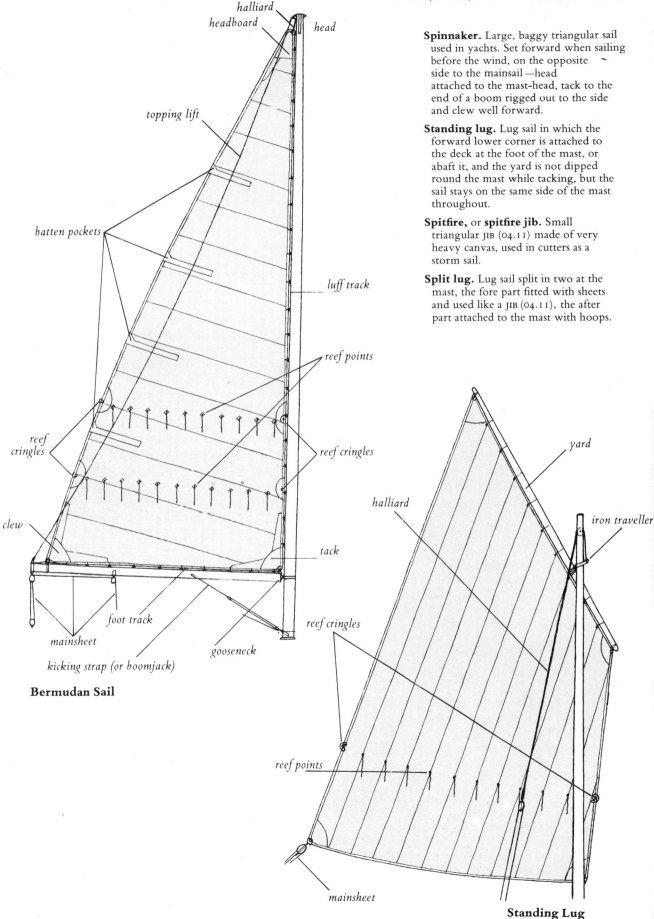

halliard
headboard
head

topping lift

batten pockets

luff track

reef points

reef cringles

reef
cringles

reef cringles

clew

tack

foot track

mainsheet

gooseneck

kicking strap (or boomjack)

**Bermudan Sail**

**Spinnaker.** Large, baggy triangular sail used in yachts. Set forward when sailing before the wind, on the opposite side to the mainsail—head attached to the mast-head, tack to the end of a boom rigged out to the side and clew well forward.

**Standing lug.** Lug sail in which the forward lower corner is attached to the deck at the foot of the mast, or abaft it, and the yard is not dipped round the mast while tacking, but the sail stays on the same side of the mast throughout.

**Spitfire,** or **spitfire jib.** Small triangular JIB (04.11) made of very heavy canvas, used in cutters as a storm sail.

**Split lug.** Lug sail split in two at the mast, the fore part fitted with sheets and used like a JIB (04.11), the after part attached to the mast with hoops.

yard

halliard

iron traveller

reef cringles

reef points

mainsheet

**Standing Lug**

# Reeving and Bousing

Ropes, blocks and tackles have a long history. Early Egyptian drawings of about 2000–1800 BC show a reed-built boat with a bipod mast carrying a short yard with a square sail and designed to sail up the Nile with the prevailing northerly wind. Obviously, this arrangement must have been controlled and adjusted by some system of ropes. From such humble beginnings evolved the apparently complex machinery of masts and sails with which the man-of-war at Trafalgar manoeuvred, and which drove the square-riggers of the nineteenth and twentieth centuries at speeds of up to twenty knots.

Until the nineteenth century, ropes were made of natural materials such as hemp, coir, leather and manila. There were, and are today, three different processes involved in laying up a rope. The fibres are first twisted into yarn – rather like spinning wool – and the yarn is in turn twisted into strands ready for making the rope. The strands are then, in the third stage, subjected to tensioning and twisting by means of the rope-maker's winch, or jack, and laid up into three-, four- or five-stranded rope with or without a heart. Today, the rope-maker's art is of a more industrialized nature; but although his materials – nylon, terylene, polypropylene and wire – may be the products of a technological revolution the principles remain the same.

Blocks, like most lasting items of nautical methodology, have a basic construction and function which have lasted throughout their history, in some cases almost unchanged. The wooden clump block would be as familiar to the seaman on the *Golden Hinde* as it is to the new entrant at a sea training school today. Again, the function of the block as a single lead or as part of a complex derrick system is enduring; the fact that it is now a massive steel affair with patent self-lubricating pins does not alter its practical significance.

Along with blocks go purchases, or tackles. The simple single or double whip with its use of single blocks is easily recognized but no more difficult to understand than the impressive threefold and fourfold purchases which can be seen on the *Cutty Sark* at Greenwich and HMS *Victory* at Portsmouth.

Blocks, ropes and wires strewn in an unseemly heap on deck may appear somewhat daunting at first sight, but a boatswain or any competent seaman can soon sort them out and put them to use. Before assembling them he must know how to join the ropes with knots and splices, tidy up the ends with whippings, protect and repair the running gear and, perhaps, indulge in some fancy knot-work in his watch below. When a

rope or wire is cut, the strands immediately begin to untwist in an exasperating fashion. This is because the inherent tension, built in when the strands are twisted up, is suddenly released and must be controlled before the whole thing unravels into an unmanageable tangle. This tension is also apparent when coiling a rope up, or down, and even more so when it is new. The answer is to treat it with respect and understanding, and allow the turns to fall easily to hand while allowing the twist to pass along the rope as you coil down on the deck, or up on a belaying pin. To stop the strands untwisting, whipping or back-splicing is used. A back-splice correctly done is hardly thicker than the original circumference of the rope and allows it to pass through the swallow of a block without jamming. Joining ropes is an exercise in selection for a particular function. The ubiquitous reef knot is fine, so is the sheet bend, for ordinary work, but if the rope is needed for a tackle or any sort of bousing gear then a short or long splice is required. Ropes often have to have eyes put in them, sometimes to take a thimble or cringle, and here the eye-splice and knots like the bowline and buntline hitch are used.

Turk's heads, sennit and other fancy-work knots were not only a decorative hobby for the watch below, they also had a utilitarian purpose. Wall knots are an attractive way of securing the end of a rope; turk's heads are aesthetically pleasing in themselves but can also be used, for instance, to cover up more obvious whippings. Baggywrinkle, which could be described as a very hairy form of sennit (plaited yarn or rope), decorated stays and shrouds as a form of protection for the sails which came into contact with them.

This basic, static background description of ropes and tackle may help explain some abstruse reeving and bousing terms, but to bring a touch of reality into this discussion let us go on board a square-rigger at sea. Imagine that we are standing on the forecastle head of the steel four-masted barque *Passat* as she sails close-hauled on the starboard tack in the helpful Trade Winds of the North Atlantic. The *Passat* sailed under the Finnish flag from the mid-1930s to 1951. Imagine her sailing homeward bound from Australia in 1948 with 5,000 tons of grain aboard. Deep laden, with a draught of 24 feet, she is 350 feet long and her masts tower some 170 feet above the listing deck. She has wire rigging, but its use is fundamentally the same as that of hemp rigging.

Looking ahead over the long steel-spike bowsprit, three jibs and a fore topmast staysail obscure our view. The lee jib sheets (wires controlling the corner of the sail) are boused down with a single whip tackle, the running part leading through a bull's-eye on the deck to the pin rail. Over the heavy jib stays (wires controlling a mast fore and aft and here taking the edge of the sail) lie the weather sheets ready to be hove down when she turns onto the other tack.

The forestay, a massive double wire which passes from the deck on the fore part of the forecastle head, round the foretop on the mast and back down to the deck, is set up with bottlescrews. Where it passes round the mast and where the ends are turned up round dead-eyes, the wire is wormed, parcelled and served in order to protect it from the sea and the weather. Here, the mnemonic, 'worm and parcel with the lay, turn and serve the other way' gives some valuable advice. Worming, in this context, means laying a light tarred line between the strands of wire, following their lay or twist; this is parcelled with strips of old canvas passed round and round, and then the whole length is served over with tarred marline bound tightly with the help of a wooden serving mallet. These heavy crucible wire stays and shrouds (supporting masts athwartships) are difficult to splice, so they are usually secured at the lower end with wire racking seizings. When the stay or shroud is bent around the dead-eye, it is done with a Spanish windlass and the seizings put on using a special type of serving mallet with a long handle providing the necessary leverage to tighten up the tough wire.

The wind forces transferred by the sails via the masts to the hull with the aid of these stays and shrouds were sufficient to drive some 8,000 tons of ship and cargo at speeds of up to seventeen knots through even the worst seas in the world, off Cape Horn, so that careful preparation and maintenance were absolutely vital. Looking aloft, up the forestay, we can see the baggywrinkle worked along the wire to prevent chafing as the sail billows out. The foresail, of course, stretching its ninety-foot length over the ship, is boused down to the forecastle head with a single wire tack (holding the lower weather corner of the sail) led to the capstan through a single built block; there is also a chain preventer tack standing by for heavy weather. Above the fore course are the lower and upper topsails, lower and upper topgallants and the royal, all with their constituent lifts, halyards, sheets, clew-lines, buntlines, gaskets, footropes and so on.

To exemplify the running rigging, we can look at lifts (controlling the angling of a yard-arm up or down) and their working. The crossjack lifts (one on each side of the crossjack – lower yard on a mizen mast), and this applies equally to the main and fore lifts, provide the vertical canting movement for the ninety-four-foot long, six-ton yards, and are heavy wires secured near the yard-arm by means of an eye-splice with a thimble, shackled to the lift band. The lift is then led through a single block on the mast at the lower topsail truss band, down through the lubber hole in the mizen top and shackled to the upper block of a rope double purchase,

which in turn is secured to the deck at the base of the mast.

Having described the function of the lift, let us now look at the fore course as it draws well on the wind and consider the various lines in action as the order comes to take in sail. The first job is to break the buntline stops. As their name suggests, buntlines pull up the bunt (middle) of the sail to the yard in bunches ready for the hands to furl. The wire buntlines are secured to the foot of the sail and pass up through cringles, wooden thimbles or bull's-eyes on the fore part, up to the yard and along to the mast. Led through single wooden blocks, they then go through another block and down to the upper block of a single whip purchase whose running part is secured to the pin rail on the ship's side. If these buntlines were allowed to remain taut there would be considerable wear on the sail due to constant chafing, so the lines are overhauled (extended) for a couple of feet, either on the yard or at the mast, and the slack secured by stops, strands of old rope which can be easily broken by a sharp tug from the deck. The overhauling of buntlines was a source of employment when the mate on watch could find nothing else for idle hands to do. It has even been known for that same watchkeeper to quietly break a few buntline stops, usually on the royals, in order, apparently, to disturb an otherwise slack Sunday morning.

Clew-lines or clew-garnets, haul up the corners, or clews, of the sail to the yard-arm. They consist of wires shackled to the clew irons, then led through a single block on the yard-arm below the yard, along to the mast and down to the deck where a rope whip provides the necessary purchase to heave the heavy sail up to the yard. Having hauled up, first the weather side, then the lee, the watch clamber up the weather shrouds on the order 'up and make fast' and furl the sail, securing it with rope gaskets passed round the yard and lashing the rolled-up sail onto the jackstays.

Descriptions such as these, of one or two parts of the rigging of a sailing ship combined with the straightforward, everyday, occurrence of taking in sail, cannot do full justice to the multifarious blocks, tackles, hitches, splices, lines, downhauls and hawsers which were used in the normal sailing of a ship. Catting the anchor with a cat-fall or checking the yards with by-the-wind hitches have not been described in practical terms here, but they, along with all the other functions, were essential for the skilful business of sailing and seamanship. Reeving and bousing terms like the Spanish burton, Matthew Walker and reef tackle may have passed substantially into history along with manoeuvres such as wearing, club-hauling and box-hauling, but we should remember that they are not just archaic terms but also the living language and technical expressions of sailors and ships.

MARTIN LEE

# Parts of the Block

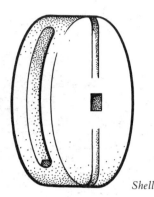

*Shell*

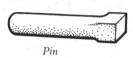

*Pin*

*Sheave*

**Strop.** Piece of rope spliced into a circular wreath, used to surround the body of a block so that it can be suspended.

**Arse.** Choke end of a wooden block (that opposite the SWALLOW); the hole through which the FALL (05.04) runs.

**Breast.** The opposite end of the block to that through which the FALL (05.04) runs.

**Cap.** Semi-circular projection from the sides and round the end of a block above the pin. Two holes are bored obliquely from the sides and the STROP passed through these to prevent chafing.

**Cheeks.** The two sides, or side pieces, of a block.

**Coak.** Cylindrical metal bush let into the middle of the SHEAVE to take the pin. The coak is held in position by two end-plates riveted to the sheave.

**Crown.** The top of the block. It is not so deeply scored as the bottom.

**Forelock.** Small iron wedge driven through a slot near the end of an iron sheave-pin to prevent it from working out.

**Gorge.** Another name for SWALLOW.

**Hook.** Plain or swivel hook attached to the rope strapping, or incorporated in the iron strapping, by which the block is attached.

**Jumpsurgee strop.** Strong rope STROP or loop passing three times round the block and once round the THIMBLE (05.03). The strop is made by unlaying the ends of the rope and plaiting these into NETTLES (05.09).

**Pin.** Steel rod through the block, upon which the SHEAVE revolves.

**Pudding chain** Chain composed of short links so that it may be reeved through a block. Used for halyards and SHEETS (04.09) before the introduction of wire rigging.

**Pulley.** Wheel turning freely on a pin, with its edge grooved to take a rope. In a block, a pulley is termed a SHEAVE.

**Roller sheave.** SHEAVE with a metal bush and rollers which revolve around the pin.

**Score.** Groove cut on the outside of the shell of a block to take the STROP. A block is either single- or double-scored.

**Selvagee strop.** Several rope yarns MARLED (05.07) together with SPUNYARN (05.09) in the form of a SLING (05.05); softer than rope and therefore less likely to slip. Used to attach the hook of a tackle to a rope.

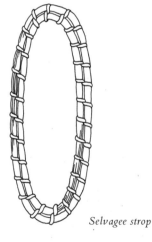

*Selvagee strop*

**Sheave.** Solid grooved wheel, fixed in a channel and revolving about an axis, which guides a rope as in a block.

**Sheave hole.** Aperture in the block shell into which the SHEAVE is fitted.

**Shell.** In a block, the outer frame or casing which contains the SHEAVE.

**Swallow.** Space between the SHEAVE and the SHELL of a block through which the rope runs.

**Tail.** Extension of rope strapping to form one or two ends by which the block may be attached to the place required.

**Web sheave.** Iron sheave with four spokes joined by a thin web. The pin-hole is usually brass-coaked.

# Types of Block

*Main topsail and main yard lift blocks*

**Bee block.** Rectangular piece of timber, usually elm, having a sheave hole fitted in the foremost end and a square mortise cut in the other. Two such blocks are bolted, one on each side of the bowsprit, the bolts also serving as sheave pins. The foretopmast stay reeves through the starboard block and the spring stay through the port block.

**Block.** Pulley used for various purposes in a ship, particularly to increase the mechanical power of the ropes used in handling the sails. Blocks can be single, double, treble or larger, depending on the number of their wheels, which can be mounted on the same axis or one above the other. A common single block comprises three main parts: the SHELL, SHEAVE (the wheel held between the two flat sides of the shell) and PIN (holding shell and sheave together and providing the sheave's axis). The block is bound with a STROP, a rope ring passing in a notch around the block and across both ends of the pin, by which the block is suspended from masts, shrouds and so on.

**Bollocks.** Those blocks in the centre portion of the topsail through which topsail ties are rove to increase lifting power.

**Built-block.** One having the SHELL or outer casing made of several pieces of wood, usually elm. The cheeks, middle parts and partitions are strongly bolted together with three bolts at each end. Large treble and fourfold blocks are built this way; smaller built-blocks are of two pieces riveted together.

**Bull's-eye.** Solid block with one or more holes drilled through its centre and a groove cut round its edge. One rope is spliced round it, held in the groove, while another is run through the hole.

**Butterfly block.** Small SNATCH BLOCK (05.02) or hinged block having a length equal to twice the circumference of the rope taken. Fitted with a STROP and rope tail, it is used for hauling in a deep-sea line.

**Cat block.** Strong iron-bound double or treble block, fitted with a bound iron hook attached to the ANCHOR (06.02) ring. To hoist the anchor, the catfall is rove alternately through the cat block and the cat-head sheaves.

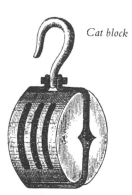

*Cat block*

**Cheek block.** Block having dimensions in proportion to the thickness of the topmast head to which it is fastened by an iron pin. This pin also serves as the SHEAVE pin. The sheave holes are coppered for durability.

**Clump block.** Wooden block with a length twice the circumference of the rope taken. In the eighteenth century clump blocks were turned on a lathe before mortising.

**Comb cleat.** Fitting used to keep ropes from fouling each other, made of ash or elm with a semi-circular back like a cockscomb. Ropes are led through two holes cut into the lower edge.

**Crowfoot.** Arrangement of small lines fanning out from one long block; used for suspending AWNINGS (03.15) and for other purposes.

**Dead-eye.** Round or pear-shaped flattish wooden block, pierced with three holes. It is encircled by a rope or

*Dead-eye*

an iron band, and a LANYARD (04.08) is run through the holes. Used mainly in the standing rigging, it creates a purchase for a shroud. One dead-eye is fastened in the lower end of the shroud, another in the upper link of a CHAIN (04.08) in the ship's side, and the two are then linked by a lanyard.

**Dee-block.** D-shaped piece of oak, 12 to 16 inches long and 8 to 10 inches wide, having a sheave hole cut through the middle fore and aft. It is bolted to the ship's sides in the channels to reeve the lift.

**Dee-sea line block.** Single block, 9 to 11 inches long, having a portion of the shell cut away like a SNATCH BLOCK. The line can be laid directly across the sheave, where it is held by a hinged portion of the iron strap.

**Double block.** Single-shelled block in which two SHEAVES (05.01) turn on the same pin. Two ropes of the same size may be worked through it.

**Euphroe,** or **euvro,** or **uphroe.** Oblong ash block without sheaves, from 9 to 30 inches long and 2 to 5 inches in diameter. It has several holes through it at equal distances. A groove round the edge takes the rope by which it hangs. Used to form the CROWFOOT (05.01) suspending an AWNING (03.15), and also as a means of separating rope strands.

**Fiddle block.** Single-shelled block having two SHEAVES (05.01) carried on separate pins one above the other. The lower portion is narrower and the whole lies flatter to a mast or yard than a DOUBLE BLOCK.

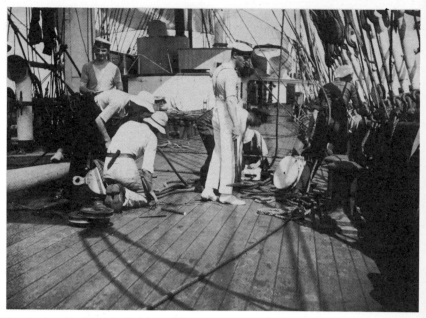

*Overhauling blocks on the deck line of the Medway, 1912*

*Fiddle block*

**Heart.** Type of DEAD-EYE (05.01), in the shape of a heart and with only one large hole through it, used as a PURCHASE (05.04) for a stay.

**Hook block.** Single or double block with a hook at the lower end for its attachment. The block may be strapped with yarn to a THIMBLE (05.03) and hook; alternatively, the strapping and hook may be formed of a single piece of metal.

**Jack block.** Single block stropped with a long leg ending in an EYE-SPLICE (05.12) (the loop) and a short leg ending in a double wall knot (the button). The strop is placed round the topgallant mast and secured by passing the button through the loop.

**Jewel block.** Small block at the end of the main and foretop yard-arms, through which a studding-sail halyard is run.

**Leading block.** The fixed block at the leading part of a TACKLE (05.05) which often serves to alter the direction of the rope led through it.

**Long tackle block.** Block with a shell, usually made of ash or elm, proportionately two-thirds longer than a single block. It carries two sheaves one above the other, the lower being two-thirds the size of the upper. Used for yard tackles or loading tackles.

**Made block.** Another name for a BUILT-BLOCK (05.01).

**Monkey block.** Small single block attached with strap and swivel to a yard, enabling it to lead the ropes in any direction. Often used on the lower yards of small ships to lead running rigging from the sails. Also, the name given to a large iron-bound block which is bolted to a chock on the deck.

*Dead-eyes of the starboard main shrouds on Nelson's Victory*

**Ninepin block.** Wooden block resembling a ninepin in shape but with flattened sides. It is fixed under the cross-pieces of the quarterdeck and forecastle BITTS (06.03), and is used to lead running rigging on a horizontal plane.

**Non-toppling block.** Ballasted or weighted block used in the lower end of a TACKLE (05.05) when rounding-up or shortening the purchase or the distance between two blocks.

**Purchase blocks.** Two blocks used as part of a purchase or TACKLE (05.05).

**Quarter block.** Another name for a THICK AND THIN BLOCK.

**Rack block.** Block or plank containing a number of sheaves. Used on the bowsprit for leading running gear.

**Ram block.** Flat-sided block having three or four holes through which LANYARDS (04.08) are rove when setting up shrouds or stays. Not used in purchases, but to keep tension in the shrouds, for which purpose it is stronger than a sheaved block. In the seventeenth century, also used in conjunction with the TYE (04.08) employed to hoist the lower yard.

**Rouse about block.** Large SNATCH BLOCK with a slotted or hinged portion of the shell allowing a rope to be laid directly on the SHEAVE (05.01).

**Running block.** In a purchase or TACKLE (05.05), the block that moves when the rope is hauled on.

**Saddle.** Section of MONKEY BLOCK, hollowed out to fit the convexity of the yard to which it is nailed.

**Secret block.** One in which the sheave is completely covered by the SHELL (05.01) except for a small lead through which the rope passes.

**Shoe block.** Block consisting of two single blocks cut out of one piece of wood, with sheave pins at right angles, one above the other. Used, though rarely, for legs and falls of the BUNTLINES (04.09).

**Shoulder block.** Large single block almost square at the *arse* or lower end and sloping in towards the SHEAVE (05.01). Used on lower yard-arms and on topsail yards. The shoulder prevents SHEETS (04.09) jamming between block and yard.

**Sister block.** Block used to reeve the LIFTS (04.09) and reef tackle PENDANTS (05.05) of the topsail yards. It consists of a cylindrical shell, usually of ash, about twenty inches long and containing two sheaves one above the other. The block is SEIZED (05.12) at

the middle and at both ends. Along its side is a groove large enough to take part of the topmast shroud to which it is seized.

*Sister blocks*

**Snatch block.** Block with an opening on one side so that a rope can be fixed round the SHEAVE (05.01).

*Snatch block*

**Span Block.** Type of block lashed around the mast in pairs to take studding sail halyards. The blocks may be SEIZED (05.12), hooked or shackled onto the span, the length of rope holding them.

**Spring block.** One having a spring connection to the RING BOLT (05.03) holding it, allowing it to yield slightly to jerks on the rope caused by the ship working.

**Standing block.** Any fixed block in a TACKLE (05.05) which does not move when the FALL (05.04) is hauled on.

**Strap-bound block.** Type of block with rope or iron strap fitted in scores from top to bottom of the CHEEKS (05.01). The strap serves to hold any hook, toggle or swivel by which the block may be slung.

**Swivel block.** One pivoted in the leg or hook by which it is attached, so that it turns easily to face in any direction.

**Tack block.** That put over the CLEW (04.12) of the sail; a STANDING BLOCK through which the sail rope is rove.

**Tail block.** Small single block with a short piece of rope attached to it so that it can be fastened to an object.

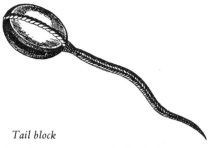

*Tail block*

**Tandem block.** Block that is double sheaved, both sheaves being in the same plane.

**Thick and thin block.** One having two sheaves in the same shell, one above the other. The upper part of the shell and its sheave are larger than the lower, allowing it to lie closer to the yard than a DOUBLE BLOCK. Used on quarters of a yard to take SHEET (04.09) and CLEW-LINE (04.09).

**Top block.** Iron-bound single block hooked to an EYE-BOLT (03.15) on one side of the mast cap. Used for reeving the top rope PENDANT (05.05) when swaying up the topmast.

*Top block*

**Treble block.** One having three SHEAVES (05.01) on one pin, the whole encased in a single shell.

**Tye block, or tie block.** Block with two small blocks strapped beneath it, and double strapped and secured with ROSE LASHINGS (05.12) to the topsail yard.

**Viol block, or voyal block.** Large double-scored block used when heaving up the anchor. The SHEAVE (05.01) is coaked or bushed with brass and the pin is of iron.

**Waist block.** One located amidships, on the bulwarks.

**Warping block.** Neatly made block, usually of ash or elm, shaped like the body of a bellows, about 16 inches long overall. The front CHEEK (05.01) is cut away to give access to the sheave, and a handle is fitted to one end of the sheave pin. Used by ropemakers to warp off yarn into hauls.

# Cringles, Thimbles and Shackles

**Becket.** Large iron hook, or short rope, used to confine large ropes, or to hang up the weather sheets and lee tacks of the mainsail and foresail to the foremost main and fore shrouds. Some beckets have an eye spliced in one end and a *walnut knot* crowned at the other; others have their ends spliced together. Also, the noose made at the end of a block to which the standing part of the fall is made fast.

**Bottle screw.** Threaded cylinder (the *bottle*) led into the outer end of a shroud or stay for setting up and tightening these ropes. It superseded the use of DEAD-EYES (05.01) and HEARTS (05.02) for this purpose.

*Bull's-eye cringle*

**Bull's-eye cringle.** Wooden BULL'S-EYE (05.01), usually made of elm or lignum vitae, with one central hole. Used at the TACK (04.09) or LEECH (04.12) of a sail.

**Chuck.** Another name for a FAIRLEAD.

**Clip hooks.** THIMBLE or ring having two hooks on it with points facing in opposite directions.

*Cringle*

**Cringle.** Small loop, sometimes with a metal ring or thimble, made in the BOLT-ROPE (04.12) of a sail to hold one of the ropes controlling the sail.

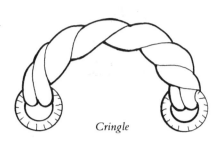

*Cringle*

*D-shackle*

**D-shackle.** SHACKLE with sides straight and parallel to one another, so giving a D-shape.

*Fairleads*

**Fairlead.** Any fixture used to lead a rope in a required direction. At its simplest, it is a wooden board pierced with holes. Leading blocks, eyes and cringles also serve the same purpose.

*Heart thimbles*

**Heart thimble.** Wooden or metal thimble with a roughly heart-shaped central hole: one end circular, the other tapering to a point.

**Krennels.** Small rope CRINGLES for the BOWLINE BRIDLES (04.09) round the edge of a square sail.

**Necklace.** Chain which is sometimes placed round the lower mast to secure the lower ends of the FUTTOCK SHROUDS (04.08).

**Reef cringle.** CRINGLE inserted in the LEECH (04.12) of a sail to take a reefing block.

**Ring-bolt.** Type of bolt with an eye and ring in its head; used especially for hooking TACKLES (05.05).

**Shackle.** Semi-circular ring of iron with an eye in each end, through which a ring or iron bolt is passed to close the fixture. Made in a variety of shapes, and used to join lengths of chain or to hook or lash a TACKLE (05.05).

**Shackle bolt.** Bolt with a shackle at one end.

*Shroud truck*

**Shroud truck.** Short cylinder used as a fairlead for running rigging, usually of ash or elm, with a hole bored lengthwise through its centre. It is grooved along its outer length to fit onto a shroud and scored round the middle so that it can be SEIZED (05.12) to the shroud.

**Sling cleat.** Cleat, usually of oak, made in various sizes, the largest serving for gammoning the bowsprit and as stops to stay collars. Other types, usually of elm, are used to secure mast-head lashings.

**Slip hook.** Hinged hook which, when opened, allows its load to be easily slipped off.

**Snap hook.** One having a spring strip across the hook mouth to prevent the load from slipping off.

**Snatch.** FAIRLEAD with a spring across its mouth to prevent slippage of the rope.

**Straining screw.** Threaded cylinder into which is screwed a swivel at one end and an eye at the other. Used to support AWNING (03.15) ridge ropes, guard chains and other fittings.

**Thimble.** Metal ring with a concave outer edge round which a rope can be spliced; used to take a hook or to guide another rope.

*Shackle keys*

**Shackle key.** Key made to unscrew flush-headed SHACKLE pins. The key is T-shaped, with a square end which fits the countersunk recessed head of the shackle pin.

**Shroud cleat.** Cleat, usually of oak, with two arms, resembling a belaying cleat. The inside face is hollowed to fit the shroud and the ends are grooved to hold the seizings which secure it to the shroud.

*Thimbles*

**Traveller.** Large, light iron ring or cylinder, able to move freely along any mast, spar or rope. The *jib-traveller* is an iron ring, up to $1\frac{1}{2}$ inches thick, encircling the boom, with a hook and shackle that slide on the ring.

**Turnbuckle.** Alternative name for a BOTTLE SCREW.

**Warwick screw.** Type of BOTTLE SCREW in which the cover is cut away to allow locking blocks to be placed on the square ends of the screws.

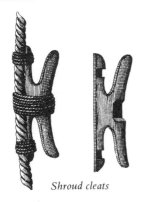

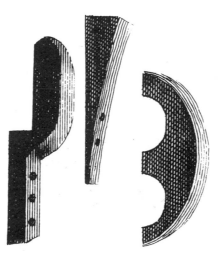

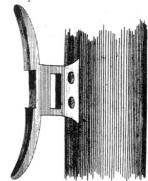

*Shroud cleats*

# Tackles and Lifts

**Bale sling.** Rope loop joined with a short splice, then SERVED (05.06) with SPUNYARN (05.09) over the splice.

*Bale sling*

*Butt sling*

**Block and block.** The situation of a tackle when two opposite blocks are drawn close together, thus nullifying their mechanical advantage until the tackle is again overhauled by increasing the distance between them.

**Bobstay purchase.** Tackle in the upper end of the BOBSTAY (04.08) and used for setting it up; consisting of a double running block, a single fixed block hooked to a SELVAGEE STROP (05.01) round a KNIGHT-HEAD (06.03) and another double block through which the fall is rove.

*Hogshead sling*

**Boom jigger.** Tackle composed of double and single blocks, stropped, with tails. Used in getting the studding sail boom in or out.

**Burton.** Type of TACKLE (05.05) using two blocks to bring the rope back on itself and thus increase the mechanical advantage. Used to tighten shrouds or lift heavy objects.

**Butt sling.** Rope with a THIMBLE (05.03) or EYE-SPLICE (05.12) in one end, with the other end whipped so that it can be run through the thimble to form a SLING.

**Chock a block.** BLOCK AND BLOCK.

**Choke the luff.** To temporarily jam a TACKLE (05.05) by passing the FALL over the sheave of a BLOCK (05.01) and under the rope entering the block. The block is freed by pulling on the fall.

**Double luff.** Tackle made up of two DOUBLE BLOCKS (05.02), one made fast, the other moving.

**Downhaul tackle.** Series of pulleys used to pull down the main or fore yard in a storm, in order to reef the sail. The tackle is needed because the force of the wind prevents the yard from descending under its own weight when released.

*Up and down tackle*

*Sail tackle*

*Gun tackle*

*Long tackle*

*Luff tackle*

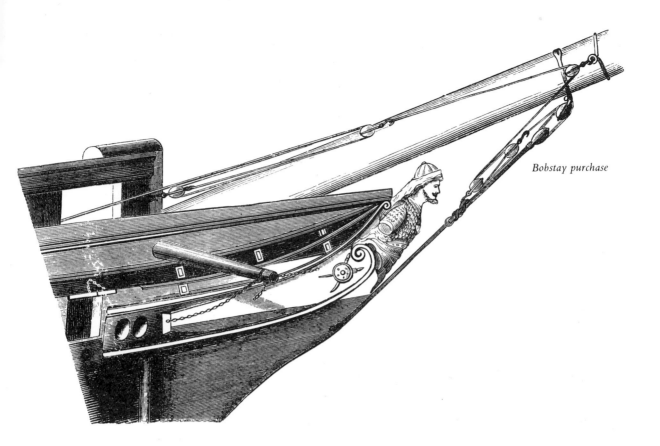

*Bobstay purchase*

**Fall.** The loose end of a TACKLE (05.05); the rope on which a seaman hauls to operate the tackle.

**Garnet.** Tackle composed of a double and a single block, stropped, with a hook and thimble. Hooked to the

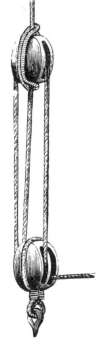

*Lower lift purchase*

TRIATIC STAY (04.08) in merchant ships, it was used for hoisting goods.

**Guy.** Rope used to steady a heavy object while it is being hoisted or lowered. Also the rope exerting lateral control on a BOOM (04.07). In addition, the term refers to a rope extending from mainmast to foremast of a merchant ship, and carrying two or three large blocks through which cargo hoisting tackle is run.

**Handy billy.** Small, light general-purpose tackle employing one single and one double block.

**Jigger tackle.** Light small tackle, comprising a single and a double block, used on various occasions by seamen.

**Luff tackle.** PURCHASE comprising a single and a double block; a large tackle used for various purposes.

**Luff upon luff.** Tackle made up by hooking the block of one LUFF TACKLE to the fall of another, thereby greatly increasing the lifting power.

**Main tackle.** Large, heavy-duty tackle, used for such purposes as securing the mast or setting up rigging and stays. It is composed of fixed single and double blocks together with a moving double block, the tackle being hooked on the main PENDANT.

**Mast tackle.** Strong tackle used for lifting a mast, composed of a fixed treble block hooked to SHEERS (06.01) and a moving double block to which the mast is attached by a SELVAGEE STROP (05.01) and TOGGLE (10.08). Alternatively, any tackle secured to the mast.

**Outhaul.** Rope forming part of the tackle used in hauling out the jib traveller. It is rove through a block strapped to an eye-bolt in the bowsprit cap, then through the sheave hole in the heel, the end taken to an eye-bolt on the other side of the cap and hitched.

**Parbuckle.** Simple contrivance used to raise a round object, and worked by securing the middle of a rope, passing both halves under and over the object and hauling on both ends.

**Pendant.** Short rope fixed under the shrouds and hanging from the head of the mainmast or the foremast, with an eye and THIMBLE (05.03) or a BLOCK (05.01) in its lower end to take main, fore and other TACKLES (05.05).

**Purchase.** Mechanism – such as a TACKLE (05.05), WINDLASS (06.03), CAPSTAN (06.03), screw or HANDSPIKE (06.03) – by which a mechanical advantage is gained in order to move heavy bodies or extend the ship's rigging.

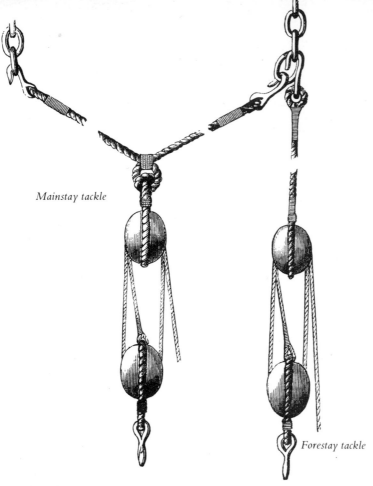

*Mainstay tackle*

*Forestay tackle*

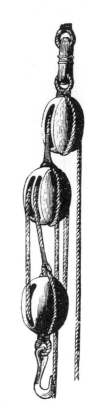

**Runner tackle.** Tackle comprising double and single blocks and a PENDANT (05.04). Used for setting up shrouds and staying the masts.

*Runner tackle*

**Purchase fall.** Rope run through a series of blocks for mechanical advantage. That part of the fall fastened to the fixed blocks is the *standing part*, while the rest is the *leading part*.

**Raise a purchase.** To arrange tackle in such a way that sufficient mechanical advantage is gained to shift a particular object.

**Relieving tackles.** Two tackles, one on either side of the tiller, fixed during bad weather or in action, designed to dampen shocks and thereby reduce stress on the tiller connections.

**Ridge tackle.** Tackle suspending the centre, or ridge, of an AWNING (03.15). Composed of a double and a single block, strapped, with an eye.

**Rolling tackle.** Gear clapped on to windward on the topgallant yards during rough weather. As the ship rolls, the tackle is BOUSED (05.07) down and belayed to restrain the yard and prevent it from chafing the mast.

**Rudder tackle.** Arrangement of LONG-TACKLE BLOCKS (05.02) and single blocks, strapped, with hooks and thimbles. Used to save or direct the RUDDER (01.01), in the case of some accident to the tiller.

**Runner.** Rope used to increase the mechanical power of a TACKLE: one or both ends are fixed, while the rope runs through a HOOK-BLOCK (05.02), which is attached to the object being moved.

*Runner*

**Running gear.** Any tackles, ropes or rigging that move or can be moved.

**Running part.** Hauling part of a simple TACKLE.

**Sail burton.** Tackle extending from the topmast heads, used to hoist sails aloft.

**Single whip.** Small simple tackle formed by reeving the FALL (05.04) through a single block. Suitable for light loads only.

**Sling.** Rope used to encircle a cask, bale or similar object so that it can be hoisted or lowered by a tackle.

**Spanish burton.** PURCHASE (05.04) of two single blocks, giving the lifting power of three but only over a short distance.

**Splay tackle.** Two-block tackle used to adjust and maintain the position of the heels of SHEER LEGS (07.01) when these are set up on deck. Tackles are led and secured both fore and aft.

*Spanish burton*

**Standing part.** Rope made fast to a block forming part of a TACKLE.

**Stay tackle.** Composed of double and single blocks, strapped, normally with hooks and THIMBLES (05.03), except when spliced into a PENDANT (05.04). Used for hoisting anything out of the main and fore holds and for hoisting boats in and out.

**Stock tackle.** Tackle used to keep the ANCHOR (06.02) stock vertical and clear of the ship's sides when the anchor is being FISHED (06.02).

**Strop and toggle.** Quick-release device used for slings and other bonds. And endless rope, the *strop*, is secured transversely by a wooden pin, the *toggle*.

**Swifting.** Method of tautening a rope by passing frapping turns (see FRAP, 05.12) round it, used particularly for setting up standing rigging.

**Tackle.** Pulley, or purchase, created by running a rope through one or more BLOCKS (05.01); used to move heavy objects and in supporting the masts and working the sails and rigging. That part of the tackle fixed to a block or to some other point is the *standing part*, the rest are *running parts*. The rope hauled to operate the tackle is the *fall*.

**Tack purchase.** Simple general-purpose tackle, made by reeving a rope through two single blocks. Also called *gun tackle purchase*.

**Tack tackle.** Arrangement composed of a double and single block, strapped, with hooks and thimbles, used for bousing down the TACKS (04.09) of the principal sails to their respective stations. In particular, attached to the mainsail tacks of brigs, sloops, cutters and schooners.

**Tail jigger.** Small light general-purpose tackle made up of a single block and a double block with a SELVAGEE (05.01) tail. (See also WATCH TACKLE.)

*Tail jigger*

**Tail tackle.** Hooked single block and double block with a SELVAGEE (05.01) tail. Similar to a LUFF TACKLE (05.04) or WATCH TACKLE.

**Threefold purchase.** Tackle in which the rope is rove through two treble blocks to increase lifting power.

**Top tackle.** Arrangement of double and treble blocks, the FALL (05.04) being rove through a leading block. Used to hoist up topmasts.

**Two blocks.** BLOCK AND BLOCK (05.04).

**Watch tackle.** Strong purchase made up of a hooked single block and a

double block with hook or tail. Used to tighten running rigging and as a general-purpose tackle.

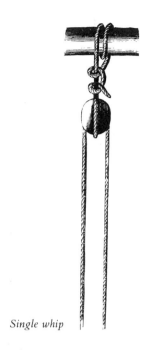

*Single whip*

**Whip.** Small tackle used for light tasks, comprising a rope run through a fixed block or through one fixed and one movable block.

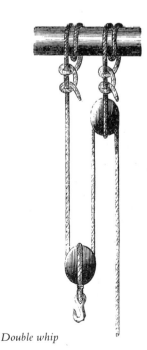

*Double whip*

**Winding tackle.** Heavy-duty tackle comprising a fixed treble block and a movable double block.

# Construction of Ropes

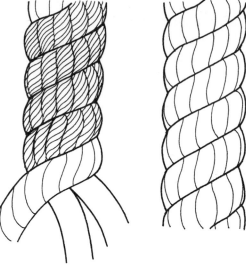

**Boatswain's plait.** Plait made up from three strands of rope, in which two strands are hitched alternately over a one-strand foundation.

**Cable-laid.** Describes a rope composed of nine strands laid first into three small ropes and then into one. It is laid LEFT-HANDED.

**Cantline.** The groove between the strands of a rope.

**Cap a rope.** To PARCEL a wormed rope by wrapping tarred canvas round the end before it is SERVED. The cap protects the end from being injured by water when the service becomes worn.

**Core.** Central strand of a four-stranded rope around which the other strands are laid.

**Hard-laid.** Cordage whose strands are tightly torsioned for added strength.

**Hawser-laid.** Describes a rope composed of three strands, laid RIGHT-HANDED.

**Heart yarns.** The inside yarns of a rope strand.

*From left to right: Cable-laid, Hawser-laid, Right-handed*

**Lay.** Direction in which strands are twisted to form various types of rope. Lay may be RIGHT-HANDED, with the sun, as in hawser-laid or shroud-laid rope. Alternatively it may be left-handed, AGAINST THE SUN (05.07), as in cable-laid rope.

**Lay up.** To apply the torsion to yarns and strands that forms them into ropes. Ropes may be HARD-LAID or SOFT-LAID, depending on the degree of torsion employed.

**Left-handed.** Direction of lay of a CABLE-LAID rope. Seen from the side, the strands lay from upper left to lower right.

**Link worming.** Method of WORMING hemp rope by passing a small chain along the CANTLINES of the rope, to reduce chafing.

**Long jaw.** Said of a rope laid with its strands forming an angle less than $45°$ from the run of the rope.

**Parcel** (vb). To wrap fabric, such as canvas or hessian, round the end of a WORMED rope to prepare it for serving and to protect the rope end from water when the service becomes worn.

**Ratline stuff.** Three-strand, loosely laid, LONG-JAW rope of tarred hemp. Normally 1 to $1\frac{1}{4}$ inches in circumference, it is used for shroud RATLINES (04.08).

*Ropemaking in the eighteenth century*

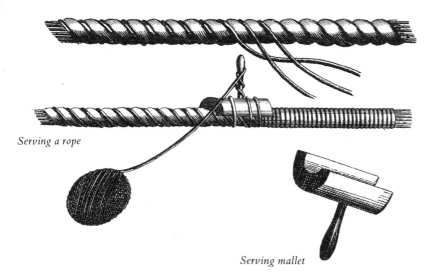

*Serving a rope*

*Serving mallet*

**Snake.** Method of securing the SEIZING (05.12) put on a single rope. Made by taking the yarn ends under and over the lower and upper parts of the seizing in such a way as to form a zig-zag pattern across them.

**Soft-laid.** Describes rope in which the strands are loosely laid with little torsion, thereby making it more pliable.

**Tapered ropes.** Ropes whose circumference diminishes towards one end, making them easier to work through blocks. Once used extensively for sheets and tacks.

**Tapering.** Gradually reducing the thickness of a rope's end so that it is more easily worked through blocks or thimbles.

**Three-stranded.** Said of a rope, such as a hawser, composed of three single strands.

**Twice-laid stuff.** Made by unlaying old rope and laying the yarns up again.

**Water-laid.** Said of a rope that is laid LEFT-HANDED.

**Worm** (vb). To pass SPUNYARN (05.09) along the CANTLINES of a rope to strengthen it or to make a smooth surface preparatory to PARCELLING or SERVING it.

**Worm.** Thin strand of SPUNYARN (05.09) laid along the CANTLINES of a rope to make it waterproof.

**Reverse laid.** Said of a rope whose yarns and strands lay in the same direction.

**Right-handed.** Direction of lay of HAWSER-LAID and SHROUD-LAID ropes. Seen from the side, the strands lay from upper right to lower left.

**Rogue's yarn,** or **marker yarn.** Coloured or white untarred yarn inserted in each strand of any rope issued by H.M. Dockyard, the East India Company, or other official bodies, to indicate their ownership of the rope.

**Salvage.** Rope made of yarns laid parallel, untwisted and bound together or MARLED (05.07).

**Serve** (vb). To bind a rope's end tightly with SPUNYARN (05.09), canvas, hide or some other suitable material, in order to prevent the end from fraying. Serving is done with a special mallet.

**Short jaw.** Said of a rope laid with its strands forming an angle greater than 45° from the run of the rope.

**Shroud-laid.** Said of a rope composed of four strands laid RIGHT-HANDED.

**Sinking a strand.** Procedure employed when splicing a three-strand rope to a four-strand rope. One strand of the extra end is split into three and these sunk where they lay before entering the splice.

# Handling of Ropes

**Against the sun.** Anti-clockwise circular motion employed when coiling down LEFT-HANDED rope (05.06).

**Belay** (vb). To fasten a rope by giving it several cross-turns alternately round two timber-heads, each end of a cleat, or any suitable fitting.

**Bend.** Any temporary secure join of one rope with another or of one rope with an object for a particular purpose.

**Bending the cable.** Attaching a cable to the anchor by taking the rope's end through the anchor ring then turning it around the BIGHT (05.10), making a CLINCH (06.03) which is then seized. These seizings are the *bends*.

**Bitt** (vb). To pass a cable or rope round the BITTS (06.03) in order to fasten it, or in order to slacken it gradually – the latter operation being called *veering away*.

**Bouse.** To pull down upon a rope or the fall of a tackle.

**Catch a turn.** To make a temporary turn with a rope.

**Check** (vb). To ease a rope and then hold it or secure it again. Also, to halt a rope's too rapid progress as it runs out by throwing a turn or two on the BITTS (06.03).

**Checking.** To ease a rope under strain carefully, a small amount at a time, so that it will not part in the process.

**Clear for running.** Said of a rope coiled down in such a way that the end is underneath and the rope able to run out freely.

**Coil.** Length of rope, usually 113 to 120 fathoms long, wound concentrically.

**Coiling.** Method of stowing a rope by winding it round in the direction appropriate to its lay.

**Douse** (vb). To lower or slacken suddenly.

**Ease off.** To gently slacken taut rope, particularly on a TACKLE (05.05).

**End for end.** Reversing the ends of a rope to get more wear from it or to ease chafing.

**Fake.** One turn of a rope when stowed away or coiled.

**Flake** (vb). To coil a rope flat on the deck so that it can run freely.

**Fleeting.** See OVERHAULING.

**Flemish coil.** Rope coiled flat on deck with its end at the centre of concentric turns of rope. Used in port as a decorative method of tidying away the falls of the running rigging.

**Freshen the nip.** To change the position of any rope that is being nipped or chafed. The rope is veered or hauled so that a fresh portion is exposed to the friction.

**Half crown.** Small circular BIGHT (05.10) or loop in a rope.

*Half crown*

**Hang taut.** Said of a rope's end, piece taut as it can be made when pulled by hand. The expression describes the tension; the rope need not have been pulled by hand.

**Hang Judas.** Said of a rope's end, piece of yarn or small line left hanging or loosely fastened.

**Haul** (vb). To pull a rope, without the assistance of blocks or other mechanical means.

**Heave** (vb). To give a horizontal pull on a rope, by hand or by turning round a capstan.

**Hoist** (vb). To draw up a weight by means of TACKLES (05.05).

**Hoist.** Extent by which a yard or sail may be raised by its tackles. Also the part of a sail which is bent to a yard or stay.

**Judas.** Any rope hanging down unfastened and so subject to buffeting by the wind.

**Keckling.** Old rope wound round a cable to protect its surface from chafing on the ship's sides or bottom.

**Kink.** Short, tight bend or curl occurring in a rope twisted too hard or drawn too hastily out of the coil.

**Lead.** Direction in which a rope may be led or turned by blocks, cleats or FAIRLEADS (05.03).

**Leading part.** Rope forming the fall and moving parts of a TACKLE (05.05); that is, all except the standing part.

**Light** (vb). To help carry any rope in the required direction.

**Light along.** To pass a rope along.

**Marl** (vb). To wind a small line round a rope, securing every turn by a hitch so that rope and marl are independent of each other and will remain fixed if either is cut. Splices are marled down for SERVING (05.06) with rope yarn or twine.

**Mend** (vb). To put an extra serving upon a rope.

**Nip** (vb). To stop a rope by attaching another to it with several turns of yarn alternately round each and the ends made fast.

**Nip.** Short turn in a rope or cable.

**Nipped.** Said of a rope or cable when it is in an undesirable position or caught up on some obstruction.

**One for coming up.** Final pull on a rope to take in the extra required for belaying it.

**Overhauling.** Act of improving the efficiency of a choked tackle by increasing the distance between its component blocks.

**Part** (vb). To break or separate a rope or cable.

**Pay out,** or **pay away.** To slacken a rope or cable and let it run out.

**Ran.** Yarns made by unlaying old cable, tarring it, then laying up three or four strands on a SPUNYARN (05.09) winch. Also called spunyarn and used for worming, seizing, serving and so on. Also, a reel wound with twenty cords of twine each parted by a knot so as to be easily separated.

**Reeve** (vb). To pass a rope's end through any sheave or block, thimble, ring or cringle. The reverse process is termed *unreeving*.

**Render** (vb). To yield without resistance; said of a rope when it runs freely through an opening or block.

**Riding turn.** A turn in a rope which rides over another.

**Round in.** To haul on the FALL (05.04) of a tackle, so closing the distance between its blocks.

**Round turn.** Single turn of rope round a timber head or bollard.

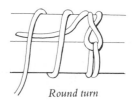

*Round turn*

**Round up.** In general, to gather in the slack of any rope passing through one or more blocks in a perpendicular direction. In particular, to close the space between the blocks when there is no weight on the tackle.

**Rouse** (vb). To pull together, for instance, on a cable or hawser, without the assistance of a capstan, windlass or any other mechanical aid.

**Settle** (vb). To ease any rope by letting it slacken a small amount.

**Shifting.** Separating the blocks of a choked tackle.

**Slack of a rope.** Any section of a rope which hangs loose, having no load or strain upon it.

*Cadets in the* Parma *hauling on the clew-lines of a sail before furling it*

**Stoppering.** Holding part of a rope under tension by means of a short rope or STOPPER (05.08), allowing the part not under tension to be handled freely.

**Sweat up.** To haul on a rope in order to bring in the last few possible inches.

**Swig.** To haul on a taut rope at right angles to its direction, taking up any slack and obtaining maximum tension.

**Take a turn.** To secure a rope quickly, and usually temporarily, by making it fast on a BELAYING PIN (10.07), CLEAT (10.07) or BITT (06.03).

**Thoroughfoot.** Method of clearing a rope which has been unduly twisted by coiling it down in the same direction as the twist, bringing its end up through the centre of the coil, then hauling out the coil. Also the fouling of a TACKLE (05.05) by catching one of the blocks in the running parts.

**Thumb cleat.** Small cleat with only one horn.

**Trice** (vb). To haul on any FALL (05.04) or rope passing through a sheave.

**Unreeve** (vb). To remove any rope passing through a block, sheave, ring or thimble.

**Veer and haul.** Method of getting greater tension on a rope by rhythmically easing and hauling on it. This was the method used in hauling on the BOWLINES (04.09) of a square-rigged vessel.

**Working strain.** The maximum load that can be borne by any working rope.

# Types of Rope

**Cable.** Heavy chain or hemp rope, usually 120 fathoms in length, to which the anchor is secured. Hemp cable is composed of nine strands, laid first into three ropes and then into one large rope.

**Cordage.** General term used to describe strands or rope of hemp or other fibres before these are laid up or finished for a specific purpose.

**Dead man.** The end of any yarn, cord or rope left hanging untidily.

**Dead ropes.** Any ropes not rove through some sheave or block.

**Dummy gantline,** or **dummy girtline.** Rope forming part of the tackle used to hoist rigging. The rope is passed through a sheaved block and the GANTLINE attached to it for reeving.

**Fag-end.** Unwhipped rope end which has become unlaid through use.

**Flax rope.** Rope made of flax, a fibre which gives a breaking strain more than double that of a manilla rope of equal size. Used particularly on yachts.

**Fourcant.** Rope composed of four strands.

**Gantline,** or **girtline.** Rope rove through a single block at a lower mast-head, used to set up the rigging. This is the first rope sent up during the rigging of a ship.

**Hawser.** Small cable used when swaying up topmasts. For this purpose it is stopped to the topmast, then rove through a large single block lashed around the head of the lower mast.

**Heaving line.** Small line thrown from a ship to some other point to establish contact, and as a means of transferring a heavier rope attached to it.

**Hook rope.** General-purpose rope, usually about ten fathoms long, with a hook secured to one end.

**In haul.** Term applied to any rope or part of a tackle bringing objects inboard.

**Junk.** Remnants of old rope, cut into pieces and used to make mats, swabs, oakum and so on.

**Lazy guy.** Single-rope GUY (05.04), used when little weight is involved, for example to steady davits, sheers or derricks.

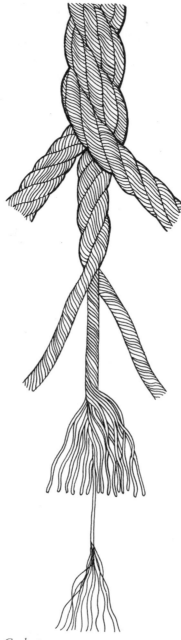

*Cordage*

**Leg.** Short rope which branches out into three or more parts; for example, bowline-legs, buntline-legs or crowfoot-legs.

**Lifeline.** Any rope attached to part of the ship for the security of the crew when working aloft or in bad weather. Also, any rope's end or buoyed rope thrown into the water for the purpose of rescuing a man overboard.

**Limber rope.** Long rope running through the LIMBERS (03.06) and pulled back and forth to clear them of any clogging dirt.

**Lizard.** Iron thimble spliced into the main BOWLINES (04.09) and pointed over one end so that a tackle may be hooked to it.

**Man ropes.** Safety ropes, rigged alongside ladders, steep steps or any hazardous area.

**Mast rope.** Rope used to hoist the upper mast.

**Monkey tail.** Rope fastened to the end of a lever so that extra men may haul on it.

**Painter.** Rope secured to the bow of a boat for the purpose of making her fast.

**Port lanyard,** or **port pendant.** Rope spliced to the ring on the outside of a port, then led through a pipe in the ship's side. Used to haul up the port-lids, with the assistance of a tackle if necessary.

**Quarter gasket.** One of the braided cords used to secure a sail to its yard when furled; specifically, that located at the quarter between the middle and end of the yard.

**Quick saver.** Rope span fixed to the fore side of a course, or lower sail, to prevent it from bellying.

**Ridge rope.** Rope forming the main support of an AWNING (03.15), rove through wooden TRUCKS (04.07) secured along the awning's centre-line.

*Ring-rope*

**Ring-rope.** Short rope fastened to a RING-BOLT (05.03) and used to secure the anchor cable or another rope when it is under heavy strain.

**Rope.** General term applied to all cordage more than one inch in diameter. Normally made of hemp yarn (sometimes tarred) twisted into strands which are then again twisted or laid into rope. The direction of lay, and the amount of torsion put into the rope, varies according to the purpose for which it was required. Until recently the dimension given of a rope referred to its circumference. Stranded wire rope was introduced towards the end of the nineteenth century.

**Rope's end.** Any short length of rope, or the end of a long rope.

**Shroud bridle.** Short rope which confines running rigging to a shroud.

*Stopper*

**Shroud stopper.** Short rope used to hold together a shroud which has parted or been otherwise damaged.

**Smiting line.** Single line of rope used for rapid unfurling of a sail. The line is attached to several rope yarn stops on a furled sail and is pulled to release the sail.

**Spurling line.** Small line connecting the tiller, or wheel, to a cabin indicator showing the amount of helm being used.

**Stage lashing.** SOFT-LAID (05.06) pliable rope used to lash STAGES (03.15) or working platforms, or for general use.

**Stopper.** Short length of rope, firmly secured at one end, used as a temporary measure to take the strain off a loaded cable. The term usually appears in a form indicating a specific use, such as anchor-stopper, deck-stopper or sheet-stopper.

**Stops.** Several turns of SPUNYARN (05.09) taken round the end of a rope, similar to a seizing, in order to fasten it to another rope. Also, projections left on the topgallant mast to prevent the rigging from sliding down.

**Tack tricing line.** Small rope, generally passed through a block or thimble, used from a yard to hoist the TACK (04.09) of a sail.

**Tew,** or **tow.** Rope used for towing. Also, process of beating hemp as a preliminary stage in rope manufacture.

**Tier.** Hemp rope which has been FLAKED (05.07) down ready for running.

**Tiller rope.** Untarred rope made of fine white 25–thread yarn. It contains three or four strands, with or without a heart, and is laid harder than other ropes.

**Timenoguy.** Rope fastened at one end to the fore shrouds and nailed at the other end to the ANCHOR (06.02) stock on the bow, to prevent the foresheet from entangling.

**Tow line.** Hawser passed from one ship to another for the purpose of towing.

**Tricing line.** Small rope or tackle used to hoist any object to a higher point.

**Twiddling line.** Small line made fast at one end, the other end passed round the spoke of the ship's wheel. It serves to ease the helmsman's arm when steering.

**Tye.** RUNNER (05.05) or large rope which conveys the motive power of the tackle used to hoist the upper yards and gaff. Small ships used one tye and tye block; large ships with heavy yards were fitted with a pair of tyes and blocks.

**Weather ropes.** Those whose yarn has been tarred.

**White rope.** Rope that has not been tarred when made. It may be tarred when put into use.

# Small Stuff

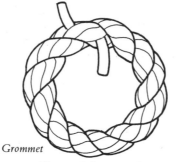

**Baggywrinkle.** Length of SENNIT wrapped round a rope to protect it from chafing against a yard or other fitting.

**Cod line.** Originally a fishing line. Made of Italian hemp in various sizes; three or six threads to the strand, three strands to the line.

**Dogging.** Thin rope or twine wound tightly around another rope.

**Drummer's plait.** PLAIT in which the bight passes through every preceding loop.

**English sennit.** Simple plait of three strands. To make it the ends are made fast, the outer strand brought down across its sister strand and laid parallel to and below the left-hand one. The upper left strand is then brought across and laid parallel to and below the right-hand strand. The process is repeated alternately.

*English sennit*

**Flat sennit.** Simple flat PLAIT made with more than three strands, each passed over two sister strands. The plait pattern has a central axis, as opposed to a FRENCH SENNIT.

**Fox.** Twisted rope yarns, used for making bands, GASKETS (04.09) and so forth. Three or more yarns are taken, according to the size required, twisted together and smoothed down.

**French sennit.** Flat plait composed of an odd or even number of strands, having a regular one-over, one-under

*Grommet*

weave. The result is an evenly woven braid.

**Garland.** Collar or ring of rope around the head of the mast, supporting the STANDING RIGGING (04.08) and preventing it from chafing the mast.

**Grommet.** Small rope ring which is made up and stitched to any hole in canvas to prevent it fraying, for example an eyelet hole at the sail-head. The grommet is made by unlaying a rope strand and placing one part over the other, with the long end following the lay, till it forms a ring. An OVERHAND KNOT (05.11) is then cast on the two ends and these tucked in.

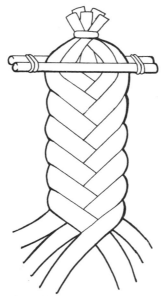

*French sennit*

**Hambro line.** Line used mainly by sail-makers for reef holes. May be composed of six, nine or twelve strands, depending on the size required.

**Hank.** Skein of SPUNYARN or other small cordage.

**Head line.** Line sewn along the upper edge of flags. Also, that used to lace the sail-head to its yard or gaff.

**House line.** Line composed of three threads, loose laid. Used for seizing STROPS (05.01) on blocks.

**Lacing.** Fastening the head of a sail to the mast, yard or gaff by a line turned spirally round them and reeved through eyelet holes in the sail.

**Lashing.** Any rope used to secure objects in place or for tying any two objects together.

**Line.** Cordage less than one inch in circumference. Formed of two or more strands of hemp.

**Marline.** Line composed of two threads laid together. Generally used for seizing STROPS (05.01) onto blocks.

**Mouse.** Large, pear-shaped knot, composed of yarns worked around the eye of a stay to prevent it chafing against the mast. Mousing a hook involves taking several turns of SPUNYARN round the back and point of a hook to prevent the load from accidentally slipping off.

*Mousing a hook*

**Nettle, or knittle.** Small line composed of two or three rope yarns twisted hard together between the finger and thumb, with the twist of the yarn beginning in the middle; the ends are whipped. Used for various purposes, particularly to fasten the service on the cable, to reef the sails by the bottom, and to sling sailors' hammocks.

**Nettle stuff.** SPUNYARN laid with two or three yarns, sometimes used for making GASKETS (04.09) and similar small fittings.

**Nine thread stuff.** Line composed of nine strands, usually one inch in circumference.

**Ocean plait.** Plaited yarns, often used to make up CHAFING MATS (04.02).

**Plait.** SENNIT or gaskets made by intertwining yarn or small line.

**Rope yarn.** Hemp threads made up in various thicknesses and termed, according to their composition, twenty-five, twenty and eighteen-thread yarn. The higher the number, the finer the yarn, since either twenty-five, twenty or eighteen threads make up a rope of the same circumference.

**Rounding.** SERVING (05.06) made of old rope yarns, wound around that part of the cable lying in the hawse or athwart the stem. Used to prevent chafing.

**Rumbo,** or **rumboline.** Line made by re-laying old yarns taken from the outside of worn rope. Having little strength, it was used for lashings and similar work.

**Sail twine,** or **seaming twine.** Made of the best long hemp, well beaten, spun fine and well dressed, made up with two or three threads. As used by the sailmakers, *extra* twine ran 360 fathoms to the lb., and was employed for seaming; *ordinary* was thicker and ran 200 fathoms to the lb., being used to sew on sail bolt-ropes.

**Samson line.** Line, usually in 30-fathom lengths and weighing about one pound.

**Seaming twine.** Alternative name for SAIL TWINE.

**Sennit.** Braided cordage composed of five to thirteen rope yarns. A variety of patterns can be made, according to the number of strands and the method of plaiting employed.

**Shakings.** Odds and ends of old rope, sacking, canvas and so on left after fitting and repair work; these could be unpicked to make OAKUM (03.02).

**Small stuff.** Any yarn, cord or line less than one inch in circumference.

**Soul and body lashing.** SPUNYARN passed round the body and round openings in oilskin garments to keep out wind and weather.

*The manufacture of spunyarn, from the Encyclopédic Méthodique, 1788*

*Spanish fox*

**Spanish fox.** Made by splitting a single yarn of rope, smoothing it down and re-laying it up in the opposite direction. Used as a SEIZING (05.12) and for weaving PAUNCH MATS (10.08).

**Spunyarn.** Small line composed of two or three rope yarns, twisted together on a winch. The yarns are usually drawn out of the strands of old ropes, knotted together and tarred. Used for many purposes including SEIZING (05.12) and SERVING (05.06).

**Strand.** Any twist of rope yarn which, with others, is laid up to form a rope or line.

**Thread.** Alternative name for yarn or a pair of yarns composed of hemp fibres twisted up for ropemaking. Four hundred threads, warped off the winches, make up a *haul* of yarn.

**Twine.** Thin line, normally made of good quality long-stranded hemp. Usually described according to its use: store twine, whipping twine and so forth.

**Yarn.** Product of one of the stages in rope making. Hemp, well cleaned, is spun into yarn on a spinning wheel. In general the yarn is spun into lengths of 160 fathoms, weighing $3\frac{1}{2}$–4 lb.

# Knots, Hitches and Bends

**Admiralty hitch,** or **marline spike hitch.** Turn of a line taken round a MARLINE SPIKE (10.08), which is then lifted and its tip slipped under the bight on the right of the standing part. Used to get a strong grip for heavy hauling when making up splices, SEIZINGS (05.12) and SERVINGS (05.06).

**Anchor clinch.** The end of a cable is passed through the HAWSE HOLE (03.07), reeved through the ANCHOR (06.02) ring, then passed round the standing part, through the bight, and a circle (the clinch) formed, the same size as the anchor ring. A throat and end bend are then clapped on opposite each other and spunyarn seizing put close to the end.

**Bend** (vb). To fasten one rope to another, often of a different diameter, or to different objects. Also, to fasten a sail to its yard.

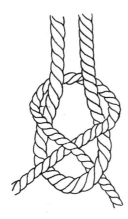

*Bend*

**Bight.** Central part of any rope, as opposed to the two ends. Alternatively, a loop or curve in the rope, usually no more than a semi-circle.

**Bowline on a bight.** Two parallel rigid loops knotted on a bight. Sometimes used to lower an injured man from aloft. He is able to put one leg through each loop and hold on to the standing part.

**Buntline hitch.** Two HALF HITCHES, the second made inside the first. On rope bent to a yard it makes a more secure knot than two normal half hitches but is more liable to jam.

*Bowline on a bight*

**Buoy rope knot.** Made by unstranding one yard of the rope end, stopping with yarn and removing one of the nine smaller strands from each of the large strands, which are then re-laid. The three smaller strands are double walled, right-handed close to the stop, and then laid up their CANTLINES (05.06).

**Carrick bend.** Quick means of joining two ropes or hawsers to lie flat. With one rope end passed over its own part, the end of the other rope is passed through the bight and over the cross of the first rope. It is then brought back through the loop opposite the one on which the first end lays.

**Chinkle,** or **half crown.** Small bight or loop made in a rope or line, with a crossing or RIDING TURN (05.07) and then seized. It is put into the middle of back ropes and passes round the end of the DOLPHIN STRIKER (04.06). Half crowns are also put into sail ropes.

*Carrick bend*

**Clove hitch.** Made by taking two turns in a rope, passing the lower over the upper and slipping both over the object to be secured. Used to fasten any part of a rope to a post or similar fitting, to tie up bales and bundles, or to secure RATLINES (04.08) to shrouds.

**Collar knot.** GRANNY KNOT, consisting of two identical half knots. It is put into the middle part of two ropes to make temporary shrouds for a JURY RIG (04.01), the knot being opened out and placed over the mast-head.

*Buoy rope knot*

**Common bend.** Made by passing the end of one rope through the bight of another, then round and under the standing part. Sometimes, the end is passed round again under the standing part to prevent jamming.

**Cuckolds knot,** or **neck.** Seized eye made with a crossing turn. Uses include being put in jib and staysail PENDANTS (05.04), in BRIDLES (14.03) and in can-hook straps.

**Figure of eight.** Made by taking the end of a rope round the standing part, under its own part, and through the bight. Sometimes put in the end of a fall to prevent it unreeving through the block.

*Figure of eight*

**Fisherman's bend.** Made by taking a round turn with the end of a rope through the ring of an anchor or similar fitting, making a HALF HITCH through both parts and another half hitch round the standing part; the end is then stopped.

**French bowline.** Similar to an ordinary bowline knot but having two turns made before passing the end up through these, round the standing part and back through the turns. Often put into stiff or slippery rope to lessen the chance of it capsizing if the knot is carelessly drawn up.

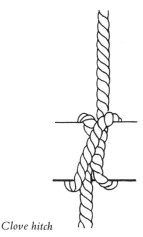

*Clove hitch*

**French shroud knot.** Method of joining the ends of three- or four-stranded shrouds. The ends are unlaid, the strands laid in a crown (see CROWNING, 05.12) over the join, and their ends tucked in. The resulting taper is then served, leaving the crown uncovered.

*Half hitch* *Two half hitches*

**Granny.** Insecure knot, easily capsized, consisting of two identical half knots.

*Granny knot*

**Half hitch.** Made by passing the end of a rope over the standing part, through the bight, and laying it up to the standing part.

*Half hitch*

*French shroud knot*

**Hitch.** Noose made on any part of a rope. The hitch may be made round a post or other object to which it is intended to fix the rope; alternatively it may be made round the rope's standing part.

**Inside clinch.** Alternative name for an ANCHOR CLINCH.

**Jury knot.** Three overlapping HITCHES are made, the inner bights of the outer hitches being led in sequence over and under to the opposite sides of the knot while the upper bight is simply pulled out. Used in JURY RIGS (04.01), where it is shipped over the mast to serve as an attachment for stays and shrouds.

**Jury mast knot.** A SHAMROCK (05.11) used for the same purpose as the JURY KNOT but having four points of attachment.

**Man harness hitch.** Loop put into the bight of a rope to give a hand or shoulder hold when it is to be hauled by manpower. A turn is made and laid across the rope, the bight on one side of which is taken over the rope and under the bight on the other side.

**Manrope knot.** Knot or knob tied onto the end of a man-line, gangway rope or side-line to provide a hand hold.

*Marline hitch*

**Marline hitch.** Single OVERHAND KNOT (05.11) normally used in series to lash bundles, hammocks and similar items. Also used when making up SELVAGEES (05.01).

**Monkey fist.** Weighted knot or knob made up on the end of a rope from three unlaid strands wound round a small heavy core of stone or iron. Used especially on the end of a heaving line to carry it from ship to shore or to another ship.

**Mouse.** Elongated knob made on a shroud or messenger to prevent nippers from slipping. SPUNYARN (05.09) is wound about the rope to form a shallow knob and small line worked through the rope strands against this. Alternatively the yarn knob is PARCELLED (05.06) and MARLED (05.07) down.

**Outside clinch.** Differs from an anchor clinch or inside clinch in that the end is passed outside, rather than through the bight, so that it may be more swiftly cast off. Used to secure a rope to an anchor ring.

**Overhand knot.** Simple knot made by taking the end of a rope across and round the rope itself, then passing it through the bight. Sometimes tied in reef points, on either side of the sail eyelet holes, or on foot-ropes, to give a grip. The knot is difficult to untie and, if used on a large rope, tends to damage the fibres.

*Sheepshank*

**Reef knot.** Composite knot made up of two half knots laid in opposite directions. Easily shaken out, it is particularly suitable for reefing, as its name suggests.

**Right knot.** Alternative name for REEF KNOT.

**Ron finish.** Method of POINTING (05.12) a rope end which incorporates a DIAMOND KNOT (05.13) over the heart.

**Rope yarn knot.** A weak knot, but useful for mending standing rigging, in place of the bulkier REEF KNOT. Made by splitting each rope yarn into two, teasing these out, and marrying the ends. With the opposing parts crossed, a half knot is tied on each pair. The ends are covered as the join is SERVED (05.06).

**Running bowline.** BOWLINE (04.09) made in the end of a rope around its own standing part, along which the bowline may slide.

**Sheepshank.** Portion of rope looped back upon itself so that each loop end is taken round the standing part in a half hitch. Used to shorten BACK-STAYS (04.08) and other ropes.

**Sheet bend.** General purpose bend in which a loop or bight is formed in one rope and the end of another passed through it, round both parts of the first rope and down through its own bight.

*Shroud knot*

**Shroud knot.** Method of joining two ropes by unlaying their ends, abutting them, and then single walling the ends of one rope, against the lay, round the standing part of the other. The ends are opened out, TAPERED (05.06), MARLED (05.07) down and served. Used to repair shrouds which have been shot or carried away.

**Slip knot.** Running knot made on, and free to travel along, its own standing part. Also an OVERHAND KNOT in which only a bight is pulled through at the end, enabling the knot to be untied simply by pulling on the free end of the rope.

**Slippery hitch.** Hitch or bend in which a rope is taken round a cleat or similar fastening, and a bight on the end passed under the standing part which presses against it. The hitch is instantly cast off by pulling the rope end or by easing the standing part. Also, the name given to any incorrectly made hitch which fails to hold.

*Overhand knot*

**Palm and needle hitching.** Series of simple HALF HITCHES (05.10) made on twine with the aid of a sailmaker's PALM (10.08) and needle.

*Reef knot*

*Running bowline*

**Shamrock knot.** Rope arranged into three loops so that these and the standing part form a cross. The loops and ends are then crowned (see CROWNING, 05.12) first to the right and then back to the left. When setting up a JURY RIG (04.01) the knot is laid over the mast-head to provide attachment for stays and shrouds.

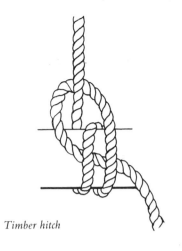

*Timber hitch*

**Timber hitch.** Means of fastening a rope end to any spar or timber head. The end is taken round the spar, under and over the standing part, then passed several times around its own part.

**Topsail halyard bend.** Method of hitching the halyard by passing the rope end three times round the yard then back under these turns, over the two outer turns and again under the first turn.

**Turn** (vb). To pass a rope once around any yard, cleat, bollard or similar fitting.

**Turn up.** To secure any rope to a cleat or bollard by simply taking several turns around it.

**Wall knot,** or **wale knot.** Knob made on a rope's end with its own three strands. These are interwoven in one of several patterns and usually CROWNED (05.12). Sometimes worked on the end of tacks, topsail sheets and STOPPERS (05.08).

**Spanish bowline.** Complex knot made on the bight of a rope to produce two permanent loops. Used to send or return a man aloft, to hold staging, or in JURY RIGS (04.01).

**Spritsail sheet knot.** Knob made on the two ends of a spritsail sheet block STROP (05.01). The rope is rove through the block and the six strands then walled to the right and topped off with an irregular crown.

**Square knot.** Means of fastening together two ropes which cross at right angles. An S-shaped bight is made in one rope and the cross-rope laced through this. Also, alternative name for a reef knot.

*Stopper knot*

**Stopper knot.** Made by single walling a three-stranded rope against the lay, and stopping or WHIPPING (05.12) the ends. Put on the end of a STOPPER (05.08).

**Studding-sail halyard bend.** Method of hitching the halyard by passing the rope end twice round the yard, round its standing part, and then under the two turns on the yard.

**Swab hitch.** Means of attaching a SWAB (10.07) to its lanyard so that after use it might be easily detached and hung to dry. The lanyard end passes through the swab grommet, round the swab head, and under its standing part.

**Tack knot.** Knob worked on the end of a tack or rope by making a double WALL KNOT and crown.

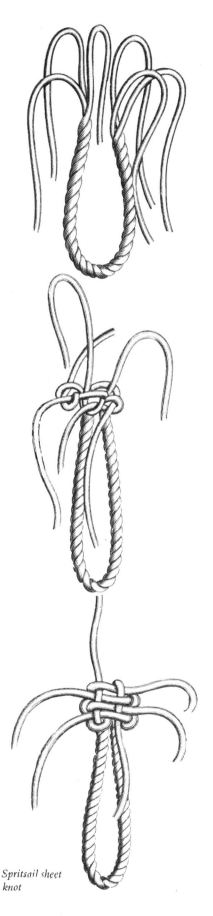

*Spritsail sheet knot*

*Wall knot*

# Splicing, Joining and Whipping

**American whipping,** or **sailor's whipping.** Method of whipping a rope's end in which the ends of the whip are pulled out at the centre and REEF KNOTTED (05.11) before being trimmed. Often put on hawsers.

**Artificial eye,** or **spindle eye.** EYE put into a rope's end by unlaying the strands and hitching them over a piece of wood or rope the size of the intended eye. The ends are then scraped down, marled, parcelled and served. Sometimes put at the end of a stay.

**Back splice.** Finishing for a rope's end that is not intended to be rove through a block. The strands are unlaid and woven into a crown, the ends being tucked in below it.

**Blackwall hitch.** Simple HITCH (05.10) used to secure a rope to a hook. The end is taken round the back of the hook and across its point, being held in position by the strain on the standing part.

**Common whipping.** WHIPPING made by laying a loop along the rope and taking a series of turns along it. The working end is then passed through the loop, pulled out of sight under the turns, and trimmed.

**Cross seizing.** SEIZING put on cross joins such as those where BATTENS (03.02) cross shrouds. The seizing is turned several times under the batten and over the shroud.

**Crowning.** Method of finishing the end of a cable. The cable is WHIPPED some distance from the end, which is then unlaid into its nine strands. The inner three strands are laid into a heart and the remaining six paired, one of each pair being fayed along the heart. The whole is then served to finish it off.

**Cut splice.** SPLICE put in standing rigging to take pendants or ropes. The ropes are overlapped the required distance and each end is then spliced into the opposite standing part and seized.

**Eye.** Loop in a rope's end. Also the loop in an EYE SPLICE.

**Eye splice.** Loop or EYE made in a rope's end by splicing the strands into the standing part the required distance back from the end.

**Flat seizing.** SEIZING binding a rope's end to its standing part by taking a series of turns around both. The end of the seizing is brought up through the eye, crossing turns are made, and the end secured with a knot.

**Flemish eye.** EYE formed by unlaying one strand from a rope end, and taking the remaining strands back along the standing part. The unlaid strand is then laid round the eye in the contrary direction. The strands are seized, untucked at the straddle, and the ends fayed and served.

**Frap** (vb). To pass a lashing tightly around some rope or object.

**Frapping.** Lashing passed round two ropes or fittings which have been seized together. The frapping serves to tighten the SEIZING.

**Grecian splice.** Technique frequently used to SPLICE standing rigging. The hearts of the two ropes are SHORT-SPLICED and served. The ends are then divided, married and tucked in twice. The splice is fayed, parcelled and served. An alternative method involves putting a cross-point at the centre of the splice.

**Horseshoe splice.** SPLICE designed to span a rope loop the leads of which diverge too much to be seized. The ends of a short cross-piece of rope are side-spliced into the loop to form a bridge. Sometimes put into shrouds or stays.

**Long splice.** Method of joining two rope ends by unlaying both, placing one within the other, and replacing each strand unlaid with one from the opposite rope. Each pair of opposing strands is knotted and the ends cut off. Used to lengthen any rope which is rove through a block, since it increases the rope circumference by very little.

**Mariner's splice.** One made on cables. The ropes and strands are unlaid, each of the nine strands being divided. The halves are then plaited.

**Marry** (vb). To unlay two ropes' ends and interlace them preparatory to SPLICING or bending them.

**Outer turns.** Those on the outside of any WHIPPING or SEIZING which is made up with two layers of turns. The outer turns are usually one less in number than the inner turns.

**Palm and needle whipping.** One made using waxed thread with the aid of a sailmaker's needle. The thread end is first stitched to a strand to secure it, the turns are then made, and WORMED (05.06) back twice along each CANTLINE (05.06). A final stitch secures the whipping.

**Point** (vb). To taper a rope's end down to a point so that it may be more easily reeved through a block or eye. The rope is unlaid, scraped down and the yarns made into NETTLES (05.09) and braided, some down to the point and the rest back up the rope. When pointing a soft rope a wooden cone is sometimes inserted.

**Racking.** Lashing or bend in which cross turns are made over the eyes or ropes to be joined. Sometimes used to form a loop on the end of a hawser, and also seen in a ROSE LASHING.

**Raddle.** Yarns braided to form a GASKET (04.09) for securing furled sails.

**Rolling hitch.** Hitch designed to allow for rolling or twisting movement by the object which it secures. When SWIFTING (05.05) capstan bars, for example, the swifter is secured to the bar by a rolling hitch. It is made in the bight of a rope by winding the rope into two backward turns and putting a hitch over the end of the bar with a bight from the working end.

*Horseshoe splice*    *Cut splice*    *Blackwall hitch*    *Flemish eye*

*Short splice*

*Eye splice*

*Long splice*

**Rose lashing.** Method commonly used to lash blocks or stays to a mast or spar. The block eyes are lashed with RACKING turns and, in finishing off, the end of the lashing is passed alternatively over and under, or in some instances between the turns, forming a spiral 'rose'. The ends are finally knotted.

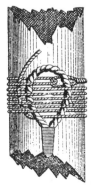

*Rose lashing*

**Round seizing.** General-purpose SEIZING formed by taking an inner and an outer layer of turns around both ropes, bringing the end down through the initial turn and adding two cross turns. The end is then brought up between the crossing turns and finished off with a wall, flat or overhand knot.

**Round spliced.** Join made by unlaying two rope ends and marrying them, scraping down if necessary. They are then woven into the opposing rope, each strand being tucked in twice.

**Sailmaker's eye splice.** Method of working an EYE into a three-strand BOLT-ROPE (04.12). Each strand is run down in turn and has some yarns cut off at each tuck so that the splice tapers back from the eye. The ends are cut to terminate in a row along the rope.

**Sailmaker's whipping.** Alternative name for PALM AND NEEDLE WHIPPING, being executed with the aid of a sailmaker's needle.

**Seizing.** Means of binding two ropes together or binding one rope to a spar or similar fitting. Made with spunyarn, twine or other small stuff. ROUND TURNS (05.07), RIDING TURNS (05.07) or racking turns are made round both ropes, the whole then being cross-turned and knotted. Seizing usually requires less material than bends or splices and does not injure the joined ropes.

**Sheer head lashing.** Fastening, similar to a SEIZING but on a much larger scale, designed to hold together the heads of SHEER LEGS (07.01). A CLOVE HITCH (05.10) is passed round one leg, then a series of round or racking turns made. Several FRAPPING turns serve to tauten the lashing which is finished off with a second clove hitch or a reef knot.

**Sheer lashing.** Method of lashing the heads of SHEER LEGS (07.01) whereby the rope is middled and turns made upwards and downwards with each end. The lashing is tightened with FRAPPING turns and finished with a knot.

**Short splice.** SPLICE in which two rope ends are unlaid, married and the strands tucked twice under strands of the opposing rope. The ends are sometimes scraped down, marled and served with spunyarn.

**Splice.** General term for the technique of joining two rope ends by unlaying them, separating their strands and tucking these through strands in the opposing rope. A wide variety of types and patterns exist, each intended to meet particular requirements of length and thickness. Splicing is carried out with the aid of fids, heavy tapered wood or metal pins, and marline-spikes, spiked iron pins having a knob head.

**Stick a cringle.** To place a thimble into a loop which has been worked in a bolt-rope or AWNING (03.15) rope.

**Tail splice.** One used to join ropes of two different materials, for example hemp and wire. Various methods are employed, according to the number of strands involved and the amount of taper required.

**Throat seizing.** Method in which a rope's turn is seized with RIDING TURNS (05.07) and the end put through the last turn of the riders, then knotted. Used for turning in dead-eyes, hearts, blocks and thimbles. A throat seizing holds the dead-eye or other fitting and the end part of the rope is turned up and fastened to its standing part with a round seizing.

**Tuck a strand.** Step in making a splice whereby strands in the opposing rope are lifted with the aid of a marline-spike in order to tuck in those brought across.

**Water splice.** Type of CUT SPLICE in which the parts between the splices are twisted round each other before the second splice is made.

**West country whipping.** Made by middling the whipping yarn, passing it round the rope and half knotting it. Each end is then brought half round the rope and the two knotted. Process is repeated so as to build up two rows of knots on alternate sides of the rope. Thus, should any part become damaged, the rest will continue to hold.

**Whipping.** Method of preventing a rope end from fraying by taking a series of turns round it with yarn, twine or other small line. The ends of the whipping are usually secured by knotting or tucking under the turns. A whipping is generally made equal in width to the diameter of the rope on which it is made.

**Woold** (vb). To reinforce a mast or spar constructed of several pieces of timber by winding several close turns of rope tightly round it. The method, known as woolding, is used when repairing a broken spar, for example.

**Woolder.** Sturdy wooden pole, used as a lever to tauten rope bound round a mast or yard.

# Decorative Ropework

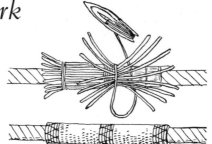

**Coach whipping.** Decorative or protective sleeve made for a rope or rail by braiding doubled or tripled strands around it. Various numbers of strands may be worked in the WHIPPING (05.12).

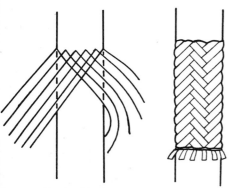

*Coach whipping*

**Cockscomb.** Ornamental cover made round a rope or rail by attaching several lines to it and half hitching them in turn round the rope.

**Crown plait.** Plait made with alternate crown and DIAMOND KNOTS. Also used to describe any plait containing crown and other knots.

*Diamond knot*

**Diamond knot.** Decorative knot formed on the bight of a rope near its end. The rope is unlaid, the knot made, and the rope laid up again. Also, a working knot, resembling a TURK'S HEAD, to put a grip on foot-ropes or side, yoke and bell ropes.

**Graft.** Originally a type of splice, later the term used to describe a woven covering made over the splice. Also used to make a decorative cover on a SAILMAKER'S EYE SPLICE (05.12).

*Grafting*

**Graft** (vb). To make up a woven cover over a splice using the rope yarns and the whipping as warp and weft respectively.

*Matthew Walker knot*

**Matthew Walker.** Knot worked on the end of a rope. Made by separating the rope strands and taking the first end round the rope and through its own bight. The second is led underneath, through the bight of the first and through its own bight. The third end is passed through the bights of the other two, and through its own bight. The whole is pulled taut and the ends trimmed.

**Pineapple knot.** Knot resembling a pineapple, made in the same way as a TURK'S HEAD.

**Rose knot.** Knob formed on a rope's end by using its strands to make a crown, following each knot round, then making a DIAMOND KNOT and tucking the ends in through the centre.

*Star knot*

**Star knot.** Knob having five-fold symmetry. It can be made on four- or six-stranded rope by adding or taking out a strand.

**Turk's head.** Knob worked on the log-line and also used ornamentally. A CLOVE HITCH (05.10) is taken with line round the rope, the top bight brought under the lower, and the end taken up through it. The bights are then crossed again and the end taken down. By following this process round, the crown is formed.

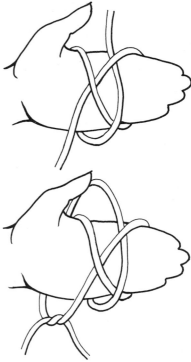

*Turk's head knot with three leads and two bights*

*Turk's head knot from a Figure-of-Eight knot*

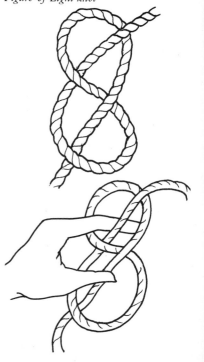

*Tying a Turk's head knot with three leads and four bights*

*Tying a standing Turk's head*

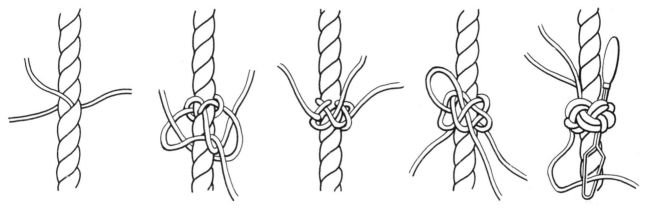

*An alternative way of tying a standing Turk's head knot*

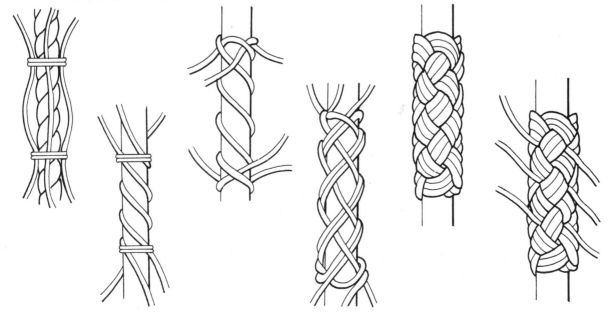

# Anchor, Capstan & Windlass

The earliest anchors were large stones, baskets full of stones, or sacks filled with sand, to which a rope was attached. This form of weight, when resting on the bed of a river or lake or on the sea-bed, and secured to a floating vessel by the rope, was intended to provide sufficient frictional resistance to prevent the vessel drifting. By enclosing the stone in a framework of wood with projecting ends, or by passing wooden stakes through holes in the stone, a ploughing action was obtained which greatly increased the holding power.

Anchors of these general types were in use during the ancient Egyptian, Greek and Roman periods and are said to date back to 2000 BC in China. In some regions, stone anchors continued in use – particularly in a modified form known as a killick – until modern times.

Ancient stone anchors recovered from Mediterranean waters have been grouped into three main functional classes. First, a simple weight anchor with the stone-pierced with a single hole for the rope, reasonably efficient on a rock bottom though it might drag on sand. Secondly, a sand anchor made from a flat stone with three or more holes in which stakes were inserted so that they projected on either side to embed in the sands. Thirdly, a combination of rock and sand anchors in which a large heavy stone, usually triangular in shape, was pierced with two holes for stakes at the base and a rope-hole at the apex.

Pliny, Strabo and other classical writers attribute the invention and development of the metal hook anchor to various individuals, but it would seem more likely that there was a natural development from the wood-framed stone anchor. An undoubted improvement over the weight anchor, the metal hook anchor has been in use from at least 600 BC. At first it consisted of a single hook, but the advantage of the double-hook form, now so familiar, was soon realized. The principal parts of a double-hook anchor were the vertical stem, known as the *shank*, the *arms* or hooks with their terminal blades or *flukes*, and the wooden cross-bar or *stock*, set at right angles to the arms and so preventing the anchor from being dragged sideways along the bottom.

Anchors with the shank and arms made of wood, but with a lead or stone stock, were used by the Greeks and Romans, and a very similar type was employed in China until recent times.

After the introduction of iron anchors with wooden stocks, little change or improvement in the form took place until the nineteenth century. From early times,

rules were laid down for the numbers and sizes of anchors to be carried by various classes of ships. The Roman triremes are said to have been equipped with eight to twelve anchors and at the end of the twelfth century AD the smaller vessels carried thirteen and the larger twenty-six anchors. Because of difficulties in handling, these anchors were probably small. As the introduction of mechanical aids – the capstan and the windlass – made possible the use of larger and heavier anchors the number per ship was reduced. Thus, in the middle of the fifteenth century a ship of about 1,000 tons required twelve anchors, while in 1637 the *Sovereign of the Seas*, at that time the largest warship in the Royal Navy, carried eleven anchors. By the end of the eighteenth century, a First Rate of 100 guns was equipped with seven anchors, the largest weighing 84 hundredweight and the smallest 5 hundredweight. Records from the end of the fifteenth century list anchors of various sizes by name and an inventory of 1514 shows that the warship *Henry Grace à Dieu* had four 'bower' anchors, four 'destrelles', one 'shot' anchor and a 'cagger' or 'kedge' anchor. In the reign of Queen Elizabeth I, anchors were known as bower, sheet, stream and kedge, and this nomenclature has survived to the present day.

Bower anchors, used for ordinary purposes of mooring, were the largest and were stowed at the bows – hence their name – ready for use. Sheet anchors, usually of about the same size as bower anchors, were used as extra anchors in case of emergency. The smaller stream anchors served for subsidiary purposes and as stern anchors, while the kedges, the smallest anchors, were only used for light work. The wrought-iron anchors with straight arms and a wooden stock, known as 'old plan long shanked' anchors, were liable to break under great strain. After tests and experiments at the end of the eighteenth century, there were improvements in the process of manufacture, a better quality iron was used and the arms of the anchor were curved. The resulting anchors were much stronger.

Kedge anchors in which the heavy fixed wooden stock was replaced by a movable iron stock were not introduced until the second half of the eighteenth century. This type of anchor, which could be stowed more readily, was first known as the common anchor, but after about 1840, when its proportions and form had been completely defined, it became the Admiralty Pattern Anchor.

A further advance in design was the self-canting anchor, in which the arms are so mounted that they can bite into the ground together. This design does not require a stock, and therefore has the extra advantage of compactness and consequent ease of stowage. First patented by R. F. Hawkins in 1821, with modified and improved designs patented by C. and A. Martin, S. Baxter and W. G. Byers in 1872, 1882 and 1887 respectively, the stockless anchor has gradually come into universal use.

The design of the C.Q.R. or ploughshare anchor, patented by Professor G. I. Taylor in 1933, was a completely new conception. This anchor has no stock and the head, which is hinged to the shank, is shaped like a double ploughshare. When used, the C.Q.R. falls on its side on the sea-bed, but with the strain of the cable turns over and digs itself into the ground. It has been claimed that this type of anchor has twice the holding power of any other anchor of the same size.

Because of the difficulties of stowing a large C.Q.R., these anchors are not used for large vessels but are considered very efficient for yachts. The American Danforth anchor is also intended principally for small craft. The Danforth anchor has pivoting flukes with a stock at their base, instead of in the usual position at the top of the shank.

Anchor cables at first appear to have been made from hide, animal membranes and withy. Later flax, hemp, jute and cotton were used. The mooring rope from a boat dating from as late as c.900 AD, found at Graveney, Kent, in 1970, was made from withy.

Julius Caesar, writing in the first century BC about the ships of the Veneti, a tribe living on the coast of what is now known as Normandy, makes the point that their anchors were secured with iron chains instead of ropes. However, until the nineteenth century chain was very rarely used as an anchor cable except for harbour moorings. About ten metres of iron chain was attached to the anchor from a Viking ship found at Ladby, Denmark, but this is thought to have been only a forerunner joining the anchor to the rope cable. Ship inventories of the late fifteenth century record the number and size of cables carried by various ships. In 1495, Henry VII's *Sovereign* is said to have had eight cables on board – two 13½ inches; two 11 inches; and four 10 inches (cables were designated by their circumference).

During the eighteenth century, British Admiralty orders laid down the number and size of anchor cables to be carried by warships of various classes. An order of 1779 stated that First and Second rates were in future to have eight cables instead of nine, as formerly, and twenty-one years later a further reduction to seven cables was ordered.

Throughout the eighteenth century, as warships became larger, the size of the cables was also increased. In 1706 a 100-gun ship's largest cables were 22½ inches, but by 1805 this size had been increased to 24 inches. Similarly, a 60-gun ship in 1706 had cables of 18 inches and by 1805 these had been increased to 20 inches.

When raising the anchor, these large hemp cables were handled in a simple and efficient manner. An endless 15-inch hemp messenger with four turns round the capstan was led forward, and back via two vertical rollers fitted just behind the hawsers. When the capstan was turned, the anchor cable was nipped (tied) to the messenger so that as the latter moved along its course the cable was hauled. A number of boys were employed in nipping, attaching the cable to the messenger at the forward end and unfastening it just before it reached the capstan.

Iron chain cable was used occasionally instead of hemp, during the early years of the nineteenth century, but its use met with opposition due to the uncertain quality of the chain. However, with improvements in welding and testing techniques, and with the introduction, for large chain, of a stud or pin in each link to increase its strength, the advantages of chain over hemp were apparent. These advantages, which combined greater strength with easier handling, longer useful life and much less space required for stowage, led by 1820 to the general adoption of chain cable for naval and merchant ships. Before 1846, Lloyd's Register Rules only specified the number of anchors and the length of chain cable required for vessels of different sizes, but in 1846 their surveyors were instructed to see that all the new chain cable supplied to classed vessels had been tested and that the load applied was stamped on each length. In 1858 Lloyd's issued a table showing the number and weight of anchors and the size and length of chain cables for various sizes of sailing ships. The safety regulations were further reinforced in 1864 by an Act of Parliament for 'Regulating the Proving and Sale of Chain Cables and Anchors'.

BASIL W. BATHE

# Anchoring the Vessel

**A-cockbill.** Said of an anchor when it hangs by its ring at the CAT-HEAD (03.07), held only by the CAT-HEAD STOPPER (06.02) and ready for letting go.

**Anchor's aweigh.** Cry indicating that the anchor has broken clear of the ground.

**Apeak.** Said of an anchor when the cable has been brought to the vertical while being hove in, so that the ship is directly above the anchor and the flukes are about to break out of the ground.

**A-stay.** Condition of an anchor cable when it is in line with the fore stay, forming a more or less acute angle with the water's edge.

**Athwart-hawse.** Said of a vessel riding across its own cable, due to tide and wind conditions, when it has only one anchor down.

**A-trip.** Said of an anchor when it has just broken out of the ground, and is hanging by the cable.

**Aweigh.** A-TRIP. Also, free of the anchor: the vessel has way.

**Back** (vb). To lay out a small anchor, such as a KEDGE (06.02) or STREAM ANCHOR (06.02), ahead of the BOWER ANCHOR (06.02), to provide more holding power and prevent the bower from breaking out or dragging.

**Becueing.** Method of securing a cable to an anchor for use on hard ground. The cable is secured to the anchor's CROWN (06.02) or FLUKES (06.02), then led and made fast to the ring with a light seizing. If the anchor is fouled, a sharp tug should break the seizing and the anchor may be hoisted by the flukes.

**Bite** (vb). An anchor bites when one fluke or both are firmly embedded in the ground.

**Break ground.** To weigh the anchor and lift it out of the ground.

**Break sheer.** Said of a vessel at anchor swung by wind or current across the line of her own anchor cable.

**Brought to.** Said of a vessel when she is anchored. Also said of the vessel's anchor CABLE (05.08) when it has been taken round a CAPSTAN (06.03) or WINDLASS (06.03) ready for HEAVING.

**Buoy rope.** Rope connecting an anchor on the sea bottom to a small buoy marking its position, and made fast to the CROWN (06.02) of the anchor.

**Cable party.** Hands detailed to work a cable.

**Catenary.** Curve of a rope or chain hanging between two points, as of an anchor cable between a vessel and the sea bottom. Also, weight attached to a hawser and producing a curve in it, in order to help it withstand sudden stresses.

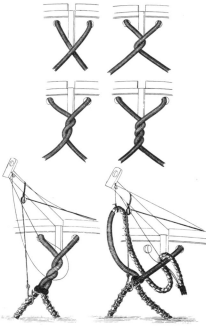

*Clear hawse*

**Clear hawse.** To disentangle anchor cables which have become crossed when the anchored ship has swung round with the tide, thus creating a temporary condition of FOUL HAWSE. Also, another name for OPEN HAWSE.

**Clear hawse slip.** Special SLIP (06.03) which temporarily secures the end of a foul cable while it is being cleared.

**Come home.** Of an anchor, to break free of the ground and come towards the ship. Also said of an anchor when its flukes are not holding and it drags along the bottom.

**Come to anchor.** To safely perform the manoeuvre of dropping an anchor, and then ride by it.

**Cross.** Condition caused when a vessel lying to two anchors swings through 180°, so that the anchor cables become crossed.

**Cut and run.** To cut through a hemp anchor cable so that the ship can get under way in an emergency. The term originated with the method used by square-rigged ships to get under way speedily, which entailed stopping furled sails with rope yarns which could be cut to quickly let the sails fall.

**Drag** (vb). To trail an anchor which has broken from the ground along the sea bottom.

**Drop anchor.** To let go the anchor on its cable.

**Elbow.** Twist formed in the cables of a vessel riding to her two BOWER ANCHORS (06.02) when the vessel swings through 360°. Each of the cables, after crossing the other before the stem, is directed outwards on the same bow from which it issued.

**Foul anchor.** Anchor which has become entangled in its own cable, or fouled in some underwater obstruction.

**Foul hawse.** Situation when both anchors of a vessel are down and the ship has swung so that one cable crosses the other.

**Girt.** Situation of a ship held so tightly by her two anchor cables that she cannot swing to wind or tide.

**Grow.** Used of an anchor cable, signifying the direction in which it leads from the vessel towards the anchor.

**Hawse.** That part of a vessel's bow where the HAWSE PIPES (03.07) are located. By extension, the space between the ship's head and the anchor to which she lies. Also, the situation of the anchor cables before the ship's stem when she lies to her two BOWER ANCHORS (06.02). A ship can be riding with a clear, or OPEN HAWSE, or with a FOUL HAWSE.

**Heave** (vb). To work bars or handspikes to operate a CAPSTAN (06.03) or WINDLASS (06.03) and thus haul in rope or cable.

**Heaving ahead.** Advancing the ship by heaving in a cable secured to an anchor some distance ahead.

**Heaving short.** Advancing the ship by heaving in a cable secured to an anchor until the ship is almost vertically above the anchor, at SHORT STAY.

**Long stay.** Said of a cable when the anchor is well away from the bows, the length of cable out being over four times the depth of the water.

**Open hawse.** Condition of a ship when her two anchor cables lead down to the anchors clear of each other, without touching or crossing. Also termed CLEAR HAWSE.

**Open hawse to the gale.** Condition of a ship when moored OPEN HAWSE while the wind is straight ahead.

**Pawl** (vb). To prevent any slipping or backward motion of the CAPSTAN (06.03) by enabling the PAWLS (06.03) to engage in the PAWL RIM (06.03).

**Proved.** Said of anchors or cables which have been tested for strength and quality and have been certified as reaching the required standard.

**Ranging cable.** Operation of laying out an anchor cable (or part of it) in order to examine it for weak links, rust or other defects. It is carried out on deck before anchoring in deep water, or on a dock before storing the cable in the chain locker. Also performed when coming to a difficult anchorage, in order to have the cable clear for running out quickly.

**Running moor.** Mooring the ship by dropping one anchor while she is still under way and dropping the second when she has gone a little further on, so that there will be an equal strain on both anchors.

**Scope.** Length of cable run out when a ship rides to an anchor.

**Sheer.** Position maintained by a ship when at single anchor; the angle between ship and anchor cable.

**Shorten in.** To take in the anchor cable, lessening the amount of cable by which a ship rides.

**Short stay.** Condition of an anchor cable when it is fairly taut and the length of cable out is one and a half times the depth of the water or less.

**Spring.** Rope run from the stern of a vessel at anchor to her anchor cable, used to turn her head in a particular direction.

**Start.** To ease an anchor out of the ground.

**Sweep** (vb). To drag the bight of a rope along the sea bottom in order to hook and recover an anchor or any object which has been sunk.

**Swing** (vb). Movement of a vessel from side to side at anchor, due to wind or tide.

**Tend.** Old term used of a ship at anchor that swings to the tidal stream.

**Tide rode.** Said of an anchored vessel swung to her anchor by the tidal current, thus with her head pointing into the tide.

**Trend.** Angle between the fore-and-aft line of a ship and the cable to which she is riding. Also, the swelling of an anchor SHANK (06.02) at its lower end to the point where it joins the arms.

**Tripping.** Freeing an anchor which has been fouled on the sea bottom by hauling on a TRIPPING LINE or on the anchor BUOY ROPE secured to the crown of the anchor.

**Tripping line.** Line fastened to the fluke of an anchor in rocky ground and used to 'trip' the anchor out, to pull it free. Also, line secured to a SEA ANCHOR (06.02) or DROGUE (06.02), by which it is hauled back on board empty of water.

**Under foot.** Situation of anchor when the vessel's FOREFOOT (03.07) is over it and the cable is almost UP AND DOWN.

**Up and down.** Condition of the cable when it is vertical and the anchor is directly under the bows of the ship.

**Veer** (vb). To slacken a cable so that it may run out; to pay out the cable.

**Weather anchor.** In a ship coming in to anchor, the anchor on its weather bow.

**Weigh** (vb). To lift the anchor out of the ground by its cable.

**Wind rode.** Said of an anchored vessel swung to her anchor by the wind, thus with her head pointing into the wind.

*Port sheet anchor on Nelson's* Victory

# Anchors, Anchor Fittings and Stowage

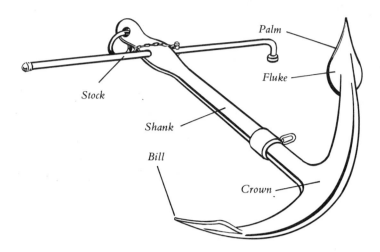

**Admiralty Pattern Anchor.** Type of anchor prevalent before the introduction of stockless anchors. The SHANK and arms are fixed and the STOCK is at right angles to the arms.

**Anchor.** Heavy iron implement dropped from a vessel and partly embedded in the sea bottom, in order to hold the vessel in a desired position regardless of wind, tide or current. It consists of a *shank* with a large ring at one end, to which the anchor cable is attached by a heavy shackle, and two curved arms at the other end terminating in flukes which engage in the sea bed. The ADMIRALTY PATTERN ANCHOR is the oldest standard type. Sailing ships were required to have three principal anchors – two BOWER ANCHORS and a SHEET ANCHOR or WAIST ANCHOR. As a verb, to anchor means to secure a vessel by letting go the anchor in good holding ground and riding to it.

**Balancing band.** Band with shackle, fitted off the centre of gravity of a stocked anchor, so that, together with the weight of the attached cable, the anchor will be horizontally balanced when hoisted.

**Bending shackle.** Heavy shackle connecting a CHAIN CABLE (06.03) to an anchor.

**Best bower.** Anchor carried on the starboard bow of the ship. It was originally slightly larger than the *port bower*, known as the *small bower*, but later both were the same size.

**Bill.** Extremity of the PALM OF AN ANCHOR. Also called *pea* or *peak*.

**Bower anchor.** One of the two principal anchors of a ship, permanently attached to a cable and stowed at the ANCHOR BED or HAWSE PIPE (03.07) when the ship is in comparatively shallow waters, ready for immediate use when required. The bower anchors are carried at the starboard and port bows.

**Breast anchor.** Anchor located at right angles to the fore-and-aft line, at either end of the vessel.

**Crown.** That part of the anchor where the arms are joined to the SHANK. In stockless anchors it is the part between the arms where they pivot on the shank.

**Fluke.** Triangular flattened barb at the end of an anchor arm, which digs in and holds the anchor in the ground. Flukes can be of various shapes – pointed flukes are usually used for grassy or rocky bottoms, spade-shaped flukes are used for muddy bottoms where a greater holding surface is required.

**Grapnel.** Shaft fitted with four prongs or large hooks, sometimes used as an anchor by small boats, more usually used to drag the bottom for items lost overboard or to hook a

wire or cable under water. Also used, in the days of wooden warships, to hook onto a vessel in order to board her.

**Grappling.** Old term for a GRAPNEL.

**Ice anchor.** Special anchor with a single fluke, designed to bite into ice.

**Kedge.** Light anchor used to keep a ship steady and support the BOWER ANCHOR when anchored in bad holding ground or when the tide or weather threaten the vessel's stability at anchor. Also used to move a ship from one berth to another in harbour; this operation is known as *kedging*.

**Killick.** Small anchor, originally a stone attached to a rope and used to anchor a small boat. Also, slang term for any type of anchor.

**Nuts.** Two protruberances on the upper part of the anchor's SHANK, fitting into corresponding notches in the STOCK and securing it in place.

**Palm of anchor.** Triangular flat face forming the holding surface of an anchor's FLUKE.

**Pea.** BILL of an anchor.

**Pick.** Naval slang term for an anchor, or for the BILL of an anchor.

**Shank.** Shaft forming the principal part of an anchor, connecting the anchor ring to the arms.

**Sheet anchor.** Third BOWER ANCHOR, the heaviest in the ship, required to be carried in reserve ready for immediate use in an emergency, such as very heavy weather in an open roadstead. The term became a synonym for dependability and security.

**Shoe.** Triangular board fixed to an anchor fluke to increase its holding ability in soft ground. Also, a small convex block of wood fitted on the sharp BILL of a fluke to prevent it from damaging the ship's side as the anchor is hoisted.

**Small.** That part of an anchor's SHANK directly below the STOCK.

**Snubber.** Short cable stopper used to temporarily secure a rope or cable.

**Square.** Upper part of the anchor SHANK, bearing the STOCK and the anchor ring.

**Stern anchor.** STREAM ANCHOR.

**Stock.** Crosspiece fitted at the top of an anchor's SHANK at right angles to the plane of the arms. When the anchor hits the bottom, the strain on the cable causes the stock to cant the anchor, bringing the arms vertical and enabling the FLUKES to bite into the

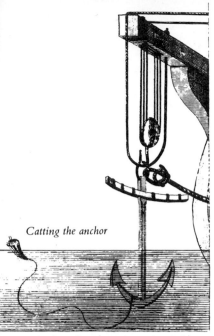

*Catting the anchor*

ground. Balls cast at the ends of the stock prevent its sinking too deeply into the ground before it is in proper position.

**Stream anchor.** Spare anchor carried at the stern and used in narrow waters where there is no room for the ship to swing with the tide. Its weight is roughly one-third that of a BOWER ANCHOR; it is sometimes used for kedging (see KEDGE).

**Tripping palm.** Projection on the arm of an anchor which causes the FLUKES to turn downward and bite into the ground. Fitted to self-canting anchors.

**Waist anchor.** Heaviest anchor of the ship, carried in reserve at the fore end of the WAIST (01.01), ready for use in an emergency. Also called *sheet anchor.*

---

**Anchor bed.** Support or platform fitted on the side of the forecastle, on which a stocked anchor is stowed and secured when at sea.

**Anchor bell.** Bell at or near the stem of a ship, rung during fog in accordance with the Regulations for Preventing Collision at Sea. Also used to indicate the number of cable shackles still out as an anchor is being hauled in. Has become one of the ship's principal bells.

**Anchor buoy.** Small buoy, attached by a rope to the CROWN of an anchor, used to mark the position of the anchor when it is on the bottom. Also used as a guide to the position of a 'lost' anchor.

**Billboard.** Sloping steel or iron plate fitted by the CAT-HEAD (03.07) to receive the flukes of a stocked anchor when it is hoisted and secured.

**Cat** (vb). To hoist an anchor by its ring to the CAT-HEAD (03.07), so that it hangs there ready either for letting go or for bringing inboard and onto the ANCHOR-BED.

**Cat back.** Small line bent on the back of the cat hook fitted at the end of the CAT-FALL, used for inserting the hook into the BALANCING BAND of the anchor in order to CAT the anchor.

**Cat block.** Heavy three-sheaved block, fitted to a CAT DAVIT or crane, used in catting the anchor.

**Cat davit.** DAVIT used to hoist the anchor from the water-line up to the BILLBOARD.

**Cat-fall.** Rope forming the tackle with which the anchor is hove up from the water's surface to the bow.

**Cat-head stopper.** Small short-linked chain or rope used to hold fast the stock of an anchor after it has been hoisted to the BILLBOARD.

**Davit.** Small derrick or crane used for hoisting the flukes of the anchor to the top of the bow. Also used occasionally in a large longboat to weigh the anchor.

**Dead head.** Rough piece of wood used as an ANCHOR BUOY.

**Fish** (vb). To hoist the flukes of an anchor upwards after it has been catted, preparatory to stowing it on the ANCHOR BED.

**Gimbleting,** or **gimletting.** To turn an anchor round by the stock so that it gets into the proper position for stowing on the ANCHOR BED. The motion resembles that of a gimlet turned by hand.

**Shank painter.** Short rope or chain securing the shank of an anchor to the BILLBOARD when stowed.

**Slip stopper.** Short length of chain with a slip or pelican hook, used to hold the anchor to the BILLBOARD. By releasing the hook the anchor is instantly freed.

**Drag sheet.** Sail or canvas attached to a spar or spars and used as a DROGUE.

**Drift anchor.** SEA ANCHOR or DROGUE.

**Drift sail.** Sail thrown overboard on a strong line to serve as a temporary DROGUE.

**Drogue.** Contraption connected to a line and cast overboard in order to slow a vessel down or hold her head to the sea in bad weather. For small boats it could be a simple canvas bag, or a hollow canvas cone which can be collapsed when no longer needed. For larger vessels it could consist of wooden spars lashed to canvas or a sail, with a weight at one corner holding it more or less vertically in the water – though this was usually called a SEA ANCHOR.

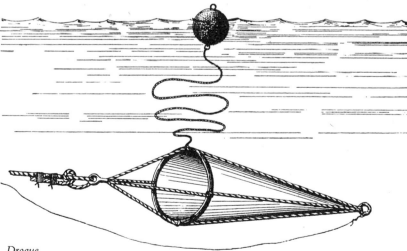

*Drogue*

**Fish.** DAVIT used to FISH the anchor.

**Fish davit.** Davit used with a CAT DAVIT to hoist the fluke end of a stocked anchor to the BILLBOARD.

**Flamming tackle.** Tackle used to haul an anchor to the ship's side when it has to be stowed vertically. It is worked through a special port in the side.

**Sea anchor.** Any contraption connected to a strong line and thrown overboard to keep the ship's bows to the direction of the sea in bad weather. It can comprise oars, spare wooden spars, loose sails lashed together or DROGUES.

**Water anchor.** SEA ANCHOR or DROGUE.

# Capstan, Windlass and Cables

**Barrel of capstan.** Main part of a capstan, cylindrical and mounted on a vertical spindle. The capstan bars fit into sockets in its upper rim, while its base carries PAWLS which fit into the pawl rim beneath.

**Capstan.** Apparatus enabling the anchor to be raised by hand. It consists of a strong upright cylindrical barrel revolving on a spindle, which took the turns of the anchor cable when this was cordage. (Later, the windlass took over this function, and was operated by means of the capstan.) A drumhead at the top takes the capstan bars, by which the capstan is worked manually. A set of PAWLS at the bottom, by dropping into notches in the pawl rim beneath, prevents the capstan from slipping back and running out the cable. Capstans were used until the end of the sailing era, often as many as seven being installed in a large square-rigger.

**Capstan bar.** Wooden lever inserted in sockets at the top of the DRUMHEAD in order to work the capstan by hand. Generally made of ash and sometimes fitted with cast-steel shoes at the inner end.

**Carrick bitts.** WINDLASS BITTS.

**Crab.** Small capstan without a drumhead, with bars inserted right through holes set on different planes in the top of the barrel. It was usually portable and used in places where a rope or cable could not be led to a fixed capstan or windlass.

**Drumhead.** Top part of the CAPSTAN BARREL, where the sockets which take the CAPSTAN BARS are located.

**Handspike.** Wooden bar used as a lever for various purposes, for instance to heave on the windlass when bringing up the anchor.

**Knight-heads.** In merchant ships, two strong pieces of timber a little behind the foremast, used to support and enclose the ends of the windlass. Occasionally used as BITTS to which the anchor cable is brought.

**Norman.** Short wooden bar, thrust into one of the holes in a capstan or windlass, to which the anchor cable can be temporarily secured. Used only when there is very little strain on the cable, as in a harbour where the ship is well sheltered from wind and tide.

**Pawl.** Short pivoted bar of iron or wood with a shaped tip, hinged at one end to the barrel of a capstan or windlass, which, by dropping into the notches in the PAWL RIM, prevents the capstan or windlass from slipping back when the cable is being hove in.

**Pawl bitt.** Vertical timber to which the PAWL governing the windlass is attached.

**Pawl rack.** Secured series of standing stops by which a PAWL can be held, thus preventing a windlass barrel from slipping back.

**Pawl rim.** Circular rim on a capstan or windlass fitted with notches into which the PAWLS fall, to prevent slipping back.

**Rundle.** Drum of the capstan.

**Saucer.** Iron bearing in which the

capstan spindle turns. It is let into a *step* bolted to the deck beams.

**Spindle.** Strong iron-shod shaft forming the axis upon which the capstan revolves.

**Swifter.** Rope with a cut splice half-way along it and a THIMBLE (05.03) at one end, which is passed over a notch in a CAPSTAN BAR and hitched over the end of other bars to provide purchase for additional men to heave at the capstan.

**Trundle-head.** The capstan head, containing the sockets which take the ends of the CAPSTAN BARS.

**Whelps.** Projections along the surface of the capstan or windlass barrel which provide a better grip for a rope or cable.

**Windlass.** Device used to lift an anchor where this can be done without recourse to the capstan. It is a horizontal cylinder supported by two KNIGHT-HEADS, one on either side, and operated by handspikes inserted in holes in the body of the cylinder. The surface of the windlass is fitted with notches into which PAWLS can fall, preventing the windlass from slipping back.

**Windlass bitts.** Upright projecting timbers supporting the shaft of a windlass. Also known as *carrick bitts* and *carrick heads*.

---

**Battledore.** Fitting running through the cable BITTS and projecting on either side, to keep the cable in place.

**Bitter.** Turn of the anchor cable about the BITTS.

**Bitter end.** Inboard end of the anchor cable, which is made fast by a slip hook or lashing to the bottom or side of the *chain locker*. Formerly it was secured to the BITTS. To pay out a rope to the bitter end is to pay it out till there is no more to let go.

**Bitt head.** Upper extremity of a heavy baulk of timber set vertically in the deck and well reinforced. Used for temporarily turning up cables or for making them fast.

**Bitting cable.** Act of passing a turn or two of the cable round a cable BITT.

**Bitt pin.** Large steel pin fitted through a cable BITT to prevent a cable or rope from coming off the bitt.

**Bitts.** Strong wooden or metal uprights used for securing heavy ropes such as anchor cables.

*Bitts*

**Bitt stopper.** Length of rope passed round the turns of a hemp anchor cable which has been secured to the BITTS, to hold it taut and prevent it slipping.

**Bower cable.** Cable fixed to a BOWER ANCHOR (06.02).

**Cable nipper.** Short length of plaited rope or SPUNYARN (05.09), used to temporarily make fast a light rope or MESSENGER to a cable when heaving in. Also, an iron nipper, hinged at one end, used for the same purpose with CHAIN CABLES.

**Cable shackle.** Shackle, with a pin flush to its sides, used for joining together lengths of cable without obstructing the cable's passage through the HAWSE PIPE (03.07).

**Chain cable.** Iron anchor cable. There are two types of chain, the stud link and open link. Each length of chain between shackles is usually $12\frac{1}{2}$ or 15 fathoms.

**Chain hook.** Hook attached to a handle, 18 to 36 inches long, used for handling lengths of CHAIN CABLE on deck or in the CABLE LOCKER (03.13).

**Clinch.** Old term for the attachment of a hemp anchor cable to the ship.

**Coir hawser.** Rope made from the fibrous husks of coconuts, about one-quarter the strength of hemp but lighter and capable of floating on the water. Used for attaching to a heavier cable to be hauled in for towing or mooring.

**Cross beam.** Heavy section of timber running across the BITTS in the bows of a vessel.

**Cross-piece.** Bar or timber connecting two KNIGHT-HEADS or BITTS.

**Deck stopper.** Rope or short length of chain, fixed to the deck at one end, with a special cable-hook at the other end, used for securing the anchor cable.

**Devil's claw.** Strong two-pronged hook used to fit into and hold a CHAIN CABLE. Its other end is attached to the deck or to the fore part of a windlass.

**Jew's harp shackle.** Lyre-shaped shackle connecting anchor cable to anchor in the days of stocked anchors. Its shape enabled another cable to be secured apart from the regular chain.

**Jigger.** Small tackle composed of a single and double block sometimes used to hold on to the cable when it was being hove into the ship by the windlass.

**Joggle shackle.** Long, slightly bent shackle with a quick-release pin, used when the chain cable of one anchor is hauled round the bows in order to fit a MOORING SWIVEL.

**Joining shackle.** Shackle with an oval pin fitted flush with the lugs, used to join lengths of CHAIN CABLE together. It is designed not to cause friction when running out.

**Messenger.** Rope passed round the capstan with its ends lashed together to form an endless line, used to heave in hemp anchor cable when it is too heavy to be brought round the capstan. It is attached to the cable by means of NIPPERS, which are cast off as the cable is stowed. Also, general term for any light line used to haul in a heavier one.

**Mooring swivel.** Large swivel shackled upon the cables forward of the stem. It consists of two triangular or three-eyed forgings to which studless links are attached. In each forging one eye is for its connection to the swivel, one for inboard and one for outboard connections of the anchor cable. Used for keeping turns out of the cables when riding to two anchors.

**Nipper.** Short length of rope used to temporarily secure a hemp anchor cable to a MESSENGER when heaving in the anchor.

**Open link.** Link of a chain which has no transverse strengthening stud; one is located at each end of a cable shackle.

**Parting strop.** Strop which will part

under excessive stress, as it is weaker than the ropes or wires to which it is attached. It is used as a safety precaution.

**Riding slip.** Short length of chain with a hinged tongue shaped to fasten on a link of the anchor cable, used to relieve strain on the cable when the vessel is riding at anchor. It is usually located above the CABLE LOCKER (03.13).

**Senhouse slip.** Short length of chain designed to secure the inboard end of the anchor cable to the CABLE LOCKER (03.13). It has a slip hook which passes through the open end-link of the cable and can be quickly released when required.

**Sheet cable.** Cable of a SHEET ANCHOR (06.02).

**Slip.** Hinged hook with a quick-release link, used to hold a rope or cable which may need to be freed instantly.

**Snub.** Suddenly stop a rope, wire or cable which is running out, by taking extra turns, by the application of a rope STOPPER (05.08), or by using the brake on a windlass.

**Surge** (vb). To slacken a rope or cable suddenly, allowing it to run out or RENDER (05.07) round a capstan.

**Swivel piece.** Short length of cable incorporating a swivel, often used to link the end of the cable and the anchor ring, and sometimes to secure the inboard end of the cable in the CABLE LOCKER (03.13).

**Tier.** Horizontal layer of coiled cable stowed in the CABLE LOCKER (03.13).

**Tumbler.** Revolving iron bar fitted with a lever and two curved pins, used to hold the end of an anchor chain. When the lever is raised the bar revolves and releases the anchor, allowing it to drop overboard.

**Unbitt.** To remove the turns of a cable from the BITTS.

**Voyal.** MESSENGER.

**Weather bitt.** An extra turn of the cable round the end of the windlass, taken as a precaution in bad weather.

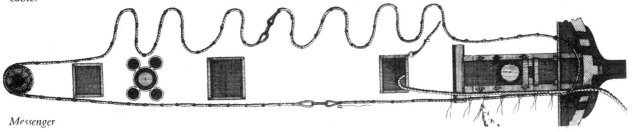

*Messenger*

# Ballast, Stowage & Cargo

Apart from the hull design, the performance of a sailing ship was greatly affected by the trim or set of the ship in the water. A ship's sailing and steering qualities and her ability to survive in rough seas depended to a large extent on the proper stowage of ballast, cargo and other heavy material. Ballast consisting of iron, lead, stone and gravel was deposited in a ship's hold when the vessel had no cargo or too little to bring her sufficiently low in the water. This ballast had to be stowed not too high or too low, too far forward or too far aft, and had to be so placed that the centre of gravity accorded with the shape and trim of the vessel, which would then float at the right depth, be able to carry a good press of sail without heeling unduly and sail well to windward. If the centre of gravity was placed too high, the ship could not carry a sufficient area of sail, if too low, the vessel would roll excessively; if placed too far forward, the ship would pitch and labour heavily and if too far aft, there was the danger of pooping by following seas. The final adjustment of the trim was made at sea by moving ballast, cargo and occasionally guns. Captain John Smith, writing in his *Sea Grammar* published in 1627, states: 'The trimming of a ship doeth much amend or impaire her sailing, and so alter her condition. To finde her trim, that is how she will saile best, is by trying her sailing with another Ship so many glasses, trimmed ahead so many and so many a sterne, and so many upon an even Keele, also the easing of her Masts and Shrouds, for some ships will saile much better when they are slacke than when they are taught.'

In a warship, the usual practice was to stow the iron ballast first. This ballast, in the form of iron *pigs*, the largest of which were 3 feet long, 6 inches wide and 6 inches deep and weighed about 3 hundredweight, was laid fore and aft on each side of the keelson. The gravel ballast was then spread and levelled over the pigs. (HMS *Victory*, after her launch in 1765, was found to have a permanent list to starboard, and an extra thirty-eight tons of ballast was placed in the port side of the hold.)

For a merchant ship to be able to carry the maximum quantity of goods, it was very necessary that the cargo and any ballast that might be required should be correctly stowed.

Dunnage consisting of loose wood, wood blocks, brushwood and other material was packed below and round the cargo to prevent it moving in rough weather and to keep it away from the sides and bottom of the vessel. When available at the port of loading, valuable materials such as redwood and rattans were used for dunnage, and when used for this purpose were usually imported free of duty.

Bulk cargoes like grain, coal and guano were each stowed in the most appropriate manner. For grain in bulk, the hold could be divided into bins strongly braced to resist the pressure of the grain. The bins were built on platforms at least 12 inches above the floors of the vessel, and nineteenth century regulations stated that no bin should contain more than 12,000 bushels of grain. When the grain was in bags, dunnage was first placed in the hold to a height of 12 inches above the floors, 15 inches above the bilges and 4 inches at the sides. This dunnage was covered with boards or canvas, and the bags were prevented from moving by strong planks extending 4 feet downwards from the beams and secured on each side of the hold stanchions.

If the cargo consisted of casks, cases, bales or boxes, these were carefully wedged aft from the bottom and sides of the vessel and from the pump well, with the heaviest goods always stowed nearest to the centre of gravity of the ship.

With a light cargo like tea, the vessel was first ballasted with heavy material, generally metal or stone. Gravel was then spread and levelled over this ballast and in turn covered with thin boards. The first tiers of tea chests were then laid. Any spaces between the tiers or between the tiers and sides of the vessel were filled with small ballast. Once a ship had been filled up with tea there was no means of altering her trim, so great care had to be taken with the ballast to ensure the draught of the vessel was correct. Dunnage up to 4 inches thick, of split bamboo interwoven trellis fashion, was sometimes placed between the tiers of chests.

A large number of sailing ships carried mixed cargoes from all parts of the world. The two examples now described are typical, but very different. The brig *Sunium*, 268 tons, left Penang for London on 23 July 1864 with a cargo consisting of

3,083 bags of black pepper
395 buffalo hides
2,822 bags of sugar
1,519 bundles of rattans
49 cases of nutmegs
2 cases of tortoise shells
2 cases of fish maws

The brig was dunnaged with thick wood from the mainmast to the fore hatch, with the rattans stowed at the ends and sides. The sugar, being only about one-third of the cargo, was first placed on double mats in the bottom, fore and aft, as a dead-weight to keep the brig stiff; the pepper, in bags each weighing about 100 lb, was stowed next, with the hides over it; and the cases of nutmeg were placed between the tiers. The *Sunium* arrived safely at London on 20 November 1864.

The second example is of a sailing ship with a mixed cargo on an Atlantic voyage. In 1864 the barque *Marinus* sailed from Newcastle to New York carrying

     106 tons of coal
     2,450 kegs of bicarbonate of soda
     20 casks of ground flints
     400 barrels of Venetian red
     450 kegs and 5 casks of red lead
     60 casks of white lead
     60 firkins of white paint
     57 casks of hypo
     200 casks of bleaching powder
     620 packages of merchandise
     50 casks of soda crystals
     19 anchors and 19 stocks
     10 chains, one length each

The coal was spread fore and aft; anchors and chains amidships on the coal; leads next, then sodas. The bleaching powder, being light, was stowed forward.

Oil was first carried by ships in barrels and in metal containers known as cases. However, the *Atlantic*, a small iron-built sailing vessel launched in 1863, was designed to carry petroleum in bulk without the aid of casks. Her tank space was sub-divided by one central and three transverse bulkheads, while the hollow iron masts served as expansion trunks. Another sailing vessel, the *Charles*, employed from 1869 to 1872 in bringing oil from the United States to Europe, was fitted with 59 separate tanks arranged along the bottom of the hold and between decks. From the 1880s, a number of sailing ships were employed in carrying oil in bulk or cased. During the period 1904–7 the Anglo-American Oil Company owned 16 oil sailers ranging in size from the *Calcutta* of 1,694 tons to the *Brilliant* of 3,765 tons. The famous *Thomas W. Lawson*, the only seven-masted schooner ever built, was converted to carry oil in bulk and was lost off the Scillies in 1907 while bringing oil to Europe.

Early efforts were made, without success, to bring New Zealand mutton to Britain packed in tallow, but in 1881 the sailing ship *Dunedin* was fitted with insulated chambers and refrigerating machinery. The fore hold and the 'tween decks abaft the fore hatch were the only parts of her carrying capacity which were insulated. The refrigerating engine was fitted forward of the main hatch, with a funnel projecting between the fore and main masts. The *Dunedin* left New Zealand in February 1882 and delivered her cargo of frozen meat in good condition at London in September 1882, after a voyage of 103 days.

BASIL W. BATHE

# Loading and Unloading

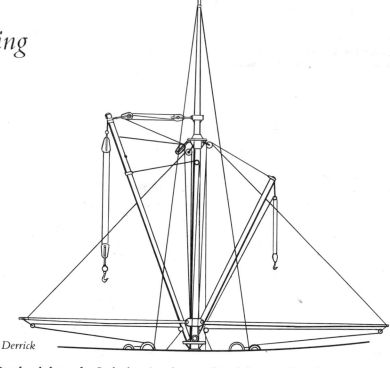

**Beam hooks.** Strong hooks used to lift HATCH BEAMS (03.14).

**Bull rope.** Rope used for hauling cargo from the ends or wings of a hold towards the cargo hatch for hoisting.

**Break bulk.** To open up a ship's holds and begin to unload her cargo.

**Burden.** Number of tons of cargo which a ship can carry.

**Cant hook.** Lever with a hook in its end, used to lift heavy cargo.

**Cargo net.** Square net of heavy rope or wire, used for hoisting cased goods or small freight packages in and out of a ship's hold.

**Deadweight.** Carrying capacity of a vessel beyond her own weight. Measure of the weight (in tons) of cargo, fuel, fresh water, provisions, stores, crew and passengers that the ship can carry when loaded to her maximum permitted DRAUGHT (03.01).

**Deadweight cargo.** Cargo that, once loaded, will take a vessel down to her maximum permitted DRAUGHT (03.01).

*Derrick*

**Deadweight scale.** Scale showing the deadweight capacities of a vessel and the corresponding DRAUGHTS (03.01) at different displacements.

**Derrick.** Form of crane used to hoist cargo or other weights. It consists of a swinging boom supported by a TOPPING LIFT (04.07) and controlled sideways by GUYS (05.04) or *guy pendants*. The name is said to derive from a seventeenth-century Tyburn hangman called Derrick.

**Derrick post.** Short heavy mast, placed roughly midway between the bulwarks and the centre-line, from which a DERRICK is supported and stayed.

**Discharge** (vb). To unload cargo from a vessel.

**Gang casks.** Medium-sized casks, larger than breakers but smaller than barrels, used to carry water from shore to ship.

**Grain space.** Total internal volume of a ship's holds, measured by the distance from side to side and from CEILING (03.06) to beams.

**Intake.** Amount of cargo taken into a ship.

**Jumper.** Person who unloads cargo by JUMPING.

**Jumping.** Method of unloading cargo from a small boat by taking hold of a rope secured to the cargo and passed through a tackle on a TRIATIC STAY (04.08), and jumping off a prepared platform, thus lifting the cargo free of the boat.

**Laden.** Old term for the state of a vessel when she is fully loaded.

**Laden in bulk.** State of a vessel loaded with bulk cargo (such as grain) in all holds.

**Lifting gear.** Overall term for cranes, derricks and all the attached equipment used for handling cargo.

**Light.** Condition of a vessel when she is not carrying her full cargo capacity.

**Liverpool hook.** Hook with inward curved bill to prevent accidental slipping, used in the end of a cargo runner.

**Load** (vb). To put cargo on board a vessel.

**Load lines.** Marks set into the ship's side at the water-line, corresponding to the maximum DRAUGHT (03.01) to which she is permitted to load by specified regulations. The Convention of 1930 laid down rules for different load lines relative to the risks of prevailing weather in different world zones: summer load line, winter load line, winter North Atlantic load line and tropical load line.

**Lumper.** Port worker paid a lump sum for his services in unloading a ship.

**Port sail.** Sail stretched between a ship and a lighter alongside, used to catch and save pieces of cargo which may break away when goods are being unloaded.

**Ramshorn hook.** Hook shaped like a ram's horn or an anchor, used to hold the ends of a cargo sling so that one end does not chafe on the other.

**Rowl.** Small crane used to unload cargo.

**Safety hook.** Cargo hook with a piece hinged to lock over the point, preventing the sling slipping off the hook.

**Samson post.** Short sturdy tubular steel mast placed about midway between the centre-line of a vessel and the bulwarks, from which a DERRICK is supported or stayed.

**Sheer legs.** Triangular structure consisting of two upright spars lashed together at the top, their lower ends spread out, the whole steadied by guys, and a hoisting tackle suspended from the apex to lift cargo or other heavy weights.

**Sheer mast.** One of the spars forming SHEER LEGS.

**Shoe.** Piece of timber housing the heel of a DERRICK or the heels of SHEER LEGS.

**Side skids.** Pieces of timber suspended over the ship's side to prevent cargo striking or scraping it during loading or unloading.

**Stevedore.** Person employed in the working of cargo when a merchant ship is being loaded or unloaded in port.

**Tally.** Count taken of the number of packages, bales and so on loaded on a vessel or unloaded from it.

**Tons burden.** Net registered tonnage of a vessel; that is, her official carrying capacity expressed in tons.

**Union purchase.** Rig to unload cargo using a pair of fixed derricks in combination. One derrick is positioned over the hatchway and is called the inboard boom. The other, positioned outboard, is the outboard boom. The runner of each derrick is shackled to the same cargo hook, so that the load is transferred from a position vertically under one derrick to a position vertically under the other.

**Weather working days.** Days during which the weather enables cargo to be unloaded without hindrance or delay; refers in particular to goods which are liable to be damaged by rain.

**Winch.** Horizontal revolving barrel used to give mechanical advantage in working a purchase to hoist cargo.

**Yard and stay.** Another term for the UNION PURCHASE method of discharging cargo. Derives from the days when one tackle was put on a stay and the other was attached to the yard-arm.

**Yard tackle.** Tackle attached to the lower yard of a square-rigged ship, used as a DERRICK in conjunction with a tackle suspended from a TRIATIC STAY (04.08).

*Sheer legs*

# Stowage; Ballast

**A-burton.** Stowage of casks sideways across a vessel's hold, in line with the deck beams, instead of in a fore-and-aft direction.

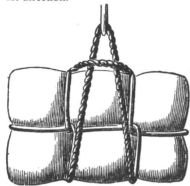

**Bale.** Package of compressed soft goods, wrapped in burlap or other fibrous material, and secured by wire, straps or rope.

**Bale space.** Volume of a cargo hold measured by the length, the distance from the CEILING (03.06) to the lower edge of the beams and the distance between the inner edges of opposite frames.

**Ballast.** Heavy material such as iron, stone or gravel placed low in a vessel's holds in order to lower her centre of gravity and provide increased stability when carrying little or no cargo.

**Batten down.** To secure hatches by means of GRATINGS (03.14) and TARPAULINS (03.02) held in place by battens.

**Beam fillings.** Small cargo stowed in the space between the beams and immediately under the deck. Also, shifting boards fixed between the beams to prevent the surface movement of a bulk grain cargo.

**Bed.** General term for a base or foundation provided for a weighty object. Specifically, timber supports placed under casks stowed in a hold to keep their bilges (middle parts) off the floor.

**Bung up and bilge free.** Proper way of stowing casks: bung staves uppermost and the bottom tier of casks resting on BEDS so that the bilges, or middles, of the casks are free of the deck.

**Cantick quoin.** QUOIN.

**Cargo battens.** Planks fitted across the inner edges of the ship's frames in order to keep the cargo in the hold from direct contact with the ship's side and allow necessary ventilation.

**Chock.** Wooden wedge used to prevent any article stowed on board from shifting when the ship is in motion.

**Deck cargo.** Goods carried on the open decks of a vessel, either because they are in any way dangerous (inflammable or explosive, for instance), or because the vessel's holds are full or cannot accommodate them due to their size (timber, for example).

**Deck load.** DECK CARGO.

**Dunnage.** Wooden blocks or other materials used to protect stowed goods from damage or from leakage, or to prevent them from shifting in the hold.

**Fardage.** DUNNAGE used particularly with bulk cargo.

**Freshen ballast.** To turn over stone or shingle ballast.

**Gangway.** Passage left in the hold when a ship is laden with cargo, to provide access so that goods can be examined en route for any possible damage.

**Ground tier.** Lowest tier of casks or cargo stowed in a hold.

**Harness cask.** Large cask kept on deck from which the daily ration of salt beef or pork was issued. The name is related to the slang term for salt beef, SALT HORSE (10.09).

*Discharging ballast on the* Passat, *1949*

**In ballast.** Condition of a vessel that is not carrying cargo, and is carrying BALLAST for stability.

**Jack screw.** Device used to move heavy pieces of cargo or to force or compress goods such as cotton into a small stowage space.

**Kentledge.** Permanent pig-iron BALLAST laid along the keelson. Also, any permanent iron ballast.

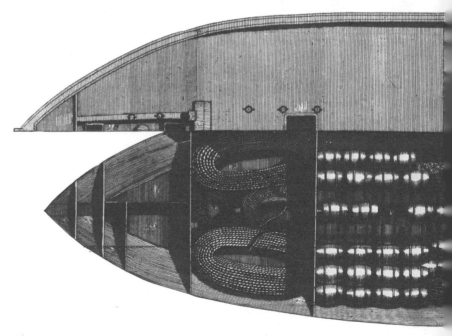

**Lagan.** Cargo or any large article thrown overboard and marked with a buoy so that it can be recovered later. Derived from old French *lagand* – lying. Also, articles lying inside a sunken ship or any goods lying on the bottom of the sea.

**Lastage.** Any cargo or ballast stowed in a ship. Also, a duty levied on a cargo ship.

**Lead ballast.** Lead used particularly in yacht keels to keep the centre of gravity low and increase stability.

**Mete stick.** Narrow plank attached horizontally to a vertical timber, used to measure height in a cargo hold or to level ballast.

**Quilting.** Wrapping of strands of rope woven round a bottle or jar to protect it.

**Quoin.** Wooden chock used as a wedge to prevent casks or other goods and containers from rolling or scraping against each other. Also called *cantick quoin.*

**Separation.** Materials used to separate different cargoes or packages of goods from each other.

**Separation cloths.** Large sheets of jute cloth, burlap or other fabric used in cargo holds to separate different grades of bulk grain or to protect special cargoes, such as sugar, from moisture.

**Shifting.** State of a ship's ballast or cargo that is shaken from side to side by the rolling of the ship.

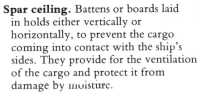

**Shifting boards.** Planks temporarily fixed to the middle-line pillars in a ship's hold to prevent a cargo from shifting. Also used to prevent the shifting of certain types of BALLAST.

**Sounding pipe.** Tube through which a SOUNDING ROD can be passed into any tank or compartment for the storage of liquid.

**Sounding rod.** Graduated rod at the end of a line, for measuring depth of liquid in a storage compartment.

**Spar ceiling.** Battens or boards laid in holds either vertically or horizontally, to prevent the cargo coming into contact with the ship's sides. They provide for the ventilation of the cargo and protect it from damage by moisture.

**Stiffening.** Ballast, weights or cargo put into a ship in order to increase her stability and prevent her capsizing. Term derives from the practice in former days of using for this purpose stiffening booms or spars lashed to the hull on each side.

**Stow.** To arrange goods compactly in a ship's hold or between decks.

**Stowage.** General disposition of goods and materials in a ship's holds. That branch of seamanship dealing with the loading of cargoes in holds, and their placing and packaging so as to avoid damage or deterioration, to assist the stability of the ship, to ensure the economy of cargo space on which the ship's earning capacity depends, and so on.

**Sweepings.** Goods which have escaped or leaked out of their containers into the hold. They are swept up and delivered to the various consignees in proportion to their claims.

**Unballast.** To unload the ballast from a vessel.

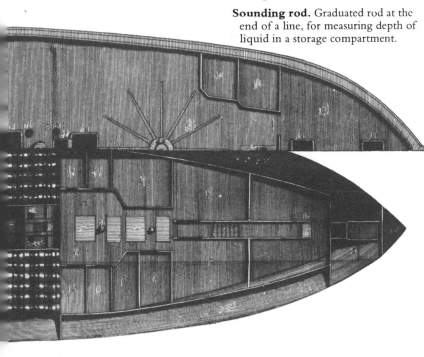

# Ship-Types

Since the greater part of the world's surface is under water, man, over the ages, has been forced to devote much thought, time and energy to devising means to travel, fight, fish and live in relative comfort and safety on the water. As a result, a multitude of types of vessels have been evolved for use on the seas, lakes and rivers of the world.

Rafts of logs, reeds or inflated skin, and dug-out canoes, together with bark and skin vessels, were the earliest and most primitive forms of water craft. The earliest known graphic representations of boats appear on Egyptian pottery of *c*3400 BC and show rafts or boats apparently built from papyrus reed and propelled by paddles.

The dug-out canoe, used wherever suitable trees were available, and canoes formed from a light wood framework covered with animal skins or tree bark were perhaps the most widely distributed form of primitive water craft. The history of the gradual development of boats and ships from these primitive origins is a long and complex one. The availability of materials, geographical conditions and the purposes for for which the craft were required all affected this development. At a time when there was no obvious communication between widely separated areas, similar conditions and resources often led to similar kinds of construction and form.

As communications between the continents and countries improved, some development in design and building techniques took place because of the consequent exchange of ideas. It is not known when a deck was first fitted to the hull, but the Egyptians possessed decked sea-going vessels from about 2600 BC. The Phoenicians, Greeks and Romans used large galleys rowed by a number of oarsmen arranged in one or more tiers. In Europe, shipbuilding developed with two main constructional practices. In those countries with a Mediterranean seaboard, carvel-built ships predominated, while in north-western Europe, until the last part of the fifteenth century, the vast majority of vessels were clinker-built. Perhaps the earliest recognizable stage in the evolution of the large clinker-built vessel of the fifteenth century is represented by the remains of a vessel of about 400 BC found in South Jutland, constructed from five wide planks sewn together. The gradual development of the keel from a centre plank is shown by the Nydam and Kvalsund boats of about 400 and 500 AD respectively, and by the true keel of the Viking ship found at Gokstad.

During the eleventh and twelfth centuries Northern vessels were of the Viking type – double-ended with high stem-post and stern-post and considerable sheer fore and aft. Temporary tower-like structures – fore and after castles – were erected for fighting purposes. The introduction, about 1200 AD, of the median rudder mounted on the stern-post, instead of a steering oar on the quarter, brought about a change in ship design. The stern-post was made straight and vertical so that the rudder could be fitted more efficiently, and this resulted in differentiation in shape between bow and stern. At the same time, the fore and after castles became a more permanent part of the ship's structure.

However, it was during the fifteenth century that the most remarkable changes in Northern ships took place. This century saw the change from clinker to carvel building, the shaping of the superstructure to the form of the hull and the complete transformation from the single mast and sail to the three-masted ship. These developments produced the large carracks of the period 1460–1560 and in turn the sixteenth century galleons designed with relatively good lines, a forecastle set well back from the stem and a long projecting beak. A number of the larger galleons were four-masted, but before the middle of the seventeenth century it was realized that additional sail-power aft could be better obtained by making the mizen mast larger and so increasing its sail-carrying capacity, rather than by adding another mast, and the four-masted rig virtually disappeared until the introduction of the four-masted barque some 200 years later.

The deployment of cannon on ships gradually brought about a distinction between warships and merchant ships. At first, when guns were small, they were mounted in the superstructure and no alterations to the structure of the hull were required; but larger and heavier guns could only be carried at a low level and gun-ports had to be cut into the side of the hull. For a period, the type of vessel could be distinguished by the number of gun-ports, but later merchant ships were frequently heavily armed, and in the eighteenth century a small frigate was very similar in appearance to an East Indiaman of about 350 tons, while the large Indiamen with a line of painted dummy ports at the lower-deck level were sometimes taken for 64-gun warships.

From the end of the seventeenth century, the warships of all European powers had the same general features: raised poop and quarterdeck aft, a square bulkhead across the bows, three masts, and additional sails below the bowsprit, with a lateen sail on the mizen mast. Improvements in armament took the form of heavier guns, rather than additions to their number for the various classes or rates, and with some structural changes fore and aft – the round bow and stern – and improvements in the rigging and sails this type of warship survived into the nineteenth century.

For warships below the rate of frigate, and for those intended for special duties, other rigs were adopted. In the second half of the eighteenth century most navies included brigs and schooners. Single-masted cutters rigged with a large gaff mainsail and square topsails were used for scouting and subsidiary services by naval forces and particularly by the British, as coastal patrol vessels to counter smuggling.

In the eastern Mediterranean, as we have seen, sea-going ships were in use before 2000 BC. The earliest fighting galleys appear to have been undecked vessels rowed by about twenty-five oarsmen a side. The bireme, with two tiers of rowers, first appeared about 700 BC, and three-tiered galleys – triremes – were the principal vessels used by both opposing forces at the Battle of Salamis in 480 BC. Vessels of the galley type continued to be the principal warships in the Mediterranean throughout the Roman and Byzantine periods, with an important change about 600 AD, when fore-and-aft lateen sails replaced the square sails which had been carried by Greek and Roman galleys as a secondary means of propulsion. Galleys remained in service in the Mediterranean until the eighteenth century.

In the Far East, junks developed within a form of construction which perhaps originated with the log raft. Longitudinal planks forming the bottom of the vessel took the place of the keel, bulkheads were used instead of frames, and transverse planking at bow and stern took the place of stem-post and stern-post. Chinese vessels made in this way range in size from the small sampan to the large ocean trader. Sea-going junks can be broadly classified into northern and southern types. Those from the north had bluff bows and flat bottoms, because trade was with river ports, where grounding was often necessary. In southern China, with deeper waters, the junks had sharper bows and greater draught, and the design showed more foreign influence. The characteristic sail of the Chinese junk was a lug-sail stiffened by battens of bamboo. Its shape varied according to the area of use. In narrow rivers, the sail was narrow and high with a nearly flat head; in more open waters and in sea-going vessels, it was wide with a high peak.

The exotic craft of Oceania can be divided into three principal types: canoes with a single outrigger, double outriggers and double canoes. The Fijian sailing canoe is said to have been one of the most successful types of outrigger canoe, and the largest could accommodate forty or fifty people and was capable of making long ocean voyages.

In the Americas, the Spanish established shipbuilding operations in the sixteenth century, and American-built galleons were carrying treasure to Spain by the 1580s. From the seventeenth century onwards a variety of ship types – including shallops, pinnaces, sloops, schooners and ketches – were built in the English colonies of North America. Towards the end of the eighteenth century the most important development in American ship design was the fast sailing schooner, which by the 1820s had become famous as the Baltimore clipper. American-built three-masted, square-rigged packets of about 500 tons were used to establish, in 1818, the first scheduled service between the United States and Britain.

By the 1840s, packets of more than 1,000 tons were sailing regular services between America and Europe. The existence in the 1850s of trades in which fast passages could earn very high freight rates brought about a demand for fast sailing ships, and began the era of the clipper ship which has attracted so much fascination, interest and controversy. The clippers were built with a hull designed for high speed and a rig that could carry a spread of sail sufficient to drive the vessel at that high speed. Vessels of this type developed in Britain and America on parallel, but independent courses.

During the later years of the nineteenth century, large schooners were employed in the coasting trade along the Atlantic seaboard of North America. Schooners with three, four, five or six masts came into use. On these vessels, the work of hoisting and trimming the sails was often done by means of winches driven by steam power. For this coastal trade the fore-and-aft rig proved superior to that of the square-rigged ship, which remained the best rig for long ocean voyages up to the end of the sailing ship era.

After about 1880, in an attempt to make ocean-going sailing ships profitable, much larger vessels were constructed, and steel-built, steel-masted and wire-rigged vessels of some 3,000 tons were built. With the increase in length an additional mast was added. The majority of these vessels were four-masted barques with the fourth mast fitted with fore-and-aft sails only, but some four-masters were square-rigged on the fourth mast and were known as four-masted ships. Right at the end of the century, even larger sailing ships up to 5,700 tons were built and rigged with five masts, but in most cases they had no square sails on the aftermost mast.

In this short introduction it has not been possible to deal with the extraordinary variety of types of small craft that have appeared on the waters of the world. In China alone, more than three hundred distinct types have been recorded; and there are now more than a thousand varieties of yacht types the world over.

BASIL W. BATHE

# Development of the Ship – Representative Types

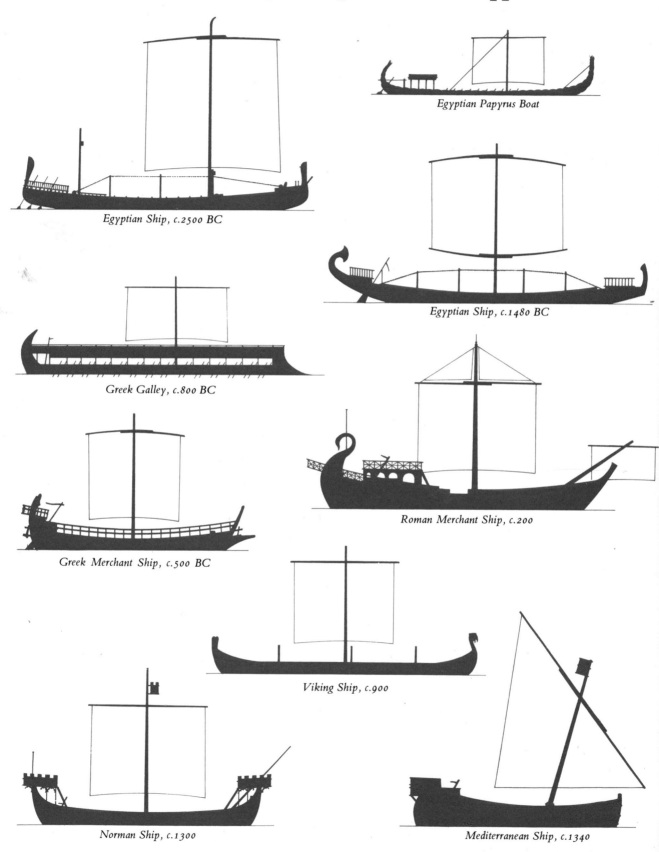

Egyptian Papyrus Boat

Egyptian Ship, c.2500 BC

Egyptian Ship, c.1480 BC

Greek Galley, c.800 BC

Greek Merchant Ship, c.500 BC

Roman Merchant Ship, c.200

Viking Ship, c.900

Norman Ship, c.1300

Mediterranean Ship, c.1340

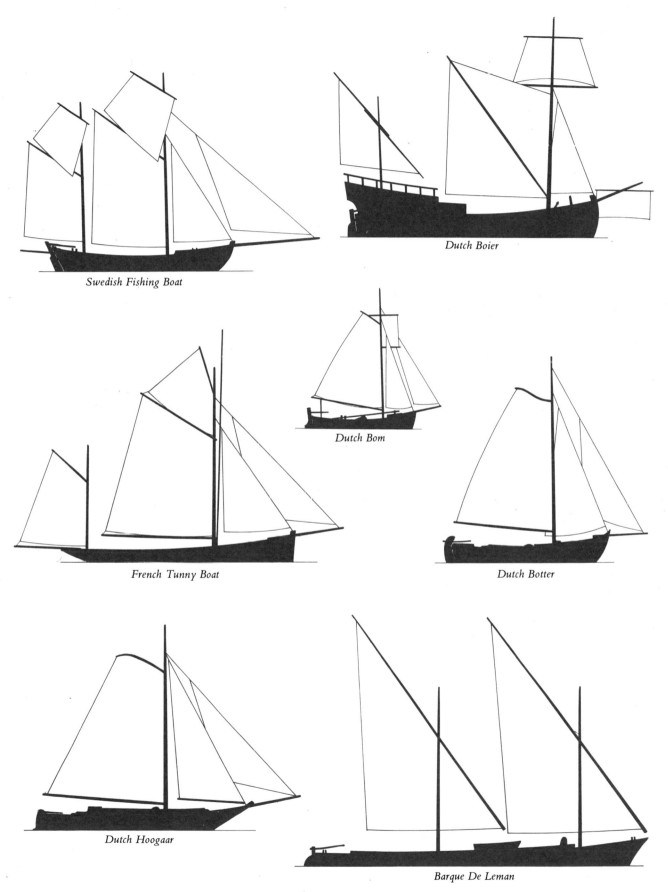

Swedish Fishing Boat

Dutch Boier

French Tunny Boat

Dutch Bom

Dutch Botter

Dutch Hoogaar

Barque De Leman

Scale 300:1

# Coastal and Fishing Craft – Europe

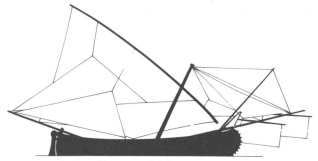

Portuguese Muletta

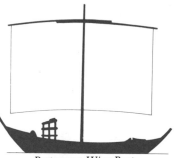

Portuguese Wine Boat

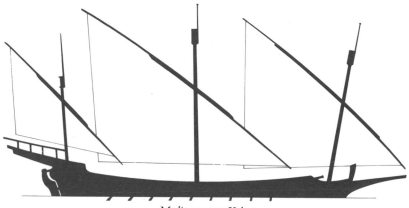

Mediterranean Xebec

Gozo Boat

Yorkshire Lugger

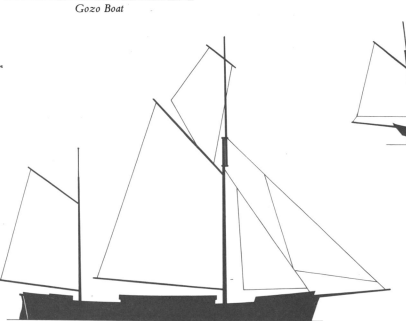

Yorkshire Billy-Boy

Yorkshire Coble

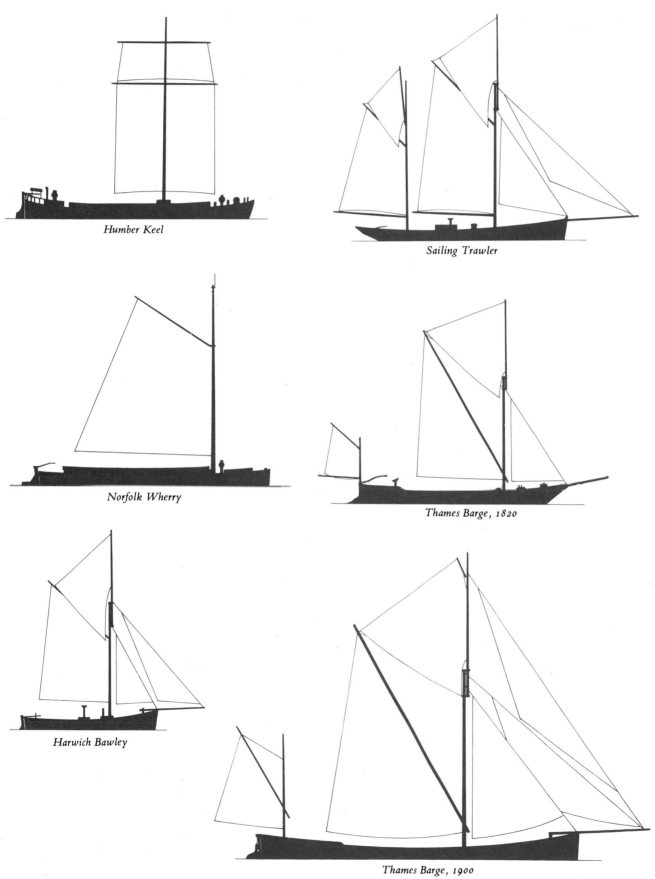

Humber Keel

Sailing Trawler

Norfolk Wherry

Thames Barge, 1820

Harwich Bawley

Thames Barge, 1900

# Coastal and Fishing Craft – Europe

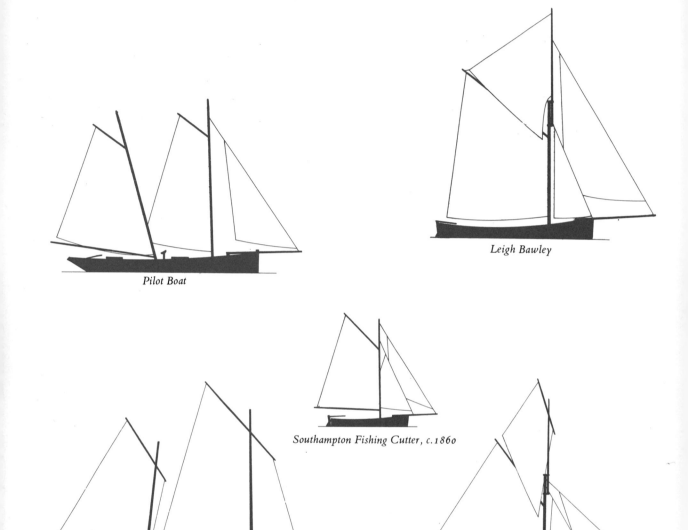

Pilot Boat

Leigh Bawley

Southampton Fishing Cutter, c.1860

Scottish Zulu

Essex Cutter Smack

Falmouth Quay Punt

Brighton Hogboat

Hastings Lugger

Lancashire Nabby

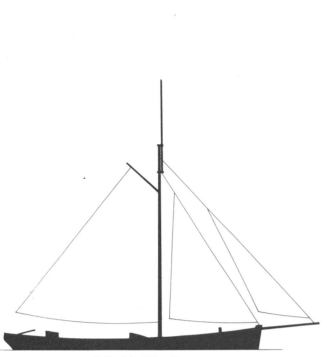

Scilly Isles Pilot Cutter

Loch Fyne Skiff

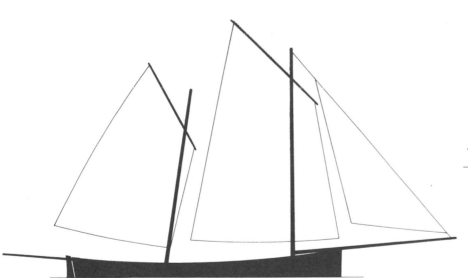

Scaffie

Shetland Sixern

Leith Baldie

Irish Curragh

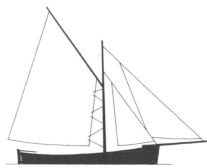

Irish Hooker

# Coastal and Fishing Craft – Africa and Asia

Ra II Raft

Egyptian Gyassa

Arab Dhow

Lama Mtepe

Bombay Prow

Ceylon Outrigger

Malay Kolek

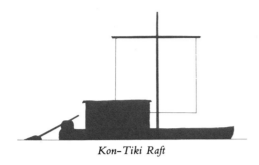

Kon-Tiki Raft

Block Island Boat

New York Pilot Schooner

Bahama Sloop

Eskimo Umiak

Barque Schooner

Scale 300:1

# Yachts

*(There are now more than 1,000 different classes of yachts and sailing dinghies, only a representative selection is listed here.)*

Cadet

International Canoe

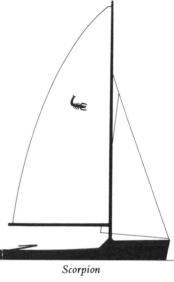

Scorpion

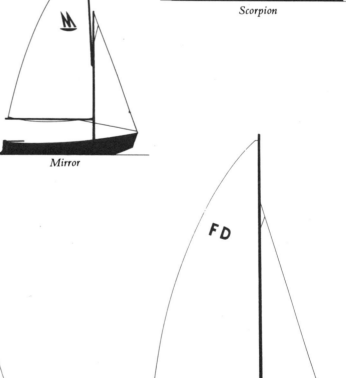

Mirror

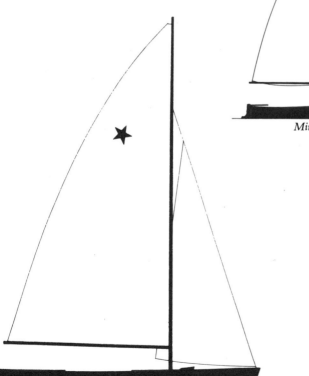

Star

Flying Dutchman

whaleboat was by far the best boat for landing through it. The use of whaleboats spread throughout the Navy, replacing yawls, and after some years they became known as whalers. Besides the whaleboat, the slave trade was responsible for another new boat, the pink-sterned launch; that is, one with a very narrow stern. It was considered to be more seaworthy for the extended cruising off the coast for which these boats were required.

The other two new types of boat were skiffs and dinghies, very small boats for small vessels or for use in harbour when only a few men needed to be transported. The dinghy, smaller than the skiff, originated in India and was first used by East Indiamen.

The design of each boat gradually developed as new ideas came into being and features found advantageous in one type were transferred to another. For example, the oar was at first constrained between two thole pins, inserted into holes in a block secured inside the gunwhale. When cutters appeared, they had an additional wash-strake which heightened the gunwale. To prevent the oars being raised too high for convenience when rowing, rowlocks were cut in this wash-strake, and closed with plugs when the boat was under sail. This arrangement proved to have advantages over thole pins, which might work out, and towards the end of the eighteenth century barges, pinnaces and yawls were fitted, first with permanent rowlocks made above the gunwale, next with removable pieces between these to make temporary wash-strakes, and finally with complete permanent wash-strakes having rowlocks cut in them.

In 1826 Lieutenant Henry Mangles Denham of the surveying vessel *Linnet* introduced swivelling metal crutches. These made it possible, when a boat was going alongside, to let go the looms so that the oars swung in and trailed beside the boat instead of having to be tossed and unshipped. The crutches were so successful that they were adopted for all single-banked boats.

The boats of men-of-war had always been used for transporting armed men, either for boarding an enemy vessel or for effecting a landing. Ships' boats were not particularly well suited to the latter purpose, and in about the year 1700 flat-bottomed boats were introduced. They had a shallow draught, enabling them to be run close inshore before the soldiers had to disembark, and very considerable beam, so that between the ten seamen rowing on each side about fifty soldiers sat on fore-and-aft benches. These boats, when inboard, could be stowed inside each other. Flat-bottomed boats were kept in the dockyards and issued to men-of-war and transports when a combined operation was imminent.

Small guns could be carried in boats. One of the earliest occasions was in 1738 when four swivels were fitted in the long-boat of the *Centurion*, under Captain George Anson, for protection while watering on the African coast. Just before the end of the century, slides were fitted down the centre-line of launches so that carronades could be carried. In the boats of the largest ships there were 24-pounders. During the nineteenth century the practice was extended, the guns varying as new types were developed.

The fitting of a boat with a single sail persisted from the earliest times, and as late as the last quarter of the nineteenth century it was still customary in some of the smaller boats. Long-boats carried a mainsail, staysail and jib as early as the 1740s; the first cutters used two masts with spritsails and there was always a great deal of latitude in the different ways in which individual captains rigged their ships' boats.

As far as merchantmen were concerned, at one time their boats were mostly limited to a long-boat and a yawl. In the nineteenth century, the larger ships usually carried two double-ended lifeboats at davits and two lighter boats on deck.

A steam-boat had first been tried in the Royal Navy in 1847 but it was not until 1864 that their issue began to become general. In spite of the obvious advantages of steam over oars and sail, the steam-boat did not, for a long time, make the impact upon the use of boats that might have been expected. Captains were enjoined to economize in the use of coal and hence steam-boats were used as little as possible. Steam-barges for the use of flag-officers did not appear until the 1890s. With the appearance of motor-boats early in the present century, and with the end of the strict economy observed during the First World War, the use of oars and sail for routine trips practically died out.

W. E. MAY

# Types of Boats; Boat Construction

**Accident boat,** or **sea boat.** Boat kept ready for lowering at sea in case of accident or emergency (such as man overboard), assisting a wrecked vessel or picking up survivors. The boat's FALLS (09.03) are always kept clear for running and lighted lanterns are kept in the boats at night, for immediate recognition. As a precaution against being separated from the parent vessel,

rigged schooner. To save space, the thwarts of the dories were taken out and they were stowed inside each other in 'nests' of dories.

**Galley.** Two masted, DIPPING-LUG (04.14) rigged boat 35 ft long and with a beam of 5 ft 11 in; formerly used by captains of the Royal Navy. It was equipped with a drop keel and oars. Large *lateen-rigged* galleys with

(09.03), stocked with provisions and medicines. Shore-based lifeboats are of special 'unsinkable' construction, and are maintained by various organizations for the rescue of shipwreck victims.

**Pram.** Two-transomed open boat developed in Scandinavia, nowadays mostly used by yachts.

**Pulling boat.** A boat which is propelled by oars.

**Quarter boat.** Emergency boat ready for immediate service, carried in DAVITS (09.03) on the quarter of a vessel.

**Row boat,** or **rowing boat.** Boat propelled by oars.

accident boats always carry survival equipment, stores and a BOAT'S BAG (09.02).

**Cock.** Medieval term for a small open boat.

**Dinghy.** Small general-purpose boat about ten to twelve feet long. Usually equipped with one pair of oars and sometimes a small LUG SAIL (04.14).

**Dory.** Type of flat-bottomed boat mostly used by the long-line fishermen of the Newfoundland Grand Banks. Usually equipped with two pairs of oars and a small spritsail, they operated *trawls* of lines and worked from a parent ship, usually a fore-and-aft

single banks of oars, known as *réales*, were used by the French as warships until 1720. *Deal galleys* were used on the coast of Kent until comparatively recent times. *Lugsail-rigged*, 30 ft long with 5 ft beam, they were one of the fastest types of sailing boat ever built.

**Jolly boat.** Small but strongly built boat used for general purposes.

**Lifeboat.** Boat intended for the saving of life at sea, or specially designed for the purpose. Lifeboats are built to rigid specifications. They are compulsorily carried on board ship in sufficient numbers to save all passengers and crew, and are kept ready at their DAVITS

*St. Ives lifeboat, Cornwall, 1870*

**Sea boat.** ACCIDENT BOAT.

**Surf boat.** Boat specially designed and equipped to operate in surf. It is usually high at stem and stern with a low FREEBOARD (03.01) amidships.

**Whaleboat.** Light, double-ended boat originally used for whaling. CLINKER-BUILT (03.17), about twenty to thirty feet long, it carries oars and a small SPRITSAIL (04.10). When carried as ship's boats, whale boats are called *whalers*. The whalers used in the Royal Navy were about 27 feet 6 inches long, *staysail-rigged* and carried a DROP KEEL (03.17).

*Longboat*

*Cutter*

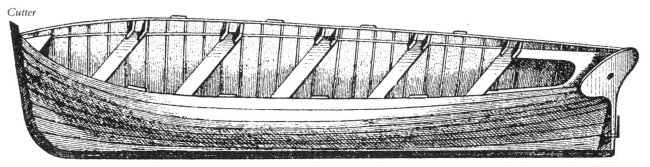

**Back board.** Board in a boat's stern just forward of the TRANSOM (01.01) and against which the COXSWAIN (10.02) leans when steering.

**Bank.** Collective term for the oars along one side of a boat when they are manned. Ancient craft such as biremes and triremes carried two and three banks or tiers of oars respectively.

**Becket rowlock.** Short length of rope securing an oar between thole pins. A feature of boats working from beaches where the breakers alongshore were liable to jerk the oars from between the THOLE PINS (09.02).

**Benches.** Curved seats in a boat's stern. Traditionally the place for ship's officers, guests and other important persons.

**Bent timbers.** The frames or ribs of a boat.

**Bilge piece,** or **bilge rail.** Fore and aft timber fitted outside the BILGE (03.10) and recessed with hand-grips to enable the crew to remain with the boat if it is capsized.

**Boat's badge.** Device, symbol or insignia on the bows of naval boats to show which vessel they belong to.

**Bottom boards.** Light planks fastened together and laid fore and aft in the boat's bottom over the frames, to take the weight of the crew off the boat's planking and timbers.

**Bow locker.** Small locker in the bow which contained the BOAT'S BAG (09.02) and the DROGUE (06.02) and oil bag of the SEA-ANCHOR (06.02).

*Lifeboat*

*Rowlock*

*Buoyancy tanks*

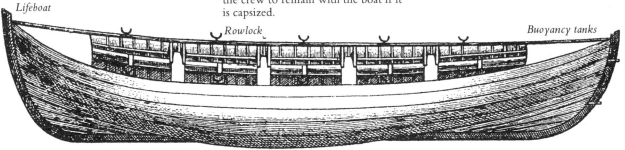

*Gig*

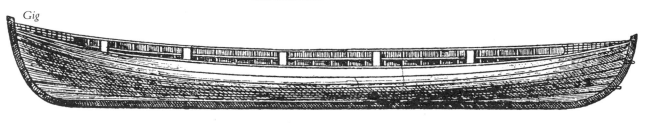

*Oar*

*Boat hook*

**Bow sheets.** Raised platform or wooden grating in the bows of a boat.

**Buoyancy tanks.** Tanks fitted to a vessel's lifeboats to keep them afloat even when swamped. The tanks are of non-corrosive metal and are required to provide one cubic foot of positive buoyancy for every person the lifeboat is certified to carry.

**Capping.** Rounded moulding finishing off a boat's gunwale.

**Chine, or chime.** The line where bottom and sides of a boat meet (particularly in a flat-bottomed boat).

**Cleading.** Wooden casing round a boat's sides which houses the internal BUOYANCY TANKS.

**Cleat.** Wooden or metal device bolted inside the gunwales of boats, to which the sheets are fastened when the boat is under sail.

**Crutch.** A U-shaped metal swivel mounted on a boat's gunwales for an oar to work in.

**Grab lines.** Lifelines hanging in regular BIGHTS (05.10) around the outside of LIFEBOATS. (09.01).

**Head sheets.** BOW SHEETS.

**High wooded.** Said of a boat with a lot of freeboard, that is, with much of its sides above the water-line.

**Hog piece.** Piece of timber secured to the inside of the keel from the fore DEAD-WOOD (03.06) to the after dead-wood and to which the GARBOARD STRAKE (03.10) the FLOORS (03.16) and the frames are secured.

**Keel band, or stem band.** Metal strip on a boat's stem which runs from the FOREFOOT (03.07) upwards.

**Keelson board.** Piece of wood running along the centre-line of the boat and over the FLOORS (03.16), extending about two-thirds of the boat's length. It holds the MAST STEPS and the THWART pillars.

**Mast clamp.** Iron clamp hinged to a boat's THWART, which locks the mast into a recess in the thwart.

**Mast step.** Wooden block on the keelson recessed to take the butt of the mast.

**Open boat.** Said of any boat which is not decked in.

**Pillar.** Moulded wooden column supporting a boat's THWARTS.

**Plug.** Stopper fitted in a boat's bottom to enable the boat to be drained when hoisted in the DAVITS (09.03) or pulled ashore.

**Poppet.** Wooden shutter which closes a ROWLOCK when not in use. It is fitted with a LANYARD (04.08) to prevent loss.

**Rising.** Fore-and-aft timber along the interior of a boat's side, which takes the ends of the THWARTS.

**Rowlock.** A U-shaped aperture cut in the WASH STRAKE of a boat to accommodate an oar.

**Rubber, or rubbing piece.** Wooden moulding running along the outside of the gunwale to protect against chafing when alongside a wharf or another vessel.

**Running hook.** Off-centre hook fitted in the bow of a boat, which takes the foresail TACK (04.09) when running before the wind.

**Sailing thwart.** Fore-and-aft THWART running along a boat's centre-line and accommodating the mast. In small boats it can be athwartships.

**Sand strake.** GARBOARD STRAKE (03.10) in a boat.

**Saxboard.** Top strake of a boat.

**Sheer strake.** Top strake or plank of a boat, to which the gunwale and CAPPING are attached.

**Side benches.** The fore-and-aft benches in a lifeboat, beneath which the BUOYANCY TANKS are housed.

**Steering crutch.** CRUTCH used to take a boat's steering oar and shipped near the stern-post.

**Stern sheets.** That part of a boat extending aft from the aftermost THWART.

**Stretcher.** Stout wooden batten housed in chocks on the bottom boards of a boat, against which an oarsman braces his feet when pulling.

**Take up.** Boat's timbers are said to 'take up' when they are swollen sufficiently to close the seams and prevent leaking. Boats kept in DAVITS (09.03) for prolonged periods should be partially filled with water from time to time to prevent the timbers shrinking.

**Thole, or thole pin.** Wooden or metal pin inserted singly or in pairs in a boat's gunwale to serve instead of a ROWLOCK or CRUTCH and hold an oar.

**Thwarts.** Planks set athwartships in a boat and which serve as seats for the oarsmen. The ends of the thwarts rest on timbers called STRINGERS (03.06) running fore and aft along the inside of the boat.

**Tilt.** Canvas awning covering the after end of a boat.

**Tingle.** Sheet of copper, lead or Muntz metal used for repairing the outside of a boat which has been holed.

**Top strake.** The plank of a boat immediately adjacent to the gunwale on both sides.

**Wash strake, or wash board.** Top strake of a boat's planking. Also, a removable plank mounted above the gunwale to increase a boat's FREEBOARD (03.01).

**Wiring clamp.** Wooden fitting on a boat's RISING OR STRINGER (03.06) to which a THWART is fastened.

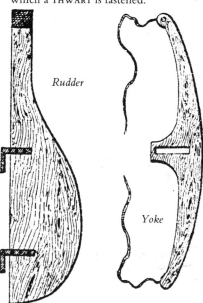

*Rudder*

*Yoke*

**Yoke.** Cross-piece of wood or metal mounted on the rudder head of a boat. It is fitted with *yoke lines*, one on each side, to control the rudder.

# *Boat Gear; Boat Handling*

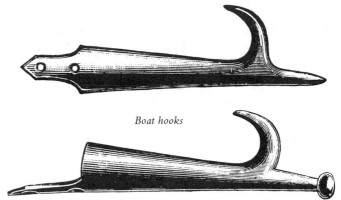

*Boat hooks*

**Bailer.** Scoop for emptying water from a boat. Some boats, particularly the light cedar boats of whale-ships, carried wooden bailers resembling shovels with short handles.

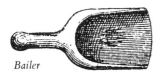

*Bailer*

**Barge pole.** Long, heavy pole, iron-shod and used aboard barges for fending off from other vessels and from obstructions. Also used to push a barge off a sandbank.

**Barricoe.** Small wooden cask used in boats to hold drinking water. Also known as a *breaker*.

**Boat hook.** Long, slender, wooden shaft with a brass or galvanized iron hook at one end. Used for picking up ropes when coming alongside, and for fending off.

**Boat lead and line.** Small tapered LEAD (05.07) weighing 7 lb, with a $2\frac{1}{2}$-lb line. The line is 10 to 12 fathoms long and marked like the HAND LEAD (19.01), though in feet up to 3 or 4 fathoms.

**Boat rope.** Rope run from forward in a vessel to a boat, such as an ACCIDENT BOAT (09.01), to keep it safely alongside.

**Boat's bag.** Bag carried in ACCIDENT BOATS (09.01). It contained emergency tools and materials such as spunyarn, tallow, palm and needle, marline spike, twine tingle, hammer, chisel, wax, tommy bar and punch.

**Bow oar.** Oar pulled immediately in the boat's bow and, because of the confined space, the most difficult one to handle. Also, another name for BOWMAN (09.03).

**Blade.** Flat extremity of an oar, which enters the water and provides the leverage to propel the boat.

**Chest rope.** Long boat rope leading from a vessel's bow to an entry port or gangway in the vessel's side.

**Dipper.** Another name for a boat's bailer, usually in the form of a wooden scoop which enables the water to be thrown from the boat at speed.

**Euloe.** Another name for SCULL (09.03). Taken from *Yuloh*, a self-feathering oar used by Taiwan surf-rafts.

**Fender.** Device used to prevent damage by impact or by chafing or rubbing.

Large rope fenders are known as puddings or pudding fenders.

**Lazy painter.** Small rope about five fathoms long, with its inboard end secured to the stem, used for mooring a small boat in quiet water when heavy stresses are not expected.

**Loom.** Inboard extremity of oar forming a hand-grip for the oarsman.

**Oar.** Wooden implement used for the propulsion of a boat. It consists of loom, shaft and blade.

**Paddle.** Short, broad-bladed oar used to propel canoes or dug-outs but held with both hands and not shipped into a ROWLOCK (09.02) or CRUTCH (09.02). Also, as a verb, to propel a boat by means of paddles; and to pull an oar with a short, easy stroke.

**Painter.** Rope attached to the stem of a boat and used to moor it to a quay, jetty or buoy, or for securing it to another vessel.

**Piggin.** Small, bucket-shaped wooden bailer.

**Puoy.** Type of QUANT with a spike instead of a flat disc at the end. Used for propelling barges and boats.

**Quant.** Long pole with a shoulder-piece and with a flat disc at the other end, used to propel barges and wherries when there is no wind.

**Scull.** Light oar with a curved blade.

**Shaft.** Long, rounded section of an oar between the LOOM (09.02) and the BLADE (09.02).

**Steering oar.** Large and powerful oar used to steer a boat when sea conditions render the rudder useless (for example, in heavy breaking sea or in a surf).

**Sweep.** Long, heavy oar once used in galleys, dromons and galleasses but now used only in barges and lighters.

---

**Back astern.** To give stern way to a boat by pushing on the oars instead of pulling on them. Going into reverse, in effect.

**Back in.** Safety measure used to land a square-sterned boat through a heavy surf. The boat is taken in stern first, to reduce the risk of its broaching-to and capsizing.

**Bail** (vb). To empty water from a boat by means of a bailer.

**Boat drill.** Compulsory mustering of passengers and crew at a vessel's lifeboats. Performed at regular intervals so that all are familiar with their stations and duties in case of emergency.

**Boat keeper.** Member of boat crew left with boat when remainder of crew have left it to go ashore or aboard another vessel.

**Boat pulling.** Seaman's term for rowing.

**Boat's recall.** Flag hoists used by vessels to recall boats. In earlier times, boats often recalled by firing cannon.

**Bowman.** Member of a boat's crew who, when the boat is under oars, pulls the oar in the boat's bow and is responsible for handling the BOAT-HOOK (09.02) when coming alongside. In an ACCIDENT BOAT (09.01), he is also responsible for letting go the BOAT ROPE (09.02). Boats under sail had two bowmen, who were responsible for

handling the TACK (04.09) of the foresail. He is also called the *bow oar*.

**Catch a crab.** To get an oar blade caught in the water with its forward edge lower than its after edge, so that the movement of the boat jams the oar in the rowlock.

**Double-banked.** Said of an oar when it is pulled by two men. Ancient slave galleys and Viking longships were usually pulled in this manner. Also said of vessels equipped with two tiers of oars; such a vessel was the heavily armed *dromon*, a warship of the twelfth century, whose two banks of oars were pulled by 150 to 200 men.

**Feather** (vb). To turn the blade of an oar horizontal when it leaves the water. This is done to lessen wind resistance and is the mark of an experienced oarsman.

**Pulling.** Seaman's term for rowing.

**Row** (vb). To propel a boat by facing aft and pulling on oars.

**Scull** (vb). To propel a boat by means of one oar shipped in a groove or in a CRUTCH (09.02) in the counter, moved in the water with a figure-of-eight action. The resulting turbulence pushes the boat forward.

**Single banked.** Said of a boat when it is pulled with one man on each oar. Also a boat where only one oar is pulled at each thwart; for example, a racing shell.

**Stroke.** Complete pulling sequence of an oar from the time it enters the water until it emerges again. Also, the distance an oar is pulled through the water.

**Stroke,** or **stroke oar.** The aftermost oarsman, who sets the rhythm for the other oarsmen. (Also, the name for the oar itself.)

**Tow.** To pull another vessel through the water by means of a HAWSER (05.08) or rope.

**Trim** (vb). To distribute the weight of the crew and any load the boat may be carrying so that the boat rides in the water to the best advantage.

**Turning short round.** Said of a boat under oars which is turning within as small a compass as possible. This is done by one bank of oars being pulled while the other is being pushed or is holding water.

**Underrun.** To haul up a submerged rope and pull a boat along it so that the rope goes in over the bow and out over the stern. Usually done to determine which way the rope is leading, but also to check for wear and chafing.

# *Hoisting and Mooring Gear*

**Block span.** Length of light wire stretched between the lower blocks of a boat's FALLS to prevent them twisting when being hauled up after the boat has been unhooked.

**Boat boom.** Spar extended from a ship's side in harbour, to which boats can be secured.

**Boat cover.** Canvas cover which, supported by the STRONGBACK, protects the interior of the boat when in the DAVITS.

**Boat skids.** Hardwood chocks upon which boats are carried.

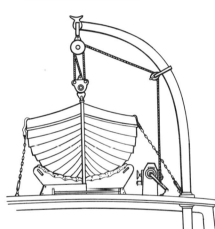

*Davits*

**Davits.** Curved wood, iron or steel pillars fitted to the deck close to a vessel's sides and from which boats are lowered and hoisted by means of two sets of tackles, one from each davit, known as FALLS.

**Disengaging gear.** Device enabling a boat's FALLS to be released quickly and simultaneously when lowering at sea, particularly from a moving vessel.

**Falls.** The ropes by which a boat is lowered and hoisted in the DAVITS.

**Gripes.** Two pieces of SWORD MATTING (10.08), the upper ends secured to the DAVIT heads and the lower ends to slips on the opposite davits. They cross diagonally over the outside of the boat and keep it hard up against the GRIPING SPAR.

**Griping spar.** Long spar equipped with canvas PUDDING (04.02) held between the DAVITS and against which the boat is firmly held.

**Lizard.** Rope or wire with a THIMBLE (05.03) spliced into the loose end, attached to a BOAT BOOM for making fast a boat's PAINTER.

**Slings.** Two spans of chain or wire by means of which boats are hoisted. The foremost sling has one end secured to a RING-BOLT (05.03) in the stem and the after span is similarly connected to the stern-post. The other ends are secured to link plates in the keel.

**Steadying lines.** Lines of hemp and chain extended from a ring in the centre of the SLINGS to the gunwale of the boat. They keep the boat upright while it is being hoisted into the DAVITS.

**Strongback.** Long stout wooden beam running fore and aft over a boat when in the crutches inboard, providing support for the BOAT COVER.

**Swinging boom.** Boom swung out from a vessel's side, to which boats were secured when the vessel was moored or anchored in smooth water.

# Sailors' Life, Customs & Tools

In describing life on board sailing ships of the seventeenth to early nineteenth centuries, we shall use the life of the British sailor as a convenient example. During this period, there was really no distinction between the seamen of the Royal and Merchant navies. It was not uncommon for merchant vessels to be armed, and the muzzle-loading guns used varied only in size and weight. The handling of sails was much the same whatever the type of vessel. The arrangement of rigging became standardized to an enormous extent, so that an experienced man knew where to put his hand on the rope required.

Service in the Royal Navy was unpopular for a number of reasons, chiefly that wages were lower than in the Merchant service and less regularly paid, and large crews caused terrible overcrowding. Nevertheless, in time of peace there seems to have been little difficulty in manning ships; since many men paid off from one ship almost immediately joined another, the service cannot have been too bad.

In time of war it was another matter, and it was necessary to invoke the press to raise the men needed. It has been estimated that in general about half the crews were volunteers and half pressed men. Volunteers were paid a bounty, which at times might reach as much as £5. The press was widely extended and was supposed to take only fit men with sea experience, but in practice these were not adhered to and in the French wars landsmen were accepted and rated as such. The best source of men was homecoming merchantmen, who were stripped of their crews in the English Channel, the Navy lending men to take them to their destinations. Protections were issued to men in employment where their loss would have been undesirable.

The greater part of the men forming a ship's company were able seamen, but there were about thirty other rates, such as gunner's, boatswain's and carpenter's mates, quartermasters, armourers and so forth. By 1806 this number had swelled to over forty, partly due to the introduction of additional petty officers as captains of the fore, main and mizen tops. The number continued to swell and by the middle of the nineteenth century there were about ninety different ratings, the increase being chiefly caused by the introduction of steam and by the general increase in mechanization. The able seamen's pay remained unaltered at 24/– a lunar month from 1653 to 1797. It then increased to 33/6, and by the middle of the next century had crept up to 47/–.

In harbour, when fresh food was available, the sailor received two pounds of meat on two days of the week, a pound of salt meat on two days and a quarter of a pound of cheese on the other three. He also got daily a pound of biscuits and a gallon of beer, and a pint of wine or half a pint of spirits. The amounts should have been ample but there were many cases of short measure and the quality often left much to be desired. In the nineteenth century matters improved considerably and meat was issued daily.

Health in ships was the greatest problem. Pressed men often came on board in a revolting condition and started epidemics of typhus. On long voyages the lack of fresh food led to many deaths from scurvy. The advantages of such remedies as lemon juice had been known to some since Elizabethan times, but it was not until 1795 that its issue was regularized by the Admiralty and scurvy virtually disappeared. The damp, crowded and badly ventilated condition of the mess decks also contributed to the incidence of disease, while in the tropics yellow fever produced its quota of deaths. The introduction of the divisional system whereby each lieutenant was responsible for his quota of men did much to improve cleanliness and consequently health.

When at sea the sailor was kept fully employed; he worked watch and watch, four hours on and four hours off, and in a sailing ship there was usually plenty to do. At times it was also necessary to call up the watch below to give aid in shortening sail. Authorities differ as to the amount of work done in harbour. Some say that a man had little or nothing to do, some that he was kept fully employed, being turned out at 6 am, if not earlier, to scrub decks and thereafter employed at drills until piped down at 8 or 9 pm. It is probable that this picture applies more to the Victorian Navy than to that of a century earlier, but in sail there must always have been much refitting of rigging to be done.

Where men were paid infrequently and had hardly any privileges to stop, the only punishment available to captains was flogging. Except by sentence of court martial, twelve strokes was the maximum that should have been given, but this rule was often ignored. On the other hand, it would seem that much that has been written on the subject is exaggerated. It has been claimed that many captains held daily flogging sessions. A few may have, but it is telling that the notorious Captain Pigot flogged fewer than two men a week. Floggings were usually entered in the log book and it is unlikely that a captain would only pick out a few for entry. It is significant that during the mutinies of 1797 the delegates made no complaints about flogging. For really serious offences, not such as to merit hanging, a man might be flogged round the fleet. He was taken in a boat alongside each ship in turn and given so many strokes, the total often reaching hundreds.

In the early part of the seventeenth century men who joined ships of the Royal Navy were usually in rags. The disadvantages of this are obvious. Men who are cold and wet, through being insufficiently clad, are at least inefficient and at worst exposed to sickness and death. To remedy this state of affairs the slop system was introduced. A contractor was appointed slopseller to the Navy and had to supply a range of clothing to every ship. The slops were in the charge of the purser, and a newly joined man could be supplied with a certain value of clothing on credit. At later dates more could be obtained and the value deducted from money due to the man when the ship was paid.

An early range of clothing consisted of Monmouth and red caps, canvas and blue suits, blue or white shirts, kersey or cotton waistcoats and drawers, stockings and shoes. As years passed the slopseller changed and the range of clothing was varied. The articles supplied reflected to a great extent fashion among the men, and one result of the slop system was that there tended to be a certain uniformity of dress. By the middle of the eighteenth century, trousers had replaced breeches and hats had replaced caps. The frock had come into use, and was rather like the jumper worn by the modern bluejacket but fuller and worn tucked into the trousers instead of being worn outside.

The advantages of a uniform were nevertheless not generally recognized, though as early as 1757 surgeon James Lind recommended that if the men were put into one there would be advantages to health. In 1807 the *Tribune* took a convoy to Gibraltar and on her return was lucky enough to snap up four valuable prizes. When the ship's company received their prize money of £76 a man, they decided that they would adopt a uniform consisting of blue trousers, a white flannel waistcoat bound with blue, a blue jacket with three rows of gilt anchor buttons, placed very close together, a black silk neckerchief, and a round black hat with a gold band bearing the ship's name in front in capital letters.

The interest in a uniform seems to have developed to a considerable extent throughout the Navy. In 1815 the men of the *Antelope* were ordered to provide themselves with a frock, trousers, black silk handkerchief and straw hat. These were mostly made by the men themselves, and to permit this sort of thing ships had long been supplied with materials, needles and thread for issue to the men. To provide time for

sewing it was usual to give men half a day a week free and this was known as a *make and mend*. This expression is still used for a free afternoon. With the return of peace in 1815 and the end of the need for impressment, a general smartness crept in and this, coupled with the conservatism of the sailor, led to the Naval man becoming much more distinctive when seen ashore. Continuous service was established in 1853, and a uniform for seamen, which did not greatly differ from what was already being commonly worn, was finally adopted in 1857.

A feature of the mentality of the British sailor was his extraordinary sense of loyalty, loyalty to his shipmates and loyalty to his officers. Of course there were mutinies, but these generally only occurred when men had been driven beyond endurance. Such a case was that of the *Hermione*, whose men mutinied in 1797 after extraordinary brutality on the part of Captain Hugh Pigot.

In 1748 an unusual event occurred. While the captain and most of the officers of the *Chesterfield* were ashore at Cape Coast Castle, the first lieutenant seized the ship and took her to sea. The ship's company obeyed the orders of the officer without demur, though they did not think it proper to put an officer in irons when ordered to confine the boatswain. When after a few days the boatswain was released, he managed to retake the ship, the men supporting him but again being troubled at the propriety of confining the first lieutenant to his cabin.

Shore leave was commonly granted in peace, but in war the pressed men so increased the number of desertions that leave had to be greatly restricted. This led to large numbers of women being allowed to sleep on board when a ship was in harbour. They were nominally seamen's wives, but few were. With mess decks already overcrowded, each man being allowed only fourteen inches for his hammock, there could be no privacy and the scene must have been indescribable! Women were not allowed to be taken to sea, but some were, and in action proved to be most valuable assistants to the surgeon. At least two children are recorded as having been born in the heat of battle, one at the Glorious First of June in 1794 and the other at the Nile in 1798.

A sideline in the history of the sailor is that from time to time women serve at sea, disguised in men's clothing, without being detected. One example was Mary Lacey, who served at sea for some years under the name of William Chandler, and then obtained employment in Portsmouth Dockyard. When her sex was detected in 1772 she was awarded the pension of a superannuated shipwright.

W. E. MAY

# The Crew – Officers

**Commander.** Naval rank between captain and lieutenant-commander. His rank is designated by three gold rings on his sleeve. Also, the MASTER of a Merchant Navy ship.

**Crew.** Men who operate a ship or any section of a ship. On a merchant vessel the crew consists of everyone except the MASTER. Ratings on naval vessels are sometimes referred to as 'crew' as distinct from officers, but legally officers are also members of the crew.

**Deck officer.** Officer who serves on deck. In the Merchant Navy, an officer who keeps watch on the bridge. In port, deck officers supervise the loading and unloading of cargo.

**First mate.** Chief officer of a vessel, next in rank to the MASTER.

**Flag lieutenant.** Royal Navy Lieutenant who acts as a personal aide to a flag officer such as an admiral, rear admiral and so on.

**Ice master.** Officer of a whaling vessel in charge of navigation when entering icy waters.

**Master.** Officer in command of a Merchant Navy vessel. Title derives from twelfth-century abbreviation for MASTER MARINER. The master of a ship is duly certified for the position and is in charge of all activities on board. He holds special disciplinary powers over all persons aboard ship. Also, title formerly used for the navigating officer in Royal Navy vessels.

**Master mariner.** Alternative and original title of MASTER.

**Mate.** Officer ranking immediately below the master. He holds a certificate of examination or TICKET (10.06). The title First Mate, Second Mate and so on denotes seniority. A mate is responsible for organizing seamen's work as well as stowage and navigating duties. In sailing ships the First Mate was often called simply the Mate.

**Midshipman.** Naval officer ranking between cadet and sub-lieutenant. He is the lowest ranking commissioned officer on board. In the Merchant Navy a midshipman is similar to apprentice in rank, though he may sometimes enjoy extra privileges such as being berthed aft and eating the same food as the officers.

**Naval cadet.** Student officer in the Royal Navy. In the Merchant Navy he is a young man who undergoes his nautical training ashore, but the term is also sometimes used for young men serving at sea.

**Rector.** Term for the MASTER of a vessel, current in the eleventh and twelfth centuries.

**Sea captain.** Officer who has a certificate of competency to be the MASTER of a sea-going vessel.

**Seaman.** Person, other than the MASTER, who serves in any capacity aboard a ship. More particularly, anyone serving on a vessel below the rank of officer. In the Royal Navy the term is reserved for a man who works on deck.

**Shipmaster.** Any person in command of a ship. Alternative term for MASTER.

**Skipper.** Title officially given to the MASTER of a fishing vessel. Term also used for any person in charge of a small vessel such as a yacht or tug. Colloquially used for any master or commanding officer.

**Young gentleman.** Traditional term for a MIDSHIPMAN in the Royal Navy.

Opposite: *'Midshipman' by Thomas Rowlandson, 1756-1827*

*The pressing of a gentleman*

# The Crew – Petty Officers and Men

**Able seaman.** A senior DECK HAND. His duties were to set up and maintain both standing and running rigging, trim sheets, braces and bowlines and take the helm when necessary. Able seamen would act as gun's crews and boarding parties when ships were in action.

*Seaman*

**Blue jacket.** Generally, sailors of the Royal Navy who wear bell-bottom trousers.

**Boatswain, or bosun, or bos'n.** Warrant officer responsible for handling the crew and for the ship's general maintenance. He was also the ship's executioner. The boatswain's badges of office were his pipe or whistle, worn about the neck by a chain and with which orders were piped to the crew, and his *cherriliccum*, a cane sheathed in the cured penis of a bull, with which he beat the crew to encourage them to work.

*Boatswain*

**Boatswain's mate.** Petty officer assisting the BOATSWAIN.

**Cabin boy.** Term used for a junior rating who sees to the needs of the officers.

**Call boy.** Boy who carried the boatswain's whistles or pipes and who relayed piped orders and calls. His duties also included taking part in the ceremonial piping aboard of visiting dignitaries.

**Captain of top.** PETTY OFFICER who led one of three groups of TOPMEN in each watch (one for each mast).

**Carpenter.** Merchant Navy PETTY OFFICER in charge of all woodwork on board. His duties are to see to the upkeep of masts and cargo booms, to repair damage to decks, boats and hull and to open and batten down hatches, cargo ports and so on. In the Royal Navy he is a commissioned officer.

**Cockswain, or coxswain, or coxen.** HELMSMAN of a ship's boat, also in charge of its crew. The term derives from the fact that boats carried on board were originally called *cockboats*.

**Conder.** Person who cons (directs) a ship by giving orders to the HELMSMAN. In fishing vessels, the man on the mast-head who points out shoals of fish appearing off the bows.

**Deck hand.** Seaman in the Merchant Navy ranking from deck boy to ORDINARY SEAMAN and ABLE SEAMAN. A RATING who works on deck under the Chief Officer or the BOATSWAIN. Also, member of the crew of a fishing vessel.

**Efficient deck hand.** DECK HAND over the age of eighteen who has passed an examination of competency and has served at sea for at least twelve months.

**Foretopman.** Seaman whose station is at the *foretop* or fore topmast. Also, Royal Navy term for a member of one of the four quarters of a watch.

**Hand.** Any member of a vessel's crew.

**Helmsman.** Seaman who steers the ship. In cargo and passenger vessels, the helmsman is usually the QUARTERMASTER. Also called *wheelman* or *steersman*.

**Idler.** Member of the crew who works during the day but does not stand the usual night watches; such as the boatswain, carpenter, storekeeper, sailmaker, lamp trimmer and so on. Such hands were envied as idlers by the rest of the crew. Also called *day worker* or *dayman*.

**Lady of the gunroom,** Term for night-watchman in the GUN-ROOM (03.13). Slang name in the Royal Navy for the member of the crew in charge of the gunner's stores, either in the gunroom or in a separate section called the after scuttle.

**Lamp trimmer.** PETTY OFFICER or seaman responsible for the upkeep of all oil lamps on board. He usually worked under the BOATSWAIN.

**Lee Helmsman.** Assistant HELMSMAN, who stands ready at the lee side of the wheel.

**Liberty man.** Royal Navy seaman permitted to go ashore for a short leave.

**Light hand.** Rather young but bright seaman, subject to banter by the crew.

**Lowerer.** Member of the crew stationed at the DAVITS (09.03) to assist in lowering a ship's boat.

**Master at arms.** Officer responsible for order aboard ship. On a passenger vessel he is in charge of general police duties. On Royal Navy ships he is a chief PETTY OFFICER charged with disciplinary duties.

**Ordinary seaman.** Member of the crew who has yet to qualify for the rank of ABLE SEAMAN by passing an examination. He performs various repairs and general maintenance aboard.

**Perforst men.** Seamen removed from merchant ships to serve in the Royal Navy. Derives from the phrase 'per force'.

**Petty officer.** Non-commissioned officer in naval vessels, in charge of RATINGS. His rank is the naval equivalent of sergeant. The term derives from French *petit* – small. In merchant

*1st Class Petty Officer*

vessels, a petty officer could be a seaman promoted from able seaman to boatswain, for instance.

**Quartermaster.** In the Royal Navy, a petty officer who supervises the HELMSMAN and occasionally steers the vessel. In the Merchant Navy he is the seaman responsible for steering. He takes a two-hour spell at the wheel and also has charge of navigating equipment such as log lines, lead lines and so on. In port, he is on duty at the gangway.

**Rating.** A seaman as distinct from an officer.

**Reeler.** Seaman whose task it is to reel in the ship's LOG (19.01) line.

**Rigger.** Person, usually a shipyard worker, who installs and repairs all stays, lifts, braces and other parts of the rigging between the time one crew is paid off and a new one engaged.

**Sailmaker.** Member of the crew who assembles and repairs canvas articles such as sails, covers, awnings and so on. Also sometimes called *sails*.

**Sailor.** Generally, anyone who goes to sea for a living. More particularly, an experienced seaman below the rank of ABLE SEAMAN, working specifically on deck.

**Sea boy.** Youth below the age of eighteen who serves on a ship.

*1st Class Boy*

**Second hand.** Rank immediately below that of SKIPPER (10.01) in a fishing vessel. He is usually responsible for the vessel's navigation.

**Ship's husband.** Person, on board ship, representing the owner of a vessel and entrusted with various business transactions in port. He concludes the necessary contracts for equipment, supplies, freight, repairs, hiring crew and so on. Originally he was the ship's BOATSWAIN.

*Steerage passengers*

**Side boy.** Member of the crew who stands at the gangway of a naval ship to salute high-ranking visiting officers. Also, member of the crew who acts as messenger boy, performs general cleaning duties and also passes ropes from the ship's side to passengers in boats alongside.

**Steerage passenger.** Passengers accommodated between decks, for example emigrants or indentured labourers. More specifically, any passenger allotted less than thirty-six superficial feet of space for his or her personal use.

**Steward.** Member of the crew who attends to the domestic needs of crew and passengers, such as provisioning, catering and seeing to the upkeep of living quarters.

**Storekeeper.** Person, carried on some merchant vessels, who is in charge of all the stores in the ship and of issuing them when needed.

**Stowaway.** Person who hides on a ship in order to obtain free passage. When discovered he can be required to work his passage without pay and may be turned over to the authorities at the ship's destination.

**Supercargo.** Representative of the owners of cargo who sails aboard a merchant vessel with authorization to carry on all business transactions concerning the cargo and to supervise its loading and unloading. The term is an abbreviation of *cargo superintendent*.

**Swabber.** Member of the crew put in charge of cleaning the deck.

**Timoneer.** Old term for the HELMSMAN deriving from the French *timonier* and from the ancient term *tymon*, meaning a staff and hence a TILLER (03.09).

**Tom Bowling.** Title of a famous sea song by Charles Dibdin (1745–1814); also a character in Smollett's earlier *Roderick Random*. The name came to signifying the ideal sailor.

**Topman.** Seaman whose station is in the *foretop* or MAINTOP (04.03). Men who worked on the masts and yards of square-rigged ships were often considered the élite of the crew.

**Warrant officer.** In the Royal Navy, the senior rank held by a non-commissioned officer. The rank was held by a warrant issued by or for the Lord High Admiral of Great Britain and Ireland. It is now obsolete.

**Yeoman.** In the Royal Navy, a rating who acts as assistant to a navigating officer or to a storekeeping officer.

# Crew's Quarters

**Berth.** Space allotted to a member of the crew or a passenger for sleeping, either in a bunk or hammock. Also, job or position on board a ship.

**Bunk.** Built-in bed. Often built up to three in a tier, on some vessels, particularly small ones, bunks have sliding doors which close on the occupant to prevent him being tossed out in bad weather.

**Cot.** Ship's bed made of canvas stretched on a wooden frame and slung like a HAMMOCK from the deck beams. Used by officers before the introduction of permanent cabins.

**Fiddles.** Strips of wood or small cords passed through wooden frames, affixed to tabletops in ship's messrooms in order to prevent dishes, mugs and so on from sliding about in bad weather.

**Hammock.** Hanging bed made of canvas, fitted with clews which are secured to iron rings attached to the deck beams at either end. Used at sea for the berthing of seamen. Said to have been first used in ships towards the end of the sixteenth century.

**Hammock clews.** Lengths of NETTLE STUFF (05.09) spread from the ends of a hammock. They are brought together and secured to a ring attached to the deck beams.

**Hammock cloth.** Tarpaulin used to cover the HAMMOCK NETTINGS (03.15), or spaces along the upper deck and the break of the poop in which hammocks were stored daily in naval vessels.

**Hammock lashing.** Ropes lashed round a hammock several times, securing it when it is not in use.

**Mess.** Group of crew members who eat together and sleep in the same quarters, usually determined by rank: officers, chief petty officers, petty officers and seamen mess separately. Also, the space and facilities available to each group.

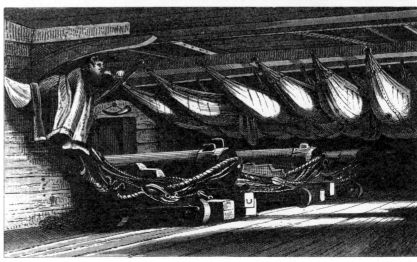

*Top, spinning a yarn in the mess;
middle, a midshipman's berth;
right, hammocks below decks*

*Above, midshipmen's mess on* HMS Caesar, *1856*

*Below, Nelson's cot on the* VICTORY

# Daily Life

*Crossing the line*

**Action stations.** The places and duties detailed to various sections of the crew for battle. Seamen slung yards with chains, doubled important control ropes such as sheets and braces, and rigged extra tiller lines. Gunners cast loose, loaded and primed cannon. Marines were detailed to the fighting tops. Powder monkeys (ship's boys) brought up powder and shot from magazines, and provided barrels of water in case of fire and barrels of vinegar for sponging cannon. Ordinary seamen doused sails with solution of alum as a fire precaution.

**Banyan day.** Any day when the crew are given a treat, extra food or grog, or an unexpected day's shore leave.

**Barbarising.** Swabbing down the deck with a mixture of sand and cleansing powder.

**Clear for action.** To prepare for battle by securing all items on board and removing obstacles in the way of the ship's guns. This includes hoisting out all boats, spreading protective nets to catch any falling debris during battle, removing cabin furniture and so on.

**Crossing the line.** Crossing the equator. Also, the initiation ceremony for crew members or passengers crossing the equator for the first time. Veteran members of the crew dress up as 'King Neptune' and his 'queen'. 'Neptune' shaves the initiate with a large wooden razor, then throws water over him.

**Deck log.** Record of a vessel's voyage kept by the officer of the watch. It should include weather conditions, currents, courses steered, ship's position each noon, distance from points on shore, work carried out on board and any unusual happenings.

**Fore bitters.** Songs sung on the fore-castle when a watch was off duty, gathered round the fore-BITTS (06.03).

**Harbour log.** Record of the work done on a ship while she is in harbour, plus routine LOG entries.

**Hornpipe.** Seamen's dance, originally danced to the old Celtic musical instrument known as a hornpipe.

**Log,** or **log book.** Official record of events on board ship as well as of the ship's movements. Several types of log are kept, such as the DECK LOG, MATE'S LOG and so on.

**Man ship.** To provide a ship's crew.

**Mate's log.** Log kept by the ship's mate into which the entries from the deck log are copied. Also called the *smooth log* – as opposed to the *rough log*. The mate is responsible for preparing it for the master's signature.

**Mustering.** Calling passengers or the ship's company together for drill or inspection. In naval sailing ships it was often done to check that no one was drawing double rations or pay by entering fictitious names in the ship's muster book.

**Piping the side.** Saluting the arrival or departure at the gangway of a high-ranking officer, by sounding a call on a BOATSWAIN'S WHISTLE (see CALL, 11.03). Originates in the days when visitors were hoisted aboard and the BOATSWAIN (10.02) controlled the operation by the varying trills on the pipe.

**Quid.** Piece off a plug of chewing tobacco. Corruption of 'cud'.

**Riding the rigging.** Working one's way down a stay in a boatswain's chair, usually when BLACKING DOWN (04.08) or performing some other work on the rigging.

**Rough log.** Alternative term for DECK LOG.

**Sea legs.** Measure of one's stability in walking about on a vessel when she is under way. A person who has 'not got his sea legs yet' is one who is inexperienced at sea.

**Shanty,** or **chanty.** Song sung on board to help hands work in unison, for instance while pulling on ropes or heaving at the capstan. Usually included short solo verses and hearty choruses.

**Short handed.** Said of a vessel which does not have a full complement of crew.

# UNMOORING

All hands on board! our boatswain cries,
His voice like thunder roaring;
All hands on board! his mates reply,
'Tis the signal for unmooring
Then your messenger bring to,
Heave your anchor to the bow,
And we'll think on those girls when we're far, far away,
And we'll think on those girls when we're far, far away.

Go loose your topsails next he cries,
Topgallant sails and courses,
Your jibs and royals see all clear,
Haul home those sheets, my hearties.
With a light and pleasant gale
We will crowd aloft our sail
And we'll think, etc.

Your anchor's now apeak he cries,
'Vast heaving, lads, 'vast heaving,
Your cat and fish now overhaul,
The capstan nimbly leaving.
Then obey your boatswain's call,
Walk away with that cat-fall.
And we'll think, etc.

Farewell to friends, farewell to foes,
Farewell to dear relations,
We're bound across the ocean blue,
Bound for a foreign station.
While we cross the raging main,
The Union Jack we will maintain.
And we'll think, etc.

# Discipline

**Bilboes.** Heavy iron bars fixed to the deck just abaft the mainmast, to which were attached iron shackles used for confining prisoners.

**Cobbing.** Punishment prevalent in the British Navy well into the nineteenth century and usually meted out for offences, such as petty theft, committed by a seaman against his shipmates. The offender was tied down and struck on the buttocks with a cobbing board or with a hammock clew.

**Cobbing board.** Flat piece of wood used in cobbing.

**Colt.** Length of rope knotted at the end, used by officers in the Royal Navy to punish minor infringements of naval discipline or merely to goad men to work. Abolished early in the nineteenth century.

**Ducking.** Form of punishment in which a rope was fastened round the offender's body and he was hauled up to the yard-arm and then immersed repeatedly in the sea. It was phased out at about the end of the seventeenth century.

**Gantlope,** or **gauntlet.** Royal Navy punishment in which the offender, sitting on a wooden grating, was pulled, up to three times, along a double line of ratings, who each struck him with a knotted cord or rope yarns as he passed. Abolished in the early nineteenth century.

**Hazing.** Practice of keeping a man or crew hard at work unnecessarily; petty tyranny of superiors which makes life on board unbearable.

**Iron garters.** Shackles used to secure an offenders' legs to an iron bar. Equivalent to the stocks in civilian punishment.

**Jump ship.** To desert or to leave a ship without proper authorization.

**Keel hauling.** Punishment in which an offender was hauled underneath the keel of the ship from one side to the other, by means of ropes attached to the port and starboard yard-arms. It was phased out in the early nineteenth century.

**Maroon.** (vb) To put a person ashore in an isolated place with no facilities for escape. Alexander Selkirk, on whose experiences the story of Robinson Crusoe was based, was so treated by the commander of his ship.

**Marry the gunner's daughter.** To undergo a flogging on Royal Navy vessels. The offender had to lean over the barrel of a gun or be tied down to it to take his punishment.

**Naval court.** Court convened by a naval or consular officer to investigate charges made against any member of the crew of a ship, or to inquire into the loss of a ship. It consisted of three to five officers of the Royal Navy, masters of ships or consular officials.

**Pierhead jump.** The joining of a ship just as she is leaving port, from the pierhead.

**Press gang.** Party of naval personnel who, under the command of an officer, went ashore to seize unwilling men and press them into naval service. Pressed men were paid for their work, but at a lower rate than that of enlisted men or volunteers.

**Sea battery.** Assault upon a seaman by the master of a ship, while at sea.

**Shanghai.** To forcibly abduct a sailor, generally with the help of drink or drugs, and enlist him aboard a ship other than his own. A practice notorious in some American ports in the nineteenth century, particularly when crew numbers had to be made up.

**Start** (vb). To use a length of rope to drive on a younger member of the crew at work or to administer summary punishment.

*Point of Honour*

*Press gang*

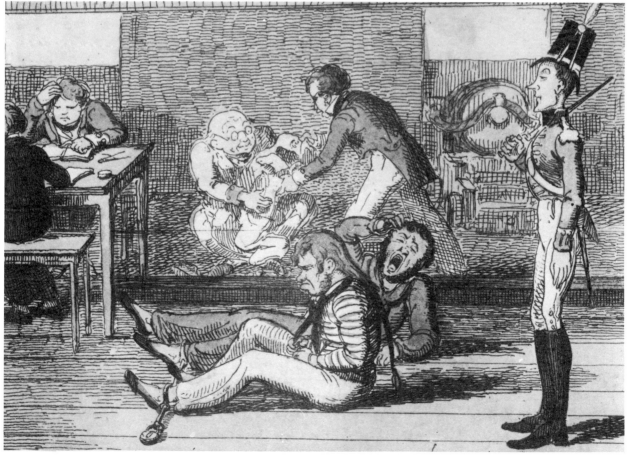

*In irons*

# Organization

**Afterguard.** Originally a term for the seaman who worked the after sails and after gear.

**Anchor watch.** Officer and a small number of seamen detailed to see that the ship did not drag while at anchor.

**Articles of agreement.** Contract between shipowners and crew. It detailed a code of conduct, disciplinary measures and penalties, entitlements to pay, rations, leave and living space aboard.

**Articles of war.** Code of discipline in the Royal Navy, specifying severe penalties for error, misjudgement or incompetence leading to the loss of a ship; also for failure to carry out proper duties. It was incorporated into English naval law in 1661.

**Blood money.** Money paid to an agent such as the keeper of an inn or boarding house for the procurement of men to fill vacancies in a ship's crew.

**Commission.** Document specifying the status of an officer in a naval vessel. It is issued by the Sovereign or Head of State or his authorized representatives. Also, period of service of a naval vessel on a particular assignment or in a particular part of the world where she is to perform her duties.

**Company.** Entire crew of a vessel including all officers and ratings.

**Complement.** Necessary number of men to man a ship.

**Deck watch.** Timepiece used for noting the time when astronomical observations are being taken. Its readings are compared with those of the ship's chronometer.

**Discharge.** Act of signing off a member of the crew, releasing him from obligations incurred in signing on for a particular voyage or period of service.

**Dog.** Another term for DOG WATCH.

**Dog watch.** Either of the two watches between 4 pm and 8 pm.

**Graveyard watch.** Term for the middle watch, from midnight to 4 am, and so called because of the quietness of this period, when most of the crew are asleep. Known sometimes as the 'gravy-eye' watch since the watch-keeper often finds it difficult to keep his eyes open.

*Paying off: a satirical treatment*

**Harbour watch.** Part of the crew on duty watch who stay on board to perform any necessary tasks when the ship is in harbour.

**Larbowlines.** Old term for the men who formed the larboard (port) watch.

**Laws of Oleron.** Early maritime code which set standards and responsibilities for ships' captains in relation to discipline, pay, cargoes and so on, as well as for pilots. The code was enacted by Eleanor of Aquitaine, who attributed it to the skilled seafaring population of the Island of Oleron, part of the Duchy of Aquitaine. It was introduced into England in 1190 by Richard I.

**Light handed.** Said of a vessel which does not have her full complement of crew.

**Little one bell.** One stroke on a ship's bell – signal for a night watch which has just come on duty to muster and be checked.

**Look-out.** Member of a vessel's crew whose duty it is to keep visual watch and report anything he sees. Look-outs are stationed aloft high on the FORE-MAST (01.01) and sometimes at the bow. In fog or where ice hazards prevail, look-outs are posted by day both at the bow and at the mast-head.

**Man the yards.** Ceremonial ranging of the crew along the yards as a salute to a visiting dignitary or in honour of some other occasion. Once customary in the Royal Navy, the practice was discontinued in 1902.

**Messmate.** Person who shares the same mess, particularly one on whom you can depend for help in times of difficulty.

**Morning watch.** That part of the watch between 4 am and 8 am.

**Paying off.** Discharging a crew and paying them all moneys outstanding at the end of a voyage on a merchant vessel. Also, ending the commission of a naval vessel.

**Portage.** Wages earned by a seaman during one complete voyage. Also, wages earned while in port.

**Proper return port.** Port to which a seaman ought to be returned on completion of his term of service on board.

**Purser's pound.** Measure of 14 ounces – 16 ounces less one-eighth.

**Quarantine.** Period of isolation for which a vessel is detained due to an outbreak of infectious disease on board, or due to her arriving from a port or area where an epidemic has occurred. During this period the flag Q, known as the *yellow jack*, is displayed, and the vessel cannot leave until a port doctor certifies her as free from disease.

**Sailing instructions.** Orders pertaining to a particular voyage. Also, specific orders by the commander of a convoy to officers of the various ships in the convoy, specifying points of rendezvous, signals and so on.

**Sailing orders.** Orders setting out precise time of sailing, speed, assigned duties and arrival time. Also, final orders given specifically to a warship.

**Sea-going.** Said of a vessel that has been certified fit to undergo deep-sea voyages, as distinct from a vessel that navigates in sheltered or inland waters.

**Ship's papers.** Documents required to be held in a vessel as a manifest of her ownership and of her compliance with legal requirements. They include the Certificate of Registry, license, muster book, log book, bill of health, ship's articles, charter party, bills of lading and so on.

**Sixty-fourth.** Share-owning system in shipping. The value of a ship was divided into sixty-four shares, each share legally constituting part-ownership in the vessel.

**Spell.** Period spent working on a particular task in a ship.

**Starbowlines.** Common term for the men of the starboard watch.

**Station bill.** List of all members of the crew, detailing their posts for purposes of fire and boat drill and other emergency duties.

**Ticket.** Merchant Navy officer's Certificate of Competency, allowing him to take up a position on board a merchant ship.

**Trick.** Period of duty at the wheel, often lasting about two hours in the case of merchant vessels. The term indicates the particular skills needed by the HELMS-MAN (10.02) in steering.

**Undermanned.** Said of a vessel that does not have a sufficient number of men to form a full complement of crew.

**Watch bill.** List of men in a particular watch, setting out each man's specific duties and station.

**Wreck Commission.** British court, consisting of one to three persons, appointed by the Lord Chancellor to investigate the causes and circumstances of shipping losses and casualties.

*Manning the yards on the flagship* St. Vincent

*Look-out*

# Tools and Equipment

**Beetle.** A heavy MAUL (03.03).

**Belaying pin.** Short bar of brass, iron or wood used to secure a rope and particularly to BELAY (05.07) the running rigging. Usually set in a socket in the PINRAILS (03.15).

**Bell.** Bell and clapper made of brass, used on a ship to announce the time every half an hour and as a signal or alarm in fog or during emergencies.

**Bell rope.** Short hand-rope secured to the clapper of the ship's bell and used to ring the bell.

**Bible.** Term used for a large HOLYSTONE.

**Bilge water alarm.** Warning device set in the ship's BILGES (03.06), consisting of a clockwork bell which strikes when the water level becomes excessive.

**Boatswain's chair.** Seat used by men working the rigging or painting where there is no secure foothold. It consists of a wooden board about twenty-four inches in length. Two lines are passed through holes in its corners to form a bridle by which it can be hoisted aloft.

**Breast band.** Rope or band of canvas passed round the LEADSMAN'S (19.01) body to prevent his falling overboard.

**Can-hooks.** Device for lifting casks, consisting of a rope or chain with two flat hooks at either end which are fitted onto the ends of the casks.

**Carpenter's stopper.** Plug of wood or OAKUM (03.02) used by ships' carpenters to plug small holes caused by gunfire during a battle.

**Check stopper.** Length of small chain used to regulate the speed of a moving wire. One end of the chain is attached to a RING-BOLT (05.03), then around the wire and back through the bolt. Hauling on the free end of the chain checks the speed of the wire.

**Cleat.** Piece of wood or metal with two projecting horns, placed at convenient locations aboard ship, around which ropes are secured.

**Collision mat.** Mat made of heavy canvas held against an accidental opening or leak in the ship's hull below the water-line, to temporarily halt incoming water.

**Creeper.** Pronged iron GRAPNEL (06.02) used for dragging the bottom to recover articles lost overboard.

**Crow.** Lever made of iron with a forked wedge end.

**Ditty bag.** Small canvas bag in which a seaman keeps the gear he needs for working round the decks.

**Ditty box.** Small wooden box in which a seaman keeps his personal valuables and mementoes from home such as letters and photographs.

**Dodger.** Canvas windshield spread to protect the man on watch from the weather.

**Dog vane.** Streamer made of bunting shaped like a conical bag, or constructed from cork and feathers and placed in the after shrouds or the mizen to show the direction of the wind to the HELMSMAN (10.02).

**Fenders.** Pieces of wood or other material, used to cushion the contact of a ship's sides with a quay or with another vessel or object.

**Flake.** Light cradle or stage hung over a ship's side for men to stand on while repairing, re-caulking and so on.

**Hag's teeth.** Strands of rope protruding from an inefficiently woven paunch mat.

**Hand organ.** Large piece of sandstone or HOLYSTONE used to clean the deck. Two seamen drag it along by means of attached lines.

**Heaver.** Wooden lever or staff used to twist or haul tight a STROP (05.01) or rope.

**Hog.** Large brush-like device used to clean the ship's bottom. It is made of twigs held between pieces of timber, attached to ropes and dragged along the hull.

**Holystone.** White soft sandstone used to scrub the ship's decks.

**Jack pin.** Pin-shaped piece of wood or BELAYING PIN used particularly for fitting across the shrouds.

**Jury mat.** Temporary or hastily constructed mat, put together by interweaving bights and ends of rope.

*Cleat*

**Lee fange.** Iron rail athwartships along which a ring or traveller attached to the lower sheet block of a fore-and-aft sail can move from side to side when TACKING (12.08).

**Lifebelt.** Buoyant belt or jacket used to support a person in the water. Originally made of cork blocks, with a cloth lining and straps to secure it round chest and shoulders. Required by British statute to be able to support $16\frac{1}{2}$ lb of iron for 24 hours, in fresh water.

**Lifebuoy.** Buoyant object thrown overboard when necessary to support a person in the water until he or she can be rescued. Usually consists of a canvas-covered cork ring. Required by British statute to be able to support 32 lb of iron for 24 hours, in fresh water.

*Flake*

**Line throwing appliances.** Life-saving pistols, guns or other devices, which can shoot or throw out a line to or from a stranded vessel to another vessel or to the shore.

**Mat.** Flat piece of fabric made of interwoven strands of rope, straw or various fibres, used on ships for sundry protective purposes.

**Mess kit.** Eating and drinking utensils used by a mess.

**Oil bag.** Canvas bag filled with OAKUM (03.02), cotton or waste saturated with oil and punctured in several places to allow the oil to drip out slowly. It is heaved over the side, attached to a SEA ANCHOR (06.02) or line, in order to provide a slick and reduce the seas in heavy weather.

**Paunch mat.** Thick mat made of interwoven strands of rope, used in the rigging and yards as a protection against chafing.

**Prayer book.** Small HOLYSTONE (10.07) used to scrub deck corners which are inaccessible to the larger holystones known as bibles.

**Purser's dirk.** Seaman's knife of uniform pattern. More especially, a midshipman's dirk.

**Purser's knife.** Seaman's clasp knife.

**Russian sennit.** Loose type of mat made of strands of small rope or yarn interwoven across, over and under themselves.

**Scoop.** Small implement used to remove water from the bottom of an open boat.

**Scraper.** Metal instrument with a particularly sharp edge, with or without a wooden handle, but with both ends tapered and one end bent at right angles. Used for scraping the ship's bottom, removing paint and so on.

**Self-mousing hook.** Hook with a mousing that allows easy hooking, but prevents accidental slippage.

**Shackle crow.** Instrument shaped like a crowbar, with a shackle at its tip, used for withdrawing bolts.

**Skeet.** Long-handled dipper used to wet the sails of a yacht in hot weather or to wet the decks and hull in a larger vessel. Also, another term for SCOOP.

**Slush bucket.** Bucket containing a mixture of linseed oil and tallow soap used to grease masts to allow easier movement for the PARRELS (04.03) as well as blocks and running gear. Also, a bucket in which skimmings accumulated from boiling salted meat are kept.

**Smoke sail.** Small sail used as a screen or protection behind the GALLEY (09.01) funnel to prevent smoke fouling the poop or quarterdeck and sparks from blowing into the foresail. Also, a similar protection rigged near a forge when it is being used on deck.

**Soogee moogee.** Mixture, usually of soap or soda and water, used to clean woodwork and paintwork.

**Spanish windlass.** Device used to heave two ropes together. Both ropes are made fast to a line which in turn is secured to a crossbar. Two MARLINE-SPIKES at either end of the crossbar are used to revolve it and draw the two ropes tautly together.

**Speaking trumpet.** Trumpet-shaped instrument used at sea before the introduction of megaphones.

**Squeegee.** Broom-shaped instrument with an edge of rubber or leather fitted to a flat piece of wood, used to push water from the deck surface after it has been cleaned.

**Squilgee.** US name for SQUEEGEE.

**Striker.** Brush attached at right angles to a long handle, used for painting in difficult places.

**Swab.** Mop made of unlaid rope, sometimes fastened to a wooden handle, used for cleaning paintwork or for scrubbing the decks. It can vary from one and a half to four feet long.

**Sword.** Long thin piece of wood used for beating down rope strands when making SWORD MATTING.

**Sword matting.** Mat made of several strands of rope through which small rope or SPUNYARN (05.09) is passed by raising alternate strands and then beating them down with the SWORD.

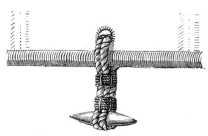

**Toggle.** Pin of wood or other material passed through the eye of a rope or a BECKET (05.03), making a rapid-release attachment.

**Tormentor.** Large fork used to lift boiled salted meat out of the pot or copper in which it is being prepared.

**Weather cloth.** Canvas cloth secured to the weather mizen rigging or around the *crow's nest* to protect the person standing watch on the bridge or aloft. Another term for a DODGER (10.07).

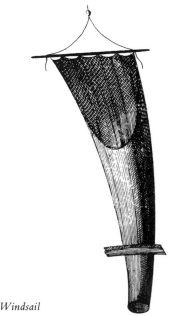

*Windsail*

**Windsail.** Funnel-like canvas tube, suspended as high as possible and held by GUYS (05.04) to face and catch the wind, so conveying fresh air to the lower decks and holds.

# *Tools and Equipment – Rigger*

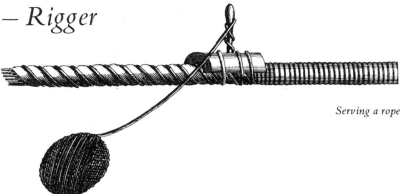

*Serving a rope*

**Fid.** Conical piece of wood, tapering to a point, sometimes used as a MARLINE-SPIKE.

# *Tools and Equipment – Sailmaker*

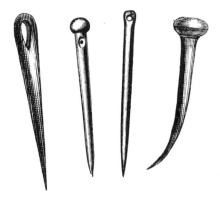

**Marline-spike.** Iron pin, about sixteen inches long and tapered to a point which is either fine or wedge-shaped, used to open and separate the strands of a rope when splicing. It has a hole at the opposite end for a LANYARD (04.08).

**Serving board.** Flat wooden board with a handle, used to wind round or SERVE (05.06) a rope or wire with SPUNYARN (05.09).

**Serving mallet.** Mallet scored with a semi-circular groove, used for serving a rope where maximum tautness is required.

**Splicing hammer.** Hammer tapered at one end, used in splicing.

**Top maul.** Heavy mallet kept in the maintop or foretops to be used to remove the topmast FID when necessary.

**Palm.** Strip of leather or rawhide worn around the hand to which is attached a metal disc or cup, which sits in the palm of the hand and is used as a thimble to force sailmakers' needles through canvas. The thimble has several indentations in its surface in which the eye of the needle sits.

**Pricker.** Small pointed implement with a wooden handle, or a small MARLINE-SPIKE, used to prick holes in canvas.

**Roping needle.** Strong needle curved towards the point, used to sew rope or wire cordage to the edges of sails or awnings.

**Roping palm.** Heavy type of PALM used in conjunction with a ROPING NEEDLE when sewing rope to a sail. The iron thimble is larger and stronger than that of a sailmaker's palm and has fewer but larger indentations to take heavier needles.

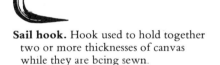

**Rubber.** Round-faced steel instrument used to flatten or smooth down the seams of sails after sewing has been completed.

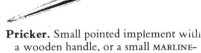

**Sail hook.** Hook used to hold together two or more thicknesses of canvas while they are being sewn.

**Sail needle.** Needle used for sewing sails, which has a triangular cross-section at the tip, and comes in four different sizes.

**Seaming palm.** Lighter PALM used in stitching together seams of canvas. The iron thimble has many small indentations to suit the lighter types of needles used.

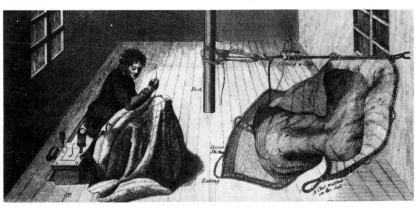

# Clothes

**Blazer.** Jacket which derives its name from HMS *Blazer*, whose captain in 1845 dressed his crew in special blue-and-white striped jerseys.

**Monkey jacket.** Heavy but short navy blue coat, reaching just below the waist, worn by petty officers and officers. Originally worn by seamen, particularly for work in cold or stormy weather, as its shortness kept their legs free for climbing.

**Oilskins.** Waterproof coat, trousers and hat made of cotton, linen or silk treated or soaked with linseed oil, affording maximum protection in bad weather.

**Pea jacket.** Short thick double-breasted coat made of coarse woollen fabric.

**Reefer.** Another term for PEA JACKET, worn particularly by midshipmen.

**Slops.** Clothing kept in the slop chest (a store of various clothes) and held by the master of a ship for sale to the crew, since many seamen embarked on a voyage without adequate clothing.

*Oilskins*

# Food and Health

**Burgoo.** Boiled oatmeal porridge, seasoned with salt, sugar and butter. Said to originate with Norse sailors of the Viking age.

**Crackerjack.** Sailor's dish consisting of preserved meat or soup, mixed with broken ship's biscuits and other ingredients.

**Dandyfunk.** Sailor's dish consisting of broken ship's biscuits mixed with molasses and other available ingredients.

**Fanny Adams.** Royal Navy term for tinned meat. Derived from the name of a child murdered in the 1860s. Later came to mean 'absolutely nothing', as in 'sweet Fanny Adams'.

**Grog.** Rum diluted with water. First introduced as a Royal Navy ration in 1740 and named after Admiral Sir Edward Vernon (1684–1757), who was nicknamed 'Old Grog' because he

habitually wore a cloak made of grogram, a type of coarse cloth.

**Hard tack.** Nickname for ship's biscuits.

**Harriet Lane.** Nickname for tinned meat. Said to derive from the name of a girl murdered in 1874, or from that of a girl who was once caught up in the machinery of a tinned meat factory.

**Lime juice.** Obligatory ration introduced on British naval ships to combat the prevalence of scurvy. British sailors were accordingly nicknamed 'lime juicers' but the practice then spread to the navies of other countries.

**Liverpool pantiles.** Hard ship's biscuits issued on sailing ships, often infested with weevils.

**Lobscouse.** Stew consisting of salt meat, potatoes, broken ship's biscuits, onions and available spices.

**Manavalins.** Odds and ends. Originally, certain foods left over from the master's table, which were prized by the ship's apprentices as luxuries.

**Midshipmen's nuts.** Slang term for broken ship's biscuits.

**Old horse.** Nickname for salt beef.

**Poor jack, poor john.** Derogatory name for dried and salted fish, mainly cod, occasionally issued on Royal Navy ships in place of pork or salt beef.

**Salt horse.** Slang for the salt beef issued at sea, referring to its toughness as it came out of the cask. It was the seaman's staple diet.

**Salt junk.** Slang for salt beef, implying that any old meat was thrown into the cask.

**Scorbutic.** Said of conditions which give rise to SCURVY.

**Scurvy.** Disease caused by the lack of Vitamin C, brought about by exclusive feeding on salted meat aboard ships with no fresh vegetables to vary the diet. Symptoms are spongy flesh, swollen gums, tiredness, and debility that can lead to death. Prevalent in ships which sailed the long Far Eastern routes, particularly in the eighteenth century.

**Sea pie.** Seaman's dish made of meat and vegetables layered between crusts of pastry, the number of layers giving it the name of 'double decker' or 'three decker'.

**Ship fever.** Name given in the eighteenth century to typhus aboard ships, caused by unhygienic conditions in overcrowded ships, particularly on long voyages.

**Soft tack.** Bread baked at sea, as distinguished from the stored ship's biscuit known as HARD TACK.

**Weevil.** Small red beetle which can live either in larval or in adult form in various stored foods. Found in ship's biscuits and often in cargoes of grain.

# Sailors' Slang

**Admiralty sweep.** A wide turn of a ship's boat to come alongside. Anything overdone.

**Adrift.** Late, absent; especially when supposed to join ship.

**All my eye and Betty Martin.** Nonsense; without foundation in fact.

**Andrew.** Short form of ANDREW MILLER.

**Andrew Miller.** Seaman's nickname for the Royal Navy, derived from the name of a notorious PRESS-GANG (10.05) officer.

**Awning.** Piecrust; particularly when made by a member of a broadside mess.

**Belay (it).** Shut up. Stop it. Pipe down. Technically, as you were; cancel it.

**Bent.** Worn in with use; particularly sails.

**Between the devil and the deep blue sea.** No choice. (The devil was a seam near the keel.)

**Bleed the monkey.** To clandestinely remove spirits from a cask through a hole, usually by sucking through a straw or pipe.

**Blood and guts.** Seaman's nickname for the Union Jack.

**The boats.** Destroyers in particular; generally, small ships.

**Bristol fashion.** Very efficient, neat and seamanlike – 'shipshape and Bristol fashion'. Derived from the period when Bristol was the main British west-coast port and her shipping was conducted in a businesslike and orderly fashion.

**Brothel creepers.** White shoes with brown leather decoration, frowned on as evidence of depraved taste.

**Bucko, or bucko mate.** Nickname for the brutal mates employed aboard American merchant ships of the late 1800s and early 1900s. Crews were worked cruelly hard to round Cape Horn in the shortest possible time.

**Bum boat.** Any local small boat providing a service, particularly accosting a ship with wares.

**Bunk with.** Share cabin or lodgings ashore.

**By and large.** All things considered.

**By the wind.** Broke, penniless.

**Cally ho.** Callao. Unduly free and easy, especially ship's routine.

**Cape horn fever.** Malingerer's feigned illness in bad weather. The weather off Cape Horn was often so bad that a feigned illness was the only way of keeping out of dangerous and uncomfortable conditions.

**Cape Stiff.** Nickname for Cape Horn.

**Carney.** Hypocrisy and cant. Said to derive from a Captain Carney who was deceptively mild when ashore but unbearably harsh at sea.

**Cheerily.** With a good will. Also, a capstan song.

**Chippy chap.** Nickname for the carpenter of a ship or a member of his crew.

**Chips.** Nickname for the ship's carpenter.

**Clewed up.** Very knowledgeable; particularly at work.

**Colonel.** A person who provides hospitality ashore.

**Copper bottomed.** Very (doubly) safe and sure.

**Crab fat.** Much used Royal Navy grey paint. From the name of an ointment often used by sailors against crab-lice.

**Crimp.** Person who would SHANGHAI (10.05) a seaman, being paid for delivering his victim to a short-handed vessel about to sail.

**Cross his bows.** To annoy someone.

**Cumshaw.** Backhander, commission, something obtained free. Used particularly in the Far East.

**Cut of his jib.** The (characteristic) way he looks (or acts).

**Cut and run.** To depart hurriedly.

**Dab toe.** A seaman. (Washes decks in bare feet.)

**Dead men.** Untidy ropes' ends over the ship's side.

**Deep-sea sailor.** One who has sailed the seven seas, rather than on coasting ships.

**Devil to pay and no pitch hot.** An apparently insoluble predicament. Derives from the outermost deck seam, the *devil*, which a sailor had to *pay*, seal with pitch.

**Dhobie, or dhobey.** The act of washing clothes and so on.

**Dicky.** A diminutive. For instance, dicky run. Short leave ashore in the evening, rather than long leave.

**Dingbat.** Slang term for a small rope mop used for drying the decks.

**Dockyard job.** Big or heavy job. A sit-down job in the lavatory.

**Doctor.** Nickname for the ship's cook. Derives from the days when the cook was in charge of the ship's medicine chest.

**Doggie.** Assistant, helper, friend.

**Doggo.** Not blessed with good looks. Also, to be quiet: lie doggo.

**Dogs.** Two-hour watches between 1600 and 2000 hours, designed to break up the sequence of four-hour watches so that the same men would not do the same watches day in day out. Also, time off for recreational games.

**Donkey's breakfast.** Very badly performed. A mess. Term for a seaman's bunk or mattress, in the days when it was made of straw.

Cut of his jib

**Dooflicker,** or **doo hickie.** A gadget or device too technical for a simple sailor.

**Drip.** To complain. A complainer, usually with no just cause.

**Duff.** Dessert. Also, bad, not good enough.

**Dunnage.** Kit or baggage of a seaman.

**Easting down.** The long sea route to Australia via the Cape of Good Hope.

**Eat the wind.** Take an opponent's wind.

**Father.** The commanding officer (captain).

**Fine trim.** In the best of spirits.

**Firm.** One or more of the crew who provide a service for payment; for instance, dhobie firm.

**First turn of the screw pays all debts.** When a port is left, so are all encumbrances.

**Fish's tit.** Useless, nothing; for instance, 'I don't give a fish's tit' (I don't give a damn).

**Flap.** Panic or confusion.

**Flogging a dead horse.** The phrase derives from seamen's slang for a month's work on board ship, called a dead horse, for which the crew was paid in advance. On the last evening of the month the crew would flog a straw-stuffed effigy of a horse as they paraded it around the ship, finally throwing it overboard.

**Foo-foo,** or **poo-poo.** Effeminate or not understood. For instance, talcum powder might be called 'foo-foo powder'; and an object whose precise technical name could not be remembered might be called a 'foo-foo box', 'foo-foo valve' and so on.

**Friday while.** Friday to Monday week-end leave.

**Full house.** A mixed grill. Everything that is going. Probably from the poker term.

**Gash.** Free, or more particularly 'left over'.

**Gilguy.** See DOOFLICKER.

**Green coat.** To wear a green coat: to feign ignorance in order to escape responsibility or retribution.

**Green rub.** Undeserved rebuke.

**Griff.** Information.

**Grippos.** Something for free.

**Growl.** Seamen's conversation in the forecastle.

**Gunnels under.** Overloaded with work, or with drink (drunk).

Horse marine

**Half seas over.** Nearly drunk.

**Half shot.** Nearly drunk.

**Handsomely.** With great care; from the technical term used in boatwork.

**Harbour style.** Easy and relaxed; no heavy sea work.

**Hard up in a clinch.** Seaman's saying indicating that he is in a difficult position and can see no clear way out of it.

**Harry flatters.** (Taking a horizontal rest. ('Harry' has no particular meaning here.)

**Heavy weather.** To make heavy weather: to exaggerate the difficulty of a job. To be inexpert.

**Hide droghing.** Carrying a cargo of hides up and down the coast of the Americas.

**Hoggin.** The sea.

**Hogwash.** Nonsense; no truth in it. Also, the sea.

**Hoist in.** To understand, to comprehend.

**Horse marine.** Clumsy or awkward seaman. Derived from the cavalry regiments which used to serve on board the old men-of-war, or from the incongruous concept of a marine on horseback.

**Hussif.** Corruption of housewife. Sailor's kit for effecting repairs to clothing.

**I'm inboard.** 'I'm all right, Jack'; provided the speaker's own welfare is ensured, everything is fine.

**It's not my part of ship.** It is not my responsibility.

**Jack nastyface.** Nickname for a sailor who is disliked by his shipmates. Derived from the pen-name of a seaman who exposed bad conditions in the Royal Navy in the early nineteenth century.

**Jack strop.** One against the establishment or authority, a SEA-LAWYER (10.12) type.

**Jack tar.** Old nickname for a sailor, now used by seamen only in a slightly derogatory sense. Said to derive from the tarred canvas seamen used to wear in bad weather.

**Jaunty.** Term for the master-at-arms in the Royal Navy. Derived from the French *gendarme*, it refers to the master-at-arms' responsibility for the maintenance of rules and regulations aboard.

**Jaw.** Insolent backchat to a superior.

Gunnels under

**Jewing.** Sailors' term for sewing or repairing clothes. (Jewing firm, and so on.)

**Jimmy bungs.** Name for the ship's cooper.

Jimmy Ducks

**Jimmy ducks.** Name for a galley boy or butcher's assistant. Derived from the rating in charge of poultry on Royal Navy ships.

**Jolly.** Name for a Royal Marine.

**Jonnick.** Honest, fair, correct, true.

**Joss.** Loosely, luck or fortune. Used in the China seas; for instance, bad joss, joss stick. An offering to bring good luck.

**Judas.** Hanging free and serving no good use.

**Keelhaul to.** Phrase representing a dire threat of reprisal.

**King's** or **queen's hard bargain.** Useless and inefficient sailor. Royal Navy term derived from army use.

**Know the ropes.** To be experienced; know the dodges.

Lash up

**Kye.** Seaman's name for cocoa made from solid slabs and served hot on watch.

**Land sharks.** Lawyers. Considered very unlucky to have aboard for any purpose.

**Lash up.** A temporary or badly performed job.

**Lazy.** Semi-technical term for a necessary but (temporarily) unused fitting.

**Lively.** Quickly and with enthusiasm; for instance, 'look lively there' (hurry up).

**Loggerheads (at).** To quarrel or not see eye to eye. (Loggerhead, a tool for sealing seams and a handy weapon in an argument.)

**Look out for.** To act as a substitute on duty.

**Lubber.** Lazy and clumsy seaman; one without sufficient experience or skill.

**Lubberland.** Imaginary land of paradise where even clumsy lubbers can be tolerated.

**Lubberly.** In an unseamanlike way; slovenly.

**Luffed.** Caught or detailed for an unpleasant task.

**Make and mend.** A half day off. Formerly, time off to mend clothes, very necessary with the hard wear experienced at sea.

**Maltese lace.** Frayed edges to trousers, sleeves and so on.

**Matelot.** Lower-deck term for a seaman in the Royal Navy. Derives from the French for 'sailor'.

**Money for old rope.** Very easy job; cheap.

**Monkey.** A diminutive; something small or little; for instance, monkey block, monkey jacket.

**Mudhook.** The anchor.

**Nelson's blood.** Ship's rum. (Nelson's body was reputedly preserved in it.)

**Nip.** A small turn to hold a rope temporarily.

**Nor'easter.** No pay on pay-day. Not Entitled.

**Now she's talking.** Referring to the sound as a boat gets under way.

**Old and bold.** Elderly officer from the lower deck.

**Old man.** Nickname for the master of a Merchant Navy ship irrespective of his age.

**Old salt.** A very experienced seaman, not necessarily aged. A retired mariner.

**Old ships.** Old shipmates; sailors who have sailed together on the same ship.

**On the make.** Making the desired course when TACKING (12.08). Also, feathering one's nest.

**On the right tack.** Making the correct approach.

Pipe down

**On the trot.** Successively; for instance, two watches on the trot.

**On the wrong tack.** To misunderstand the underlying purpose.

**Oppo.** Shipboard pal and shore-going companion.

**Paddy's purchase.** Derogatory term for a rope LEAD (05.07) that increases work rather than saves it.

Part brass rags

**Prick.** Plug of pipe tobacco made up from duty-free tobacco leaves; sometimes flavoured with rum.

**Pump ship.** Urinate.

**Purser's dip.** A candle.

**Purser's grin.** Insincere or sarcastic smile or sneer.

**Put your ears back.** Eat to the full, usually said to a guest. Anything run 'by the book', over-zealous.

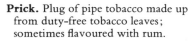

**Rig.** Clothing worn, uniform; for instance, 'Rig of the day will be . . .'

**Rogue's yarn.** The tell-tale Admiralty thread in ships' rope. Hence, a giveaway.

**Rorty.** Bellicose; particularly because of drink.

**Round the buoy.** To take a second helping at meals.

**Sail close to the wind.** To take a chance, especially with authority or accepted ship standards.

Sail close to the wind

**Panic stations.** Ready for an emergency.

**Part brass rags.** Break a friendship in anger. Said to derive from the fact that close friends in the Royal Navy would share cleaning rags.

**Peggy.** Nickname for a seaman detailed to clean the mess. Originally, an apprentice who acted as unpaid steward to seamen or other apprentices, fetching their meals, cleaning the deck and so on.

The quack

**Pipe down.** Shut up. Also, a proper order to be silent.

**Point beacher.** Old Portsmouth prostitute.

**Poodle faking.** Going ashore to meet the young ladies.

**Poop off.** Fire a small cannon. Also, perform an ineffectual action.

**Poor as piss and twice as nasty.** Anything really bad.

**The quack.** Ship's medical officer (a friendly term).

**Quarterdecker.** Officer excessively conscious of his rank and prerogatives.

**Queen of the road.** A vessel close-hauled and having the right of way.

**Quid.** A wad of chewing tobacco.

**Rattle (in the).** To be in official trouble; to be run in.

**Sailor's disgrace.** Seaman's name for the 'foul anchor' badge of the Lords of the Admiralty. Derived from the arms of Lord Howard of Effingham, commander of the English fleet which defeated the Spanish Armada.

**Salt beef squire.** Royal Navy nickname for an officer who has come up from the lower deck (from the ranks).

**Salt horse.** Royal Navy term for an officer who has not specialized in any professional branch such as gunnery or signals.

**Scouse.** Food; especially ships' meals.

**Scran.** Food; originally ship's biscuits.

**Scranbag.** Depository for articles carelessly left lying about (left *loafing*). The payment for retrieval was a bar of soap.

**Scrimshaw.** A hobby to while away the time off watch. Now the name of whale's-teeth carvings, usually made by whalemen.

**Scrub** (vb). To cancel.

**Scrub round.** To perform a task inadequately or superficially.

## Scuppered

**Scuppered.** Frustrated, defeated or killed.

**Sea lawyer.** A know-all on board ship; a trouble-maker who argues against authority but seldom follows his own advice.

**Second greaser.** Nickname for a second mate.

**Sell before the mast.** To auction off a dead man's effects. His messmates usually bought in at inflated prices, to look after his dependants and to avoid the stigma of charity.

## Shellback

**Shellback.** Old sailor who spins well-embroidered yarns of his sea experiences.

**Ship it green.** To run into unexpected trouble. Specifically, to have the sea breaking onto the forecastle.

**Shonky.** A mean messmate, who will drink but avoid paying his round.

**Shot across the bows.** Verbal warning to someone treading on dangerous conversational ground, usually women or reputation.

**Shot in the locker.** Money left unspent towards the end of a run ashore.

---

**Skate.** One who misbehaves ashore, though usually very good at his job.

**Sky pilot.** A clergyman.

**Sling your hammock.** To go, usually for good; pack up.

**Slip one's cable.** To die.

**Snotty.** Royal Navy nickname for a midshipman. It was said that Nelson first ordered three buttons sewn on midshipmen's sleeves to prevent them from wiping their noses on their sleeves.

**Snowball hitch.** A badly made knot that will not hold.

## Sod's law

**Sod's law.** Unfortunate things always happen at the worst time and in the worst place. Sometimes known as the Law of Imbuggerance.

**Sod's opera.** The ship's concert; very often impromptu and highly libellous of authority.

**Sojering.** Hanging back when work is to be done.

**Soldier's wind.** Sailing with the wind abaft.

**Son of a gun.** Complimentary term originally meaning a seaman born at sea. Derived from the period when wives of seamen lived on board in harbour and even, occasionally, at sea, and had to give birth in between the guns, since other deck space had to be kept clear.

## Stonnicky

---

**Sparnyarn job.** A temporary job. A badly performed task.

**Spidereen,** or **spidereen frigate.** Mythical ship. 'The spidereen frigate with nine decks' would be the flippant reply of a reluctant sailor pressed for the name of his ship.

**Spithead pheasant.** Smoked herring; kipper or bloater.

**Splice the main brace.** To issue a special ration of rum to the crew, on the occasion of some rare celebration. Derived from the fact that the main BRACE (04.09) was very rarely spliced or rejoined if damaged.

**Spouter.** Whaleman.

**Square off.** Make tidy; especially caps or clothing.

**Sticks.** The ship's masts. Also, old term for a Royal Marine drummer.

**Stone frigate.** Shore establishment.

**Stonnicky.** Rope's end used to chase sluggards.

*Swing the lead.*

**Stow it.** Shut up.

**Stretch off the land.** A short nap. Derived from old sailing days when the crew of a ship TACKING (12.08) along a coast could relax their attention when the vessel stretched on the seaward LEG (12.08).

*Suck the monkey*

**Suck the monkey.** To sneak spirits from a cask by sucking through a straw. Originally, to suck out rum surreptitiously inserted into a coconut, whose end was said to resemble a monkey's face.

**Sun over the foreyard.** Phrase meaning 'time for a dink'. Derived from the fact that the sun would appear over the foreyard towards noon, indicating that the officers could allow themselves their first drink of the day.

*Trim the dish*

**Swallow the anchor.** To leave the sea; or to retire.

**Swing the lamp.** To tell a tall sea story.

**Swing the lead.** To pretend to be sick; or not to pull one's weight.

**Swipes.** Drinks; mostly the overlooked portions left in used glasses.

**Swordspoint (at).** Quarrelling.

**Tack.** Food, particularly ship's biscuits (hard tack).

**Taken aback.** Surprised, stopped short.

**Tally.** Sailor's name; anyone's name.

**Tarpaulin muster.** Collection for some joint, often charitable, purpose. Money would be collected in a piece of tarpaulin.

**Taut.** Very efficient, smart; for instance, taut ship (no loose rigging), or taut hand.

**Tea boat.** The provision of mugs of tea; 'tea-boat time' means stand easy.

**Three half hitches (are more than the king's yacht wants).** Comment to someone who makes too many unnecessary fastenings in ropes or takes excessive precautions.

**Three sheets in the wind.** Drunk.

**Tidley.** Very smart. (Sometimes, 'very efficient', but TAUT would be more usual in that case.)

**Tom Cox's traverse.** Tricks of an artful dodger, a sailor who gives the appearance of working but in fact accomplishes nothing.

**Top gear.** Upper garments.

**Tricks.** Watches.

**Trim the dish.** Level things up. Specifically, rearrange the passengers in a small boat to preserve an even keel.

**Tub** (vb). To disconcert or puzzle; particularly if done deliberately to teach someone a lesson.

**Vast heaving.** 'Stop pulling my leg. I don't believe you.'

**Warm the bell.** To stop work too early.

**Wash out.** Cancel.

**Watch below.** General term for time off.

**Watch on, stop on.** Always working.

**Water bewitched and tea begrudged.** Seaman's description of the tea served below as his main hot drink.

**Weigh off.** To give an inferior in rank a good telling off for a misdeed or mistake.

**Wet as a scrubber.** Foolish or daft.

**Whack.** Regular ration of provisions, as supplied to each seaman according to regulations.

*Whistle up a wind*

**Whistle up a wind.** To indulge in vain hopes of something; especially when trying to raise money for shore-going.

**Whistling psalms to the taffrail.** Providing advice that will be ignored.

**White rat.** A lower-deck spy for authority.

**Winger.** A protégé or sidekick. The 'junior hand' of a twosome.

**Wrinkle.** A smart way of doing something or, perhaps, of dodging it.

**Wrist-watch and motor-bike navy.** Older hands' scathing term for the newer entries between the two world wars.

**Yellow bellies.** Term for Chinese ashore as opposed to Chinese who were entered on the ship's books, that is, went with the ship. The latter were regarded with a great deal of affection by the crew.

**Zizz.** To sleep; in particular to get one's head down between watches.

**Zob.** To moan in a whining way.

**Zobbing match.** A concerted duet by two moaners. Also, an argument for the sake of it.

# Calls & Commands

The big square-rigged ship looked and very often was a complicated and difficult creation, requiring skilled and experienced masters, officers and crews, and above all needing expert handling. She lived by the wind, and good winds were noisy, often shrieking and screaming through the gigantic maze of the standing rigging, especially deafening in anything of a gale.

The merchant-man differed greatly from the wind-blown ship-of-war, in that, after the first third or so of the nineteenth century, she did not often get involved in battles. The sea and its storms were her enemies, though they could be friendly, too, especially the storms from astern of her if she was able to shorten canvas in time. Unlike the old sailing ships-of-war, which often looked like lumbering great galleons with tiered decks pierced for guns (the ship herself often grossly over-manned for everything but the guns' service), the merchant-man was a slim racehorse, lithe and lean and sinewy in all her 3,000 tons, with a sail area of 50,000 or 60,000 square feet or more to drive her, and crew enough (and no more) to handle a few sails at a time while keeping all under control.

It was the sailing warships, very naturally, which developed the drill – drill on deck, sail-handling drill aloft, gunnery drill all the time. Merchant seamen quickly learned their business, because it was limited to pure seamanship alow and aloft, and because crews usually comprised just enough seamen to handle the essential work, in two watches – four-hour stretches of duty, one on and one off, throughout a whole voyage of anything from 6,000 to 16,000 miles, on one non-stop run. Whatever else the merchant seaman of the last century of square-rigged ships had to master, it included little or no drill. Naval ships had to allow for casualties, of course, often at a heavy rate; and the working of the ship, her sails and gear, and of her guns had to go on while battle lasted, and after that.

So the system of organized, standardized orders of command was of necessity introduced into the Navy and carefully developed there. Pipes and calls on the bos'n's whistle and standardized, distinctive phrases loudly shouted were the backbone of it all, and these were learned almost as holy writ. This sort of semi-mechanization of the mind kept things going in action, too, and that was vital. In the merchant-man, the wind shouted and roared in the rigging for all to hear and understand: her war was with storm and sea, and she fought back with good officers and good men.

The following are just about all the effective standardized orders I ever heard, in half-a-dozen ocean-going square-rigged ships on deep-water voyages:

All hands on deck!
Call out the watch!
Ready about!
Stand-by to wear ship!
Stand-by to tack ship!
Lee-oh! (Helm is down: she is coming up; alert there now!)
Mains'l haul! (Swing the main yards and the mizen!)

These were all very meaningful orders, to be obeyed immediately. 'Call out the watch!' referred to the watch below, of course; for it often took both watches – the whole crew – to deal swiftly and effectively with emergencies. 'Stand-by!' meant to get ready for the intended manoeuvre, and for small crews this always involved a lot of work just to get the gear clear for running.

Other orders included:

Haul round the head yards! (To the other tack.)
Lee fore brace! (Sharpen the yards up – the fore first – for a heading wind.)
Weather main brace! (Square in a bit for a fairing wind.)
Stand-by the royal halyards! or Stand-by the topgallant! (Prepare swiftly to reduce sail.)
Aloft and furl!
Set the . . . . . . . . . . . ! (Whatever upper sail is not set at the time.)
Splice the main brace! (Lay aft for a tot after herculean efforts, well made.)

The last was an order not often heard in merchant-men in my experience, and unknown internationally. Decent food throughout the voyage was of far more importance than the rare tot.

The old-time sailing warship, however, often had to manoeuvre skilfully in formations hard to maintain, to keep careful station under sail, to carry out fleet manoeuvres. On board such a warship in battle, the naval seaman might become a casualty at any time. Moreover, his ship's main purpose was to function as a sort of floating fortress with as many heavy guns as possible, with a sufficiency of well-drilled and courageous men to handle them at a maximum rate of fire for as long as possible. So the ship-of-war and her people needed standardized orders drilled into them. It was vital to have uniform calls and commands, whether trilled upon a bos'n's pipe or shouted by stentorian voices. Obey at once! That was the essential thing.

The merchant-man, on the other hand, made her voyages using the bare forces of nature directly and constantly, from beginning to end of the voyage; for the wind gave her way through the water, and her master and his officers (usually only two) knew how to use that wind. So did the long-voyage crews, following minimal orders. 'Lee fore brace!' or 'Weather main brace!', such curtly phrased orders, though concise, were clear to all; for the first meant that the wind was heading (which was bad) and the second that the wind was fairing (which was good). Just the three words of each order told the merchant crew all they needed to know, and the handful aboard and on watch jumped to the job.

The commerical square-rigged ships or the long-voyage great barques depended on the seaman's quick understanding of what was required, in the light of his experience. His 'calls' came from wind and sails and the thunder of their tremendous noise. What had to be done was immediately obvious to such seamen. They well knew how to get on with it safely and at once. The whistle of pipes or the standardized shouts of leather-lunged bos'n's, mates, et al, were quite superfluous. The ship in a gale screamed her needs, and her crew knew how to respond to them. Get the great sails off her to ease the strain; if too late to save them, let the kites blow away with a thunder of wildly flapping, torn canvas. Let it go! You can do nothing

about it anyway once it splits. Get on with the real job of saving what can be saved! Above all, save the ship.

The mates will direct you if you cannot see; and you cannot hear, either, such is the fury and the tumult of the wild gale and the noise of all its damage to the over-press of canvas the ship is carrying. Noise won't hurt you. Get on with the real job – cope, save, and live! Cope properly, save what can be saved (under your officers' direction). Let the rest go, and hope to be brought safely to another morning. There are other good sails in the sail locker: you may bend them when the ugly gale hurls itself away across the horizon, and be damned to it.

Looking back on the wild night, you may realize that you heard no man-made calls or commands at all. Nor did you need them, for the true seaman could see (and hear, at times almost to the depths of desperation) what needed to be done and get on with it if he possibly could, without any shouting or piping at all. He lived in and served his beautiful and (potentially) dangerous ship as a man close to his creator but cut off from all else.

ALAN VILLIERS

# Hails and Cries

**Abandon ship.** Order to leave ship, given when facing disaster and when there is no hope of saving the ship.

**Ahoy.** Standard hailing cry to attract attention.

**All hands,** or **All hands on deck.** Summons to the entire crew.

**All hands to quarters.** Order to officers and crew to take up their allotted stations and prepare for action. This was done either by beating the drum or by the boatswain and his mates piping at the hatchways.

**All's well.** Affirmation of safety or security proclaimed by the sentinel every half-hour (when the bell is struck) during the night watches. (In effect, the call shows that the sentinel is awake.)

**Avast.** Stop, or pause, in any operation; for instance, 'avast heaving'.

**Aye, aye, sir.** Standard naval acknowledgement that an order has been understood and will be executed.

**Bear a hand.** Exclamation generally meaning 'assist', 'give a hand'.

**Belay.** Order or exclamation meaning 'stop' or instructing hands to secure a line round a belaying pin.

**Cheerily,** or **Cheerly.** Encouragement to work heartily, vigorously or quickly; for instance, 'Row cheerily in the boats' or 'Lower away cheerily'.

**Easy.** Lessen the effort put into a particular action; or take care.

**Hands.** Used in calling the hands to take up position or to stand by to perform a particular operation, as in 'Hands by the topgallant sheets'.

**Helm's alee.** Cry uttered when going about under sail. It warns hands that the vessel is coming up to the wind, for the helmsman has put the helm down, that is, towards the wind's direction to swing the vessel across it.

**Lower cheerily.** Order to lower rapidly.

**Lower handsomely.** Order to lower very carefully, gradually.

**Man.** Used in ordering hands to stand by at a particular place in the vessel or to handle a particular part of the running rigging, as in 'Man the weather after-braces'.

**Man overboard.** Alarm cry when a person has been seen to fall overboard.

**Off.** Used in ordering the release or removal of a particular item, as in 'Off nippers'.

**Off and fair.** Instruction to remove a damaged part, repair it (*fair* it in the sense of returning it to its right form) and put it back in position.

**Sail ho.** Cry of the LOOK-OUT (10.06) on catching sight of a sailing vessel.

**Show a leg.** Traditional Royal Navy order to hands to make some show of getting out of their hammocks. Often explained as a relic of the time when women were allowed on board while the ship was in port, and boatswain's mates would check the sex of a hammock's occupant in this way.

**Stow.** Used in ordering a particular item put away, as in 'Stow the jib'.

**Together.** Injunction to hands to work together or simultaneously, in heaving, rowing, hoisting and so on.

**Turn.** When heaving the hand LOG (19.01), the order to turn the sand-glass and start timing in order to calculate the ship's speed.

**Vast.** Shortened form of AVAST.

**Watch there watch.** When using a deep-sea LEAD (05.07), warning that line is about to run out.

**Where away?** Enquiry to a LOOK-OUT (10.06) reporting an object or sail he has sighted; a request for its precise bearings.

# Handling Sails

**Aboard main tack.** Order given when CLOSE-HAULING (12.11), instructing the hands to haul the TACK (04.09) of the mainsail down to the CHESS-TREE (03.15).

**About-ship.** Order to the crew to prepare to TACK (12.08), or GO ABOUT (12.08).

**Aloft.** Used in ordering hands aloft to handle sails and rigging; for instance, 'Foretop men aloft furl the topgallant sail'.

**Attend,** or **'tend.** Used in ordering hands to ensure smooth functioning of a certain component; for instance, 'Attend the weather topsail braces', when reefing topsails.

**Away aloft.** Order to hands to climb aloft preparatory to handling sails and rigging.

**Bend.** Used in ordering hands to attach particular parts of the rigging; for instance, 'Bend the topgallant and royal gear'.

**Brace.** Used in ordering hands to adjust the BRACES (04.09) controlling horizontal movement of the yards; for instance, 'Brace up the after yards' or 'Brace in the foreyard'.

**Brail.** Used in ordering a fore-and-aft sail gathered in to its mast, as in 'Brail in the spanker'.

**Haul of haul.** Order given prior to going about; all the necessary ropes and tackle are to be pulled as tight as possible.

**Hoist,** or **hoist away.** Order to hands manning the relevant lines to pull and lift a yard or sail into place, as in 'Hoist the topsails'. Also, the order to hoist in a boat from overside.

**In.** Used as an order to shorten sail (with the word 'take' understood); usually applied to upper square sails, as in 'In topgallant sails'.

**Lay in.** Order to hands aloft on yard FOOT-ROPES (04.04) to move in towards the mast.

**Lay out.** Order to hands to spread out on the FOOT-ROPES (04.04) along the yard.

**Let draw.** Release the weather FORE-SHEET (04.09) of a head sail during TACKING (12.08), leaving the sail under control of the lee SHEET (04.09).

**Let fall.** Let a sail drop and extend from the yard.

**Let fly.** Order, in an emergency, to release the SHEETS (04.09) completely, as quickly as possible.

**Let go.** Release a mooring line or other rope, as in 'Let go the brails'.

**Lower and dip.** Order given when a DIPPING LUG (04.14) has to be lowered and dipped round to the other side of the mast while GOING ABOUT (12.08).

**Lower away.** Lower a yard or sail when sails are being taken in.

**Mainsail haul.** Order given on a square-rigged ship when tacking; foremast yards are braced ABACK (12.11), the after yards are braced round and the mainsail is set for the new TACK (12.08).

**Raise tacks and sheets.** Order, given when TACKING (12.08), to raise the CLEWS (04.12) high enough to allow the lower sails and their tack and sheet blocks to clear the bulwarks and any other obstructions when the yards are swung.

**Ready about,** or **ready all.** Warning given to the crew to stand by, alert at their stations, ready for TACKING (12.08).

**Reef.** Used in ordering REEFING (12.12) operations to start, as in 'Reef topsails'.

**Rig in.** Used in ordering a BOOM (04.07) withdrawn from its position at the end of a yard or bowsprit, as in 'Rig in the topmast studding-sail booms'.

**Rig out.** Used in ordering a BOOM (04.07) run out at the end of a yard or bowsprit, to extend the foot of a sail, as in 'Rig out the topgallant studding-sail booms'.

**Set.** Used in ordering the setting of a particular sail, as in 'Set the mainsail'.

**Sheet home.** Haul on the SHEETS (04.09) of a given and fully extend it.

**Shorten and trim sail.** Order given to take in lesser sails and re-BRACE (12.09) the yards to improve their set.

**Shorten sail.** Reduce the sail area set.

**Slack.** Used in ordering parts of the running rigging slackened off to facilitate the handling of yards and sails, as in 'Slack lifts and trusses'.

**Square.** Used in ordering yards squared, adjusted at right angles to the fore-and-aft line of the ship, as in 'Square the main yard'.

**Sway.** Used in ordering yards and masts hoisted, as in 'Sway up the lower yards'

**Sway away.** Hoist up an upper mast or a yard.

**Trice up.** Haul lines, blocks or tackle out of the way and secure them temporarily while performing a particular operation in handling sails or yards.

**Trim.** Used in ordering a spar or sail adjusted to make better use of the wind, as in 'Trim the lower boom'.

**Trim and make sail.** Adjust yards and sails and set further sail.

**Trim sails.** Commence the operation of adjusting sails for the wind.

**Unbend.** Used in ordering part of the running rigging sent down in order, for instance, to unbend sail (to remove the fastenings at the head of the sail from the yard and send the sail down).

**Way aloft.** Shortened form of AWAY ALOFT.

*Aloft*

# Helm Orders

**Helm orders.** Orders given by whoever is CONNING (12.04). When the vessel is CLOSE-HAULED (12.11), these may refer to the weather (upper) and lee (lower) sides; when before the wind, to port and starboard. (The orders below were used in the given senses until some time after the First World War.)

**Come to,** or **Come up a little.** Bring the vessel's head nearer to the wind (with great care).

**Down with the helm,** or **a-lee the helm,** or **luff round.** Push the helm down to the lee side to put the vessel ABOUT (12.08) or lay her to windward. The helmsman answers *helm's a-lee.*

**Hard a-lee.** Order to helmsman for maximum helm: the helm should be put as far to the lee side as possible.

**Up with the helm,** or **bear up the helm,** or **bear away.** Pull the helm so that the vessel may go more LARGE (12.03) before the wind.

**Hard a-weather.** Maximum helm to the weather side.

**Port the helm.** Place the helm to carry the rudder and the ship's head to starboard. (The word 'port' was used in helm orders long before it superseded 'larboard' in the nineteenth century in other contexts.)

**Hard a-port.** Maximum helm to port (rudder and ship's head to starboard).

**Starboard the helm** and **hard a-starboard.** The reverse of the two orders listed above.

**Ease the helm.** Let the helm come more amidships.

**Helm amidships,** or **midships,** or **right the helm.** Bring the helm amidships after it has been put to starboard or port.

**Meet her.** Reverse the helm to stop the vessel swinging any further round.

**Thus,** or **very well thus,** or **very well dyce,** or **keep her so.** When sailing CLOSE-HAULED (12.11), keep the vessel in the present direction.

**No near,** or **no nearer,** or **keep her away,** or **keep her full.** Warning to the helmsman when too close to the wind.

**Nothing off,** or **fall not off.** Do not let the vessel fall off the wind.

**Luff,** or **keep your luff,** or **keep your wind,** or **spring the luff.** Come closer to the wind.

**Full and by.** Steer the vessel so that the sails are not too close to the wind but reasonably full, and thus do not shake.

**Luff and touch her.** See how close to the wind the vessel will sail.

**Steady.** When sailing LARGE (12.03), keep the present course. The response is *steady it is, sir.*

**Steer east north east.** Steer the given compass course.

**How's her head?** Report the compass course.

# Weighing Anchor

**Pay out the cable,** or **veer away the cable.** Slacken the cable so that it will run out of the vessel.

**Come up the capstan.** Reverse direction in turning the capstan, in order to slacken the cable or let it out.

**Man the capstan.** Hands are ordered to stand by to work the CAPSTAN (06.03).

**Heave taut.** The hands take the strain of the cable by heaving on the capstan.

**Unbitt.** The cable is released from the BITTS (06.03).

**Heave round,** or **heave away.** Order to start turning the capstan.

**Up and down.** Admonition given to the capstan heavers when the cable is perpendicular and the anchor should be about to break out of the ground, and it is therefore important to have the ship under control.

**Pawl the capstan.** Once the anchor is up to the HAWSE (06.01) the PAWLS (06.03) are engaged to hold the capstan temporarily.

**Hook the cat.** The CAT (05.01) tackle is attached.

**Man the cat – haul taut.** The cat tackle is manned and the hands haul to take the weight of the anchor.

**Off nippers – surge the messenger.** The NIPPERS (06.03) holding the cable to the MESSENGER (06.03) are taken off and the messenger released.

**Stopper before all.** When enough cable is up, the STOPPERS (05.08) are applied to hold it temporarily while the anchor is stowed.

**Hook the fish.** Once the cat tackle has been removed, the *fish tackle* is attached and the anchor is fished; its arms brought up so that it lies on the ANCHOR BED (06.02) or BILLBOARD (06.02).

**Bitt the cable.** With the anchor fished, the stoppers are removed and the cable bitted (secured to prevent it running out again accidentally).

# Handling Ropes

**Bouse.** Used in ordering hands to haul downward on particular ropes; for instance. 'Bouse taut lifts and trusses'.

**By the run.** Order to release a rope and let it run freely; or to run up a lighter halyard, as for royals, jib or upper staysails.

**Come up.** Order to hands to stop hauling on a rope or FALL (05.04) and slacken it off; or to let go sail handling gear, BRACES (04.09) and so on.

**Ease away.** Slacken a rope or TACKLE (05.05) gradually.

**Every inch of it.** Order to hands hauling on a rope to take up any vestige of slack.

**Hand over hand.** Order to men to haul in a continuous and rapid motion, by alternating one hand in front of the other along the rope.

**Haul.** Order to hands to heave on a particular rope or FALL (05.04), as in 'Haul aft the head and fore sheets'.

**Haul taut.** Take up the slack on a rope.

**Heave and hold.** Pull vigorously and hold onto any gain.

**Heave and rally.** Encouragement to heave well and heartily.

**Overhaul the gear.** Order to go aloft and loosen BUNTLINES (04.09) and other gear to prevent chafing the sail.

**Tail on.** Lend a hand in hauling on the FALL (05.04) of a tackle.

**Walk away.** Haul on a rope by holding onto it and walking away with it against the strain.

**Walk back.** Walk back towards a pulley or tackle while holding onto its FALL (05.04) thus allowing the load to descend or pull away.

# *Handling Boats*

**Up oars.** Crew of a boat waiting to move off seize their oars and raise them to the vertical. (Bowmen handle BOAT-HOOKS (09.02), HEAVING-LINE (05.08) or PAINTER (05.08), and do not raise their oars until the order LET FALL.)

**Bear off,** or **shove off.** Bowmen cast off heaving-line or painter and push the bow clear of the wharf or ship.

**Out oars,** or **let fall.** Once the boat is well clear, the oars are eased down into the ROWLOCKS (09.02) and levelled, and the FENDERS (09.02) are taken in. (The boat can then be turned in the right direction by ordering oars on one side rowed or BACKED (12.11), as necessary.)

**Up together,** or **give way together.** Taking the stroke from the starboard after-oar, the crew commence rowing.

**In bows,** or **bows.** On approaching the landing point, the bowmen raise their oars to the vertical, boat them (bring them into the boat), and then seize their boat-hooks.

**Way enough – toss and boat oars.** When sufficient headway remains to reach the landing point, the crew stop rowing, raise their oars to the vertical and lay them in the boat, blades forward; the fenders are then thrown out and a line held ready to throw ashore.

**Stand by to lay on your oars – oars – give way.** In saluting other boats, stopping to hail or checking headway, the stand by order is given, followed by 'oars', on which the crew take one more stroke, bring their oars out of the water, FEATHER (09.03) them and hold them horizontally at gunwale height. Pulling is resumed on 'give way'.

**Stand by to toss oars – toss.** In saluting or in going alongside another vessel to deliver a brief message, following the 'stand by', on the order 'toss' the oars are brought out of the water and raised to a vertical position.

**Stand by to trail – trail.** Given when oars are to be dropped out of their rowlocks and trailed in the water alongside the boat, held either by the LOOMS (09.02) or by special lines called trailing lines.

**Oars – hold water – stern all.** When a boat's headway has to be stopped, at 'oars' the crew lay on their oars, holding them horizontal, and at the second order they drop the blades into the water to check headway. When necessary, the order 'stern all' is given, at which the crew pull backwards on their oars.

**Give way starboard** (or **port**), **back port** (or **starboard**), **oars.** Order given when the boat has to be turned suddenly, one side pulling while the other backs.

*Hauling on a halliard*

# Calls

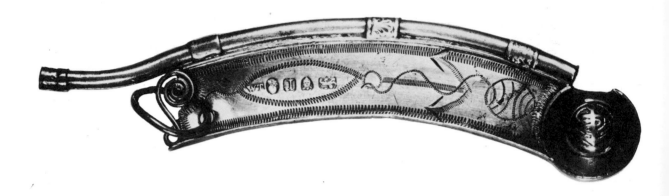

**Call,** or **boatswain's call,** or **boatswain's whistle.** Special whistle blown by boatswain's mates in the Royal Navy to pass along particular orders or pay salute. Its four parts are *buoy*, *gun*, *keel* and *shackle*.

The note made by the call is produced by a) blowing with an even pressure, or b) blowing with a varying pressure to give a warbling sound, or c) blowing evenly while making a trilling sound by vibrating the tongue. This note is further modified by opening, closing or partially closing the hand round the buoy, so producing a variable 'throttling' effect.

The term 'call' also applies to the signal sounded. Each call varies in duration and speed, being given its own special expressive form by a combination of the methods of producing and modifying the note.

**Call boatswain's mates.** Meant to gather boatswain's mates in preparation for a long call that has to be piped in unison.

# *Pipes*

**Belay.** Order to cease hauling and make the line fast.

**Avast**, or **High enough.** Stop.

**Sweepers.** Summons deck sweepers.

**Dinner**, or **supper.** Chorused for a meal.

**Heave round the capstan.** Turn the capstan. (Lasts about a minute, with boatswain's mates carrying on from each other in turn.)

**Veer and haul.** Consists of WALK BACK, followed by HEAVE ROUND THE CAPSTAN; repeated.

**Haul and veer.** Consists of HEAVE ROUND THE CAPSTAN, followed by WALK BACK; repeated.

**All together.** An officer's order to be obeyed 'all together'; similar to PIPE STILL, but one-quarter the length.

**'Away galley'.** PIPE THE SIDE, followed by the words 'away galley' in a long-drawn-out cry; as the GALLEY (09.01) boat leaves the side.

**'Away . . .'** (any other boat). Short call, followed by 'away first cutter [or any other boat]'. Also used before a short pipe.

**'D'ye hear, there'.** Long call, followed by 'd'ye hear, there'. Used before a long pipe such as 'call the . . . watch', 'call the hands' and so on.

**Pipe the side.** A mark of respect for an admiral, captain or other commanding officer as he boards or leaves ship; always piped twice – once on the officer's approach or as he moves away and once on his actual entrance or exit. Also piped during a funeral as the coffin passes over the side.

**Pipe still.** Calls for the hands to stand still or to attention.

**Pipe down.** Calls a) for hands to turn in; or b) for hands to come down from aloft; or c) to signify that hands will not be required until further orders.

**Reelers.** Called to summon hands working the sounding machine; later became the call summoning hands to heave the hand LOG (19.01).

**Haul taut.** Calls on hands to pull hard on a rope or FALL (05.04).

**Haul.** Instructs all to haul together.

**Hoist**, or **haul away.** Originally, instructed all to WALK AWAY (11.02) with a rope or FALL (05.04); later used in its literal sense.

**Walk back.** Instructs hands to ease a rope.

**Light to.** Order to stop hauling on a particular rope.

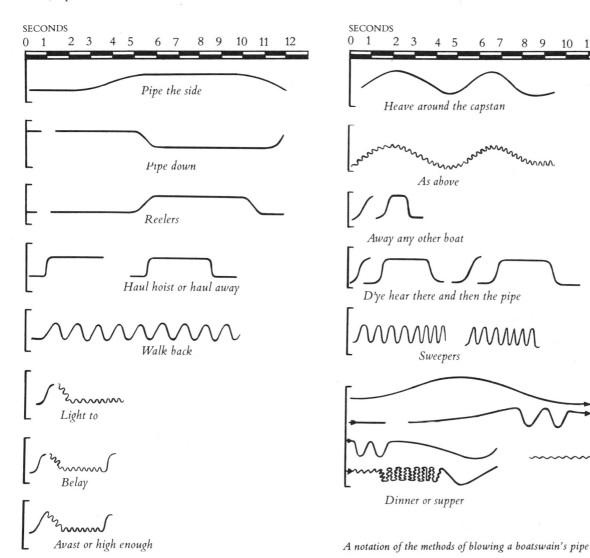

*A notation of the methods of blowing a boatswain's pipe*

# Sailing & Seamanship

I write of the only form of sailing I really know, and that means the inducement of shapely sea-borne craft called ships (or barques, brigs, schooners, full-riggers, barquentines and so forth, each in its own category according to its rig) on long voyages driven only by the wind to and from the ends of the Earth, handled by men known as sailors in the full meaning of that ancient term – a race of men skilled aloft and on deck in sailing ships. Masters, aided by watch-keeping mates, did the actual sailing, which means, briefly, to make the best possible safe use of the prevailing winds to blow a ship on whatever voyage she is required to make – across the Atlantic, round half the world, past Cape Horn to windward or to leeward, or whatever – economically and as fast as possible, without undue loss of men or sails – without loss at all if that·be possible.

I write as a twentieth-century big square-rigger man. These were the ultimate ships in efficient ocean-going sailing. But I have also sailed in other types, such as Indian Ocean dhows (shapely fellows from the Persian Gulf in the Zanzibar trade) or four-masted Portuguese cod-fishing schooners which kept at sea for six months or so on the Grand Banks and off Greenland in their tough trade; and in a Maldivian *baggala* and a Tasmanian Ketch in the rough Tasman Sea. Here I shall write mainly of the great deep-watermen, the 2,000-ton full-riggers and the 3,000-ton (and more) four-masted barques which lasted as viable ships until the outbreak of the Second World War.

By that time, there was just a handful of big Finnish ships, all bought from either Britain or Germany – the classic big square-riggers, battlers against the Roaring Forties and Shrieking Fifties to whom almost every voyage (except the South American) meant taking on a tough assignment including battles not just with Cape Horn but, during a complete circumnavigation of the watery globe at its worst, the whole windy lot south of Forty South, much of it south of Fifty.

These were the ships, ships sailed by the last real sailors of this world – with mighty small crews: maybe twenty or twenty-four men to a great barque or full-rigger, with an average age of sixteen or seventeen. Towards the end of the era these ships flew the Finnish flag mainly, a few the German. They were commercial ships earning their keep. Their needs were wind, cargoes to carry, and enterprising charterers and merchants to use them. There were then also (and still are) sailing-school ships, but with one exception these are now powerful auxiliaries, and they do not take on Cape Horn. Very wisely, they are largely limited to fine-weather sailing, for they are crewed by boys, and

too many have been lost in the past.

The work of the sailing-ship crews demanded great skill and could be dangerous: the handling of great square-rigged ships was not for the incompetent or the weak-willed. There were a few bully-boys, 'bucko-mates' and suchlike, on board some of these vessels, but there was only a handful of them, and their failings were offset by the merits of the hundreds of others. For the latter were the men who got the consistent best out of the best of the square-rigged ships in the real Cape Horn trades – Chilean nitrates and gold-rush traffic to California and even as far north as Alaska. The Cape Horn way was the classic run, demanding the ultimate in courage, skill and endurance. It made supreme demands on the ships themselves, too – the magnificent wind-driven ships that were often undermanned but always bravely sailed.

These ships required skilful handling by their masters, officers and crew. The master's job was based on comprehensive knowledge not just of his ship (she could be over 3,000 tons, net register), but also of the ocean winds and currents – winds such as the Trades and the Roaring Forties and zones such as the Horse Latitudes and the Doldrums – and how to minimize the delay they could cause.

The development of the great ships (some of them might be regarded almost as perfect sailing machines, among them the great five-masters of the Chile trade, *Potosí* and *Preussen*, and a few of the British, American and French vessels) kept pace with the growth of knowledge of the ocean winds and the best ways of using them, for lack of wind could be the ship's greatest curse. It is odd how essential developments in the ships and the best manner of using them kept pace for so long; and even as late as the 1950s real great square-rigged sea-battlers still fought their way deep-loaded round the stormy Horn, homeward-bound for Europe from Chile or Australia. In the end, it was their trades that slipped away from them (by, for example, the development of artificial nitrates), never their brave endurance, wonderful sailing qualities, or the skills of their masters and crews.

They had developed slowly through earlier centuries, when seamen and merchants had to grope along not very efficiently, largely ignorant of both the ocean wind systems and the most effective rigs with which to use them. It was the mid-nineteenth century before they caught up, in the form of the wonderful clippers racing through the seas with the teas of China, gold from Australia and passengers to California. These were the thoroughbred racehorses, marvellous and sometimes glorious, but short in stamina perhaps; good for racing under great masters and splendid crews but vulnerable, especially later when jammed full of heavy cargoes such as iron ore or nitrates after the Suez Canal was opened and the tea and passengers went by steam.

Something of the traditions these ships set up lasted to the end of the era, into the 1930s. By then, a mere handful of 3,500-ton four-masted barques and 3,000-ton full-rigged ships survived – a dozen in the Australian grain trade, half a dozen others still taking on the Horn to windward every voyage, bound out from Europe for the odd cargo of Chilean nitrates or fertilizing guano. They were lucky to find charters for even these tough cargoes, now that they had to compete against the Panama Canal and the economic efficiency of the big steam or motor cargo-tramps. The few charters to and from the Australian wheat-fields kept the last handful of big square-riggers going. By the late 1930s, there were only ten of these, mainly big Finnish ships, left in sailing commission in the world.

The ships got their charters because they were both well established in the Australian trade and, with their boy crews (whose average age was about 16) and fine young officers, very economical to run. They were good ships, well handled, well sailed, and some of them were making their ocean voyages in near-

Clipper time right to the end, though few shore-dwellers heard of them. There were no prizes for them, and little publicity outside the shipping press, and not much even there.

I was there, an able seaman in those glorious ships – the swift *Herzogin Cecilie*, the battling old Scots *Lawhill* of ungainly rig and superb performance, the killer full-rigger *Grace Harwar* (she killed my shipmate down there near the Horn). The *Grace Harwar* was a beautiful ship – glorious in the sea but old, maybe creaky aloft here and there by the 1930s, for she had been battling the savage sea for over half a century. Later, I was in the *Parma* too, a big four-masted barque that carried well over 5,000 tons, with a crew of two-dozen lads. I sailed with her into the late 1930s. She was a grand ship, a tremendous racer through tremendous seas. That outstanding master of these last of the great square-rigged ships, the famous Captain Ruben de Cloux, was in command; he never had a bad passage.

What men! And what ships! Gone now for ever, one fears, from a heedless world, for their places cannot be taken by auxiliaries nor by summer-sailing school-ships of any kind, though these are indeed a great deal better than nothing.

ALAN VILLIERS

# State of a Vessel

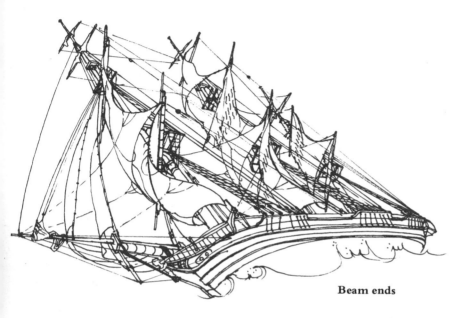

**Beam ends**

**Beam ends.** Position of a ship which has LISTED (02.03) to an angle where her deck BEAMS (01.01) are almost vertical and she is unable to right herself. This may be caused by heavy seas or squalls or by her cargo shifting.

**Close aboard.** Said of anything nearby.

**Clubbing.** Drifting downstream or with the current, with the anchor down.

**Collision.** The colliding of two moving vessels.

**Dismasted.** Said of a vessel which has lost its masts (as in a storm) or has had them removed.

**Encumbered vessel.** Vessel so burdened that she cannot take full advantage of her sail power.

**End on.** Said of a vessel when only her bows can be seen. Also said of an object whose longitudinal axis is directly in line with the keel of the observer's vessel. Generally, any object facing directly towards the observer.

*The* Hougomont *under jury rig after dismasting*

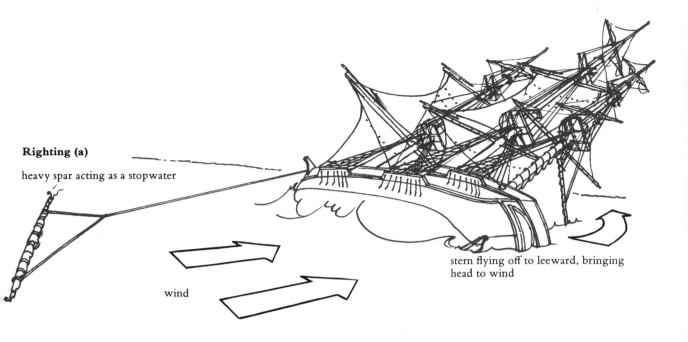

**Righting (a)**

heavy spar acting as a stopwater

wind

stern flying off to leeward, bringing head to wind

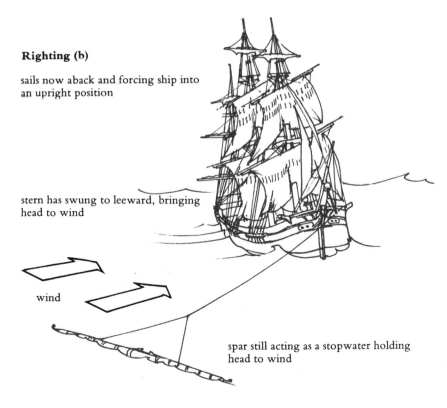

**Righting (b)**

sails now aback and forcing ship into an upright position

stern has swung to leeward, bringing head to wind

wind

spar still acting as a stopwater holding head to wind

**Four s's.** Four points that should be kept in mind before sailing: steering gear, side-lights, side ports and stow-aways.

**Heave astern.** To haul a vessel in a sternwise direction by means of anchor cable or SPRING (06.01).

**Hull down.** Said of a vessel when only its masts and upper works are showing above the horizon.

**Laid-up.** Said of a vessel when she has been unrigged and her gear dismantled.

**Lie** (vb). To keep a vessel in a secure position.

**Out of trim.** Said of a vessel whose yards (or cargo) are not properly TRIMMED (09.03). Also said of a vessel which is not floating horizontally and may be drawing more water at the stern (*trimmed by the stern*) or at the head (*trimmed by the head*).

**Righting.** Bringing a vessel upright after she has capsized. Also said of a vessel coming upright after a heavy roll.

**Sailing trim.** Said of a vessel when she is in the best state for sailing.

**Sea kindliness.** Ability of a vessel to cope well with different conditions, particularly heavy weather.

**Seaworthy.** Said of a vessel when she is in a fit condition to go to sea: properly built and maintained, fully equipped and manned, and able to carry the required cargo.

**Shipshape.** Everything aboard a vessel stowed neatly in its proper place. A well-known expression in British ships is 'everything shipshape and Bristol fashion'.

**Spend** (vb). To allow a sail, yard or mast to be broken or carried away in bad weather.

**Unseaworthy.** Said of a vessel which is unfit to go to sea because of her condition and equipment, or because of deficiencies in cargo stowage or in her crew.

# In Sight of Other Vessels or in Sight of Land

**Athwart-hawse.** Said of a vessel which is lying across the bows of another vessel, roughly at right angles to the latter's fore-and-aft line.

**Claw off.** To BEAT (12.08) to windward of a lee shore or of a hazard.

**Dip a light.** To sail away from a navigational beacon so that it dips below the horizon.

**Double** (vb). To sail round a cape or promontory.

**Drop astern.** To fall behind in a chase or a race.

**Fall astern.** Said of the land when a vessel is sailing away from it. Also said of a vessel being left behind because she is slower than others or because she deliberately reduces speed.

**Fall foul of.** To be obstructed by another vessel.

**Fall in with.** To meet another vessel by chance.

**Gather way.** To begin to move through the water.

**Go ahead.** To proceed straight ahead.

**Keep off.** To keep a vessel at a distance from the land or from another vessel.

**Keep the land aboard.** To keep a vessel in sight of land as much as possible.

**Lay aboard.** Said of a sailing warship which has manoeuvred itself close alongside an enemy vessel. In more recent times it became an order for a boat to come alongside.

**Lay the land.** To sail away from the land, thus making it sink below the horizon.

**Lee gage.** Position to leeward of another vessel.

**Lie by.** To keep close alongside another vessel.

**Manoeuvre.** Movement of a vessel involving change of speed, position or direction for a given purpose.

**Outsail.** To sail faster or manoeuvre more efficiently than another vessel.

**Overtake,** or **overhaul.** To come up from abaft the beam of another vessel under way and pass it.

To claw off and to weather

wind

**Range alongside.** To come close to another vessel on the beam while both are under way.

**Round** (vb). To sail round a headland, lighthouse or any sea mark, keeping a constant distance from it.

**Run.** The distance a vessel travels over the ground. Also, a regular voyage between particular ports, or a given trade route, as for example the *China Run* for tea, the *Australia Run* for wool, or the *West Coat Run* for Chilean nitrates.

**Running the easting down.** Said of a vessel sailing to the east before westerly winds. This is a 'deep-water' term and implies great distances such as those sailed by the clippers.

**Settle the land.** To lose sight of the land by sailing away from it, when the land appears to sink below the horizon.

Weather gage

wind

*The barquentine* Waterwitch

**Sheer off.** To move the vessel away at an angle.

**Stern chase.** The pursuit of another vessel from directly astern, often a long and tedious operation.

**Under way.** Strictly speaking, not moored to a buoy or to the shore, or not at anchor. More commonly, on course and moving through the water.

**Van.** Vessel or vessels at the head of a fleet or squadron. In the days of wooden warships, also the leading squadron in line of battle.

**Weather** (vb). To pass clear to windward of a cape, headland, rock or reef. Sometimes a risky manoeuvre, especially in vessels with poor windward performance.

**Weather gage.** The position held by a vessel which is to windward of another. An advantageous position in battle or in a race. Also said if a vessel is well to windward of any hazard such as shoals or rocks.

**Yard arm and yard arm.** Said of square-rigged vessels so close alongside each other that the tips of their yard-arms are almost touching.

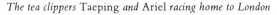

*The tea clippers* Taeping *and* Ariel *racing home to London*

# Before the Wind

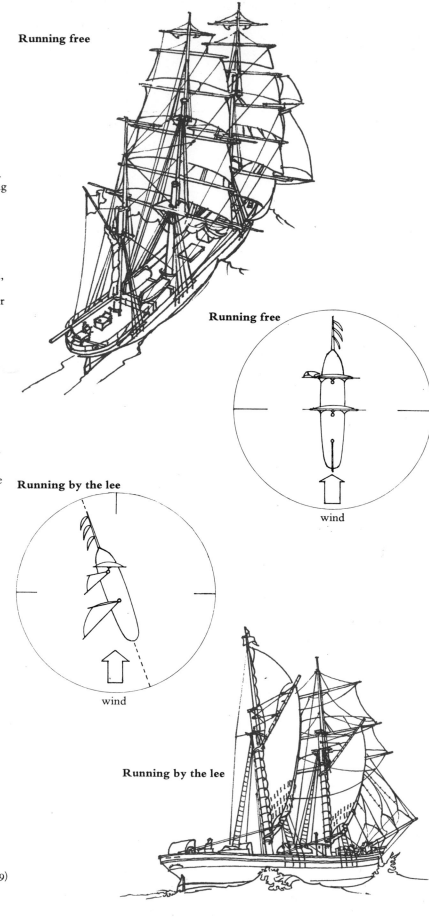

**Running free**

**Bear away,** or **bear up.** To change a ship's course to make her run before the wind.

**Bear down.** To keep closer to the wind. Also said when one vessel is approaching another. In general terms, to move directly towards something.

**Both sheets aft.** Said of a square-rigged vessel that is sailing directly before the wind.

**Bring by the lee.** Said of a vessel which, when running with the wind, has the wind change suddenly from one quarter to another. This is sometimes the result of bad steering and in heavy weather can be dangerous: the vessel could BROACH-TO (12.05) and risk capsizing.

**By and large.** Sailing close to the wind but not too close. Also used as a colloquialism meaning 'on the whole' or 'all things considered'.

**Crowd** (vb). To set every stitch of canvas a vessel could carry, sometimes to her danger. This is done to sail as fast as possible in a race, to catch or escape from an enemy vessel and, in the days of the great clippers, to make or break records.

**Crowd on.** Increase sail.

**Drive** (vb). To be forced to leeward by wind and sea, or to run before a gale. Also said of reckless captains who sometimes had their vessels carry large spreads of canvas to make fast passages, for personal prestige and for bonus payments.

**Forge ahead.** To move ahead rapidly under PRESS OF CANVAS (12.09).

**Forge over.** To force a vessel, under press of canvas, to sail over a shoal.

**Free.** Said of a vessel which is sailing with the wind abaft the beam.

**Going free.** Sailing with the wind; not CLOSE-HAULED (12.11).

**Going large.** Proceeding with a fair wind and all sails drawing.

**Haul off.** To sail with the wind before the beam.

**Large.** Said of a vessel sailing with the wind abaft the beam but not dead aft.

**Lask** (vb). To make good speed with a quarterly winds, yards BRACED UP (12.09) and SHEETS (04.09) eased out.

**Running free**

wind

**Running by the lee**

wind

**Running by the lee**

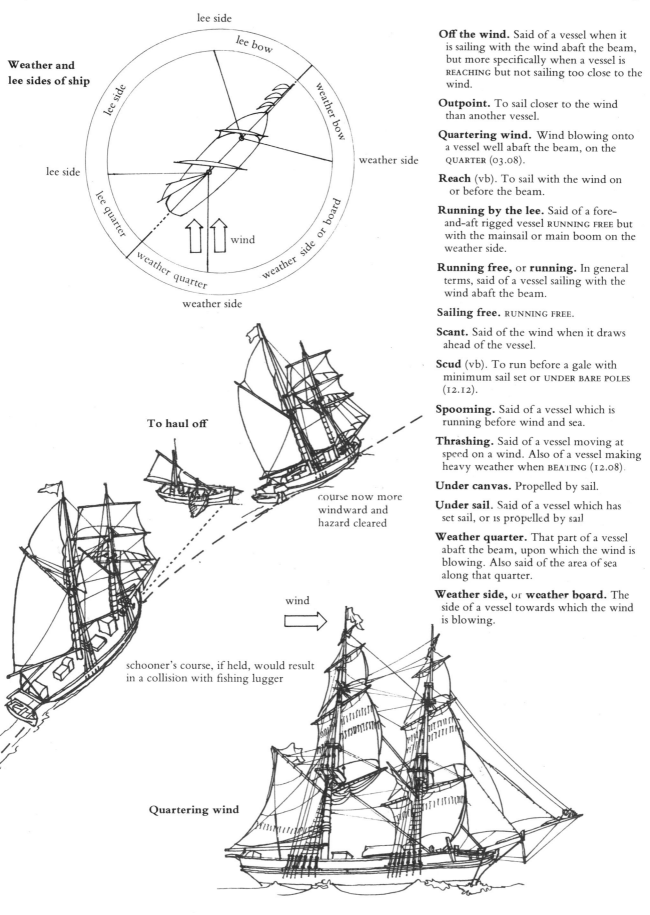

**Weather and lee sides of ship**

lee side

lee bow

lee side

weather bow

weather side

lee side

weather side or board

lee quarter

weather quarter

wind

weather side

**To haul off**

course now more windward and hazard cleared

schooner's course, if held, would result in a collision with fishing lugger

wind

**Quartering wind**

**Off the wind.** Said of a vessel when it is sailing with the wind abaft the beam, but more specifically when a vessel is REACHING but not sailing too close to the wind.

**Outpoint.** To sail closer to the wind than another vessel.

**Quartering wind.** Wind blowing onto a vessel well abaft the beam, on the QUARTER (03.08).

**Reach** (vb). To sail with the wind on or before the beam.

**Running by the lee.** Said of a fore-and-aft rigged vessel RUNNING FREE but with the mainsail or main boom on the weather side.

**Running free,** or **running.** In general terms, said of a vessel sailing with the wind abaft the beam.

**Sailing free.** RUNNING FREE.

**Scant.** Said of the wind when it draws ahead of the vessel.

**Scud** (vb). To run before a gale with minimum sail set or UNDER BARE POLES (12.12).

**Spooming.** Said of a vessel which is running before wind and sea.

**Thrashing.** Said of a vessel moving at speed on a wind. Also of a vessel making heavy weather when BEATING (12.08).

**Under canvas.** Propelled by sail.

**Under sail.** Said of a vessel which has set sail, or is propelled by sail.

**Weather quarter.** That part of a vessel abaft the beam, upon which the wind is blowing. Also said of the area of sea along that quarter.

**Weather side,** or **weather board.** The side of a vessel towards which the wind is blowing.

# Steering a Course

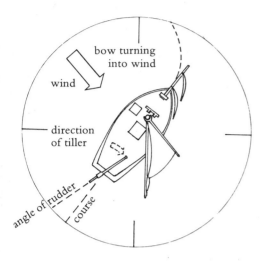

wind

bow turning into wind

direction of tiller

angle of rudder

course

**A-lee or lee helm**

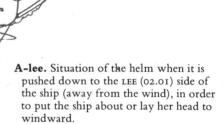

**A-lee and lee helm**

wind

angle of rudder

course

*Two seamen at the midships wheel of the* Passat

**A-lee.** Situation of the helm when it is pushed down to the LEE (02.01) side of the ship (away from the wind), in order to put the ship about or lay her head to windward.

**Cast** (vb). To make a vessel PAY OFF (12.08) in the direction required. Also to turn a vessel in the required direction when she has just weighed anchor.

**Con** (vb). To direct a vessel by giving specific orders to the HELMSMAN (10.02).

**Crossing.** Said of a vessel on a course which will intersect that of another vessel.

**Cruise.** Extended voyage made to a series of destinations or on a series of different courses.

**Heave in sight.** To become visible to an observer.

**Hold on.** To keep a vessel to her course.

**Homeward bound.** Said of a vessel proceeding to its home port.

**Lay the course.** Maintain a given course.

**Lee helm.** Tiller to leeward, rudder and and wheel to windward, in order to bring the vessel into the wind.

**Pivoting point,** or **turning centre.** The point on which a vessel pivots when answering the helm.

**Right the helm.** Bring the helm amidships.

**Rise** (vb). To come above the horizon.

**Rooming.** Safe water to leeward of a vessel.

**To right the helm**

**Pivoting point or turning centre**

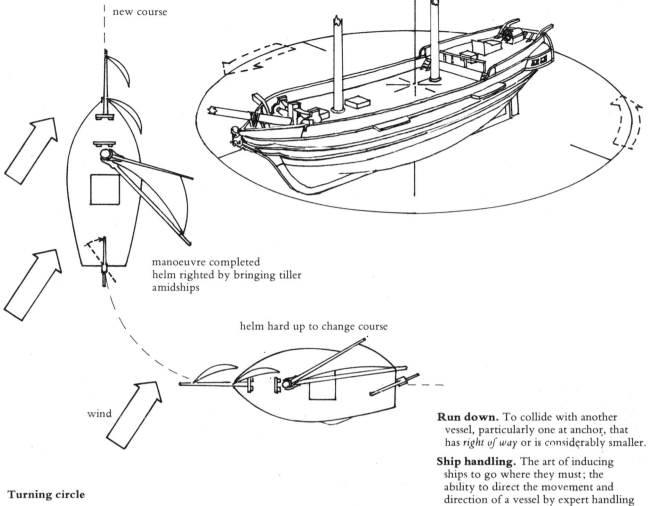

new course

manoeuvre completed
helm righted by bringing tiller
amidships

helm hard up to change course

wind

**Turning circle**

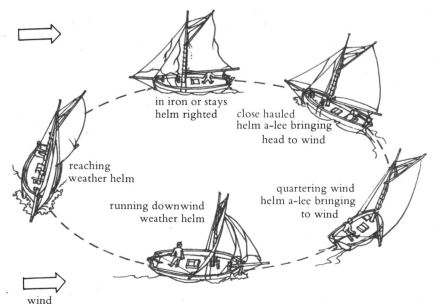

in iron or stays
helm righted

close hauled
helm a-lee bringing
head to wind

reaching
weather helm

quartering wind
helm a-lee bringing
to wind

running downwind
weather helm

wind

**Run down.** To collide with another vessel, particularly one at anchor, that has *right of way* or is considerably smaller.

**Ship handling.** The art of inducing ships to go where they must; the ability to direct the movement and direction of a vessel by expert handling of sails and helm.

**Stand on.** To continue on course towards the land, or towards any other destination.

**Steer.** To direct the course of a vessel by means of rudder (controlled by tiller or wheel) or steering oar.

**Steerage way.** Said of a vessel when she has sufficient way, or movement through the water, to enable her to answer the helm and come under control.

**Try back.** To veer or change direction slightly.

**Turning circle.** The path a vessel follows when turning, but not necessarily with the helm hard over. It varies according to the speed, draught, handiness and trim of the vessel.

**Wide berth.** Ample clearance. To 'give a wide berth' is to manoeuvre well clear of something.

# Sheering Off Course

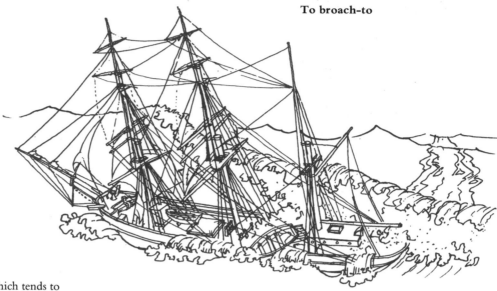

**To broach-to**

**Ardent.** Said of a vessel which tends to fly into the wind, demanding an excess of WEATHER HELM. This tendency is influenced by the shape of the bow the amount of HEEL (12.06) and other factors.

**Broach-to.** To fall into the trough of a running sea; to be suddenly brought broadside to the sea when running before a heavy wind. Due occasionally to careless steering, but more often to loss of rudder power occasioned by the vessel lifting her stern out of the water in a following sea.

**Chapelling.** Putting a vessel's head through the wind without BRACING (12.09) her yards, through careless steering or because of a sudden change of wind.

**Crab** (vb). To move sideways through the water, to make LEEWAY.

**Drift** (vb). To be carried by the tide or current, without being controlled by the helm. Also, the distance over the ground and the direction in which the vessel drifts, her LEEWAY.

**Fall down.** To drift with the current or stream in an estuary or river.

**Fall off,** or **fall away.** Said of a vessel when its head is deflected away from the wind, to leeward of its course.

**Gripe** (vb). Said of a vessel which tends to go to windward of her course when sailing with the wind on her beam or quarter.

**Leeway.** Sideways drift of a vessel to leeward of her course, caused by the wind. Also, the angle between a vessel's course as drawn on a chart and her actual track through the water.

**To sheer**

wind

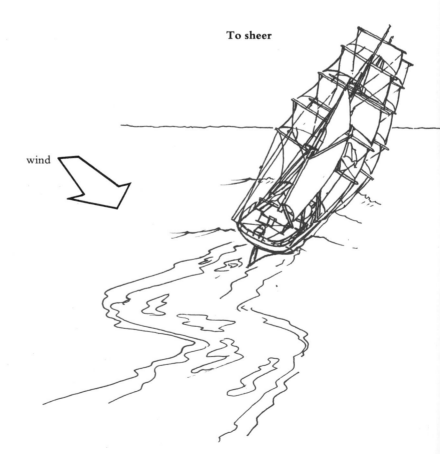

**Sag to leeward.** To drift to leeward; to make excessive LEEWAY.

**Sheer** (vb). To deviate or stray off course in an irregular manner. This can happen through difficulties in steering the vessel, or because of a negligent or inexperienced helmsman.

**Weather helm.** The degree to which the helm has to be kept to windward to prevent a vessel coming up into the wind and to keep her on a steady course.

**Yaw** (vb). Of a vessel, to deviate from a given course because of the effects of wind and sea. Often the result of a following wind or sea.

**Weather helm**

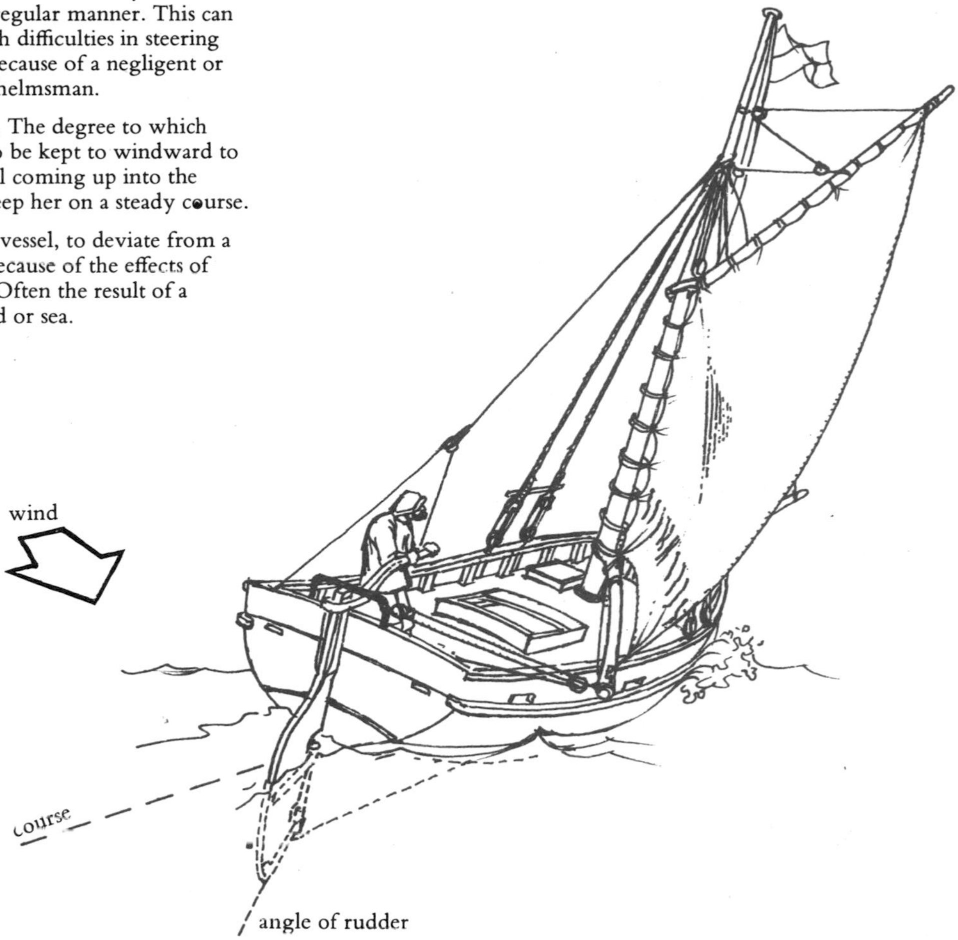

wind

course

angle of rudder

**To gripe**

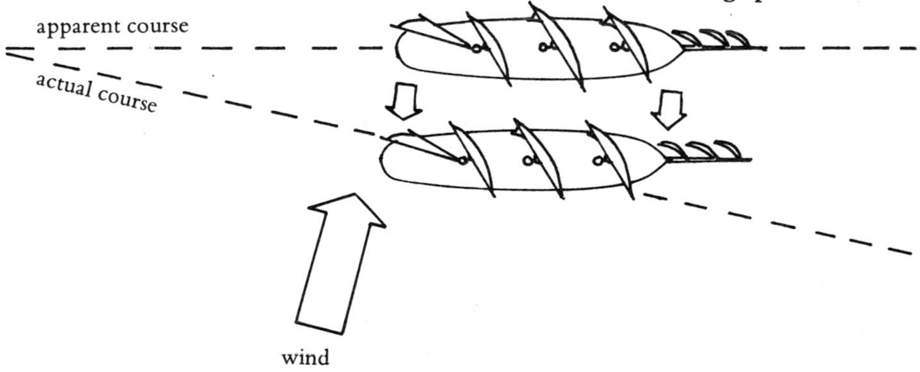

apparent course

actual course

wind

**To yaw**

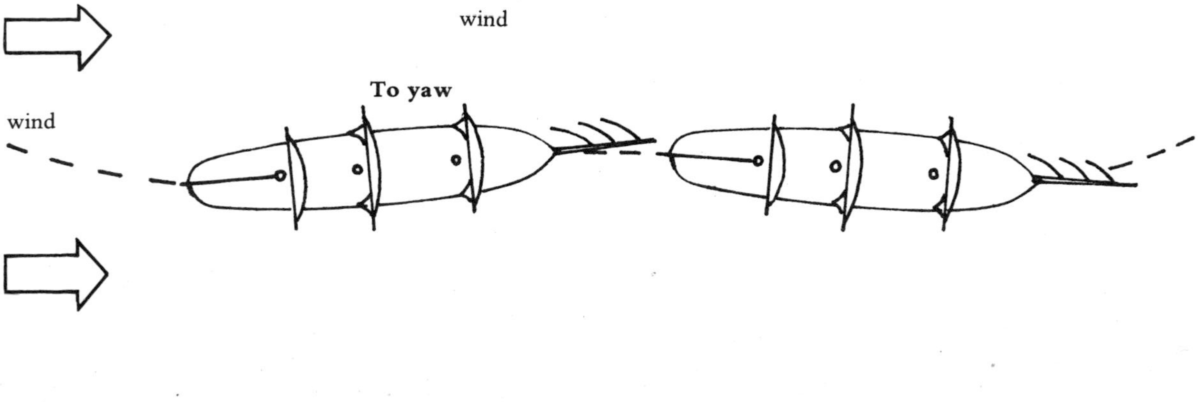

wind

# Motions of a Ship at Sea

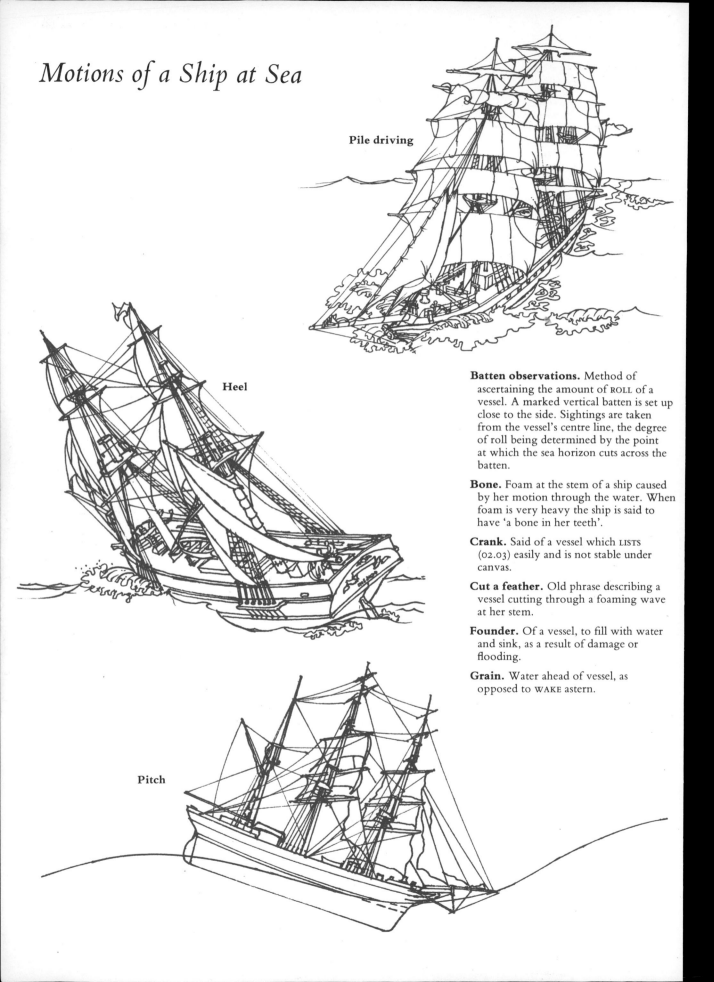

**Pile driving**

**Heel**

**Pitch**

**Batten observations.** Method of ascertaining the amount of ROLL of a vessel. A marked vertical batten is set up close to the side. Sightings are taken from the vessel's centre line, the degree of roll being determined by the point at which the sea horizon cuts across the batten.

**Bone.** Foam at the stem of a ship caused by her motion through the water. When foam is very heavy the ship is said to have 'a bone in her teeth'.

**Crank.** Said of a vessel which LISTS (02.03) easily and is not stable under canvas.

**Cut a feather.** Old phrase describing a vessel cutting through a foaming wave at her stem.

**Founder.** Of a vessel, to fill with water and sink, as a result of damage or flooding.

**Grain.** Water ahead of vessel, as opposed to WAKE astern.

**Hawse fallen.** Said of a vessel which is pitching heavily and therefore taking in water through her HAWSE HOLES (03.07).

**Heave** (vb). Of a vessel, to move violently up and down because of a heavy sea.

**Heel,** or **heel over.** To lean over to port or starboard due to wind pressure, heavy seas or the shifting of cargo.

**Labour** (vb). Of a vessel, to roll and pitch heavily, with a laborious motion.

**Lay along.** To LIST (02.03).

**Lee lurch.** A sudden and heavy roll to leeward.

**Lie along,** or **lie over.** To heel over with the wind.

**Pile driving.** Said of a vessel which plunges her bow down violently in heavy seas, particularly into the troughs of the waves.

**Pitch** (vb). Said of a vessel when her bow falls into the trough of a wave.

**Pooping.** Said of a vessel running before the wind in a heavy following sea when the sea breaks over her stern. This is a very dangerous condition to be in.

**Pound** (vb). Of a vessel, to drop heavily back into the sea or to hit the shore, having been lifted by action of the waves.

**Ride** (vb). Of a vessel, to give easily to the motion of wind and sea.

**Roll.** Pendulum-like thwartship movement of a vessel from the perpendicular to each side in a heavy sea or swell.

Pound

**Scend.** The movement of a vessel in a heavy sea when her stern falls into a trough and her bow is thrown violently upwards.

**Seel** (vb). Of a vessel, to make a sudden roll or to suddenly lurch to one side.

**Slam** (vb). Of a vessel, to strike the waves heavily with the FOREFOOT (03.07) when PITCHING in a head sea.

**Stiff.** Said of a very stable vessel which does not roll or list easily, or of a heavily laden vessel with a low centre of gravity.

**Wake.** Disturbed water stretching astern of a moving vessel.

**Wake current.** The current of water disturbed by the motion of a vessel that flows back into place astern.

**Washing down.** Said of a vessel shipping heavy seas which run off through the SCUPPERS (03.16) and WASH PORTS (03.16).

**Waterlogged.** Said of a vessel so flooded and saturated with water that she barely manages to stay afloat.

**Weather lurch.** The sudden roll of a vessel to windward.

**Work** (vb). Said of a vessel straining her timbers when labouring in a heavy sea.

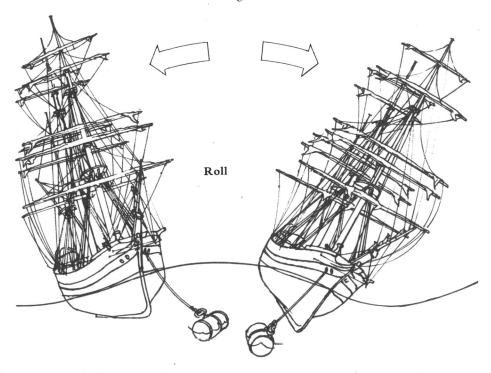

Roll

# Hove-To

**To bring-to**

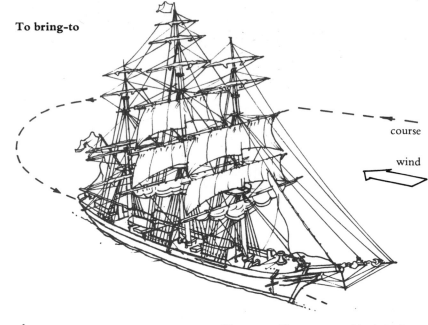

course

wind

**A-hull.** Said of a vessel riding out heavy weather at sea UNDER BARE POLES (12.12) and with her HELM'S A-LEE (11.01).

**Becalmed.** Said of a vessel delayed without sailing wind, unable to make way.

**Bring-to.** To stop a vessel's way by bringing her head to the wind.

**Brought up.** Said of a vessel when she is stopped but not at anchor.

**Brought up all standing.** Said of a vessel which stops suddenly when her sails are put ABACK (12.11) by a sudden change of wind.

**Check** (vb). To stop a vessel's headway.

**To heave-to**

wind

**Heave-to.** To stop a vessel by bringing her head near to the wind yet trimming sail so that she will fall off the wind and make no headway. Particularly necessary in bad weather, to keep the vessel riding safely.

**Hulling.** Said of a ship which is floating free without rudder or sail.

**Lie-to,** or **lie a-hull.** To HEAVE-TO in heavy weather.

**Riding a try.** Said of a vessel LYING-TO under BARE POLES (04.01) in very bad weather.

**Try** (vb). To LIE-TO in heavy weather, with reduced sail or, sometimes, UNDER BARE POLES (12.12).

**Weather bound.** Said of a vessel which cannot leave harbour or an anchorage because of heavy weather.

**Wholesome.** Said of a vessel which will LIE-TO reasonably comfortably in bad weather, lie safely broadside to the sea under BARE POLES (04.01), or ride well at anchor.

**To lie-to**

# Tacking and Wearing

1 Barque on the wind on the starboard
tack kept off slightly to increase
speed.

wind

2 Helm has been put down, head has
come into the wind and sails are aback
but must still have way, and main yard
about to be hauled round

wind

**To tack.** Going about as at point 2

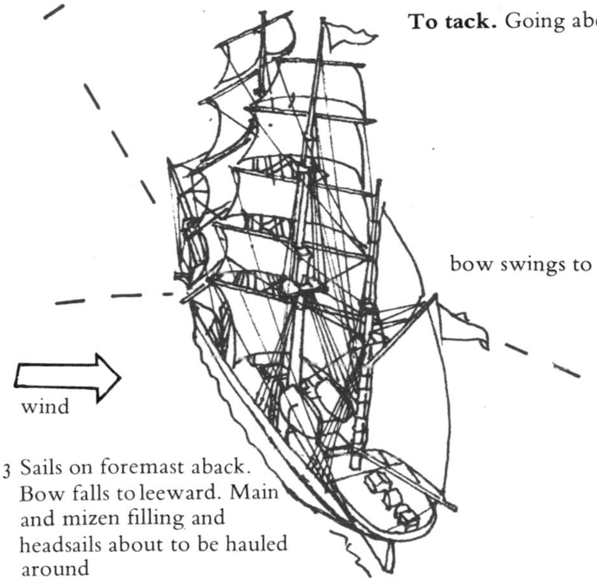

bow swings to lee

3 Sails on foremast aback.
Bow falls to leeward. Main
and mizen filling and
headsails about to be hauled
around

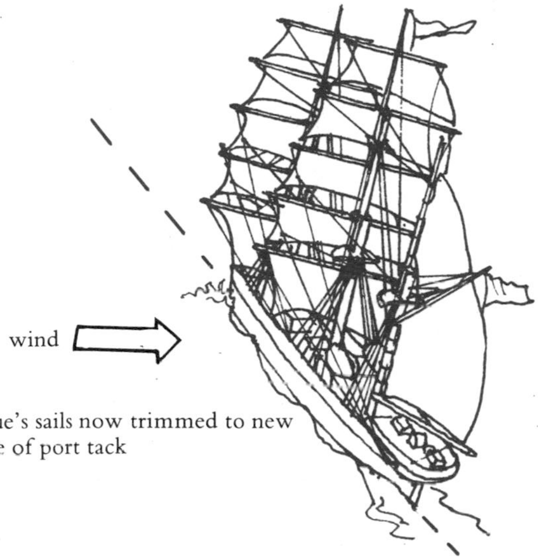

wind

wind

4 Barque's sails now trimmed to new
course of port tack

5 Barque pays off as
sheets are trimmed
and gathers way on
port tack (as at 4)

**Tacking** (going about)

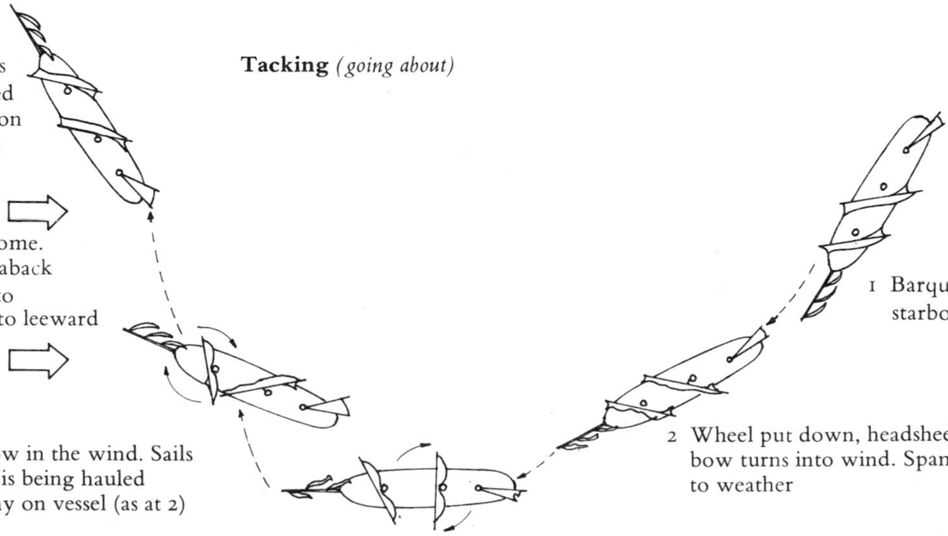

1 Barque sailing on
starboard tack

4 Jibs are sheeted home.
Sails on foremast aback
as mainsails start to
fill. Bow flies off to leeward
(as at 3)

3 Barque's head now in the wind. Sails
aback, mainyard is being hauled
around. Little way on vessel (as at 2)

2 Wheel put down, headsheets let go,
bow turns into wind. Spanker hauled
to weather

**All in the wind.** Said of a vessel's sails when going from one TACK to the other and the luffs are shaking. Can also be due to bad steering when sailing close to the wind.

**Back sailing.** Form of BOX-HAULING, in which the boom of a mainsail or mizen is hauled to windward when a vessel loses way while GOING ABOUT, thus forcing her head onto a new tack.

**Beat** (vb). To make progress to windward (against a foul wind) by a series of TACKS, sometimes also called LEGS.

**Blanket** (vb). Said of a vessel which, when TACKING, sails to windward of another vessel which is also tacking, and so robs it of the wind.

**Board.** The distance sailed between TACKS when a vessel is BEATING to windward.

**Board and board.** Said of vessels which are on the same TACK, BOARD or LEG.

**Box-hauling.** Method of WEARING a vessel in a confined area. Done by throwing ABACK (12.11) the sails on the foremast and putting the helm down (to the leeside, thus bringing the ship's head into the wind) when the vessel begins to go astern.

**Brace to.** In TACKING or WEARING, to swing a yard round so that the sail is marginally ABACK (12.11) the wind partly striking its forward side.

**Club haul.** To TACK a vessel with the anchor down in case of an emergency.

**Coming-up tack.** TACK on which a ship will be brought to windward of her course by changes in the wind, when she is riding out a cyclonic storm.

**Fore-reach.** To shoot ahead when going about under sail, or to continue moving forward while close to the wind.

**Full and by.** Sailing close to the wind but with the sails full.

**Go about.** To go from one TACK to the other, turning the vessel's head into the wind.

**Hank for hank.** Said of two vessels which are TACKING and make progress to windward together without either getting to windward of the other.

**Heave in stays.** To bring a vessel into the wind when TACKING.

**In irons.** Said of a vessel when her head is to the wind and she will not PAY OFF on either TACK. Also said of a vessel which is not able to turn freely because of some impediment such as a towing rope out aft.

**In stays.** Situation of a vessel under sail with her head to the wind as she is GOING ABOUT from one TACK to the other.

**Leg.** The distance a vessel sails on a single TACK.

**Make a board.** To make a short TACK; the distance made good while on one tack.

**Make a good board.** To sail to windward almost on a straight line, with minimum LEEWAY (12.05).

**Missing stays.** Said of a vessel when it is TACKING and fails to complete the manoeuvre, often because of too light a wind.

**Pay off.** Said of a vessel's head when it falls away from the wind when TACKING.

**Peg to windward.** To beat to windward, to make way to windward by sailing CLOSE-HAULED (12.11) on alternate TACKS. Describes a situation where the vessel's progress has to be worked hard for.

**Ply** (vb). To work to windward, putting the vessel about frequently, TACKING.

**Port tack.** Situation of a vessel under sail with the wind on the port side.

**Round to.** To bring a vessel's head to the wind.

**Shooting in stays.** Said of a vessel with plenty of way on as she GOES ABOUT from one TACK to the other.

**Slack in stays.** Said of a vessel which is slow in going from one TACK to the other.

**Splitting tacks.** In yacht racing, going about from one TACK to another on the LEE (02.01) bow of another vessel.

**Starboard tack.** Situation of a vessel under sail with the wind on the starboard side.

**Tack.** The vessel's direction in relation to the wind while under sail. Also, the distance sailed in that direction.

**Tack** (vb). To work a vessel to windward, changing course alternately from starboard to port tack (with the wind on the starboard and port sides respectively). *Tacking* is the zigzag manoeuvre by which the ship makes a progression to windward. It is also the operation of bringing a vessel's head into the wind and bringing her as rapidly as possible to the other tack.

**Traverse.** The zig-zag movement of a vessel plying to windward when TACKING.

**Traverse sailing.** Getting a vessel to windward by a series of TACKS.

**Trip.** Another term for LEG.

**Veer** (vb). To WEAR.

**Wear** (vb). To put a vessel on to the other TACK by putting its stern into the wind; that is, by running off before the wind and sailing round to the other tack while trimming sail.

**Wending.** Old term for going from one TACK to the other.

**Work to windward.** To BEAT or to TACK. Also, to get a vessel under way in foul winds.

**Diagram of sail positions during wearing, as illustrated opposite**

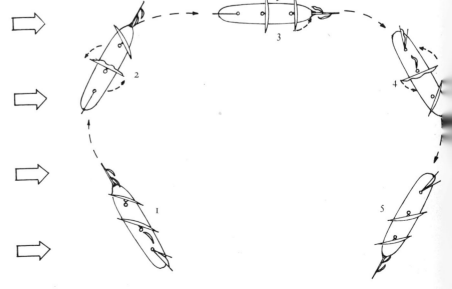

**Wear**

2 Spanker and mizen staysail taken in, helm put to weather and mainyard squared. Without spanker, head flies to leeward

1 Barque on the wind. Port tack

3 Running downwind. Foresails being braced round and jibs sheeted to port

4 Coming round to starboard tack. Spanker and mizen staysail being set, bringing head into wind. Mainyard being braced round

5 Barque on starboard tack, on the wind. All sails retrimmed and drawing

# Handling Sails

**A-box.** Said of a square-rigged ship when the yards are BRACED in opposite directions.

**A-cockbill, or cockbill.** Said of a yard when it is topped by one LIFT (04.09) so that it is at an angle to the mast.

**Belly.** The bulging part of a sail which is holding the wind.

**Bend sail.** To attach a sail to its yard, stay, gaff or BOOM (04.07).

**Box off.** To cause a vessel's head to PAY OFF (12.08) or move away from the wind by hauling aft on the SHEETS (04.09) of the jibs (sails extending from the foremast to the bowsprit) and BRACING back the yards of the sails on the foremast. This procedure is carried out in an emergency, as when the wind shifts ahead suddenly.

**Brace** (vb). To adjust a yard horizontally, by using the BRACES.

**Brace in.** To adjust a yard by means of the BRACES so that it is brought more ATHWARTSHIPS (02.01).

**Brace up.** To adjust a yard so that it lies closer to the fore and aft line of the ship.

**Carry on.** To increase sail when the wind is still strong, despite the risk.

**Chaffer.** Said of a JIB (04.12) when it SHIVERS (12.10) in the wind.

**Counter-brace.** To BRACE fore-yards and main yards in opposite directions, thus taking the way off the vessel.

**Crack on.** To set all sail and proceed at top speed.

**Draw** (vb). Of a sail, to be full of wind.

**Fill** (vb). To TRIM a vessel's sails to catch the wind.

**Flake a mainsail.** To take in a gaff mainsail and secure it in bights on either side of the BOOM (04.07).

**Flowing sheet.** Said of the SHEET (04.09) of a sail that is eased off when the sail is full and the vessel is RUNNING FREE (12.03).

**Gybe** (vb). To shift a boom-sail (extending fore and aft) from one side of the mast to the other while sailing with the wind abaft the beam.

**Make sail.** To prepare and set the sails ready for sailing. Also, to increase the amount of sail already set.

**Out.** Situation of the sails when they are set, or extended, in order to propel the ship.

**Press of canvas.** All sails set and drawing well.

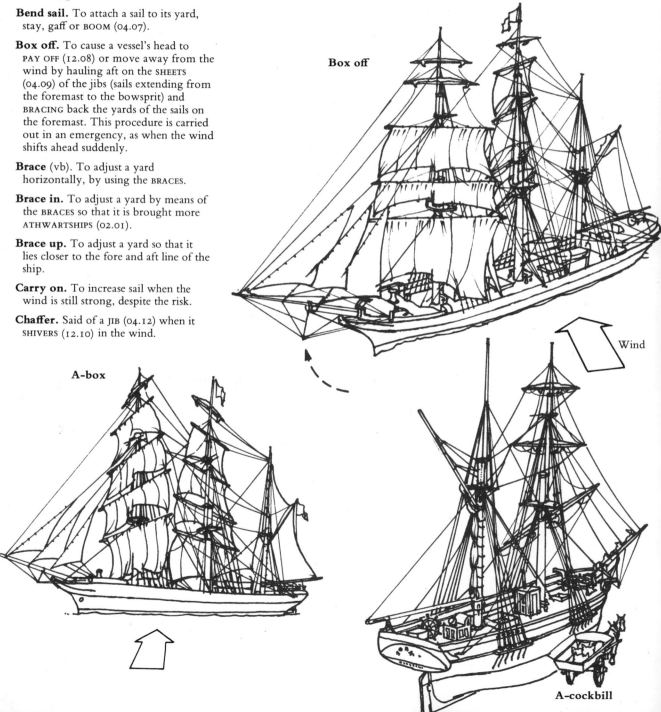

Box off

Wind

A-box

A-cockbill

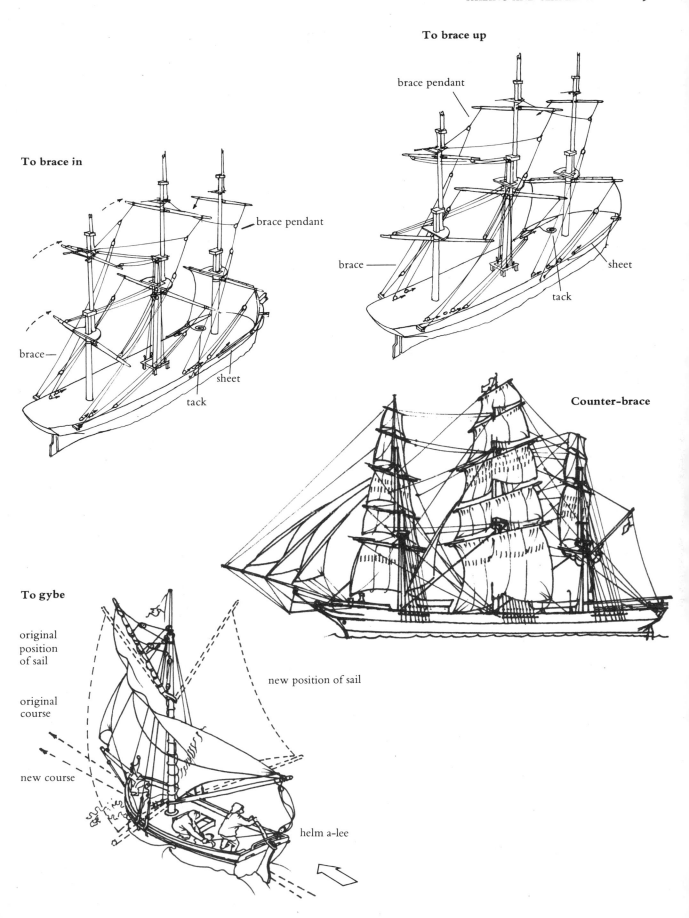

**To brace up**

brace pendant

brace

tack

sheet

**To brace in**

brace pendant

brace

tack

sheet

**Counter-brace**

**To gybe**

original
position
of sail

original
course

new course

new position of sail

helm a-lee

# Handling Sails

**Rap full.** Said of a vessel's sails when they are drawing to their fullest extent.

**Scandalize.** To deliberately set a vessel's yards and sails in disarray, by trimming the yards in different directions and letting the sails hang loose in the BUNTLINES (04.09). It was a traditional way of mourning the dead.

**Set sail.** To loose sail and extend it fully by hauling the SHEETS (04.09) taut.

**Shiver** (vb). Said of the LUFF (11.02) of a sail when the vessel comes head to wind and the luffs begin to shake, indicating that if no correction is made the vessel will soon be ALL ABACK (12.11).

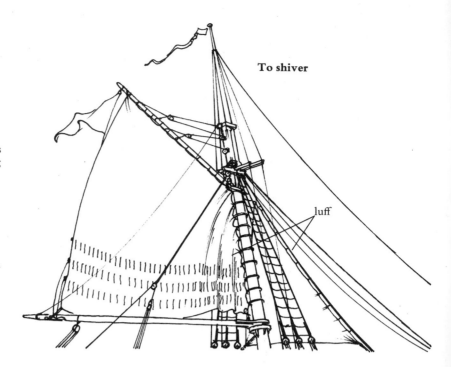

**To shiver**

luff

*Unbending the fore topsail*

**Slatting.** Said of sails which are slapping against the mast or any other nearby object, or of the LUFF (11.02) of a sail which beats back and forth when a vessel comes too close to the wind. Also used to describe the noise made when a sailing ship rolls and pitches about in a calm.

**Spill** (vb). To make the weather LEECH (04.12) of a sail shake out the wind by bringing the ship up close to the wind.

**Square the yards.** To adjust the yards so that they are BRACED (12.09) at right angles to the ship's fore-and-aft line and are brought to the horizontal by the LIFTS.(04.09).

**Stand.** Said of a sail when it has been correctly set and is drawing well.

**Strike sail.** To lower a sail as a mark of respect or as a salute.

**Strip to a gantline.** To send down all upper masts and yards and all running rigging, leaving only lower masts with GANTLINES (05.08) rigged, the gantlines being left for re-rigging.

**Sway** (vb). To hoist an upper mast or yard into position.

**Taut leech.** Said of a sail which is well set and drawing as it should.

**Topping.** The act of raising one end of a yard higher than the other, by slackening one LIFT (04.09) and pulling on the other.

**Touch** (vb). Said of a sail when it first begins to shiver, with its LUFF (11.02) just beginning to catch the wind, as the ship alters course or as the wind changes.

**Trim.** When applied to sails and yards, means the general arrangement and adjustment calculated to make the most of the wind.

**Unbend.** To unreeve the lacings through the eyelet-holes of sails and remove the sails from the yards, booms or gaffs.

**Wing and wing.** Said of a fore-and-aft-rigged vessel running before the wind with the sails set on both sides, foresail to port, *mainsail* to starboard, both full and pulling. Also called *goose-winged.*

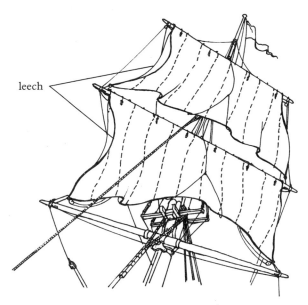

leech

To spill
(foremast of a
topsail schooner)

Square the yards

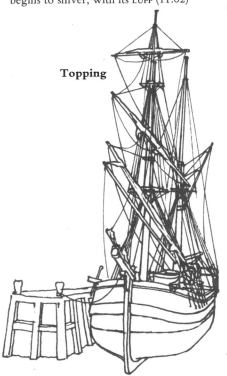

Topping

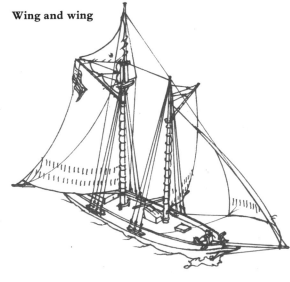

Wing and wing

# Close-Hauling; Backing and Filling

**Aback—back**

Wind

**Bagpipe the mizen.** To lay the mizen ABACK by bringing the weather SHEET (04.09) to the weather mizen rigging in order to slow a vessel down or bring her to a stop.

**Board a tack.** To haul in the TACK (04.09) of a square sail in order to sail closer to the wind.

**Brace aback.** To swing a yard round by means of the BRACES (04.09) so that the wind strikes the forward side of the sail.

**By the wind.** Sailing as close to the wind as possible without the luffs of the sails shaking.

**Close-hauled.** The general arrangement, or trim, of a ship's sails when she is trying to sail as closely as possible towards the compass point from which the wind is blowing. The greater the wind and the more turbulent the sea, the more the angle of leeway (off course and away from the wind) will increase. The ship is said to be close-hauled because her tacks, the lower corners of the principal sails, are drawn close down to her side to windward; the SHEETS (04.09) hauled close aft; and all the BOWLINES (04.09) drawn to their greatest extension in order to keep the sails steady.

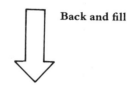

**Back and fill**

movement of barque

**Aback,** or **all aback.** Said of a vessel when the wind suddenly shifts onto the fore side of the sails.

**Back** (vb). To trim the sails so that the wind is on their fore side, in order to bring the vessel's head round or take way off.

**Back and fill.** Trimming the sails of a vessel so that they are alternately ABACK and filled, so that the vessel maintains her position.

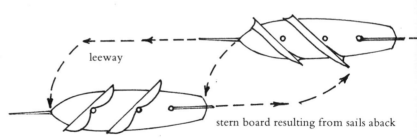

leeway

stern board resulting from sails aback

in a confined area this manoeuvre can be used to negotiate narrow passages, often using drift of tide

**Bagpipe the mizen**

**Closed-hauled.** Board down the Tack. On a Bowline. Sharp up. Taut Bowline.

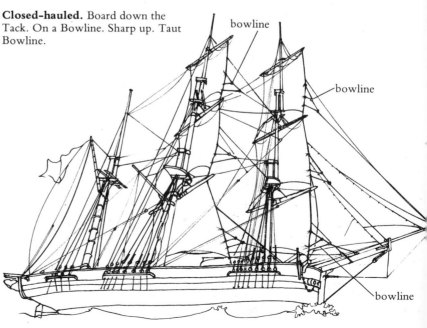

bowline

bowline

bowline

**Closed-hauled**

**Close-hauled** (leeway)

point of departure

actual course

apparent course

leeway

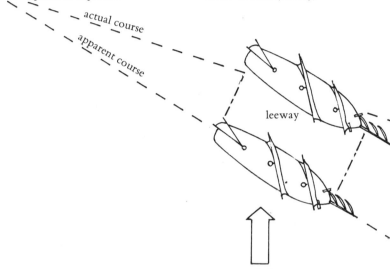

wind

**Close-hauled**

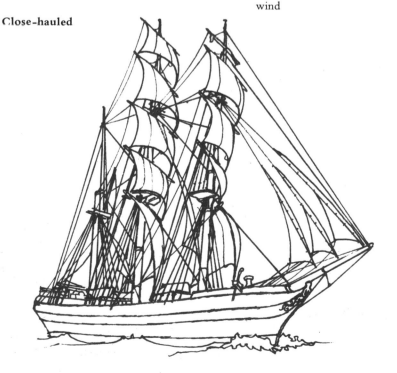

**Close-jammed.** Close-hauled to such an extent that the vessel cannot come nearer the wind without putting the sails ABACK.

**Flat aback.** Said of a vessel or its sails when the sails are taken ABACK and pressed against the mast. Also a colloquialism meaning to be suddenly surprised or disconcerted.

**Flat aft.** Said of a fore-and aft sail when the SHEET (04.09) is hauled as taut as possible.

**Flat-in, or flatten.** To haul ropes aft, particularly the SHEETS (04.09) and thus the CLEWS (04.13) of a fore-and-aft sail, as far as possible.

**Haul the wind.** To sail closer to the wind.

**Hold a luff.** To keep a vessel close to the wind.

**Lay a hold.** To put the helm down and come near to the wind.

**Luff** (vb). To come closer to the wind.

**Make sternway.** To retreat or move with the stern foremost.

**On a bowline.** Said of a square-rigged vessel sailing CLOSE-HAULED and with the weather BOWLINES (04.09) taut.

**Sharp up, or sharp trimmed.** Said of the yards of a square-rigged vessel when they are BRACED (12.09) as far forward as they will go. The ship is then 'sharp up' by the wind.

**Sheet home.** To haul on the sheet(s) of a sail until the sail is drawing fully and there is no more slack to haul in.

**Spring a luff.** To come nearer to the wind while sailing CLOSE-HAULED. Also to sail into the wind and then drive to leeward, done when the vessel has lost some headway.

**Stand up.** To sail close to the wind.

**Stretch** (vb). To sail CLOSE-HAULED while crowding on every stitch of sail.

**Taken by the lee.** Said of a vessel when she is caught ABACK by a sudden shift of wind. In a square-rigged vessel the sails would be blown against the mast. In a fore-and-aft-rigged vessel the booms would slam over.

**Taut bowline.** Said of the BOWLINE (04.09) and BRIDLES (20.03) at the LEECH (04.12) of the sails of a square-rigged vessel when that vessel is sailing CLOSE-HAULED. A vessel is said to be *on a taut bowline* when it is sailing as near to the wind as it can go while still making headway.

**Traverse the yards.** To BRACE (12.09) the yards as far aft as possible.

# Reefing and Furling

**Balance.** Method of further reducing the the area of fore-and-aft sails in very bad weather, after they have been reefed. It involves gathering up slack at PEAK (04.12) or CLEW (04.12) and lashing it to the yard or boom.

**Brail up,** or **brail in.** To gather a TRYSAIL (04.11), GAFF TOPSAIL (04.10) or spanker into the mast by hauling on the BRAILS (04.09).

**Clew to earing.** Situation of a sail when the CLEW (04.13) has been hoisted up by CLEW-LINE (04.09) or CLEW-GARNET (04.09) as far as the EARING (04.12).

**Clew up.** In furling a sail, to haul its CLEWS (04.12) up to the yard by means of their CLEW-LINES (04.09).

**Close-reefed.** Said of sails when all the REEFS (04.13) have been taken in and the sails can be reefed no further.

**Cut** (vb.) To loosen the GASKETS (04.09) securing a furled sail in order to set it.

**Ducking.** Clearing sail out of the way to give the HELMSMAN (10.02) an unobstructed view.

**Embrail.** To use the BRAILS (04.09); to BRAIL UP a sail.

**Furl** (vb). To gather in a sail, rolling it up and securing it with GASKETS (04.09) to the yard, boom, spar or mast.

**Furling in a body.** Method of furling a square sail when in port; the sail is loosened at the yard-arms and gathered neatly at the centre of the yard.

**Goose-wing.** In a square-rigged vessel, a COURSE (04.10) or topsail with its weather clew hauled up to the yard and its lee clew (corner) hauled down and spread. In fore-and-aft rigged vessels, the term is synonymous with WING AND WING (12.10).

**Hand a sail.** To FURL a sail.

**Loose** (vb). To cast off the GASKETS (04.09) of a furled sail preparatory to setting it.

**Reef** (vb). To reduce sail area by gathering up part of the sail and securing it by means of fitted REEF-POINTS (04.09).

**Settle** (vb). To lower a sail slightly for reefing purposes.

**Shake out a reef.** To take a REEF (04.12) out of a sail and reset the enlarged sail.

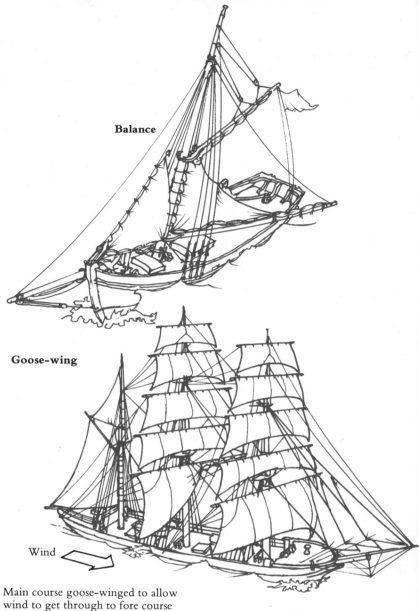

Balance

Goose-wing

Wind

Main course goose-winged to allow wind to get through to fore course

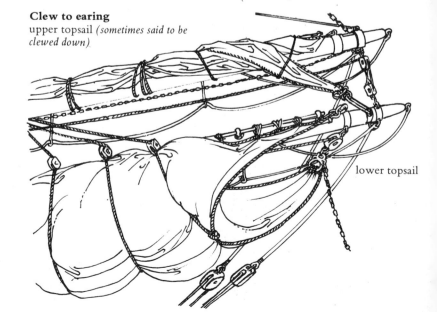

**Clew to earing**
upper topsail *(sometimes said to be clewed down)*

lower topsail

**Shorten sail.** To reduce the sail area of vessel under way by reefing or furling, or both.

**Skinning a sail.** Making the surface or skin of a sail taut and smooth when furling, particularly that area of canvas still exposed after the sail is furled and secured on its yard.

**Snug down.** To prepare a vessel for heavy weather, especially by reducing sail.

**Spanish reef.** Slovenly reef in a sail, occasionally done for expediency by lubberly seamen. It was done by lowering either the yard of a square sail or the gaff of a fore-and-aft sail, or by knotting the head of a triangular sail.

**Stop** (vb). To lightly tie up a sail or awning with SPUNYARN (05.09) or other small lines.

**Take in.** To lower or FURL a vessel's sails and secure them.

**Under bare poles.** Said of a vessel under way with no sail set.

**Unfurl.** To release sail which has been furled along a yard or on a boom, in order to dry the sail or set it again.

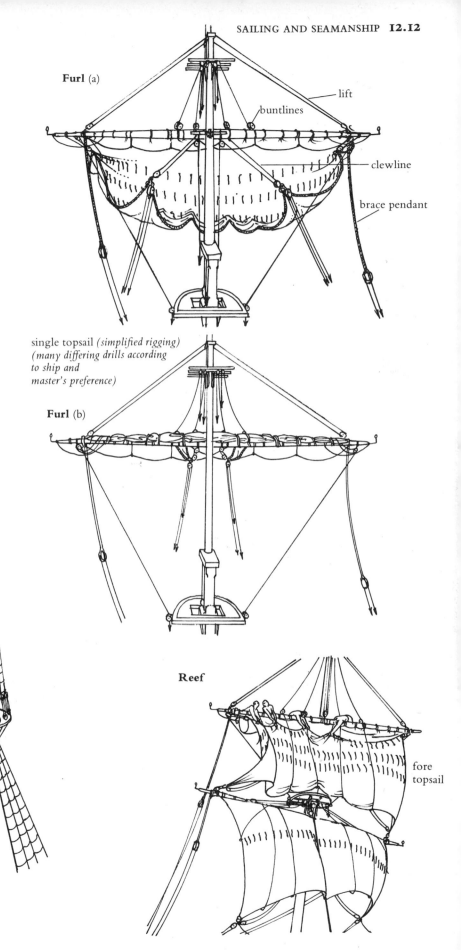

**Furl** (a)

lift

buntlines

clewline

brace pendant

single topsail *(simplified rigging)*
*(many differing drills according to ship and master's preference)*

**Furl** (b)

**To brail up**

downhaul

brail

**Reef**

fore topsail

# Maintenance

**Chain pump.** Pump used in large wooden sailing ships, consisting of an endless chain equipped with valves, operated by several men working at a roller or winch, and making it possible to pump large quantities of water in a short period.

**Fetching the pump.** Act of pouring water into the upper part of the ship's pump, to expel the air contained above the plunger and make the pump easier to use.

**Fother** (vb). To stop a leak in a vessel's hull by drawing a large piece of canvas or a spare sail over the hole.

**Make water.** To take in water through leaks in the side or bottom of the vessel.

**Pump, or bilge pump.** Device used in sailing ships to draw up water from the lower part of the hull for discharge into the sea. It was a long wooden tube operated from the main deck by the PUMP BRAKE and two pistons to

which valves or clappers were attached. In large ships a CHAIN PUMP could be used.

**Pump box.** Valved piston forming part of a ship's PUMP.

**Pump brake.** Handle or lever by which an old bilge pump is worked.

**Pump spear.** Long iron bar running between PUMP BRAKE and PUMP BOX, by means of which the latter is operated.

**Tend** (vb). To attend to the working of a vessel's equipment, such as the running rigging and ground tackle when at anchor.

*The port sea-water pump on the upper deck of HMS* Victory

**Undergird, or Frap.** To pass a chain, hawser or heavy cable under a vessel and heave it taut across the deck, as an emergency measure when a vessel's seams are liable to open through strain.

**Weeding.** Clearing the rigging of any temporary or unnecessary lines, STOPS (05.08) and so on.

**Weeping butts.** Said of a vessel's timbers when there is water seepage throughout their BUTTED (03.10) joints.

*'Short-handed'. Engraved after Lionel Smythe, 1874*

*'All Hands to the Pump' by H. S. Tuke*

# The Language of Flags

There is no doubt that from the beginning – the prime function of flags was not merely decorative, but to indicate authority and, secondly, to order or encourage action in battle. Perhaps the earliest representation of what appears to be a flag is that on a ship depicted on a funeral vase from the Nile Valley of approximately 5000 BC. On a Greek fifty-oared two-masted ship of the time of the Persian Wars (about fifth century BC), also painted on a vase, we find a very definite flag at the bow, while several similar flags appear on ancient Greek and Roman coins.

Flags as we know them today began to develop with the rise of heraldry in the thirteenth and fourteenth centuries, particularly among the Mediterranean maritime powers. These were mainly mast-head flags but, corresponding to modern stern ensigns, they were used to denote nationality. The earliest recorded document concerning English maritime flags is an order dating from 1297 requiring that all English ships sailing to Flanders should fly a banner of the royal arms. In 1492 there is a record of Columbus not only flying the royal arms of Spain at the mainmast-head, but also a special flag at the fore displaying the initials of his Spanish royal patrons, Ferdinand and Isabella.

In Elizabethan times, English ships began to wear stern ensigns of various patterns, usually striped blue and white or green and white, with a red cross of St. George either in the canton (the top corner nearest the mast) or overall. The Honourable East India Company, chartered in 1600, used a red and white striped ensign of its own, at first with the St. George's cross, and later the Union Flag, in the canton. Tolerated but never authorized, this flag is mainly interesting as a possible inspiration for the later American flag.

With the introduction of the first Union Flag in 1606, we have a definite British national flag. This was carried at the mainmast-head of both English and Scottish ships, the former having the St. George's cross, red on a white field, at the foremast, while the latter flew the flag of St. Andrew, blue with a white diagonal cross.

The modern stern ensign denoting nationality developed from the striped ensigns. In 1621, there is a record of a plain red ensign with a St. George's cross in the canton. In 1633, plain white or blue ensigns with a St. George's cross made their appearance. The normal British stern ensign was red, but ensigns of each colour were used in a large fleet to identify the centre, van and rear squadrons.

A proclamation was issued in 1634 that none but naval ships and ships in the king's service were to fly the Union Flag. Merchant ships were to fly either the St. George's cross or the St. Andrew's cross at the main, according to their nationality. This proclamation did not prohibit the use of the Red Ensign, but the first record of its legally permitted use by British merchant ships is dated 1674. Naval vessels continued to fly the Union Flag, at the main, and the Union Jack (technically only so called when flown at the jackstaff in the bows).

The plain white ensign was first given its overall St. George's cross in 1702, while in 1707, at the legislative union with Scotland, the 1606 Union Flag replaced the St. George's cross in the canton on all ensigns. The modern Union Flag, with its red diagonal cross, came into being in 1801, and has since appeared in all British ensigns.

The New England colonists may have been influenced by the unofficial red and white striped ensign flown by East Indiamen when choosing a common flag for the thirteen States. Known as the Grand Union, or Cambridge flag, this came into existence in January 1776 with thirteen such stripes (representing the colonies) and the 1606 Union Flag in the canton. It was the basis for the first 'Stars and Stripes' instituted by Congress on 14 June 1777, with thirteen white stars in the blue canton. Both stars and stripes were gradually added to as more States joined the Union, but in 1818, when the stars were increased from fifteen to twenty, the stripes were stabilized at the original thirteen.

A complete revision of British ensigns took place in 1864, when the senior ensign, the red, was given solely to the merchant navy and privately owned British ships in general, the Royal Navy was allocated the White Ensign, while the Blue Ensign was given to the Royal Naval Reserve.

While house flags, as an indication of ownership, developed mainly in the early nineteenth century, they have an older origin, some examples dating from the sixteenth and seventeenth centuries. A charter was granted in 1581 to the Levant Company, under which its ships could fly a flag of the royal arms of England surmounted by a St. George's cross. However, it was in the days of the clipper ships in the mid-nineteenth century that house flags really came to the fore. Not only the clippers and windjammers had their distinguishing flags; even humble craft, like fishing smacks, proudly flew their owners' house flags.

In addition to their function as symbols of nationality or ownership, flags have played an important part in indicating command or rank. Admirals' flags originated in Tudor times, and from the seventeenth century the general practice was for an Admiral of the Fleet to fly a Union Flag at the main, while other admirals flew a flag of their squadronal colour – vice-admirals' flags at the foremast and those of rear-admirals at the mizen. When squadronal colours were abolished in 1864, the St. George's cross was used for all admirals' flags, vice-admirals and rear-admirals flying them at the fore and mizen mast-heads respectively.

The use of flags for communication – signalling – also dates back to early times. During the fourteenth century a flag, probably a royal standard, was displayed in a flagship's rigging in order to call a council of the captains and masters of the fleet. Most orders were given at these councils and therefore the need for action signals did not usually arise in those days.

By the sixteenth century, many nations had developed a simple code of signals for calling councils, for warning of danger, or for indicating the sighting of land or of other ships; but it is not until 1672 that we find the first English document detailing sailing and fighting instructions with appropriate flag signals. The flags had various meanings according to where they were hoisted. Thus a red flag at the admiral's fore topmast-head meant 'Engage the enemy', while at the mizen it signified 'Vice-admiral and ships of the starboard squadron to come to the starboard tack'. This system proved impractical in battle: owing to enemy action, the mast or yard-arm on which a signal flag had to be hoisted might be shot away, and the signal could not be made.

During the second half of the eighteenth century some navies introduced 'numerary' signal codes, which Britain adopted in about 1778. Lord Howe's second signal book, of 1790, had flags covering the numbers 1 to 9 and 0, also a substitute flag and a few special flags. In 1799, an improved signal book appeared, with two substitute flags, one repeating the flag immediately above and the other duplicating the top flag of the hoist. This book remained in use until 1808, although the numerical values of the flags were changed in 1803, the revised form being the one used at Trafalgar. In addition to the numerical series of set signals, which covered mainly sailing and fighting instructions, a supplementary book (using the ordinary numeral flags but with a special 'Telegraph' flag) was compiled in 1800 by Sir Home Popham. This enabled other words and sentences to be signalled, and it was from this book that Nelson took his famous signal 'England expects . . . . .'

During the Napoleonic wars, when British warships often had to protect convoys of merchant ships, it was found that there was no way of communicating by signals, as there was no mercantile code book. (The same obviously applied to communications between the merchant ships themselves.) In many cases lives could have been saved if a message had been sent. To remedy this, Captain Frederick Marryat RN produced the first edition of his *Code of Signals for the Merchant Service* in 1817. Using flags for numbers 1 to 0, with a few additional flags and pendants, Marryat's code not only included hundreds of words and sentences, but also place-names (ports, headlands, lighthouses and so on) and a register of shipping, mainly British. In 1841, it underwent complete revision, and thus we have two sets of flags for most of the signal hoists.

By 1855 it was felt that neither Marryat's code nor any of the existing foreign codes fulfilled the then current requirements, and a committee appointed by the British Board of Trade devised a code which would provide not less than 70,000 signals using hoists of not more than four flags. They designed a code of eighteen flags, lettered B to W, omitting the vowels in order to avoid 'every objectionable word composed of four letters or less'. Fourteen of the flags were taken from Marryat's designs, with very small alterations to only two. Named *The Commercial Code of Signals*, the new code came into use in 1857, and in about 1871 it became known as *The International Code of Signals*. After some thirty years, a new code, with a wider range of signals, was needed, and this was duly devised, with twenty-six flags covering the whole alphabet. All the 1857 flags were retained, with two small alterations. The new code same into use on 1 January 1901, and was eventually replaced by the 1931 Code, which was first used in 1934. This present code comprises twenty-six lettered flags as in 1901 (but providing C, D, E, F and G with rectangular flags instead of pendants), ten numeral pendants and three triangular substitute flags.

There are many special uses for flags in addition to those already described, but space permits only a few of these to be mentioned. When a ship was captured by an enemy, it was customary to hoist the captor's ensign over that of the victim. An ensign hoisted upside-down was generally recognized as an (unofficial) signal of distress, but this did depend on the design being suitable. Flags have for ages been flown at half-mast as a sign of mourning, supposedly leaving room above for the invisible flag of Death. It is doubtful if the traditional Jolly Roger design of a black flag with a white skull and crossed bones was actually used by pirates, but certainly in the seventeenth and eighteenth centuries pirates did use some bizarre designs, incorporating a skeleton, an hour glass, Father Time or other figures intended to strike fear into their victims.

ALEC A. PURVES

**Early Maritime Flags**

*Greek galley, fifth century BC (from a funeral vase)*

*Two fourteenth-century flags: from Venice (left) and Genoa*

*English royal arms, thirteenth century*

*Columbus's flags, 1492: the arms of Castile and Leon (left) and the 'Expedition' flag carrying the initials of Ferdinand and Isabella*

*Elizabethan stern ensign*

*Jacobean ensign, 1618*

*First Red Ensign, 1621*

*Red Ensign, 1707*

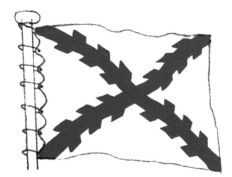

*Spanish Netherlands (fifteenth-sixteenth centuries)*

*France: Dunkirk and Marseille (seventeenth-eighteenth centuries)*

*France: galleys (sixteenth-seventeenth centuries)*

## Uses of Flags

*Admirals' flags, 1596: Admiral of the Fleet (left)*
*and Rear-Admiral of the Third Squadron*

*Union Jack at the jackstaff of a warship*

*Commodore's Broad Pendant*

*Mast-head Pendants: Common or Union*
*Pendant, 1661-1864 (left), and Commissioning Pendant*

## Methods of Hoisting

*Canvas sleeve on pole*  *Rings or riband ties round mast*  *Roped and toggled flag*  *Inglefield clips*

## Flags of the Chief Seaports of the Hansa

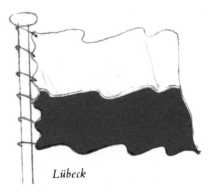

*Lübeck*

*Stralsund
(seventeenth century)*

*Rostock
(seventeenth century)*

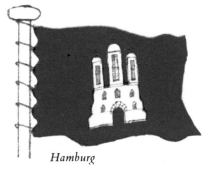

*Hamburg*

*Bremen*

## Some Early Company Flags

*The Levant Company, 1581*

*Guinea Company jack, 1662*

*The Honourable East India
Company, 1600-1707*

*Dutch East India Company
(seventeenth century)*

*The visibility of the orange band in the flag
adopted by the independent Dutch in the
seventeenth century proved to be poor, and by
the eighteenth century it had been replaced by a
red band. The modern South African flag has
revived the old colours of the United Provinces.*

*Dutch West India Company
(eighteenth century)*

## Some Fishing Boat House Flags

*Denmark: Greenland whalers (nineteenth century)*

*Netherlands: Pernis, near Rotterdam*

*Netherlands: Zierikzee, Zeeland*

*H. F. Eastick, Great Yarmouth*

*William Harrison, Great Yarmouth*

*Saml. Smith & Sons ('Old Coffee Smith'), Great Yarmouth*

*Fleming Hewett, Great Yarmouth*

*E. A. Durrant's 'Red, White & Blue Fleet', Great Yarmouth*

## Some House Flags of the Days of Sail

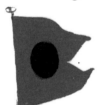

*James Baines's Black Ball Line*

*American Black Ball Line*

*T. & J. Brocklebank (flown at foremast)*

*Green's Blackwall Line*

*Money, Wigram & Co.*

*S. B. Guion's Black Star Line*

*Lamport & Holt*

*Pilkington & Wilson*

*Devitt & Moore*

*Aberdeen Line*

*A. H. Meursing, Amsterdam*

*C. A. van Vessem, Rotterdam*

*A. D. Bordes & Fils, Bordeaux*

*Siedenberg, Wendt & Co., Bremen*

*J. F. Arens, Bremen*

*Rickmers Line, Bremerhaven*

*M. A. & A. Dall'Orso, Genoa*

*B. Wenke & Sons, Hamburg*

*F. Laeisz, Hamburg*

*W. Thomson & Co., St. John, NB.*

**Some Special Uses of Flags**

British sloop Alert *captured by US frigate* Essex *(1812)*

*Ensign at half-mast as a sign of mourning*

*Inverted ensign, an unofficial signal of distress*

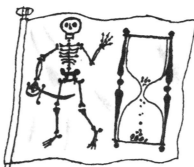

*The traditional (if apocryphal) Jolly Roger*

*Pirate flag of the seventeenth and eighteenth centuries*

*Liverpool Shipmasters' Association flag, with a master's personal number (1840)*

*Revenue cutter's jack (1694-1784) and ensign (1731-84)*

ROYAL MAIL

*US Revenue ensign (1799)*

*Royal Mail pendant (1884-1902)*

*Trinity House ensign, late nineteenth century*

*Wreck buoy and flag*

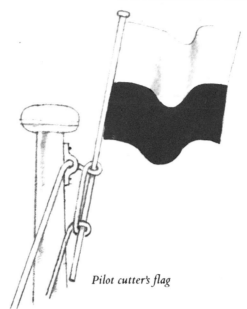

*Pilot cutter's flag*

## Some Nineteenth-Century Signals for Pilots

*Great Britain*

*France*

*Spain*

*Denmark*

*Brazil*

*Japan*

*Sweden*

*Norway*

*Italy*

*Netherlands*

*Netherlands: Pilot already on board*

*Netherlands: Flushing pilot cutter*

**Early Signals**

Red flag at fore topmast-head: 'Engage the enemy' (in use from mid-seventeenth to late eighteenth century)

Yellow-and-white-striped flag at the fore yardarm: for fireships in the Admiral of the White's Division (mid-eighteenth century)

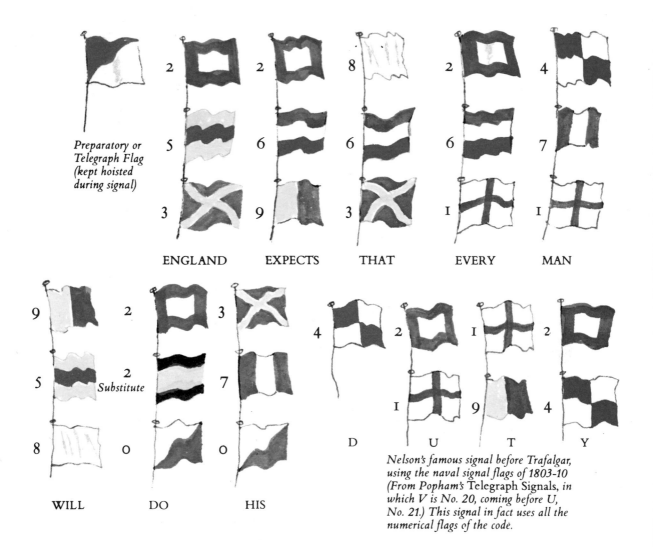

Nelson's famous signal before Trafalgar, using the naval signal flags of 1803-10 (From Popham's Telegraph Signals, in which V is No. 20, coming before U, No. 21.) This signal in fact uses all the numerical flags of the code.

## Maryatt's Signal Code Flags, 1817 to about 1880

1   2   3   4   .5   6   7

8   9   0   Telegraph flag   Rendezvous flag   Union Jack for warships' numbers (prior to 1826, without white border)

*1st distinguishing pendant*   *2nd distinguishing pendant*   *3rd distinguishing pendant (1854)*   *4th distinguishing pendant (1869)*   *Numeral pendant*

### Some Signal Hoists from Maryatt's Code

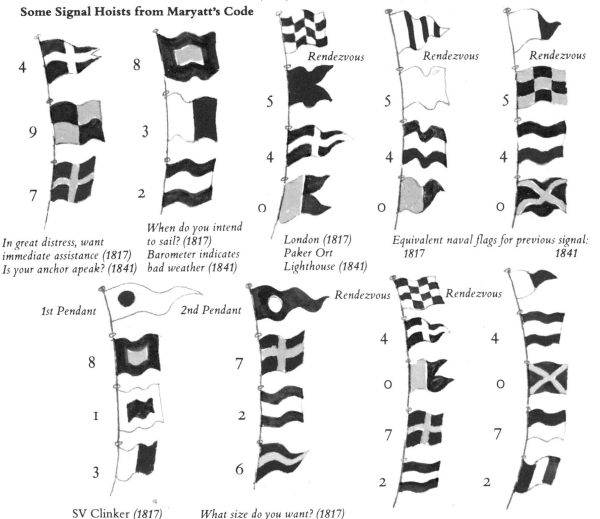

4 9 7

In great distress, want immediate assistance (1817)
Is your anchor apeak? (1841)

8 3 2

When do you intend to sail? (1817)
Barometer indicates bad weather (1841)

Rendezvous
5 4 0

London (1817)
Paker Ort
Lighthouse (1841)

Rendezvous
5 4 0

Rendezvous
5 4 0

Equivalent naval flags for previous signal:
1817                    1841

1st Pendant   8 1 3   2nd Pendant

SV Clinker (1817)
SV Beccles (1841)

7 2 6

What size do you want? (1817)
SS Scotia (1841)

Rendezvous
4 0 7 2

London (1869)

Rendezvous
4 0 7 2

Equivalent naval flags

## 1857 Commercial (later International) Signal Code

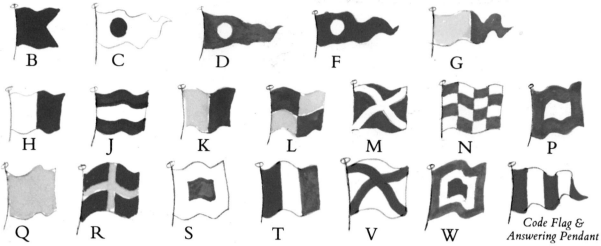

B C D F G

H J K L M N P

Q R S T V W

*Code Flag &
Answering Pendant*

## Some Signal Hoists from the 1857 Commercial Code

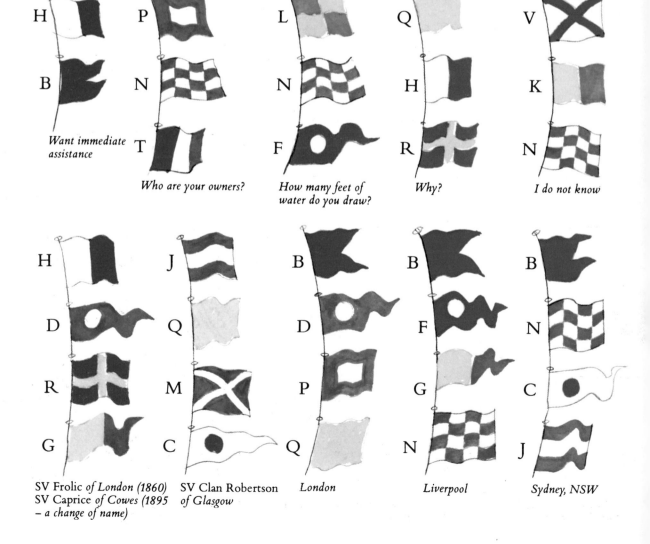

H
B

*Want immediate
assistance*

P
N
T

*Who are your owners?*

L
N
F

*How many feet of
water do you draw?*

Q
H
R

*Why?*

V
K
N

*I do not know*

H
D
R
G

SV Frolic *of London (1860)*
SV Caprice *of Cowes (1895
– a change of name)*

J
Q
M
C

SV Clan Robertson
*of Glasgow*

B
D
P
Q

*London*

B
F
G
N

*Liverpool*

B
N
C
J

*Sydney, NSW*

## 1931 International Code Flags (instituted 1934)

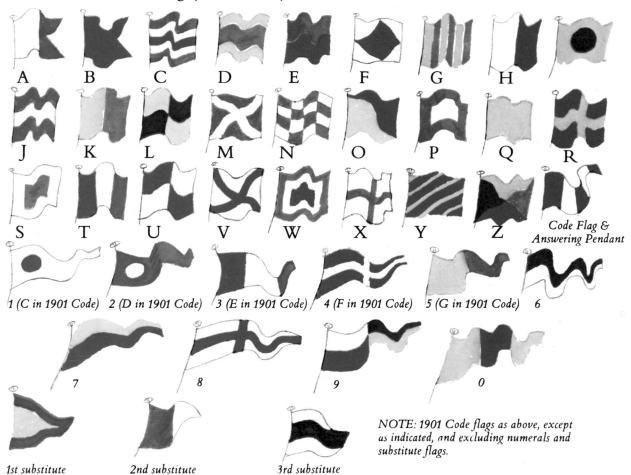

A  B  C  D  E  F  G  H

J  K  L  M  N  O  P  Q  R

S  T  U  V  W  X  Y  Z  *Code Flag & Answering Pendant*

*1 (C in 1901 Code)*  *2 (D in 1901 Code)*  *3 (E in 1901 Code)*  *4 (F in 1901 Code)*  *5 (G in 1901 Code)*  *6*

*7*  *8*  *9*  *0*

*1st substitute*  *2nd substitute*  *3rd substitute*

NOTE: 1901 Code flags as above, except as indicated, and excluding numerals and substitute flags.

## Some Signal Hoists from the 1901 and 1931 Codes

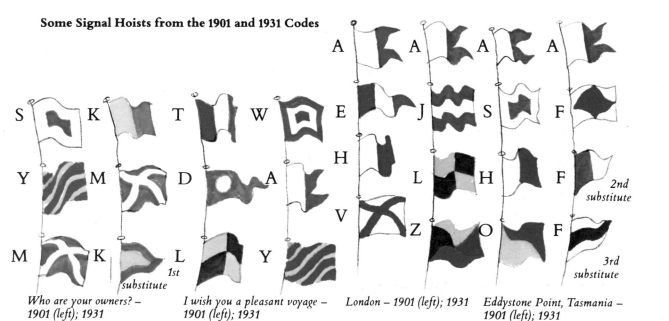

*Who are your owners? – 1901 (left); 1931*

*I wish you a pleasant voyage – 1901 (left); 1931*

*London – 1901 (left); 1931*

*Eddystone Point, Tasmania – 1901 (left); 1931*

# Fishing & Whaling

Early man apparently first caught fish by hand or by using a pointed stick as a spear. From very early times a fixed barrier of stones or wickerwork across a narrow tidal channel enabled primitive man to catch fish in some quantity. At some time, bait attached to a line came into use, and nets were invented. Eventually came the *seine*, a movable net supported by floats at the top and weighted at the bottom, which could be dragged towards the shore to form a bag, from which the fish were unable to escape. The next advance was to take the seine into deeper water by boat and then bring the ends ashore to be hauled.

Further progress was made when the net was worked entirely afloat and towed behind a boat or boats. The employment for salmon fishing, until recent times, of a net towed between two coracles is a survival of one of the earliest forms of trawl-net fishing. The trawl net, towed behind a single vessel and with its mouth extended by a wooden spar or beam, evolved from the dredge used for oyster fishing by the Romans. This type of net was in common use from the fourteenth century at least, but its employment for intensive fishing dates only from comparatively recent times.

During the second half of the nineteenth century, when large numbers of sailing trawlers worked from several English ports, the trawl normally employed was about 80 feet long, made of tarred hemp twine, with a mesh about 4 inches square at the mouth and only 1½ inches wide at the *cod* or narrow end. The wide end or mouth was extended by a beam of beech, elm or oak varying from 30 to 45 feet in length. The precise length of the beam was determined principally by the distance between the stern and the aftermost shroud of the fishing boat, as, when not in use, the beam was lashed alongside with one end projecting just beyond the stern and the other just in front of the after shroud.

Iron frames called *head-irons* were fitted to each end of the beam to raise it above the bottom and so allow the fish to enter. A ground rope made of stout hawser covered with small rope was fastened to the curved lower edge of the mouth of the trawl to protect it from chafing and, by its weight, keep the edge of the net on the ground and so disturb the fish. The net was towed by a strong *warp* of 6-inch rope some 900 feet long.

When working a beam trawl from a sailing vessel, one of the conditions required was a favourable tide, preferably one of moderate strength, as the trawl, which was always towed in the same general direction but a little faster than the tide-stream, would then work steadily and keep to the bottom. When the boat arrived at the fishing ground, work began at the early part of the tide, as the net could then be towed for several hours in the same direction. The vessel was first put under easy sail in the direction in which the tow was to be made, depending on the wind suiting the tide, as a fairly straight course had to be kept. This could only be done when the wind was generally fair, or more or less abaft the beam. The net was then thrown overboard, or *shot*, beginning at the cod end, until all of it was clear of the vessel and hanging from the beam, which was still in place, hoisted up alongside. With everything ready for lowering, the *fore bridle* was first slacked away until the end of the beam was well clear and stood out at a considerable angle from the vessel, the after part being still kept in place by the *dandy bridle*, which was brought inboard over the taffrail to a small windlass or *dandy wink* by which it was worked. This rope was then slacked away until the whole beam was in the water. The beam was now held by the two parts of the *main bridle*, and these were slowly let out until it hung evenly from them. The speed of the vessel was then increased and the warp given out so as to allow the trawl to sink to the bottom, which, as the vessel was under way, it would do at some distance astern. After that the amount of extra warp allowed was determined by the judgement of the master, according to the conditions of weather and tide and the type of fish expected to be caught. The warp was finally made fast by a small rope called the *stopper*. The purpose of this stopper was to save the warp if the trawl was fouled, for being a thin rope it would, under any sudden strain, snap or part before the warp, and the trawl would not be lost. When the trawl reached the bottom and was working properly, the warp was kept at such an angle with the length of the vessel as to make her steer herself on the desired course.

During trawling, one member of the crew stayed on deck to look out for any change of wind, to trim the sails and, by occasionally feeling the warp, learn if the trawl was working perfectly. Feeling the warp was a simple but effective test, for if all was well a regular vibration was felt, while an irregular jerking action would show that the trawl was going over rough ground or not keeping steadily to the bottom. The rest of the crew went below and turned in till the watch had to be relieved or it was time to get the trawl up. For the latter operation, the stopper or the trawl-warp was first cast off, the slack of the warp sent overboard and the vessel swung round with her head to the trawl. The foresail and other light sails being got in, the boy was sent below to the rope-room, while two hands went to the winch to heave in the warp. This was a tedious process at the best of times, seldom taking less than an hour and in bad weather sometimes taking two or three hours, with the vessel rolling and pitching heavily all the time. As the warp was brought inboard by the winch it was coiled away below by the boy in readiness for the net again being shot. As soon as the shackle joining the warp to the main bridles came in, the end of the dandy bridle was brought in over the stern to the dandy wink. The men at the winch continued heaving until the beam appeared at the surface. The after end was then hoisted up astern by the dandy bridle and secured. A tackle was then hooked to the fore end of the beam and hauled up until the head-iron was over the gunwale and made fast between the shrouds. The net was then gathered in by hand and stowed on the beam and gunwale until only the cod end with the catch of fish remained. This bag was attached to the fore halyards and hoisted up with the aid of the winch; then the net end was finally opened and the fish fell onto the deck.

The trawl-net was especially developed and constructed to catch demersal fish – sole, plaice, haddock and so on – which keep near or on the sea-bed. For pelagic fish such as herring, mackerel, pilchard and sprat which at certain times swim at or near the surface, an entirely different method of fishing, known as *drifting*, evolved. This method uses a screen or wall of mesh extending a considerable distance and allowed to drift with the tide. The fish, when their shoals attempt to pass this barrier, are caught by their gills.

Although nothing is known of the origin of this method of fishing, it has certainly been practised for many hundreds of years. Drift-nets varied in accordance with their use, the species to be caught, the size of the vessel and the season of the year. During the second part of the nineteenth century, a sailing fishing boat, probably rigged as a two-masted lugger, could have used a *fleet* of 70 to 90 nets, each about 62 feet long by 25 feet deep and extending for more than a mile. The nets were buoyed so as to hang at any desired depth.

When setting the nets, the vessel sailed to leeward while the nets were attached one after the other to a warp of strong tarred rope and then paid over the side. When the whole fleet had been shot, the vessel came round head to wind and rode to the fleet of nets as to a sea anchor. To prevent the warp chafing, the strain was taken by the *tissot*, a strong rope which was passed from the fishing vessel to the warp. The nets were hauled in by a capstan, the warp fastenings, or seizings, being released as the warp came inboard.

## Whaling

Said to be one of the oldest industries, whaling dates back to very early times, when whales were driven ashore and cut up for their blubber and bones. The Phoenicians took whales in the Mediterranean, but the first regular whaling industry was probably that established in the twelfth century by the Basques, who pursued the whale first in the Bay of Biscay and later as far as the coasts of Newfoundland. By the sixteenth century, English and Dutch whalers were operating in Arctic waters, and by the end of seventeenth century more than 200 Dutch whaleships were based at Spitsbergen. For about 100 years, from 1730, British whalers sailed from London, Hull, Liverpool, Whitby and Dundee; but it was the nineteenth-century fleets of American whaleships from Nantucket, New Bedford and Boston which achieved the greatest fame. A typical American whaler of the 1850s would have been about 350 tons and ship-rigged. On the upper deck the *tryworks*, a brick furnace with large iron cauldrons, was used to reduce the whale blubber to oil. The whaler carried a number of 30-foot boats equipped with oars, harpoons and lances and about 800 feet of *whale-line* coiled in tubs. When whales were sighted, the boats were lowered and, each with a crew of six men, rowed near enough for a harpoon to be darted into the whale so that the animal was attached to the boat by the line. The whale was killed with lances once it was exhausted by its efforts to escape. The carcase was then towed back to the whaleship, where it was cut up while lying in the water alongside, and the strips of blubber were fed into the tryworks.

BASIL W. BATHE

# Fishing craft and fishing grounds

**Abroad.** Out at sea. For example, 'the wind is getting abroad the night' was a way of saying bad weather was coming.

**Blinder.** Hidden, uncharted reef. The Iceland coast is notorious among trawlermen for these hazards.

**Bulk fleeting.** Method of fishing used by trawlers when there were rival trawler fleets fishing the North Sea, notably the *Red Cross*, *Gamecocks* and *Hewitts Short Blues* (named after the company house-flags the trawlers flew), trawler fleets sailing from Hull, Grimsby and Great Yarmouth. The trawler fleets would remain on the fishing grounds months at a time, fishing night and day. The catches would be sent ashore by fast fish cutters and thence galloped by relays of horses to Billingsgate Market in London. The rivalry for the limited space of the fish cutters was bitter and frequently violent.

**The cemetery.** North-eastern edge of the Dogger Bank, where during north-westerly gales a confused and destructive sea can pile up owing to the submerged cliff-faces of the Dogger Bank. In March 1883 this was the scene of the worst fishing disaster in Britain's history. Forty-five sailing trawlers, from 30 to 80 tons each, were lost in one night, with a total loss of 255 men and boys.

**Cod banger.** General term used by all other fishermen and seamen to describe vessels which line-fish for cod. The name is also used for the crews of these vessels.

**Copers.** Name given to vessels, usually converted trawlers, which carried duty-free schnapps and tobacco to sell to trawler crews when they were BULK FLEETING. This name was also given to those who owned and operated the vessels. Coping was the greatest anti-social activity in the history of the North-Sea fisheries, since both lives and vessels were lost because of drunkenness. This evil was eventually eradicated by the efforts of the Royal National Missions to Deep-Sea Fishermen, whose vessels and hospital ships accompanied the trawler fleets and helped keep the trawlermen in contact with their families.

**Cow killer.** Said of a successful fishing vessel.

**Dodge.** Said of a trawler when it heaves to in heavy weather, keeping under slow way, more or less head to sea.

**Drifter.** Vessel which catches pelagic fish, such as herring, sprats, mackerel and pilchard, by means of a drift net which hangs down in the water like a weighted curtain and traps the fishes by their gills.

**Driving.** Said of herring and sprat DRIFTERS with their nets out and moving with the tide.

**Grand bankers.** Line-fishing schooners from America, Canada, Newfoundland, France, Spain and Portugal, which fish for cod on the Grand Banks of Newfoundland, generally using dories carrying one or two men to set and haul the long-lines.

**Heft.** Said of a trawl net when it is caught on some obstruction on the sea-bed. More reckless skippers release the net by heaving down on the TRAWL WARP (14.03) with the steam capstan. This method lays the vessel on her beam ends and, although it frequently rips the trawl net badly, it usually works. The obstruction itself is often called a heft.

**Herring lugger.** Two- or three-masted, lugsail-rigged herring DRIFTER, crewed usually by eleven men, who work as follows:
*master* – takes charge of the helm and the handling of the vessel during shooting and hauling the net;
*mate* – generally supervises from the bows; the master and mate scud out the net, that is, shake the herring out into the fish hold;
*hawse man* – unleashes the floats from the net rope as the net is hauled in;
*wale man* – hauls in the fish-laden part of the net, known as the *lint*;
*net-rope man* – hauls in the main net rope;
*net stower* – stands down in the hold and stows the emptied net;
*all-work man* – works where he is most needed;
*capstan men* – three men who work the capstan hauling in the net;
*rope boy* – coils down the net rope in the hold as the net is released from it.

**Kids.** Compartments aboard a herring DRIFTER into which the herrings are shovelled.

**Law.** Wind is said to 'blow against the law' when it blows herring DRIFTERS back upon their fleets of nets.

**Loguy.** Said of a vessel that is heavy and slow.

**Long-boomer.** Name given to the yawl-rigged well smacks of Aldeburgh, Suffolk, because of the long retractable bowsprit they carried.

**Mother.** Term for a fishing vessel which is so successful that another vessel can be built from its profits.

**Silver pits.** Virgin fishing grounds whose accidental discovery opened up the North Sea trawl fisheries, the world's richest fishing grounds.
There are two traditional accounts of the discovery of the Silver Pits, a deep, narrow sea valley south of the Dogger Bank. One is that the Silver Pits were discovered in 1837 by Mr. William Sudds, a Ramsgate trawler skipper working out of Hull, who in a single haul caught 2,040 pairs of soles averaging $12\frac{3}{4}$ lbs the pair. The other story is that the Silver Pits were discovered in 1850 by a Brixham skipper who had spent the summer fishing close to the Dogger Bank.

**Towed under.** Said of a trawler which founders when the net suddenly becomes fast on an obstruction while the trawler is fishing in a heavy following sea.

**Trawler.** Vessel which drags a large net called a trawl along the sea-bed to catch demersal, or bottom-feeding, fish such as cod, haddock, plaice, soles, skate, turbot, brill and halibut.

# Fishing crews

**Admiral.** Senior skipper of a trawler fleet, who directs the fishing operations. Signals to manoeuvre used to be given by flag by day and rocket by night.

**Backer-in.** Crew member of a line-smack who stands in the small boat facing aft and coils the lines back into the HORSES (14.03) after the boardsman has removed the fish. The lines are then horsed.

**Balker.** A man who stood on a cliff top or any other prominent place and, using a type of semaphore, guided fishing craft to where he saw shoals of herring, pilchard or mackerel.

**Barm skin.** Oilskin apron used by fishermen when shooting and hauling lines and nets, also worn when shaking fish from the nets.

**Bete** (vb). To mend nets. Women were generally much more adept at this.

**Betester.** Person who does the BETE-ing.

**Boardsman.** Crew member of a line-smack who baits and shoots the lines,

and also hauls them. The lines are usually shot from a small boat or dory.

**Dole.** Portion of profits due to a SHAREMAN.

**Elsinore cap.** Cap with ear flaps, made of dog's hide with the hair still attached.

**Flewers.** Term used for fishermen who poach inside the lawful limit; for those who take fish under the legal size limit; or for river fishermen.

**Frost.** 'The frost has set in' – said when the monotony and grind of trawling is beginning to tell on the tempers of the crew.

**Gaffer.** Trawler owner.

**Gaffers.** Name given to cod smacksmen by herring driftermen, and obviously derived from the fact that the former use gaffs to secure their catch when hauling it in.

**Gast-cope.** Volunteer without pay aboard a cod smack or a herring drifter. Taken from the Icelandic *gesta kaup*, meaning literally 'the cheap bargain of the guest'.

**Gyp.** To gut a fish.

**Half-and-half.** The principle of the owner having one half of a fishing vessel's profits and the crew the other half.

**Jumbo wrists.** Trawlermen's term for wrists swollen by endless heaving and hauling of the nets. They are not worried by this occupational complaint as it signifies a successful voyage.

**Kid.** To make known, to signify by action. A method used to signal from a herring DRIFTER how many herrings have been caught. An arm stuck straight forward signified a *last*, that is 10,000 herrings. Waved round the head, 1,000 herrings; held straight above the head and brought sharply down, less than 1,000 herrings. The word kid was also used to indicate the premonition of an event. The stomachs of those prone to sea-sickness were able to 'kid' a coming wind. These sufferers by anticipation were called *weather-kidden*.

**Knock out.** Order given by the trawler skipper to knock the pin from the towing block and thus release the warp, preparatory to hauling the net.

**Macklantan.** Said of anything poor or scanty.

**Make up.** To conclude a fishing voyage and settle wage and expense accounts.

**Mardle** (vb). To gossip, particularly when two vessels meet at sea and the crew discuss fishing matters.

**Mopus.** Herring driftermen's name for money.

**Pricker.** Skilled crew member aboard a Well smack whose work consists of pricking cod brought up from deep water, in order to release the air from their sounds, after their sudden decompression. The cod are then placed in the well where they soon recover. *Pricker* is also the name of the instrument – the handle of a sterling silver spoon filed to a point – with which the operation is performed.

**Sharemen.** Trawlermen who receive shares of the value of the vessel's catch rather than set wages. This system of pay was an iniquitous one, since at the end of a bad voyage the crew could find themselves in debt to the owner for food.

**Shoot,** or **shot.** Said of all nets and lines when they are going and have gone into the water.

**Trawler crew.** Consisted of skipper, mate, third hand and three boys, these last usually taken from orphanages.

**Wesley hunters.** Dock-side scroungers on the look-out for fishermen who may have money in their pocket. So called after John Wesley, who was always trying to raise money for his church.

# The Fish

**Blowfish.** Fishermen's name for any species of whale. Large numbers of killer whales would frequently congregate round drifters when the herring nets were being hauled; their continuous blowing at night was an eerie sound.

**Cade.** Archaic term for a measure of sprats or herrings. About 1,000 sprats.

**Cran.** About 1000 herrings. Also, the basket which holds them.

**Dogs.** Fishermen's term for all species of dog-fish. All the species (but particularly the spur-dog) are a menace to herring fishermen, for they devour or mutilate the meshed herring and in doing so tear the nets to tatters.

**Ducks.** Haddocks.

**Fake.** Another name for a haul of fish.

**Flats.** Any form of flat fish, particularly sole, plaice and dabs.

**Gildings.** Fish which have been mutilated by dog fish when caught in nets or on lines.

**Homer.** Large spotted ray.

**Joalies.** Another name for young herrings.

**Kickling string.** String or cord which is worked through the gills of herrings so that they may be conveniently carried.

**Last.** Ten thousand herrings.

**Lipper.** Flurry on the surface of the water caused by a shoal of fish.

**Mand,** or **maund.** Large wicker basket used for measuring sprats. It holds about 1,000; thus 1,000 sprats are called a mand or maund of sprats; also, a *cade* of sprats.

**Mazy.** Said of herrings out of condition after spawning.

**Net eyes.** Young herrings which swim inshore in autumn.

**Shimmer.** Silvery gleam of fish caught in the net, seen below the surface – a sign driftermen are always looking for.

**Stinkers.** Fish which are useless because they have fed off food impregnated with iodine from seaweed.

**Swim.** Inexplicable sudden movement of vast numbers of herrings or sprats, usually in the evening, at daybreak, at slack tide or at low water. The greatest herring swims are near the full moon, when the spring tides are running strongly. Generally, a swim may occur over an area of several square miles or in patches of various sizes over a large area. During such a swim, a single drifter can net something like half a million herrings in less than one hour.

**Turkey.** General term for fish.

*'Pilchards' by Charles Napier Hemy, 1897*

# Nets and catches

**Beam trawl.** Purse-shaped net which sailing trawlers drag along the bottom, and so named because of the long wooden beam to which the net is attached. Believed to have been brought to Britain by William of Orange. Others say Brixham (Devon) fishermen invented it.

**Belly.** Main body of the trawl net between the wings.

**Bet-ups.** Nets which have been mended.

**Bowls.** Small, black-painted wooden tubs fitted with a short length of rope and secured to the headlines of drift nets to keep them afloat. To distinguish the inner and outer ends of the fleet of nets, the bowls at each end are sometimes painted in different colours.

**Bridles.** Two ropes shackled to each LUTE HEAD, to which the main towing warp of the trawl is secured.

**Buffs.** Air-filled leather spheres, about twice the size of a football, which were sometimes used in place of BOWLS. Sometimes blue, green, white or orange air-filled glass spheres about the size of coconuts and contained in net snoods were also used. Today these attractive glass spheres are sold as decorative antiques.

**Cod end.** Tapered end of the trawl net, which holds the catch. Its underside is often protected with rawhide.

**Cod-end knot.** Knot at the COD END which is released when the net is hauled up the mizen mast to permit the catch to fall on the deck.

**Cod knocker, or priest.** Short heavy club with which the live cod are despatched when taken from the well on arrival at the smack's destination.

**Dan.** Buoy bearing a long pole and some form of flag and used to mark a fleet of lines, nets or lobster pots. The dan is said 'to watch well' if it remains upright against the wind and waves.

**Dandy score.** FAIRLEAD (05.03) with rollers fitted on to the port bulwark of a sailing trawler and through which the dandy bridle, used to bring the end of the BEAM TRAWL alongside, was led inboard.

**Danish seine.** Form of long-haul net used principally for catching flat-fish on the seabed at a depth of about 50 fathoms (300 feet). Worked by a single vessel, the net has long narrow wings and a long bag.

**Donkey boiler.** Coal-fired boiler aboard a sailing trawler, which drives the steam capstan used for hauling the net.

**Draw sail.** Spare sail spread beneath the keel of a becalmed sailing trawler to catch the moving tide and thus give the trawler sufficient way to tow her net.

**Dredge.** Drag net consisting of a bag supported by an iron frame. Oysters and mussels are scraped off the sea bed by the sharp 'scythe' fitted at the bottom of the mouth of the dredge.

**Gang.** Row of meshes in a net.

**Ground rope.** Lower rope of the D-shaped mouth of the trawl net.

Usually, it is fitted with round wooden rollers called bobbins. If, however, such fish as sole, plaice or megrims are being fished for, chains are wrapped around the ground rope to disturb the mud or sand in which such fish live.

**Hand line.** Fishing line, usually with a few baited hooks, which is attended constantly and hauled in as soon as fish are hooked.

**Head rope.** Upper rope of the opening of the trawl net. It is fitted with corks or small floats to keep the mouth of the net open.

**Horse.** Shallow, three-sided wooden tray into which the lines are coiled when baited for shooting and again when hauled. When the lines have been lashed in the horses they are said to be *horsed*.

**Huddies.** The spaces between the top of the net and the net rope.

**Hues.** Tannin solution in which new nets are soaked to preserve them.

**Lade-net.** Net on an iron hoop fitted to a long handle, used to pick up fish which have fallen out of the nets. Also known as a *dydle*.

**Lint.** Name for the meshes of herring nets.

**Long line.** Fishing line with from 20 to 4,000 baited hooks. The hooks are attached to the main line by means of thin lines known as *snoods*. The line is worked from boats or set at low tide on the sands.

**Look on.** To haul part of the net out of the water; that is, under-run a short length to see if the fish are swimming.

**Lute heads.** The iron frames at each end of the trawl beam on which the entire net is dragged along the bottom.

**Molgogger.** Portable roller FAIRLEAD (05.03) which could be fitted to the port or starboard bulwarks, near the bows, and through which the warp of a drift net was led.

**Murderer.** Iron bar carrying a number of hooks, which is dragged along the bottom so that fish are impaled on the hooks; also known as a *fluke bar*.

**Net needle.** Wooden needle on which net twine is wound, used for making, or *breeding*, net and repairing net.

**Purse seine.** Used to catch fish swimming above the sea-bed. The fish are encircled by a wall of netting, the lower edges of which are gathered together or 'pursed' to stop the fish escaping downwards.

*Long-line fishing for cod*

**Satchel.** Trawlerman's name for the trawl net.

**Seine.** Fishing net in the form of a long bag with the upper part buoyed and the lower weighted.

**Spiller.** Light line with up to 2,000 baited hooks used by North Cornish fishermen.

**Split belly.** Said of a trawl net when the body of the net is torn.

**Take the ground.** Said of a fleet of drift nets so full of herring or sprats that it sinks to the bottom, and such is the weight of fish that any attempt to lift the net inevitably destroys it.

**Towing block.** Block which keeps the TRAWL WARP close alongside the trawler when it is fishing.

**Towing post.** Strong post fitted amidships on a trawler and around which the warp of a BEAM TRAWL was

passed. The pump handle was frequently hinged to the top of this post.

**Trawl warp.** Rope by which the trawl net is towed along the bottom. Usually about three times the amount of trawl warp to the depth of water is required.

**Wings.** Side pockets of the main body of the trawl net, so tapered as to keep the fish moving further into the net.

*Hauling in trawl*

# Whaleboats and their crews

**Boat header.** American term for an experienced whaleman who steered the boat when approaching the whale. After the whale had been darted, he exchanged places with the harpooner in the bows and killed the whale with lances.

**Boat steerer-harpooner.** American term for the seaman manning the HARPOONER OAR.

**Camboose.** American whalesman's name for the galley or cookhouse.

**Clumsy cleat.** Thwartship plank at the bows of an American WHALEBOAT. The after edge was notched to take the whaleman's left thigh and so steady him when darting the harpoon or using a whale lance to kill the whale.

**Cranes.** Form of davit made from hinged wooden brackets, which swung out to support a WHALEBOAT on an American whaleship.

**Gaff man.** Member of the crew who holds the blubber with a gaff while the *spade man* uses his spade to cut the blubber into HORSE PIECES (14.05).

**Gam.** Social meeting of two or more whaleships when they were on the whaling grounds in good weather. There would be an exchange visit of boats' crews, with the captains remaining on one ship and the mates on the other. The corresponding British term is *foy*.

**Harpooner oar.** The foremost oar in a WHALEBOAT, pulled by the harpooner or whale fastener. The harpooner, once he had thrown his harpoon, moved aft to steer the boat. The BOW OAR (09.02) was in fact the second oar in whaleboats.

**Kicking strap.** In American whaling, a rope fastened across the CLUMSY CLEAT, under which the WHALE-LINE (14.05) passed to prevent it sweeping aft if it jumped from the groove in the stem of the whaleboat.

**Nantucket sleigh ride.** Whalemen's term for the first wild dash of the open boat behind a freshly harpooned whale.

**Scrimshaw.** Pictorial, ornamental and useful things made by whalemen from the teeth and bone of the whale.

**Skee-man.** On a whaleship, the officer in charge of the hold.

**Specksynder.** Officer who, in the early days of Dutch whaleships, shared command with the captain. The word means literally 'fat (or blubber) cutter', but through general usage was later applied to the chief harpooner.

**Spring.** Word used by captains and officers of whaleships to their boat crews in calling for the utmost effort, as in 'spring your oars, men!'

**Steerage.** In an American whaling ship, the living quarters of the boat steerers.

**Towing drugg.** Two heavy squares of wood let into each other and attached to a harpoon with a length of line. This device was used to slow down and exhaust whales while the whaleboats chased other whales.

**Whaleboat.** Boat used for chasing, harpooning and killing whales. It was usually a lithe and graceful craft built of white cedar and so light that two men could lift it and five oarsmen could propel it at ten knots. Five whaleboats were swung from the usual whaleship's davits, and spare boats were stowed bottom-up on heavy beams above the main deck between the main and mizen masts.

**Whaleship.** Square-rigged vessel of 200–300 tons built for durability and seaworthiness. Whaleships sailed from Aberdeen, Nantucket, Easthampton and New Bedford up until about 1870. They were flush-decked and broad in the beam, with big holds to stow up to 2,400 barrels of whale oil. Space for cutting up whales was provided for by building the deck-house aft in two sections. These lumbering, often smelly, vessels were frequently pioneers in wide ocean waters, for they ranged far and wide and charted many hitherto unknown shoals and reefs. Whaling crews established the post restante of the Pacific Ocean on the Galapagos Islands, then known as the Porter Islands. The 'post box' was a large turtle-shell where the crews left and collected their mail – some written years previously.

*The whaleship* James Arnold *1852*

# The Whale

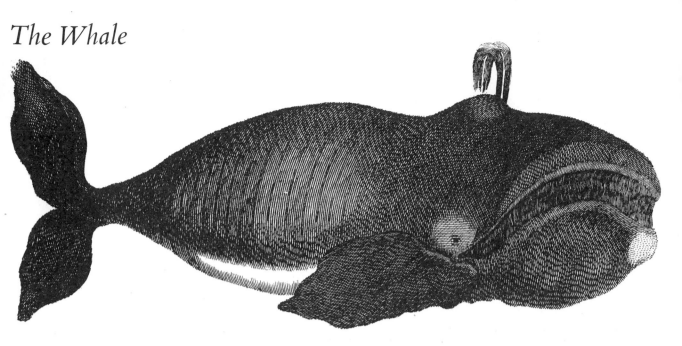

**Breaching.** Said of a whale rushing to the surface from a great depth. The animal sometimes does this with such speed and power that the entire 100-ton mammal leaps from the water like a salmon.

**Driving the spigot out.** Phrase used by whalemen to describe the moment when the whale spouts blood after it has been successfully lanced.

**Fast fish.** Whale which has been harpooned and which is thus the legal property of those who are *fast* to it. A whale was also a fast fish when it was marked with a waif-pole bearing the mark of those who had harpooned it.

**Flukes.** The whale's tail, which in a fully grown sperm whale can be 20 feet across.

**Flurry.** Final convulsion of a whale when it has been lanced.

**Funeral.** Moment when the useless remnants of the whale's carcass were cut adrift from the whaleship.

**Gallied whale.** Whale which has panicked. In this condition, whales swim madly about giving short quick spouts or just float paralysed with fear on the surface, an easy mark for the harpooner.

**Grandissimus.** Whalemen's term for the penis of the whale. This organ is sometimes between six feet and seven feet long and up to a foot in diameter.

**Heidelberg tun.** Cavity about 26–30 feet long in the top of the sperm whale's head which holds about 500 gallons of the finest sperm oil. Also called the *case*.

**Lobtailing.** Said of the sperm whale when at play. It lies on the surface idly hitting the water with its flukes. The sound resembles gunfire and can be heard for miles.

**Loose fish.** Whale which is not yet harpooned and so fair game for anyone who can harpoon it.

**Peaked flukes.** Said of a whale when it has thrown its flukes and body into a vertical position preparatory to a deep dive.

**Sweeping.** Sideways movement of a sperm whale's flukes when it is lying on the surface. Should the whale sense the presence of a boat or even a man in the water at this time, the flukes will be raised vertically and brought down like a gigantic mace.

**Town ho!** Older whale-sighting cry used before the phrase 'there she blows' became more popular.

*A whaler at Spitsbergen, 1905*

# Catching and processing the whale

**Bible leaves.** Thin slices of blubber produced by the mincing machine. Mincing the blubber accelerated the boiling out of the oil, increasing its quantity and enhancing its quality.

**Blanket, or blanket-piece.** Continuous strip of blubber which was peeled from the whale's carcass rather like the rind cut in one piece from an apple or orange.

**Blubber room.** Space below decks into which the BLANKET-PIECE was lowered before being cut into HORSE-PIECES for the mincer.

**Boarding sword.** Long sword-like instrument used to dismember the whale, and for cutting a hole in the carcass before inserting the blubber hook – by means of which the blubber was hoisted in strips out of the water.

**Bomb gun.** In American whaling, a shoulder gun which fired a metal tube (*bomb lance*) about 14 inches long fitted with explosives, with a short fuse so that it exploded inside the whale.

**Cant piece.** A two-foot wide strip of blubber. It could be 30 to 40 feet long, according to the size of the whale.

**Cant purchase.** Strong tackle extended from the mainmast head and used to haul the CANT PIECE inboard. The American term is *cutting tackle*.

**Cutting stage.** On American whalers, a platform consisting of three planks with a handrail, slung outboard amidships and used by the men cutting up the dead whale lying in the water alongside the whaler.

**Cutting tackle.** American term for CANT PURCHASE.

**Dart.** Action of throwing the harpoon into the whale. It was said that on an average less than five darts out of every fifty attempts were successful.

**Darting gun.** On American whalers, a stockless gun mounted on the HARPOON pole. When the harpoon penetrated the whale, the gun was triggered, shooting a bomb into the animal.

**Flensing.** Cutting the blubber from the whale.

**Fore-ganger.** Eighteen feet of $2\frac{1}{4}$-inch hemp rope made fast at one end to the HARPOON and the other end joined to the WHALE-LINE.

**Fore-line beck.** Box or tub amidships in the whaleship, in which the WHALE-LINE is coiled.

**Grains.** Barbed HARPOON used for taking seals and fish (American term).

**Greener gun.** American swivel gun used for shooting HARPOONS.

**Harpoon.** Spear with a single razor-sharp barb and a three-foot socketed shank onto which a wooden shaft was fitted. Attached to the WHALE-LINE, it was used to 'fasten' the whale to the whaleboat; thus the harpooner was sometimes called the *whale fastener*. The two harpoons, which were carried in a wooden crotch at the bows of the whaleboat, were known as the *first* and *second irons*.

**Horse pieces.** Blubber cut to a convenient size for the blubber-mincing machine.

**Iron.** Whaleman's name for the HARPOON. 'Sinking the iron' was the act of harpooning the whale.

**Monkey rope.** Safety-line consisting of a broad canvas belt attached to a long rope, worn by whalemen working on the carcasses of whales lashed alongside the whaleship. This precaution was essential in tropical waters owing to the hordes of sharks which often swam round whaleships, attracted by the blood and offal.

**Nipper.** In American whaling, a quilted piece of cloth about 9 inches square, which was used to protect the

*Flensing the whale*

whaleman's hand if it was necessary for him to handle the line fastening the whale to the boat.

**Pitchpoling.** Manner in which the WHALE-LANCE was thrown to kill the harpooned whale once it had exhausted itself. The butt of the lance was held in the right hand, with the left hand along the pine shaft. The lance was pitched in a high arc to give maximum penetration into the whale's vital organs. This was the crucial moment of the whale hunt, and required considerable skill and strength.

**Scarf.** Lines cut with WHALING-SPADES into the carcass of the whale, enabling the BLANKET-PIECE to be removed.

**Skead.** Wooden racking to hold barrels in the hold.

**Spurs.** Iron spikes worn on a whale-man's boots when cutting up the whale.

**Steering oar.** In American whaling, a 23-foot-long oar used for steering a whaleboat. There was a grip at right angles to the loom for the left hand of the boat steerer.

**Temple toggle-iron.** HARPOON invented by Lewis Temple of New Bedford, Mass., in 1848 and said to have been the most widely used and successful whaling iron.

**Try-works.** Structure in which the blubber was rendered down into whale oil. The try-works consisted of a brick structure about 10 feet by 8 feet by 5 feet high, built on special strengthening beams between the foremast and the mainmast and secured to the deck by massive angle-irons. The sides of the brick structure were cased in wood and the top covered by a sloping battened hatchway. Inside this structure were two huge, highly polished iron cauldrons, the *try-pots*, in which the sliced blubber was rendered down. Beneath the try-pots was the iron furnace, which was started with wood and then maintained with pieces of blubber from which the oil had been extracted.

**Waif-pole.** Tall pole thrust into the carcass of a dead whale and bearing the mark of the whaleboat whose crew has harpooned it.

**Whale lance.** Light steel lance with a ten-foot pine shaft, used to kill the whale after it had been harpooned.

**Whale-line.** Line attached to the HARPOON. Originally the line was of hemp, cured with tar smoke but not impregnated, as this would stiffen the line. Later, hemp line became obsolete and manilla was used. American whaleships carried about 300 fathoms of whale-line in a single tub, while British whaleships carried 230 fathoms in the main tub and 75 fathoms in a reserve tub. After the whale had been harpooned, the line was slowed down by turning it around a wooden post, the *loggerhead*, in the bows of the whaleboat. Such was the friction of the turns that one of the boat's crew stood by to pour water on the wood to prevent it catching fire. The inboard end of the whaleline was never fastened to the boat, to prevent a wounded but fighting whale taking the boat and crew down with it when it sounded. In such instances, the end of the whale-line was quickly made fast to the line of another boat, which then took up the chase when the whale surfaced again.

**Whaling spade.** Razor-sharp spade not unlike a garden spade, but flat at the sides and narrower at the top than at the bottom and fitted with a 20- to 30-foot shaft. It was used to loosen the whale blubber so that it could be stripped in pieces from the carcass and hauled inboard for rendering down.

**Wooden horse.** Structure to which the blubber-mincer was fastened.

# Navigation

In order to appreciate the momentous advances in navigation which took place during the eighteenth and nineteenth centuries, it is necessary to describe the slow progress of navigational methods during the previous centuries of discovery and trade.

In the fifteenth century, the Portuguese began their voyages of exploration southward down the African coast under the direction of Prince Henry the Navigator. By 1497 Vasco da Gama had rounded the Cape of Good Hope and made the first voyage to India. New techniques were developed which made voyages of this duration possible and also allowed the navigator to record the latitude and chart the new discoveries accurately. At first, measuring the height of the Pole Star with a simple wooden quadrant and converting its daily difference in height into leagues helped to keep a reckoning of progress north or south. Rules had to be learned to allow for the Pole Star's then daily 3½° radius circle round the pole, and later the altitude of the star was used to find the latitude north of the equator. But once the equator was approached and the Pole Star could no longer be seen at night, solar declination tables were constructed so that seamen could take the sun's altitude at noon in order to find their latitude.

By 1500 charts were marked with a latitude scale, and the position of newly discovered continents could be determined increasingly accurately in a north and south direction. Soon some charts carried longitude scales, but these were almost always in error, because it was not yet possible to find longitude at sea. By 1700 ships of many nations were trading regularly across the Atlantic Ocean and to India and the Far East round the Cape of Good Hope. Countless numbers were wrecked through their inability to find longitude, but the possibility of improving existing navigational techniques seemed remote. In making a landfall, a ship's navigator attempted to get into the latitude of his destination in good time and 'ran down his latitude' until land was sighted. Unless the navigator was certain whether he was to the east or west of his destination, he could sail in completely the wrong direction when running down his latitude, thus prolonging his voyage by many days through being unable to retrace his tracks because of the prevailing winds. This problem induced Charles II to found the Royal Observatory at Greenwich in 1675, '. . . so as to find out the so much desired longitude of places, for perfecting the art of navigation', with the first priority being the accurate plotting of the star positions and a study of the motion of the Moon.

Rewards for methods of finding longitude at sea had been offered by several nations over the years, principally France and Spain. However, that offered by the British Parliament in 1714, which promised £20,000 to the person who could find a practical method, proved to be the incentive which produced the desired result. A Board of Longitude was set up at the same time, to evaluate the methods and apportion the prize money.

Longitude is basically difference in time between two places on the Earth's surface, so that in order to find how far east or west his ship has sailed, a navigator must be able to find the time at the ship and at the same instant be able to calculate the time at his place of departure, or the time at a standard or prime meridian. A theoretically correct answer to the problem, the lunar-distance method, had been put forward as early as 1514 by Johannes Werner. He suggested using the Moon as a clock as it moved across the star background, by measuring its distance from certain fixed stars, or from the sun, in order to find the time at a prime meridian. This solution was defeated by an inexact knowledge of the position of the stars, an inability to predict the Moon's motion for several years in advance and the lack of a sufficiently accurate instrument to take the required measurements. These short-comings were not sur-mounted until the mid-eighteenth century. An alternative method was the 'meckanicks' answer, put forward by Gemma Frisius in 1530. This involved constructing a clock that would keep time under sea-going conditions and variable temperatures. In this way, a standard time could be carried in the ship and compared with local time, the difference in time being the longitude. Again, the technology of the period was not sufficiently advanced for such a clock to be made.

In 1730 a country gentleman and Fellow of the Royal Society, John Hadley, invented his reflecting octant, and described it to the Royal Society on 13 May 1731. Hadley was confident that when the theory of lunar prediction was perfected his octant could be used to measure the necessary lunar distances at sea. In 1755 Tobias Mayer, a Gottingen Professor, sent his lunar prediction tables to England to be considered for the longitude prize. They were tested at sea by Nevil Maskelyne, later Astronomer Royal, on a voyage to St. Helena in 1761, and Mayer's widow was eventually paid £3,000.

Maskelyne proved the feasibility of the lunar-distance method using Hadley's octant, but realized that the length of the computation, some four hours, put the method beyond the powers of ordinary navigators. He attempted to rectify this by publishing his *British Mariners' Guide* (1763), in which he explained his method and computations. However, it was not until *The Nautical Almanac* was published for 1767, based on Mayer's revised tables sent by his widow in 1763, that the method became available for seamen in general. At much the same time that Hadley's quadrant and lunar prediction tables were being worked at, a Yorkshire carpenter and self-trained clockmaker was developing a series of clocks, and later watches, that won him the longitude prize. John Harrison finished his first sea clock (known as H.1) in 1735, incorporating in it many original ideas – temperature compensation by his 'grid iron' compensator, interconnected balances to nullify the motion of the ship, a near frictionless escapement and much original thought on the elimination of friction throughout its movement. Two other clocks followed; the last (H.3) was completed in 1757. But it was Harrison's large silver watch known as H.4, completed in 1759 and tested by the Board of Longitude on voyages to Jamaica in 1762 and Barbados in 1764, that eventually won him the prize.

The initial high cost of chronometers was soon reduced by the inventions and commercial production of John Arnold and Thomas Earnshaw in England, so that an increasing number of ships began to carry them. However, it was not until 1825 that they were generally issued to ships of the Royal Navy. With the increasing use of chronometers it became necessary to devise some method of checking their rate of gaining or losing, so that time-signals were set up at most major ports around the world, the time ball at Greenwich being the first, in 1833. Today, of course, radio time-signals enable a ship's chronometer or deck watch to be checked several times daily if necessary, making the carrying of several expensive chronometers to compare with each other during a voyage a thing of the past.

In 1843 an American merchant captain, Thomas Sumner, published a pamphlet describing a new method of interpreting the astronomical time sight. Sumner's method, now generally known as position-line navigation, enabled latitude and longitude to be found at the same time by combining the information found at one sight with that of another taken several hours later. Due allowance had to be made for the course and distance covered by the ship between

the two observations. This method was further improved by the French naval officer, Marc St. Hilaire, who in 1876 devised a method of comparing the altitude of a heavenly body as actually observed with that calculated for the supposed position of the ship. The resulting differences enabled the position lines of several selected stars to be plotted around the estimated position of the ship and the ship's actual position determined. Combined with these improvements in navigational expertise was a dramatic increase in the accuracy of charts, brought about in Britain by the tireless service of the Hydrographic Department of the Royal Navy, founded in 1795. They charted much of the Earth's surface during the nineteenth century, for it was early realized that the new methods of navigation were of no use unless accompanied by accurate charts.

Contrasting the navigation methods available to prudent navigators out of sight of land in 1750 with those available in 1850, it can be seen that the earlier men relied almost entirely on estimating the ship's movements, taking into account such things as tides and currents when known, leeway, the estimated speed of the ship and courses steered. They were able to check only the latitude of their reckoning, by observing the altitude of the sun at noon or of a transiting star at twilight. One hundred years later, as long as they had the necessary mathematical skills, navigators could fix the ship's position astronomically during the course of a day in a variety of ways, provided of course the sky remained clear. Although the noon position was the important one from the point of view of maintaining the ship's log, the most accurate position finding was at morning and evening 'stars', when both latitude and longitude could be found at the same time.

It must not be forgotten that by the middle of the nineteenth century the profits to be made by the master of a merchant vessel were considerably less than in the affluent days of the East India Company at the turn of the century, so that the quality of Merchant Navy officers had fallen considerably. The British Merchant Shipping Act of 1854 made examinations for masters and mates compulsory, to remedy this state of affairs. It is from this time that a gradual improvement in navigational skills in the Merchant Service at large took place.

ALAN STIMSON

# Methods of expressing position

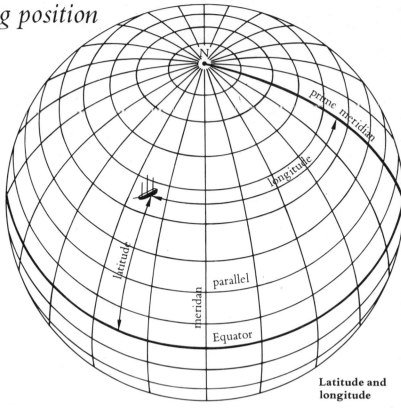

**Navigation.** The art of conducting a vessel from place to place in safety.

**Latitude** (Lat.). Angular distance of a place north or south of the equator, measured along the MERIDIAN of the place in degrees, minutes and seconds of arc.

**Parallel of latitude.** SMALL CIRCLE (15.07) on the terrestrial sphere parallel to the equator, joining all places with the same latitude.

**Longitude** (Long.). Angular distance of a place east or west of a chosen PRIME MERIDIAN, today usually Greenwich, measured either in degrees, minutes and seconds of arc, or (in astronomical calculations) in hours, minutes and seconds of time. Generally, a 180°W – 0° – 180°E notation is used, but eighteenth-century charts occasionally use 0°–360° either eastward or westward.

**Meridian.** Semi-GREAT-CIRCLE (15.07) on the terrestrial sphere from pole to pole, perpendicular to the equator. All places on the same meridian have noon at the same instant and have the same longitude.

**Prime meridian,** or **first meridian.** MERIDIAN from which LONGITUDE is reckoned. The choice is purely arbitrary, and many different meridians were used in the past, varying from country to country. The second-century geographer Ptolemy chose the Fortunate Isles (now the Canary Islands) as the most westerly land known. French charts of the 1750s had five different longitude scales – from Teneriffe and from the Isle de Fer (Hierro) in the Canaries, from the Lizard (the point of departure for many ocean voyages), from London (St. Paul's), and from Paris Observatory. The *Greenwich Meridian* was not used by British mapmakers until the British *Nautical Almanac* was first published in 1767. It was adopted internationally in 1884.

**Known position.** A vessel's position can be determined by referring to the bearing and distance of a known position. This might be a prominent landmark, the ship's point of departure, or the place for which she is bound. For example, 'Lizard N 28° 30′ E, dist. 990 m.' or 'Porto Santo S by W ½ W, 140 leagues.'

**Latitude and longitude**

**Inshore,** or **onshore.** Close to the land, in contrast to OFFSHORE.

**In mid-stream.** In the middle line of the stream or current.

**In mid-channel.** Half-way across any channel, river or similar stretch of water.

**On a lee shore.** Said of a ship near the shore with the wind blowing right onto it. Figuratively, a dangerous situation.

**In soundings.** So near the land that the DEEP-SEA LEAD (19.01) will reach the bottom. Not in deep water.

**Having sea room.** At sufficient distance from the land, rocks or shoals that a ship may DRIVE (12.03) or SCUD (12.03) without danger.

**Offing.** Far from the land but visible from it. *To keep a good offing* is to keep a safe distance off the coast.

**Offshore.** Far from the land, usually out of sight of it, in contrast to INSHORE.

**Position defined by bearing and distance**
*In the days of sail, bearing would be given to the landmark thus: 'Lizard NNW, 3½ leagues'.*

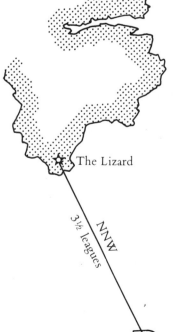

# Types of position

**Fix**

angle of cut

cocked hat

070°

085° ○ beacon

115°

☆ lighthouse

✝ church

**Dead reckoning** (D.R.), or **position by account.** Calculation of the ship's position by consideration of the distances logged and courses steered, allowing for current, leeway and so on. Some modern authorities define this as *estimated position*, reserving dead reckoning for the ship's position calculated without the allowances mentioned.

**Observed position** (Obs. or Obs. Pos.), or **position by observation.** Position obtained by astronomical means.

**Position line,** or **line of position.** Line (which may be drawn on a chart) on which the ship must surely lie. It may be a line of bearing, or an arc of a circle of equal latitude (that is, a *position circle* or *circle of position*).

**Fix.** Position determined by the intersection of two or more POSITION LINES. Where all are terrestrial position lines, it is a *land fix*; where astronomical, an OBSERVED POSITION.

**Angle of cut.** The smaller angle at which a pair of POSITION LINES intersect. For a good FIX, the larger the angle, the better

**Cocked hat.** Small triangle where, owing to errors of observation or errors in the chart, three POSITION LINES fail to meet in a point.

**Running fix.** When the POSITION LINES are not obtained more or less simultaneously, an allowance has to be made for the ship's run between observations; the position line on which this allowance has been made is a *transferred position line*. Special cases of running fixes are *doubling the angle on the bow* and *four-point bearing*.

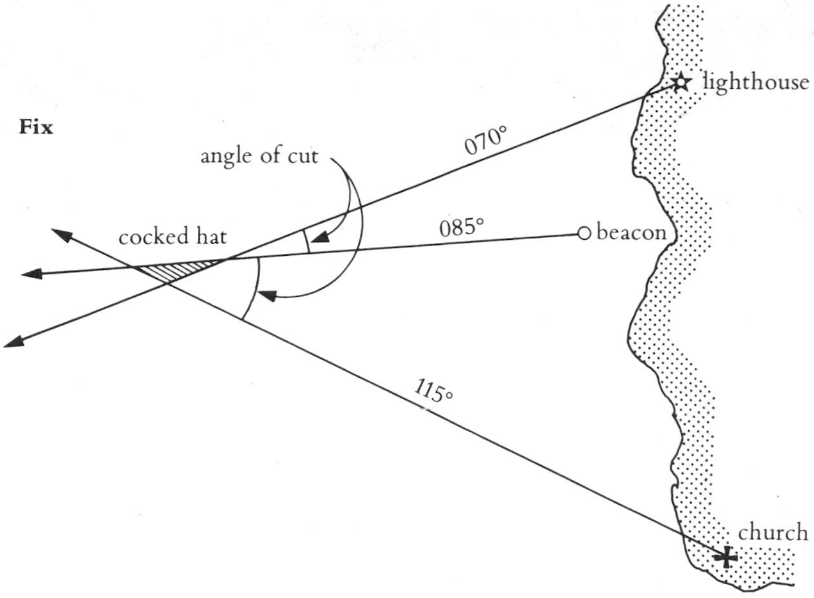

**Running fix**

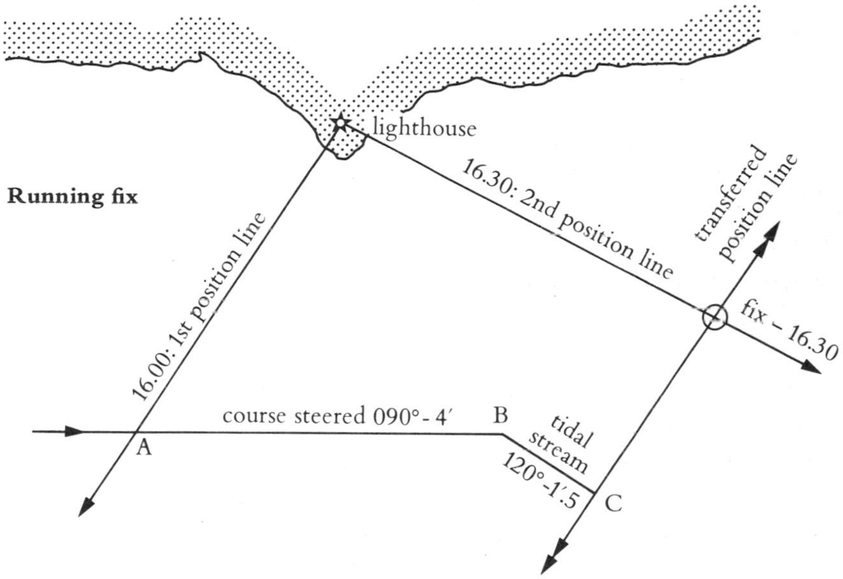

☆ lighthouse

16.00: 1st position line

16.30: 2nd position line

transferred position line

fix – 16.30

course steered 090°- 4′    B    tidal stream

A

120°-1′.5    C

## Doubling the angle on the bow
*If the angle taken at B is double that taken at A, then the distance of the ship from the object at the second bearing (BL) is equal to the distance run between the two bearings (AB).*

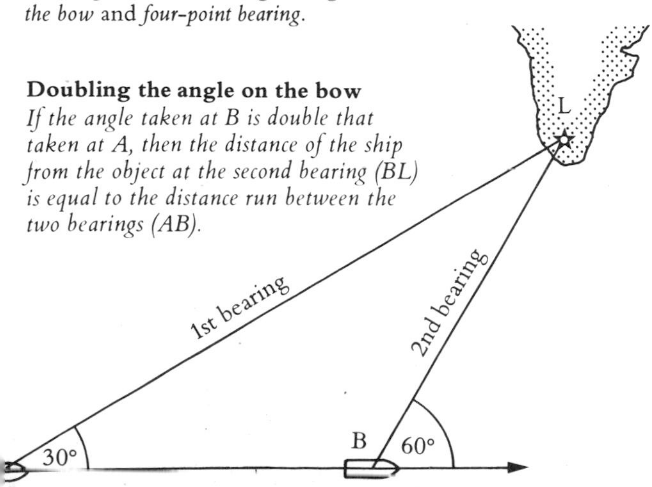

L

1st bearing

2nd bearing

30°    B    60°

## Four-point bearing
*The first bearing is taken when the object is 4 points (45°) on the bow, and the second when abeam (90°). The distance between the two bearings is equal to the distance off the object.*

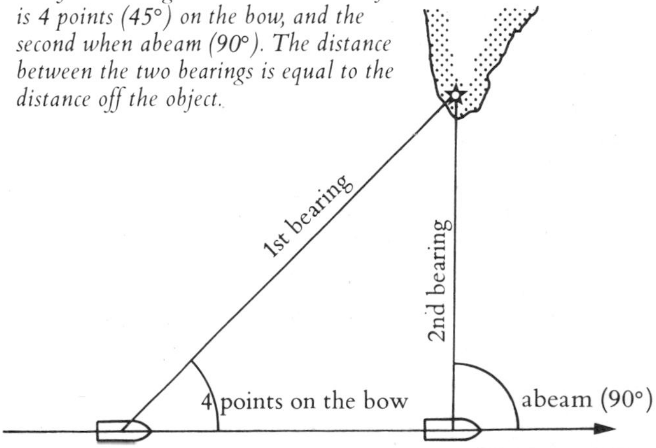

1st bearing

2nd bearing

4 points on the bow    abeam (90°)

# Compass bearings and courses

**Bearing.** Direction of one terrestrial object from another, measured from a reference direction in degrees or in POINTS OF THE COMPASS. It is designated *true, magnetic, compass* or *relative* according to whether the principal reference direction is TRUE NORTH, MAGNETIC NORTH, COMPASS NORTH, or the ship's HEADING. The angular difference between the MERIDIAN (15.01) and the initial direction of a GREAT CIRCLE (15.07) is a *great-circle bearing*. Bearings (and courses) can be expressed in points of the compass, for example NW; or in degrees, in a 0°–360° notion, for example 315° (= NW); or in degrees quadrantally from N and S, for example N 45°W (= NW).

**Azimuth.** The bearing of a celestial body.

**Course.** The intended direction steered by a vessel. This may be *true, magnetic, compass* or *great circle course*, according to the reference direction (see BEARING). The navigator *sets course* for his destination.

**Heading,** or **ship's head.** The direction in which a ship points at any instant.

**True north.** The direction of the north geographical pole on the observer's meridian.

**Magnetic north.** The direction indicated by the north-seeking pole of a magnetic needle influenced only by the Earth's magnetic field. Its angular difference from true north is the magnetic variation.

**Compass north.** The direction indicated by the compass in your own ship. Its angular difference from magnetic north is the DEVIATION OF THE COMPASS (19.06).

**Course made good.** The actual direction made good over a period.

**Track.** The actual path of a vessel over the ground.

**Courses and tracks**

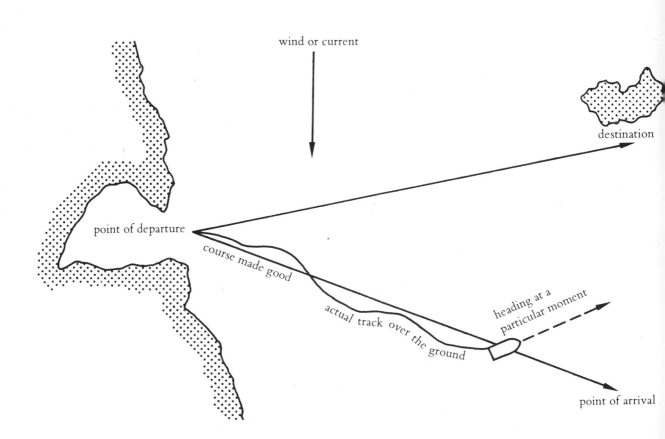

wind or current

point of departure

course made good

actual track over the ground

heading at a particular moment

destination

point of arrival

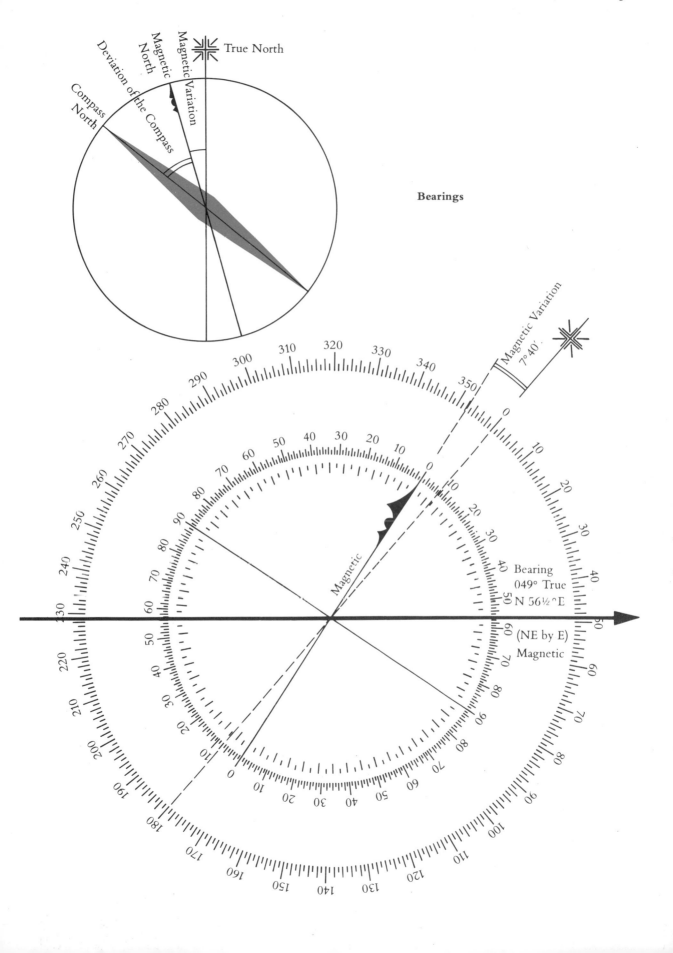

True North

Magnetic Variation

Magnetic North

Magnetic North

Deviation of the Compass

Compass North

**Bearings**

Magnetic Variation 7°40′

Magnetic

Bearing
049° True
N 56½°E

(NE by E)
Magnetic

**Points of the compass**, or **rhumbs.** In the days of sail, the compass circle was divided into 32 points, each of $11\frac{1}{4}°$. Thus, a ship reversing her course was said to be turning 16 points; and a bearing 2 points abaft the beam signified $112\frac{1}{2}°$ from right ahead. The *cardinal points* are north, south, east and west; the *intercardinal* or *half-cardinal* or *quadrantal points* are those midway between – NE, SE, SW, NW; the *intermediate points* are those between cardinals and intercardinals – NNE, ESE and so on. The remaining 16 points are called *by-points*, all containing the word 'by' – NW by N, S by E and so on. Points are further divided into *quarter* ($2°$ $48'$ $45''$ each) and *half points* ($5°$ $37'$ $30''$ each) – NE by E $\frac{1}{2}$ E, S $\frac{3}{4}$ E and so on.

**Boxing the compass.** Reciting the points and quarter points in the correct order, starting at any named point.

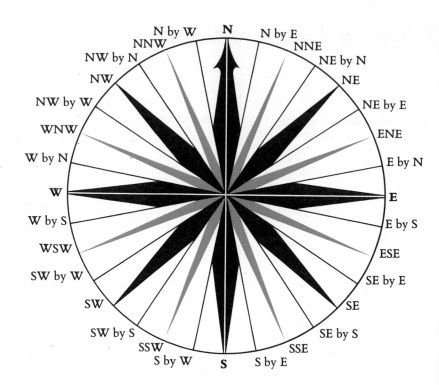

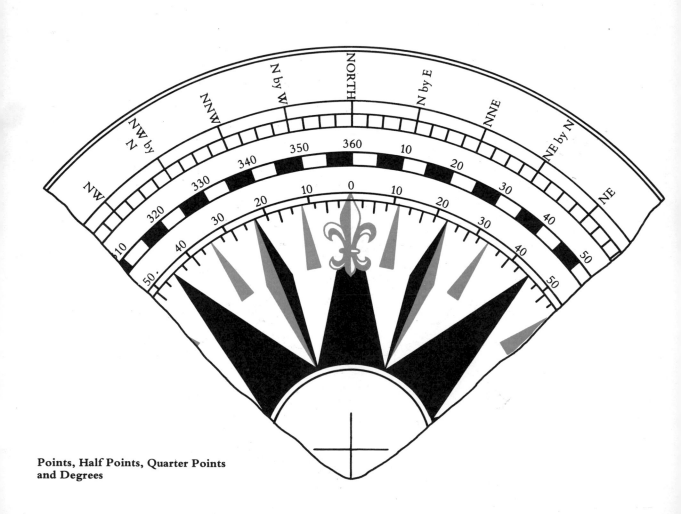

**Points, Half Points, Quarter Points and Degrees**

# Direction relative to the ship

**Relative bearings.** Though for navigation the seaman usually uses compass bearings to indicate direction, for day-to-day purposes he more often uses relative bearings based on the ship's fore-and-aft line.

There are eight principal directions (each separated by four points): *ahead, starboard bow, starboard beam, starboard quarter, astern, larboard quarter, larboard beam* and *larboard bow.* For greater precision, these can be qualified by saying: *right astern; fine on the larboard bow; broad on the starboard quarter; abaft the starboard beam; before the larboard beam* and so on. For greater precision still, the basic directions can be qualified by points: for example, *2 points [22½°] before the larboard beam;* or *3 points [33¼°] on the starboard bow.* The use of degrees instead of points to indicate relative bearings is a comparatively modern innovation. (Note: From the 1840s, 'port' would have been used instead of 'larboard'.)

## OF LAND, WIND AND TIDE

**Landward,** or **shoreward.** In the direction of the land.

**Seaward.** In a direction away from the land.

**Eye of the wind,** or **the wind's eye.** The direction from which the wind is blowing. Directly to windward.

**To windward,** or **on the weather side,** or **a-weather,** or **upwind.** Towards the direction from which the wind is blowing.

**To leeward,** or **on the lee side,** or **a-lee,** or **downwind.** Away from the direction from which the wind is blowing.

**Upstream.** On the side from which the stream is setting. If tidal, *uptide.*

**Downstream.** On the side towards which the stream is setting. If tidal, *downtide.*

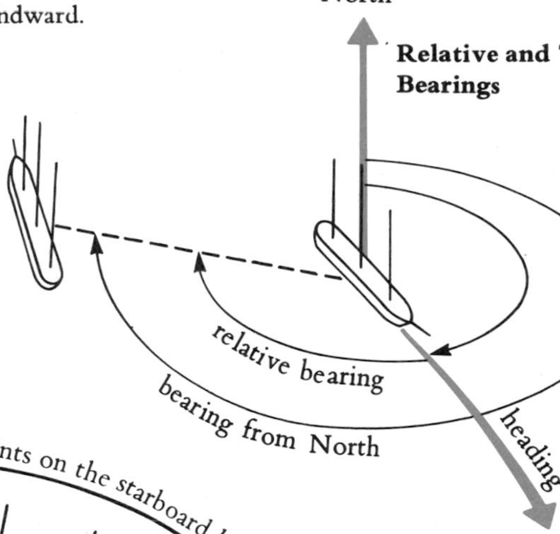

North

**Relative and True Bearings**

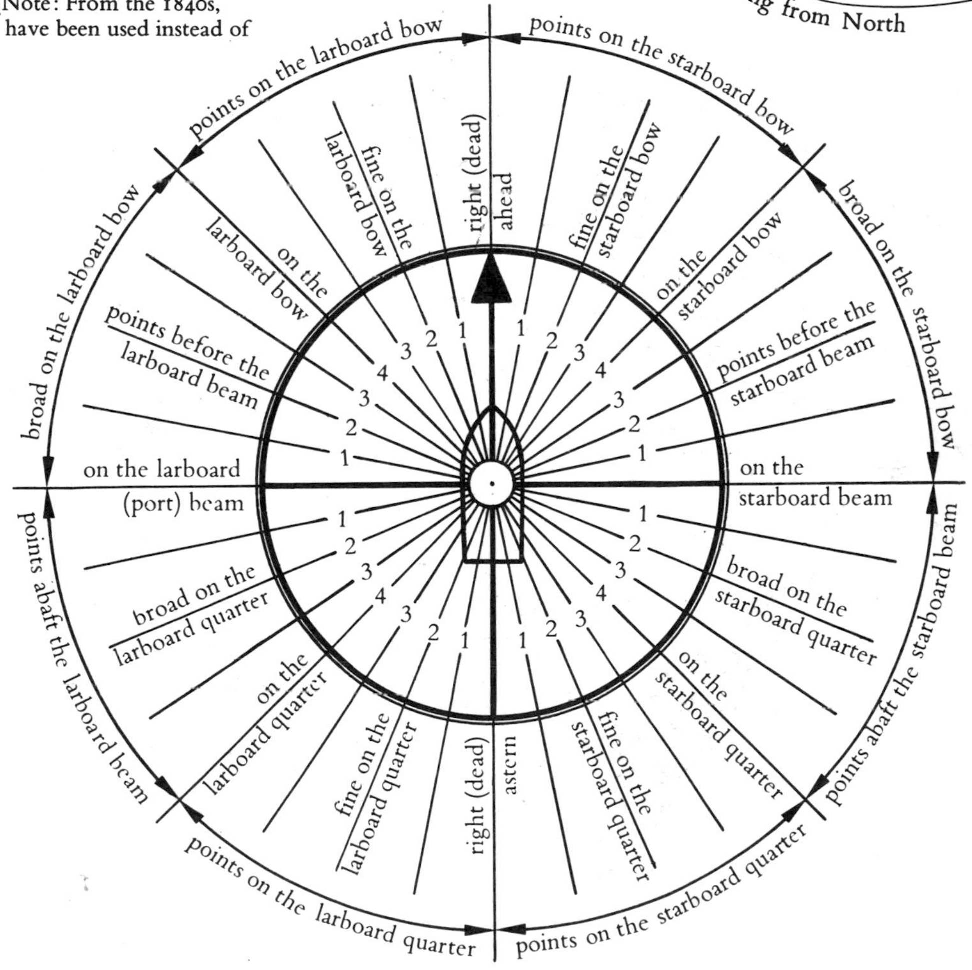

relative bearing

bearing from North

heading

# Length, depth and speed

**Fathom.** Six English feet. A very ancient method of measuring rope was to pass it between both arms outstretched, each pass constituting a fathom. The Latin equivalents make this obvious by their names – the French *brasse* (5 French feet, about 5 feet 4 inches), the Spanish *braza* and the Italian *braccio*. Fathoms are used for measuring lengths of rope, cable and, because the method described was used for sounding lines, for depth of water.

**Metre.** French charts with soundings entirely in metres began to be published in the 1820s. A chart with a conversion table from French feet into metres was published in 1802.

**Cable's length,** or **cable.** Measure of 120 fathoms, by which the distances of ships in a fleet were often estimated. It approximates to a tenth of a nautical mile and cable is often so defined in British practice.

**Nautical mile,** or **sea mile.** Length of 1′ of arc of the MERIDIAN (15.01), or 1/60 of a degree of LATITUDE (15.01). Because the Earth is flattened at the poles (the shape is known as the *figure of the earth*), the length of the nautical mile varies between 6,046 feet at the equator and 6,108 feet at the poles. For practical navigation, a standard sea mile of 6,080 feet (based on latitude 48°) was used for many years. Since 1929, the *International Nautical Mile* has been defined as 1,852 metres (about 6,076 feet).

**Geographical mile.** Length of 1′ of arc of the equator, about 6,087 feet; invariable because the equator is for all practical purposes a circle.

**Statute mile,** or **land mile.** Distance of 5,280 feet.

**League.** Three nautical miles, or 1/20 of a degree of latitude. Until the nineteenth century, the league was generally used for estimating distances at sea; except in navigation, where the mile was often used. The actual length of the league varied according to the country, English, French, Breton, Italian, Spanish, Catalan and German leagues all being different.

**Kenning.** Sixteenth-century term for the distance high land could be seen from seaward. It varied between 14 and 22 miles.

**Hull down.** Said of a distant ship when her hull was below the horizon but her upperworks or sails could be seen.

**Knot.** Speed of 1 nautical mile per hour. Derived from the COMMON LOG (19.01), where the number of knots (about 50 feet apart) which ran out in half a minute gave a direct reading of the ship's speed. The knots were subdivided into ten fathoms, each of five feet. Thus, if the log was streamed and six knots and four fathoms ran out before the half-minute glass was turned, the ship's speed was 6.4 nautical miles per hour, or 6.4 knots. (To say '6.4 knots per hour' is, strictly speaking, incorrect.)

# Logs and journals

**Day's work,** or **day's works.** Reckoning or account of the ship's courses and distances run from noon to noon according to DEAD RECKONING (15.01), due allowance being made for LEEWAY (12.05) and heave of the sea, as well as variation of the compass. This is computed according to one or other of the SAILINGS (15.06).

**Log board.** Two hinged boards, folded together like a book. They were painted black and ruled. Details of distances by log, and of courses, winds and occurrences were chalked on the board as they happened, being rubbed out daily after they had been transcribed into the LOG BOOK. Sometimes, a *log slate* fulfilled a similar function. A TRAVERSE BOARD (19.06) was used in smaller ships to record information watch by watch. In the nineteenth century, the log board gave way to the *scrap log, rough log* or *deck log*.

**Log,** or **log book,** or **day book.** Book ruled in columns (like the LOG BOARD), into which the account on the log board was transcribed every day at noon, together with all occurrences of interest and the results of any observations. From this, the navigator made the necessary deductions for his DAY'S WORK and, taking any *observations* into account, worked up his *noon position*, which was effectively the end product of the day's work. When in port, the remarks in the log were called *harbour work* and the *civil day* (from midnight to midnight) was used. For *sea work*, the *nautical day*, which started twelve hours before the civil day and ran from noon to noon, was used.

**Journal.** In some larger ships, the contents of the log book were summarized in the journal, or *fair log*, which was often the record forwarded to higher authority.

Fore Topmast going out    Ship Betsey.    with her Jury Topmast.

Right and overleaf: *sections of the log book from three voyages of the* Betsey

# in the Ship Betsey. 1770

| H | K | fth | Courses | Winds | Sunday 25th March 1770 |
|---|---|---|---|---|---|
| 2 | 5 | 1 | NE | NE | |
| 4 | 5 | 1 | SE | | |
| 6 | 6 | | SbE | EbN | |
| 8 | 6 | 1 | SE | NbE | |
| 10 | 6 | 1 | | | |
| 12 | 7 | | | | |
| 2 | 7 | | | | |
| 4 | 7 | | | | |
| 6 | 7 | | | | |
| 8 | 7 | | | | |
| 10 | 13 | | Miles ♁Log | | |
| 12 | | | | | |

The first and Middle parts of these 24 hours fresh Breezes and Squally, the latter pleasant Gales & fair Weather.

At 6 P.M. Cape Rock bore NNW distant 6 miles. at 8 A.M. Cape Roque, or the Rock of Lisbon bore EbS distant 5 or 6 Leagues.

| Course | SE ½ E |
|---|---|
| Distance | 104 |
| Λ Lat | 1" 32 South |
| Depart | 124 East |
| Δ Long | 2" 40 East |
| Long in | 10" 16 West |
| Merr D | 1 Mile West |
| D L. | 36 West |

**Latitude Observed 38° 30' North**

at Cape Roxent

When Cape Roque commonly call'd the Rock of Lisbon bears EbS. If you dist 13 or 14 Leagues it Shews thus

A View of Cape Roxent East half South dist 4 or 10 Leagues

Thus Appears Cape Spiell, or Spichell, Bearing EbS dist 7 Leagues

| Sunday 25th March continued | At 4 in the Afternoon, Cape Spichelo bore NEbE dist 9 Leagues. at 6 d° light Breezes at NW & pleasant Wr a sudden Gust or Whirlwind carryed away our Foretopmast, & a William Fitler Seaman who was furling the Fore topgallt Sail, was drownd. Suppose he was killd in the fall as we Nither saw or heard any thing of him Afterwards Employd Clearing the Wreck & Making Sail again |

# From Bristol towards S.t Carolina

| H | K | IK | Course | Winds | Tuesday Jan.y 12.th 1768. |
|---|---|---|---|---|---|
| 2 | 3 | 1 | N.W.. | S.W.. | The first part thick foggy W.r with Little wind from S.N |
| 4 | 3 | 1 | NW b W.. | SW b W.. | out 2.d Reef Topsails |
| 6 | 3 | 1 | | | spoke a Snow call'd the Portland George Higgins M.r from Ced Town |
| 8 | 3 | 1 | W b N ½ N.. | S.W.. | bound to Cowes.. at 10 P.M. Strong Gales Down M.n Stays.s. |
| 10 | 4 | | | | at 12 in all R.M.s.s hand.d Mizen s.s. at 2 A M h. M.n Y.d E S.d |
| 12 | 3 | 1 | | | at 8 M Reef'd the F.S.l Set it. |
| 2 | 4 | 1 | W b N.. | SW b S.. | |
| 4 | 4 | | | | |
| 6 | 2 | | | | |
| 8 | 2 | | | | |
| 10 | 2 | | W. N W.. | S W.. | |
| 12 | 2 | | | | |
| | 76 | plog | | | |

Thick W.r
No Observ.
Latt. p
Account
48..41 N.o

| Co.. | W ½ N.. |
|---|---|
| Dis.. | 76 |
| X Latt. | 23 N.o |
| Dep.t | 70 W.. |
| X Long.s | 1..47.do |
| Long in | 13..13 |
| Me. Dis | 330 W.. |
| Long M.d | 8..33 |

| H | K | IK | Course | Winds | Wednesday January 13.th 1768. |
|---|---|---|---|---|---|
| 2 | 2 | ..... | W b N.. | S W b S.. | The first and Latter parts of this 24 hours Strong |
| 4 | 2 | ..... | | | Gales with heavy Squalls. the Middle it has Blown a |
| 6 | 2 | 1 | W. N W.. | S.W.. | hard Storm with a very lofty dangerous Sea Running |
| 8 | 2 | ..... | | | at 8 P.M handed Main Sail Lay too under y.e Reef'd F.S.l |
| 10 | | | up W b N.. | off N.W.. | at 8 A.M set M.n Sail Something moderate. a sail in sight by S.d |
| 12 | | | up N W b N.. | off N W b N.. | |
| 2 | | | up N W.. | off N. N W.. | |
| 4 | | | up N W b N.. | off N W b S.. | |
| 6 | | | up d.o.. | d.o.. | |
| 8 | 2 | 1 | N W b N.. | W b S.. | |
| 10 | 2 | 1 | N W b N.. | S W b W.. | |
| 12 | 2 | | N N W.. | West.. | |
| | 31 | log | | | |

Latt. Obs.d 19..3

| Co.. | N W b N.. |
|---|---|
| Dis.. | 36.. |
| X Latt. | 22 N.o |
| Depart | 28 W.. |
| X Long.s | 43 d.o |
| Long in | 13..56 |
| Me. Dis | 358.. |
| Long M.d | 9..16 |

| H | K | IK | Course | Winds | Thursday January 14.th 1768. |
|---|---|---|---|---|---|
| 2 | 1 | ..... | N S W.s | West.. | Wore Ship. Strong Gales. at 4 P.M out Reef F.S. |
| 4 | 3 | 1 | South.. | N W.. | the Middle Squally with heavy Showers of Rain & hail |
| 6 | 2 | 1 | S ½ E.. | | at 4 A.M set F.s. at 6 d.o set Mizen Topsail M.n Stays.l & Jib |
| 8 | 2 | 1 | S b W.. | W b S.. | the latter part. Moderate Gales at 10 A.M out 3 R.Z.s.. |
| 10 | 2 | 1 | | | |
| 12 | 2 | 1 | South.. | N S W.. | |
| 2 | 2 | 1 | | | |
| 4 | 2 | 1 | S b W.. | W b S.. | |
| 6 | 3 | | S S W.. | West.. | |
| 8 | 3 | ..... | | | |
| 10 | 3 | 1 | | | |
| 12 | 3 | 1 | | | |
| | 68 | log | | | |

| Co.. | S 46 ¾ |
|---|---|
| Dist.. | 70.. |
| X Latt. | 54 S.o |
| Depu.. | 44 East.. |
| X Long.s | 1..7 d.o |
| Long in | 12..49 W.. |
| Me. D.s | 314 do |
| L. M.. | 8..9 |
| Latt.d Obser.d 18..9 | |

# From Bristol towards Charles Town

| H | K | HK | Courses | Winds | Friday, July 8th 1768 |
|---|---|----|---------|-------|------------------------|
| 2 | 5 | 1 | West | East | Fresh Breezes with Pleasant Wr. & cast'y |
| 4 | 6 | | | | |
| 6 | 6 | 1 | | ENE | |
| 8 | 6 | 1 | | | |
| 10 | 6 | 1 | | | |
| 12 | 6 | 1 | | | |
| 2 | 6 | 1 | | | |
| 4 | 6 | 1 | | | |
| 6 | 6 | | | | |
| 8 | 5 | 1 | | | |
| 10 | 5 | | | | |
| 12 | 5 | 144 | Miles ♦ Log | | Lattd. Observd 23. 50 No. |

Albacore
3 Feet Round the Body 4½ in Length weighs four Score Pounds sometimes 130.

| | |
|---|---|
| Cours | W. 4. So. |
| Dist | 144 |
| Δ Latt | 9 South |
| Depart | 144 w. |
| D Long | 2. 39 d. |
| Long in | 39. 28 d. |
| No. D. | 1. 74 d. |
| Δ Mer | 22. 2 |

| H | K | HK | Courses | Winds | Saturday, July 9th 1768 |
|---|---|----|---------|-------|-------------------------|
| 2 | 6 | | West | NE | Fresh Breezes and ♦ as ♦ day Past. Spoke |
| 4 | 6 | 1 | | | two Dutch East India Men homeward bound |
| 6 | 7 | | | NNE | out from St. Helena 6 weeks. |
| 8 | 7 | | | | |
| 10 | 7 | 1 | | | |
| 12 | 7 | 7 | | | |
| 2 | 7 | | | | |
| 4 | 7 | | | NE | |
| 6 | 6 | 1 | | | |
| 8 | 6 | 1 | | | |
| 10 | 5 | | NWBd. | ENE | |
| 12 | 5 | 157 | Miles | | Lattd. Observd 28. 21 North |

| | |
|---|---|
| Cours | WBS. |
| Dist | 157 |
| Δ Latt | 29 South |
| Dep | 154 w. |
| Δ Long | 2. 49 d. |
| Long in | 42. 17 d. |
| No. D. | 1. 28 d. |
| Δ Me | 24. 51 |

| H | K | HK | Courses | Winds | Sunday July 10th 1768 |
|---|---|----|---------|-------|-----------------------|
| 2 | 5 | 1 | West | NE | The first part fresh Breezes, the Middle & latter |
| 4 | 5 | 1 | | | Light Breezes and Squally with heavy Showers |
| 6 | 5 | 1 | | NNE | |
| 8 | 5 | 1 | | | |
| 10 | 6 | | | No. | |
| 12 | 6 | | | | |
| 2 | 4 | 1 | | | |
| 4 | 4 | | | EbN. | |
| 6 | 4 | | | | |
| 8 | 4 | | | | |
| 10 | 4 | 1 | | So. | |
| 12 | 4 | 1 | | NE. | |
| 420 | 119 | Miles ♦ Log | | 378 | Lattd. Observd 24. 15 No. |

| | |
|---|---|
| Co. | West'y |
| Dist | 119 |
| Δ latt | 6 South |
| Dep | 119 w. |
| D Long | 2. 9 d. |
| Long in | 44. 26 d. |
| No. D. | 1. 27 d. |
| Δ Me | 27. 0 |

# The sailings

**The sailings.** Different ways in which the path of a ship at sea can be represented on paper, either graphically or by calculation.

In essence, what the sailings did in varying degrees of sophistication was to solve the problem, 'given the starting position, and the courses and distances sailed thereafter, find the final position'; or its converse 'given the present position and the destination, find the course and distance'. Today, these problems would generally be solved by plotting them out on a chart, but in the eighteenth century this was often done by trigonometry, using tables or GUNTER'S SCALES (19.05).

**Rhumb, or rumb, or romb, or wind.** One of the points of the compass other than the cardinal points.

**Rhumb line, or loxodrome.** Line on the surface of the Earth which cuts all MERIDIANS (15.01) at a constant angle, other than a right angle. Because of the *convergence of the meridians*, a rhumb line is a spiral (though this only becomes critical at high latitudes). The COURSE (15.02) sailed by a ship is normally a rhumb line.

**Parallel sailing.** Before longitude could be found at sea, ships would often sail northwards or southwards until they were in the same latitude as their destination (latitude was easy to find), and then sail east or west along the parallel until they reached it. Parallel sailing gave the distance or difference of longitude for a ship sailing along a parallel, using the formula: D. long. = Distance run (in miles) × secant latitude.

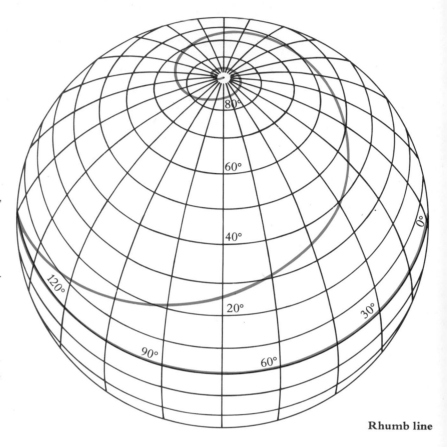

**Rhumb line**

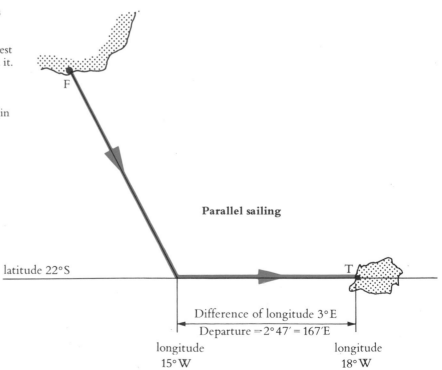

**Parallel sailing**

latitude 22°S

Difference of longitude 3°E

Departure = 2°47′ = 167′E

longitude 15°W

longitude 18°W

## TRAVERSE TABLE

| Courses. | Dist. | Diff. of Lat. | | Departure | |
|---|---|---|---|---|---|
| | | N. | S. | E. | W. |
| N. E. | 35 | 24.7 | | 24.7 | |
| E. b. S. | 25 | | 4.9 | 24.5 | |
| N. E. b. E. ½ E. | 40 | 18.9 | | 35.3 | |
| North. | 21 | 21.0 | | | |
| N. W. b. W. | 30 | 16.7 | | | 24.9 |
| | | 81.3 | 4.9 | 84.5 | 24.9 |
| | | 4.9 | | 24.9 | |
| Diff. of Lat. | | 76.4 | Dep. | 59.6 | |

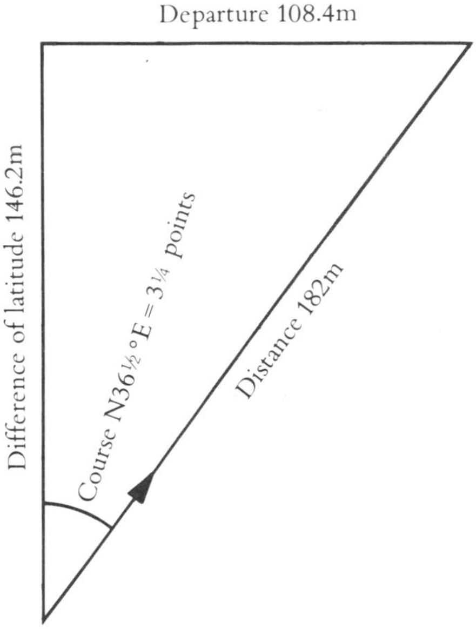

Departure 108.4m

Difference of latitude 146.2m

Course N36½°E = 3¼ points

Distance 182m

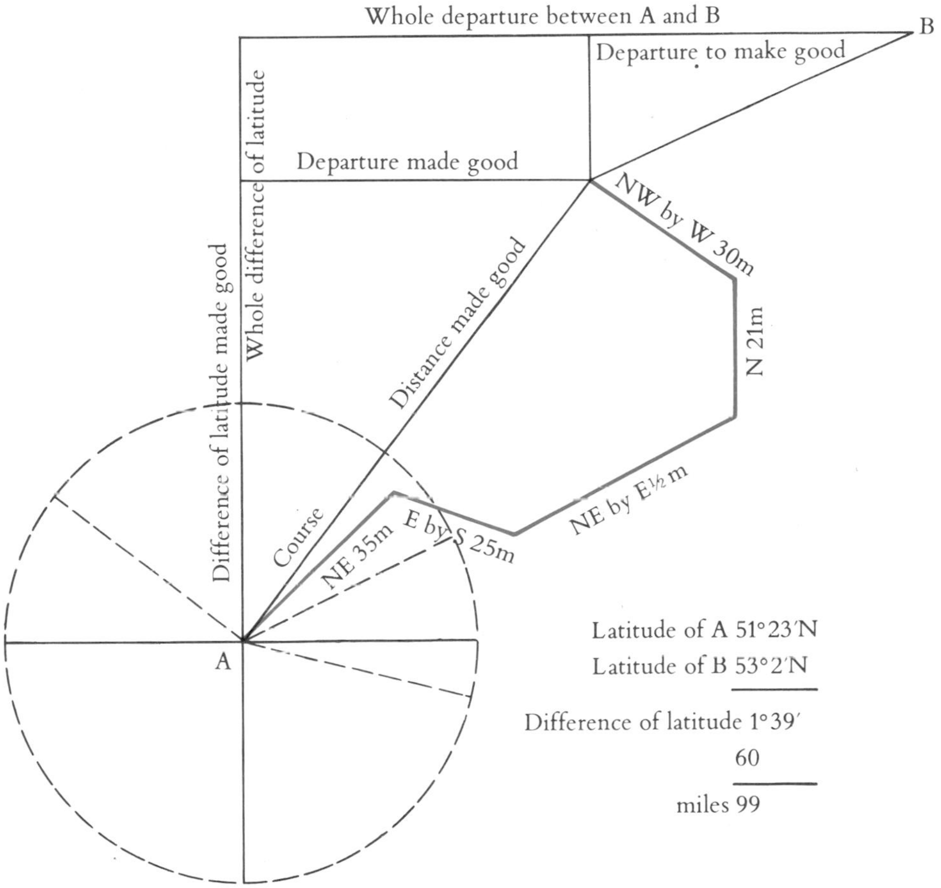

**Traverse sailing**

Whole departure between A and B

Departure to make good

Departure made good

Whole difference of latitude

Difference of latitude made good

Distance made good

Course

NW by W 30m

N 21m

NE by E ½ m

NE 35m   E by S 25m

A

B

Latitude of A 51°23′N
Latitude of B 53°2′N

Difference of latitude 1°39′
60

miles 99

**Plane sailing,** or (erroneously) **plain sailing.** The assumption is made that, over the area concerned, the Earth is flat. On this supposition, MERIDIANS (15.01) are considered as being parallel to each other, whereas in fact they converge. There are four principal components:
*Course* (Co.), or rhumb. In degrees or points.
*Distance* (Dist.). The number of miles sailed, or between places.

*Difference of latitude* (D. lat.), or northing/southing. Distance made good north or south on any course, in miles.
*Departure* (Dep.), or easting/westing, or meridional distance. Distance made good east or west on any course. This can be converted into *difference of longitude* (D. long.) for other sailings. Calculations are made by resolving a right-angled triangle in which the hypotenuse represents the *distance* and

the two sides *difference of latitude* and *departure*.

**Traverse sailing,** or **compound course.** In practice, a ship often sails a zig-zag track during a DAY'S WORK (15.04). The method of reducing the several courses and distances to a resultant single course and distance is called *resolving a traverse*. This is done by making a table and then applying PLANE SAILING, using the published *traverse table*.

**Middle latitude sailing,** or **tangent sailing.** A compound of PLANE SAILING (15.06) and PARALLEL SAILING (15.06), middle latitude being the mean of the latitudes of starting and finishing. Plane sailing gives the departure for a given course and distance. The formula is: Dep. = D. long. × cos mid. lat. gives the equivalent D. long.

**Mercator's sailing,** or **rhumb line sailing,** or **Wright's sailing.** By using the principles of the construction of a MERCATOR CHART (18.04), Mercator sailing solved the problem, 'given the latitudes and longitudes of two places, find the course and distance between them'. The method makes use of the formula: D. long. = D. mer. parts × tan course. In practice, this was generally applied to traverse sailing.

**Meridional parts** (Mer. parts). The lengths of the arc of the MERIDIAN (15.01) between the equator and a given parallel on a MERCATOR CHART (18.04), expressed in units of 1′ of longitude on the equator.

**Oblique sailing.** Using trigonometry to solve terrestrial fixes by cross bearings or RUNNING FIXES (15.01).

**Current sailing.** Essentially, traverse sailing, taking into account set and drift of the current, tidal or otherwise.

**Spherical sailing,** or **globular sailing.** Any sailing taking into account the spherical (or spheroidal) shape of the Earth.

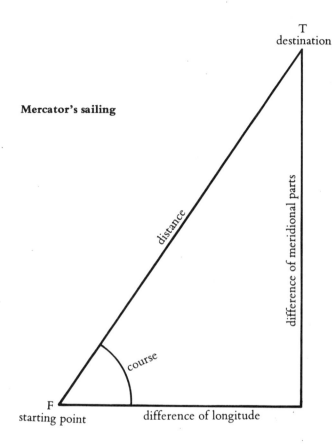

**Mercator's sailing**

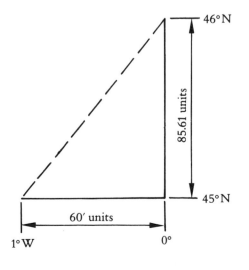

*from table of* Meridional parts

Lat 45°  m.p. 3029.94
Lat 46°  m.p. 3115.55

difference = 85.61

# Astronomical Navigation

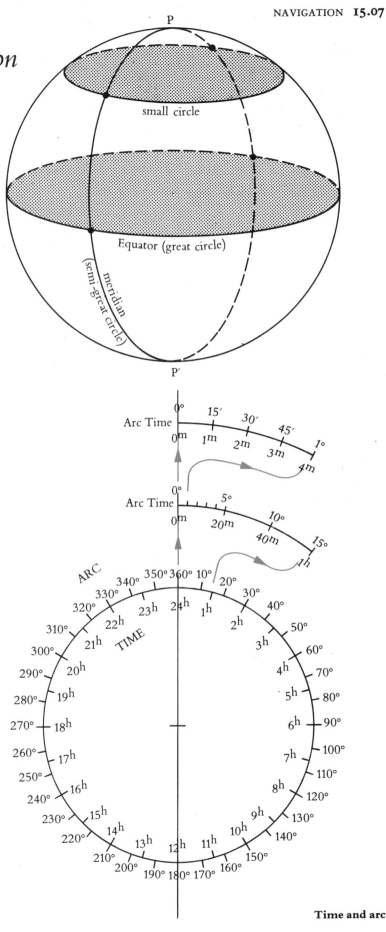

## THE CELESTIAL SPHERE

**Heavenly body,** or **celestial body** (X).
Any body on the celestial sphere –
star, sun, moon, planet or comet.

**Great circle.** Circle on the surface of
a sphere whose plane passes through
the centre of that sphere. The equator
is a great circle; meridians are semi-
great circles.

**Small circle.** Circle on the surface of
a sphere whose plane does not pass
through the centre. Parallels of
latitude, altitude and declination are
small circles.

**Spherical triangle.** Closed figure on
the surface of a sphere having the arcs
of three great circles as sides.

**Angular distance** (along the sides of a
spherical triangle). Length of an arc
of a great circle, expressed in degrees,
minutes and seconds of arc.

**Spherical angle.** Can be expressed
either in *arc* or in *time*.

**Time and arc.** $1^d = 24^h = 360°$.
$1^h = 15°$. $4^m = 1°$. $1^m = 15'$. $4^s = 1'$.
$1^s = 15''$.
Almanacs and nautical tables contain
conversion tables for time and arc.
Nautical trigonometry tables usually
have arguments in both arc and time.

**Celestial sphere.** To an observer on
Earth, the sky has the appearance of
an inverted bowl, so that heavenly
bodies appear to be situated on the
inside of a sphere of immense radius,
with the Earth as centre.

**Time and arc**

**Celestial coordinates.** Positions of heavenly bodies on the celestial sphere can be referred to the celestial equator (*right ascension* and *declination*), or to the observer's horizon (*altitude* and *azimuth*). There are also systems based on the ecliptic and the galactic equator, but these are not used at sea.

**(1) Ecliptic coordinate system.** System devised with reference to the ECLIPTIC. Though the coordinates are not used at sea, the frame of reference is important.

*Frame of reference*

**Ecliptic.** Apparent yearly path of the sun among the stars; it is a GREAT CIRCLE (15.07) making an angle of 23°27′ with the celestial equator.

**Equinoxes** (first points of Aries and Libra) (γ, ♎). The points where the planes of the ecliptic and equator intersect, with the sun's declination at 0I. This occurs at the *vernal* (or spring) *equinox* on 21 March when the sun is at the *first point of Aries* (γ), and at the *autumnal equinox* on 23 September at the *first point of Libra* (♎). On these dates, day and night are of equal length, hence the word 'equinox'.

**Zodiac.** Band 8° either side of the ECLIPTIC, within which the Moon and the planets will always be found.

*Coordinates*

**Celestial latitude.** Body's apparent angular distance north or south of the ECLIPTIC.

**Celestial longitude.** Angular distance between γ and a perpendicular dropped from the body onto the ECLIPTIC, measured eastwards. In the past, generally expressed in *degrees of the Zodiac*, for instance Aquarius 27°; today in a 0°–360° notation.

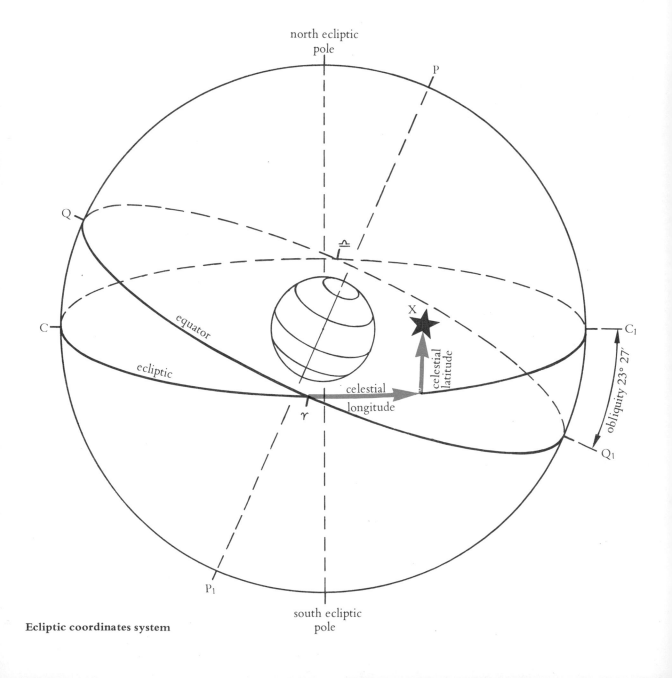

**Ecliptic coordinates system**

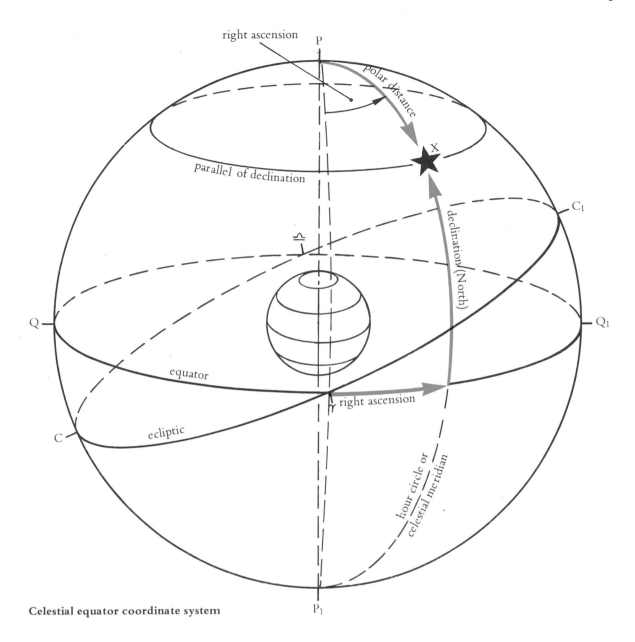

**Celestial equator coordinate system**

### (2) Celestial equator coordinate system.

System based on the projection of the terrestrial frame of reference – poles, equator, meridians – onto the CELESTIAL SPHERE (15.07).

*Frame of reference*

**Celestial poles.** The two north and south poles ($P$, $P'$).

**Celestial equator,** or **equinoctial** ($QQ'$). The word 'equinoctial' stems from the fact that, when the sun is on the equator, day and night are equal in length.

**Hour circles,** or **celestial meridians.** GREAT CIRCLES (15.07) through the celestial poles, projections of terrestrial meridians.

**Polar distance** (PD). Body's angular distance from the pole, the complement of declination. North-south coordinates are occasionally expressed in *north polar distance* (NPD), which is always positive, whereas declination may be positive (north) or negative (south).

**Right ascension** (RA, or AR). East-west coordinate equivalent to terrestrial longitude; angle at the

celestial pole between the hour circle through and that of the body, measured eastwards in time. Today, *sidereal hour angle* (SHA), which is 360°-RA, measured westwards in arc from , is used in navigation instead of RA.

*Coordinates*, exactly analogous to terrestrial latitude and longitude.

**Declination** (Dec., or *d*). Measurement northward or southward from the celestial equator, equivalent to latitude on Earth. SMALL CIRCLES (15.07) parallel to the equator are *parallels of declination*.

**(3) Horizon coordinate system.**
System based on the observer.

*Frame of reference*

**Zenith** (*Z*). Point in the heavens directly overhead.

**Nadir** (*Z'*). Point in the heavens directly opposite the ZENITH; the lowest point on the CELESTIAL SPHERE (15.07).

**Celestial horizon,** or **rational horizon** (HH'). Great circle half-way between the ZENITH and NADIR. It does not coincide exactly with the *observer's sea horizon,* or *visible horizon* (the line along which earth and sky appear to meet), because of refraction and because the observer is at the surface and not at the centre of the Earth. The vertical angle between the observer's horizontal plane and the visible horizon is the *dip* or *depression of the horizon.*

**Vertical circle.** GREAT CIRCLE (15.07) through the ZENITH and NADIR, perpendicular to the horizon.

**Observer's meridian,** or **principal vertical circle.** VERTICAL CIRCLE through the north and south points of the horizon.

**Prime vertical.** Vertical circle through the east and west points.

*Coordinates*

**Altitude** (Alt., or *h*). Angular distance of a body above the horizon. *Sextant altitude* is that measured directly with the sextant; *observed altitude* is the measurement corrected for instrumental errors, and therefore above the sea horizon; *true altitude* is the measurement corrected for instrumental errors, dip, refraction, semi-diameter and parallax (see SIGHT, (15.10), and therefore above the celestial horizon.

**Zenith distance** (ZD, or *z*). Angular distance of a body from the ZENITH. Complement of altitude.

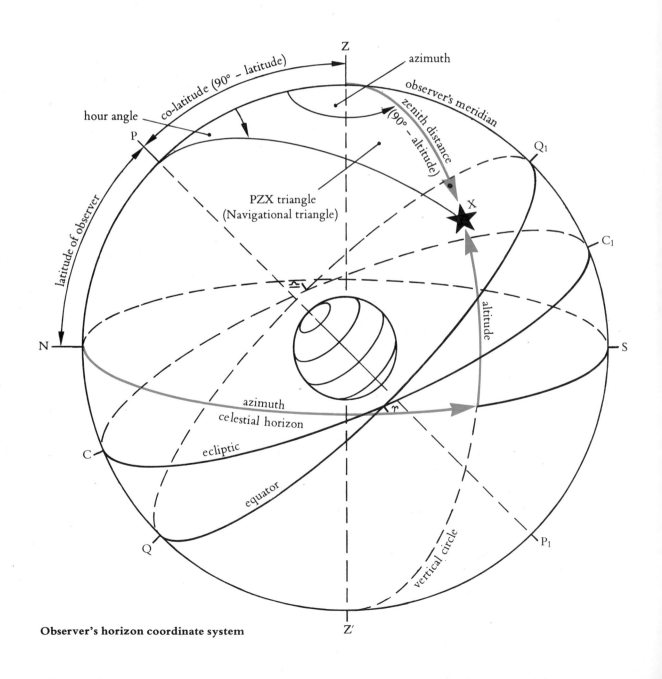

**Observer's horizon coordinate system**

**Navigational triangle, or PZX triangle.** SPHERICAL TRIANGLE (15.07) with great circles connecting the elevated pole P, observer's zenith Z and heavenly body X, the trigonometrical solution of which is the basis of much nautical astronomy. In the past, each triangle was solved individually. Today, use is generally made of *Tables of Computed Altitude and Azimuth*.

**Azimuth** (Az), or **bearing.** Angle at the ZENITH between the observer's MERIDIAN (15.01) and the VERTICAL CIRCLE through the observed body.

**Amplitude.** The angle a celestial body rises or sets north or south of the PRIME VERTICAL.

**Geographical position** (GP), or sub-celestial point, of a heavenly body. Point on the Earth's surface where a celestial body is directly overhead at a given instant. Sometimes called the *sub-solar point, sub-lunar point, sub-stellar point* or *sub-astral point*, according to the body concerned.

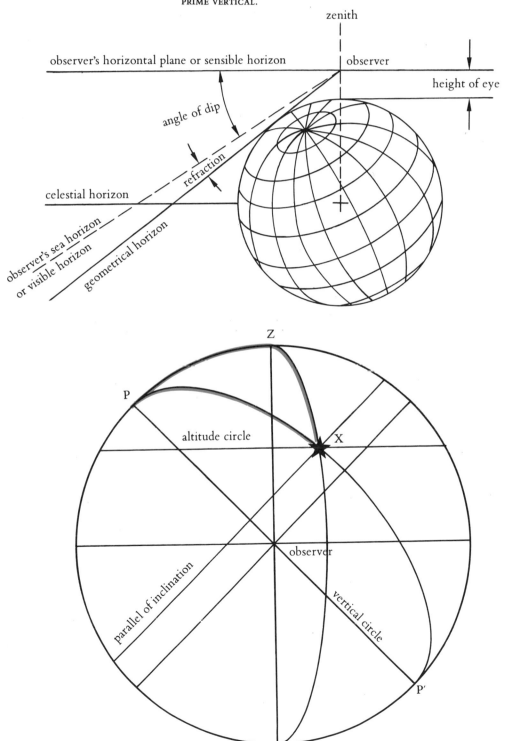

**Navigational triangle**

# Time

**Hour angle** (HA). Angle at the pole between the observer's MERIDIAN (15.01) and the meridian through a celestial body at any instant, measured westwards from the former in either arc or time, as convenient. When the body is on the meridian, HA is zero. As the Earth rotates, so a body's HA increases uniformly, hence HA is an expression of time.

**Day.** Interval that elapses between successive transits of a heavenly body across the same MERIDIAN (15.01).

**Apparent solar day.** Interval between two successive transits of the *true sun* across the observer's MERIDIAN (15.01), at which times it is *apparent noon*. Because the Earth's orbital motion is not uniform, the length of the apparent day is not constant.

**Apparent solar time,** or **true solar time,** or **astronomical time.** Time based on the hour angle of the true sun; sundial time.

**Mean sun.** To achieve a day of uniform length, a fictitious body called the mean sun is invoked. This travels along the equator at a constant speed and in the same time as the true sun takes to travel at a variable speed around the ecliptic (that is, one year). Hence the concepts of *mean solar time* (clock time), *mean solar day* and *mean moon*.

**Equation of time.** Difference between mean and apparent time – or between the clock and the sundial – at any instant. It can be as much as $16\frac{3}{4}^{m}$, and is zero on about 15 April, 15 June, 1 September and 24 December.

**Local mean time** (LMT). Mean time kept at any place. Sometimes the place is named (for instance *Paris Mean Time* or *Washington Mean Time*), and generally the reference is to the MERIDIAN (15.01) of the principal observatory.

**Greenwich mean time** (GMT), or **universal time.** LOCAL MEAN TIME instead of the meridian of Greenwich. Important to navigation because, since 1767, the British Nautical Almanac has been based on the Greenwich meridian and, since 1884, it has been recognized inter-nationally as the PRIME MERIDIAN (15.01) from which longitudes are reckoned. The difference between

local time and Greenwich time is equal to the longitude difference between the two meridians, summarized by this mnemonic:

Longitude west, Greenwich time best;
Longitude east, Greenwich time least.

Thus, if one's local time is found to be 4.25 and Greenwich time is known to be 7.25, then one's longitude is $3^{h}$ ($= 45°$) west.

**Standard time.** In the old days, each community regulated its activities by local apparent time, as shown on the sundial. With the advent of railways, it became convenient for a whole province or country to keep the same standard time. Since the 1880s, more and more countries have based their time on meridians an integral number of hours from Greenwich – called the *time zone system*. Thus, the East Coast of the United States keeps a time based (in winter) upon the meridian of 75°W, precisely $5^{h}$ behind GMT.

**Ship's time** (for domestic purposes). Until the 1920s, generally the local time of the previous noon, changing daily at noon. Since then, afloat, *zone time* has become more common.

**Civil day.** Begins at midnight.

**Astronomical day.** Until 1925, this began at noon on the CIVIL DAY concerned, and was $12^{h}$ behind the civil day.

**Nautical day.** Began at noon $12^{h}$ before the CIVIL DAY, so was $24^{h}$ ahead of the ASTRONOMICAL DAY (which was used in the Nautical Almanac) – all of which caused the navigator considerable confusion, so that the nautical day began to fall out of use early in the nineteenth century. (In the Royal Navy, 1805.)

**Sidereal time,** or **right ascension of the meridian** (RAM). Time based on the rotation of the Earth relative to the stars. Defined as the hour angle of ♈. The *sidereal day* is some $3^{m}56^{s}$ shorter than the mean solar day because of the movement of the Earth in its orbit.

# Sights

## (1) General

**Sight,** or **observation.** Measuring the vertical angle (altitude) between the horizon and a celestial body, or the angular distance between two bodies (generally the lunar distance). Sights can be *sun sights* (*shooting the sun*), *star sights* or *Moon sights*. Altitude measurements have to be corrected for:
*Index error.* Inherent in the instrument used.
*Dip.* Because of the observer's *height of eye*.
*Refraction.* Due to the bending of light as it passes through the different layers of the Earth's atmosphere.
*Semi-diameter* of the sun and Moon, because it is the *limb* of the body that is observed, not the centre.
*Parallax.* Because the observer is at the surface and not the centre of the Earth.

**Parallax**

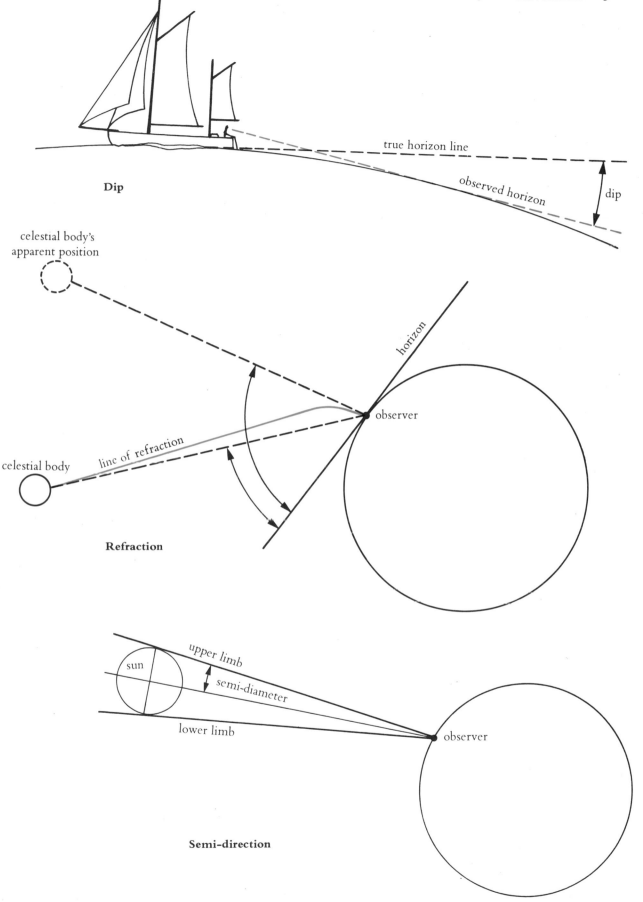

**Dip**

true horizon line

observed horizon

dip

celestial body's
apparent position

horizon

observer

celestial body

line of refraction

**Refraction**

upper limb

sun

semi-diameter

lower limb

observer

**Semi-direction**

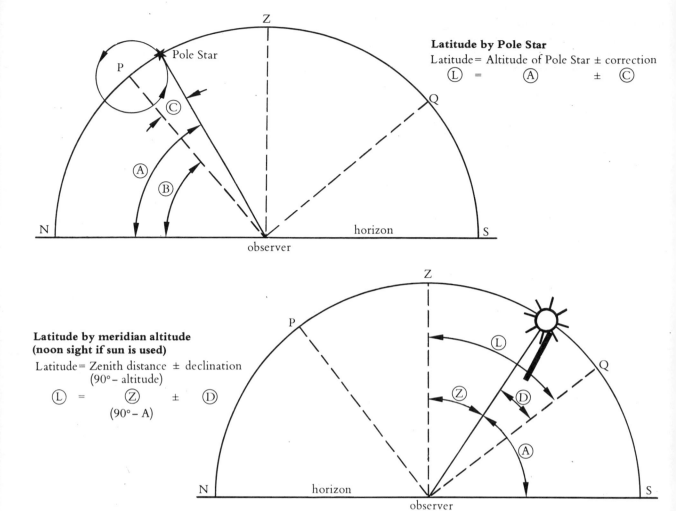

**Latitude by Pole Star**

Latitude = Altitude of Pole Star ± correction

$$\textcircled{L} \quad = \quad \textcircled{A} \quad \pm \quad \textcircled{C}$$

**Latitude by meridian altitude (noon sight if sun is used)**

Latitude = Zenith distance ± declination
(90° − altitude)

$$\textcircled{L} \quad = \quad \textcircled{Z} \quad \pm \quad \textcircled{D}$$
$$(90° − A)$$

**Reducing an observation, or sight reduction.** Process of deriving an end product (generally a position) from the raw observations. The principal books needed are:
*Nautical Almanac,* or *Ephemeris.* Annual publication giving the celestial position of bodies for every moment of the year.
*Nautical Tables,* or *Epitome.* Primarily trigonometrical. In the nineteenth century, the principal tables in the UK and US were those of Norie, Raper, Bowditch and Inman. Trigonometrical functions peculiar to spherical trigonometry were *versines,* versed sines, or (1-cos); and *haversines,* half versines, or ½(1-cos).

**Twilight.** Periods of incomplete darkness before sunrise (*morning twilight*) and after sunset (*evening twilight*), beginning and ending when the sun is 18° below the horizon. In high latitudes in summer, twilight may last all night. Only at twilight can both the horizon and the stars (or planets) be seen clearly enough to permit accurate altitudes being measured with an ordinary sextant. Star SIGHTS and star lunar distances are thus only possible at twilight, if a sea horizon is to be used.

**Dawn,** or **first light,** or **daybreak.** First appearance of light in the eastern sky before sunrise.

**Dusk.** The darker part of twilight, morning and evening.

**(2) Sights for Finding Latitude**

**Meridian altitude** (Mer. Alt.), or **noon sight.** Latitude can easily be found by measuring the altitude of the sun (or any other heavenly body) at *meridian passage* (Mer. Pass.), when it is on the MERIDIAN (15.01) at its *culmination* (the highest point of its circuit), and then adding or subtracting the DECLINATION (15.08) of the body.

**Latitude by Polaris,** or **by North Star.** At any place, the celestial pole is elevated above the horizon by an amount exactly equal to the latitude of the place. Therefore, the altitude of Polaris, suitably corrected for the fact that it is near but not exactly at the pole, can be used in the northern hemisphere (at twilight) to find latitude. There are tables from which, for a given sidereal time, Polaris's angular distance above or below the celestial pole can be found.

**Ex-meridian altitude** (Ex. Mer. Alt.). If clouds preclude a sight being taken exactly at meridian passage, there are tables which will *reduce the sight to the meridian,* given the interval from Mer. Pass.

**Latitude by single altitude,** or **by double altitude.** Methods requiring the solution of SPHERICAL TRIANGLES (15.07).

## (3) Sights for Finding Longitude

**Longitude by lunar distance.** Method of finding Greenwich time. The Moon moves comparatively quickly against the background of the stars, approximately 1° or her own diameter in two hours. Her angular distance from a particular star in the zodiac (or from the sun) can be predicted (in the almanac) for any moment of Greenwich time. If the navigator measures the *lunar distance* between the Moon and one of the predicted stars or the sun, he has, in theory, the Greenwich time of the observation – and therefore his longitude. However, *clearing the distance* – the calculations involved in allowing for the facts that refraction is different for each body, that the observer is not at the Earth's centre and that measurements are being taken from the Moon's limb – was a most laborious business, taking an hour or more. Also, the altitude of both bodies above the horizon had to be measured at the same time, so, for a Moon-star observation, the lunar-distance sight was restricted to twilight.

**Longitude by chronometer,** or **by timekeeper.** The easiest way to discover Greenwich time is for the ship to carry a timekeeper which can be set to GMT at the start of the voyage and will then keep time to sufficient accuracy for months on end, despite the vagaries of climate and ship motion. The marine chronometer became a practical and economic possibility by about 1800, and eventually the measurement of lunar distances was superseded. In essence, the navigator took an altitude observation and, using an assumed latitude, found his local mean time by solving the NAVIGATIONAL TRIANGLE (15.09). Then, LMT ± GMT = longitude.

## (4) Position-Line Methods

**Sumner line,** or **line of bearing.** The fact that an altitude observation yields not just the quantity of latitude or longitude (based on an assumed longitude or latitude) but also a POSITION LINE (15.01) was first pointed out by the American Capt. Thomas Sumner in 1837. In fact, such lines are the arcs of circles of large radius with the centre the body's GEOGRAPHICAL POSITION (15.09), and the radius the true ZENITH DISTANCE (15.09).

**Sumner method.** Establishing a POSITION LINE (15.01) by computing two or more positions at different latitudes and joining them.

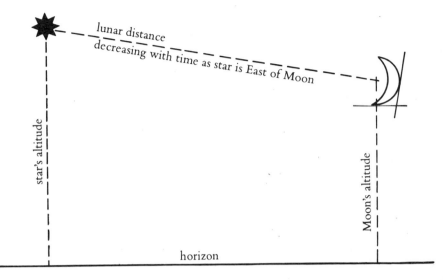

**Longitude by lunar distance**

lunar distance decreasing with time as star is East of Moon

star's altitude

Moon's altitude

horizon

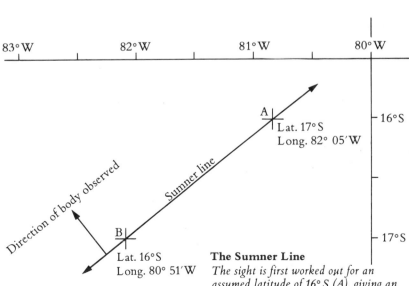

83° W   82° W   81° W   80° W

16° S

17° S

A — Lat. 17° S
Long. 82° 05′ W

Direction of body observed

Sumner line

B — Lat. 16° S
Long. 80° 51′ W

**The Sumner Line**
*The sight is first worked out for an assumed latitude of 16° S (A), giving an observed longitude of 80° 51′ W. It is then reworked for an assumed latitude of 17° S (B), giving an observed longitude of 82° 05′ W. The Sumner line joining A and B is a position line, perpendicular to the azimuth of the body being observed.*

**Marc St. Hilaire method,** or **intercept method,** or **the new navigation.** Commandant Marc St. Hilaire of the French Navy introduced this, the basis of all modern methods of astronomical navigation, in 1874. Getting a fix from the arcs of position circles based on the summer line is easy in theory but difficult in practice, because, unless the body observed is practically overhead, one cannot draw the circle since its centre will not lie on the chart being used. St. Hilaire pointed out that, with the enormous radii involved, the relevant arc of the position circle could be considered as a straight line perpendicular to the body's AZIMUTH (15.02) at the time of the sight. His *intercept method* required that the navigator compute the body's *calculated zenith distance* (CZD) using an *assumed position* (generally chosen to simplify calculation), and at the same time work out its *true zenith distance* (TZD) from his observations. Then, the difference between TZD and CZD is the *intercept*, which can be plotted on the chart towards or away from the body's azimuth according to whether CZD or TZD is the greater. This gives the *J-point*, through which the position line is drawn, perpendicular to the body's azimuth.

**Sun sights,** or **shooting the sun.** These can be taken at any time of day, but will yield only a single POSITION LINE (15.01), necessitating a RUNNING FIX (15.01), except in the last quarter, when it is possible to take near-simultaneous sights of sun and Moon.

**Star sights.** At twilight, near-simultaneous sights of several stars and planets – preferably not less than four – can be taken to yield a FIX (15.01).

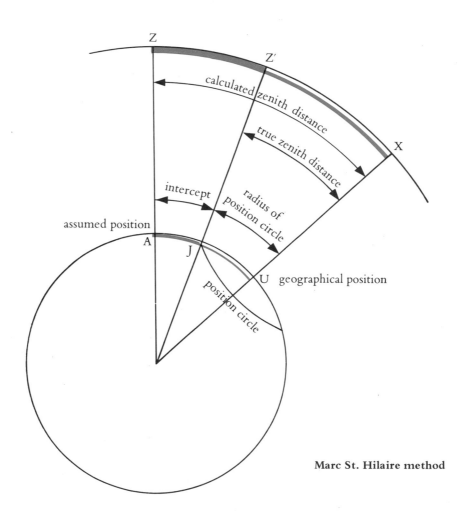

**Marc St. Hilaire method**

would seem possible, and thereby make faster and more profitable voyages.

Equally important to a sailing ship master was his knowledge of the ocean currents, whose set and drift could affect the ship's daily run by many miles and if ignored could precipitate or delay his estimated time of arrival by many days. Ocean currents had first been experienced and recognized by the explorers of the early sixteenth century on their voyages of discovery in the Atlantic and Indian oceans, but their causes long remained a mystery to seaman and scientist alike. It was thought at one time that the drift of water from east to west across the equatorial regions was caused, like the tides, by the Moon and that the continents deflected this movement of water in other directions, thus setting up other currents.

William Bourne, writing in 1578 in *The Treasure for Travellers*, was able to give comparatively accurate descriptions of the currents to be found in the Atlantic Ocean, based almost entirely on the experiences of seamen. But the rate at which these currents flowed, their drift, was still a mystery. The dangers of not knowing the drift were ably illustrated by Sir Richard Hawkins, describing an event in his voyage of 1593. Having taken a departure from the Cape Verde Islands and sailed to within 5° of the equator, he and his navigators confidently supposed themselves to be 70 leagues (210 miles) off the coast of Guinea. A change of colour in the water caused a sounding to be taken and 14 fathoms was found. Shortly afterwards they found themselves to be only 15 miles from the shore. Hawkins explained that 'the error which we fell into in our accompts was such that all men fall into where are currents that set east or west, and are not knowne, for there is no certaine rule yet practised for triall of the longitude . . .' He had in fact entered the Doldrums and been set many miles by the Counter Equatorial Current.

William Dampier, in his discourse on tides, winds and currents in *A Collection of Voyages* first published in 1699, is the first person known to have suggested that the Trade Winds were the cause of the currents, 'in all places that the Trade blows we find a current setting with the wind'. But it was many years before this theory was generally accepted by the scientific world. The accepted method for discovering what current a ship was experiencing was first described in the early seventeenth century and was still being put forward in 1844 as the 'most usual method' in the thirteenth edition of J. W. Norie's *Practical Navigation*. There, the procedure is described as follows: '. . . take a boat, in calm weather, a small distance from the ship, and being provided with a half minute glass, a log, a heavy iron pot. . . and a small boat compass, to let down the pot . . . by a rope fastened to the boat's stem, to the depth of about 100 fathoms, by which the boat will remain as steady as at anchor; then the log being hove, its bearing will be the setting of the current and the number of knots run out in half a minute will be its drift per hour.'

The perfection of marine chronometers and the lunar-distance method of finding longitude in the second half of the eighteenth century enabled seamen to accurately fix their position at sea for the first time. This meant that they could compare their 'position by account' or dead reckoning position with the position the ship was actually to be in by astronomical means. The difference between these two positions on an ocean passage was caused primarily by a current, so that it was now possible to work out not only the set of a current but its drift as well. Major James Rennell, formerly a surveyor for the East India Company, became interested in the study of ocean currents and began examining the log books of ships navigated by chronometers. His studies eventually led to a book, *Currents of the Atlantic Ocean* (1832), published after his death, which set out for the first time the accepted modern view of the causes of ocean currents. It is ironic that he is mainly remembered for the Rennell Current, supposed to set north-westward across the entrance to the English Channel, and which in modern times has been proved not to exist.

ALAN STIMSON

# Tides

**Tide.** The rising and falling of the sea due to the gravitational attraction of the sun and Moon – principally the latter – acting on the waters of the rotating Earth. Thus, *rise and fall of tide, rising tide,* or *falling tide.* Also, colloquially used to describe horizontal water movements from the same cause, that is, *tidal streams.*

**High water** (HW), or **high tide,** or **full sea;** and **low water** (LW), or **low tide.** The highest and lowest levels reached during one tidal oscillation.

**Half tide.** Level, or time, midway between HIGH WATER and low water.

**The tide making.** If unqualified, refers to a rising tide. The phrases *the ebb is making* (that is, has started) and *tide making to the eastward* are also used. Sometimes erroneously used to describe the tide increasing from neaps to springs (converse of *taking off*).

**Stand of the tide.** Period at high and low water when there is no appreciable change of level.

**Double tides.** Period when, due to local conditions, there is a high tide consisting of two maxima (as at Southampton), or a low tide with two minima (as at the Hook of Holland).

**Range of the tide.** Difference in height between consecutive high and low waters.

## Types of Tides

**Tide-raising forces.** The Moon's force of attraction tends to create high tides, or *tidal waves,* on the points on Earth nearest to and furthest from it. (Tidal wave is also the name sometimes erroneously given to a *tsunami,* an often destructive wave caused by underwater earthquakes.) As the Earth rotates, so the two tidal waves move around. The sun causes similar tidal waves but, since it is further from Earth, they are of less amplitude. The tides actually experienced are the cumulative result of both lunar and solar tidal waves, modified by the shape and size of the land masses, ocean basins and water-ways.

**Diurnal, single-day, semi-diurnal** and **mixed tides.** If the Earth's surface were entirely water-covered, the lunar tidal wave when the Moon was at zero DECLINATION (15.08) would produce two high waters of equal height daily at any given place on Earth; when the Moon has north or south declination, the two high waters would be of different heights for a given place. However, the Earth's water surfaces are restricted by land, and each body of water has a natural period of oscillation dependent upon its dimensions. The Atlantic, for example, responds more readily to the semi-diurnal component, so there are generally *semi-diurnal tides*; in the Pacific, there are more often *diurnal tides,* or *mixed tides.* In a few Pacific islands and places in Indonesia there are *solar tides,* in which high and low waters occur at the same time each day because the lunar tidal wave is almost swamped by the solar tidal wave. In enclosed bodies of water, such as the Baltic, Mediterranean and Caspian seas, there are hardly any tides.

**Spring tides.** Tides of increased range occurring near times of New and Full Moon, when the lunar and solar tidal waves reinforce each other.

**Neap tides.** Tides of decreased range occurring near the first and last quarters.

**Neaped,** or **beneaped.** Situation of a ship aground or behind a bar and unable to move until the next SPRING TIDES.

**Equinoctial tides.** Tides occurring near the equinoxes, in March and September, when the spring range is greater than the average.

**Tropic tides.** Tides occurring approximately every two weeks, when the effect of the Moon's maximum declination north or south of the equator is greatest.

**Solsticial tides.** Tides occurring near the solstices, in June and September, when the tropic range is especially large.

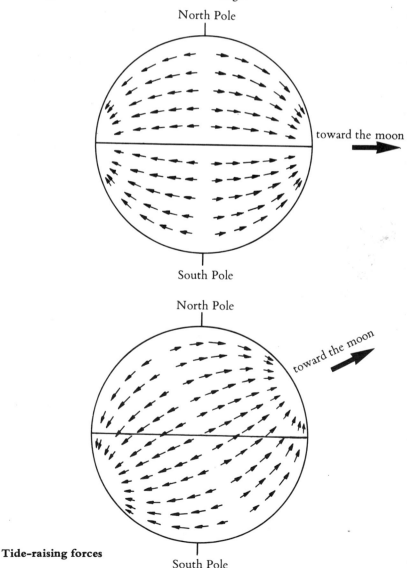

**Tide-raising forces**

# Tidal prediction

**Tidal prediction.** Except in the Mediterranean, the ability to predict the tides – their times, heights and strengths – was a necessary accomplishment for any navigator, particularly local pilots. From the earliest times, man has realized that the tides 'follow the Moon', with the times of high and low water correlating with the bearing of the Moon, and the dates of springs and neaps correlating with the phases of the Moon. The following technical terms were used in connection with methods of tidal prediction in north-west Europe (where the tides are primarily semi-diurnal) up to the nineteenth century:

**Change of the Moon.** When the Moon's age becomes zero again; that is, the New Moon.

**Age of the tide.** Mean period between the New Moon or Full Moon and the next SPRING TIDE: about one and a half days.

**Age of the Moon.** Elapsed time, usually expressed in days, since the last New Moon.

**Epact for the year.** The Moon's age at $0^h$ on 1 January. To find it, divide the year by 19; whatever remains, multiply by 11. Thus, for 1977:
$$\frac{1977}{19} = 104 + 1; 1 \times 11 = 11,$$
which is the epact for 1977.

**Epact (or number) for the month.** The Moon's age on the first day of the month, assuming the EPACT FOR THE YEAR is at $0^h$ on 1 January. Given in the following table:

**Lunar month,** or **lunation,** or **synodical month.** Period from one New Moon to the next; approximately $29\frac{1}{2}$ days.

**Lunar day,** or **tidal day.** Interval between two successive transits of the Moon across the meridian; it averages $24^h 50^m$.

**Moon's southing.** The Moon's transit across the MERIDIAN (15.01).

**Interval,** or **lunitidal interval.** Interval between the MOON'S SOUTHING and the next HIGH WATER.

**High water full and change** (HWF&C), or **establishment of the port,** or **vulgar establishment.** Lunitidal interval at a given port on the days of full and change. It varies slightly between springs and neaps; that at springs being the *corrected* or *mean establishment*. From the nineteenth century, generally expressed thus: Gravesend $I^h 30^m$; Milford Haven $V^h 15^m$; the Lizard $VII^h 30^m$.

**Moon's bearing.** Ancient way to reckon the time of high water (HW) by the point of the compass the Moon bore at that time. Thus, if HW is at noon on days of full and change, then the tide is said to flow north and south; if at 9 am, it flows south-east and north-west; and if at 3 pm, south-west and north-east. This method of expressing the establishment fell out of use early in the eighteenth century, except for local pilots and fishermen.

**Tide tables.** Tables giving HIGH WATER FULL AND CHANGE or the MOON'S BEARING for the various ports, and/or predicted times and heights of high and low water.

## Time of High Water by Eighteenth-Century Methods

Comparison of results obtained using the method in Hamilton Moore (1776) with modern tide tables. He assumes HIGH WATER gets later by $49^m$ for each day of the Moon's age.

*Required*: Time of high water at Milford Haven on 29 August 1977
*Given*: Milford Haven, long. $5°(20^m)W$; HWF&C $5^h 15^m$.
Epact for 1977 = 11
Equation of time = $-1^m$ (clock before sun)
Table for monthly epact as above.

### (1) To find the Moon's age

| | |
|---|---|
| Epact for 1977 | 11 |
| No. for month (Aug) | +6 |
| Day of month | +29 |
| | 46 |
| Over $29^d$ | −30 |
| Moon's age | 16 days |

### (2) To find time of Moon's southing

Moon's southing = Moon's age =
$$16 \times \frac{49}{60} = 13^h.067 = 13^h 04^m.$$

### (3) To find time of high water

| | |
|---|---|
| Moon's southing | $13^h 04^m$ |
| HWF&C Milford | +5 15 |
| | 18 19 |
| Over $12^h$ | −12 24 |
| Local apparent time | 05 55 |
| Equation of time | −1 |
| Local mean time | 05 54 |
| Longitude 5° west | +20 |
| Greenwich mean time | 06 14 |

The prediction in the *Admiralty Tide Tables for 1977* is 0614 GMT – precisely the same. That was near springs, a prediction for 23 September 1977 (near neaps) gave 0217 by Moore's method, 0229 by modern tables.

| | Jan | Feb | Mar | Apr | May | Jun | Jul | Aug | Sep | Oct | Nov | Dec |
|---|---|---|---|---|---|---|---|---|---|---|---|---|
| Common years | 0 | 2 | 0 | 2 | 2 | 4 | 4 | 6 | 7 | 8 | 10 | 10 |
| Leap years | 0 | 2 | 1 | 3 | 3 | 5 | 5 | 7 | 8 | 9 | 10 | 11 |

# Tidal datum

**Chart datum.** Sea level to which soundings on charts and in tide tables are reduced, chosen to be a level such that the tide at springs will seldom fall below it. (Though the word 'datum' did not come into use in this context till the nineteenth century, the principle that charted soundings should show low-water heights goes back at least to 1600.)

**Height of tide.** Vertical distance of the actual water level above CHART DATUM at a particular moment.

**Height datum.** While soundings on charts are reduced to the lowest possible level (to give a margin of safety), heights of objects such as lighthouses and hills are measured from the highest possible tidal level, generally *mean high water springs*. The British *ordnance datum* used on land maps approximates to *mean sea level*.

**Tide gauge.** Instrument for measuring, or indicating, the present water level.

### Tidal Streams

**Tidal streams, or tidal currents.** Periodical horizontal water movements due to tidal action. Offshore they are generally *rotary*, flowing continuously but with their direction changing through all the points of the compass during the tidal period. In rivers and straits, they are *rectilinear*, or *reversing*, flowing alternately in approximately opposite directions, with *slack water*, or *slack tide*, an instant of little or no stream, at each *turn of the tide*.

**Flood tide, or flow, or flux.** Movement towards the shore or upstream, with the rising tide.

**Ebb tide, or re–flux.** Movement away from the shore or downstream, with the falling tide.

**Set.** Direction in which a stream or current flows.

**Drift.** Speed in knots of a stream or current flow.

**Weather tide.** Tide against the wind.

**Lee tide.** Tide going in the same direction as the wind.

**Head tide.** Contrary tide.

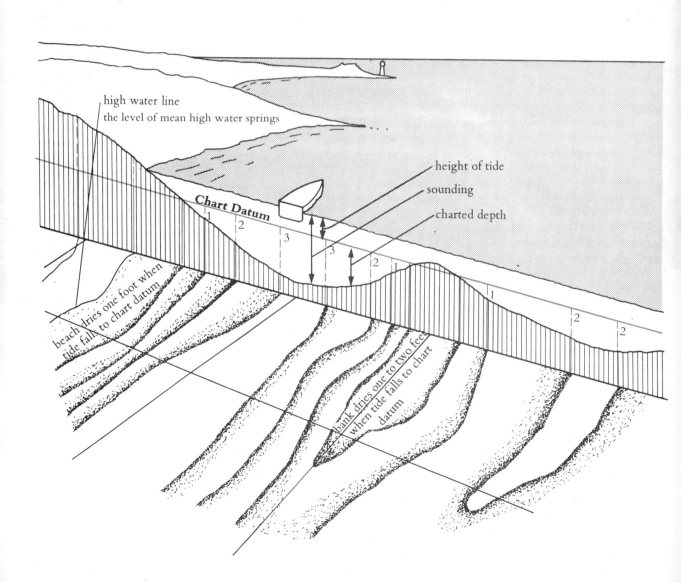

high water line
the level of mean high water springs

Chart Datum

height of tide
sounding
charted depth

beach dries one foot when tide falls to chart datum

bank dries one to two feet when tide falls to chart datum

**Tide** (vb). To work a ship in or out of a river, anchoring whenever the tide is adverse.

**Tide it (up).** With contrary winds, sailing with the tide, anchoring when the tide is contrary.

**It flows tide and half tide.** The ebb will start three hours sooner inshore than offshore. Also said of TIDAL STREAMS when their directions are reversed at half-flood and half-ebb.

**Tideway.** Where the tide ebbs and flows strongly in a channel.

**Tidal waters.** Waters affected by ebb and flow.

**Eddy.** Circular movement of water, the diameter of which may be anything from a few inches to a few miles. If strong it may form a whirlpool.

**Tide-rip.** Small ripples and waves on the surface of the water where opposing currents meet or where the current passes over an irregular bottom. Violent rips with breaking water are known as *overfalls.*

**Race,** or **tide race.** Exceptionally strong stream, usually caused by the constriction of water passing round a headland or where tidal streams from different directions converge. Where it passes through a very narrow channel, it is sometimes called a *tide gate.*

**Bore,** or **eagre.** Steep tidal wave at springs in some rivers, due to the narrowing of the channel and a decrease in depth. Occurs in the Severn, Seine, Trent and Ganges rivers.

*Low tide in Swansea harbour, 1840s*

**Currents,** or **non-tidal currents.** Horizontal water movements not due to tides. They may be either *seasonal currents* or *permanent currents*; *ocean currents* or *coastal currents*; or *surface currents* or *sub-surface currents.*

**Stream current.** Relatively narrow, deep, fast-moving current.

**Drift current.** Relatively broad, shallow, slow-moving current.

**Countercurrent.** Secondary current flowing alongside but in an opposite direction to the main current.

**Wind current.** One set up by the wind.

**Longshore current.** One parallel to the shore, inside the surf zone, generated by waves striking the beach at an angle.

# Ocean currents

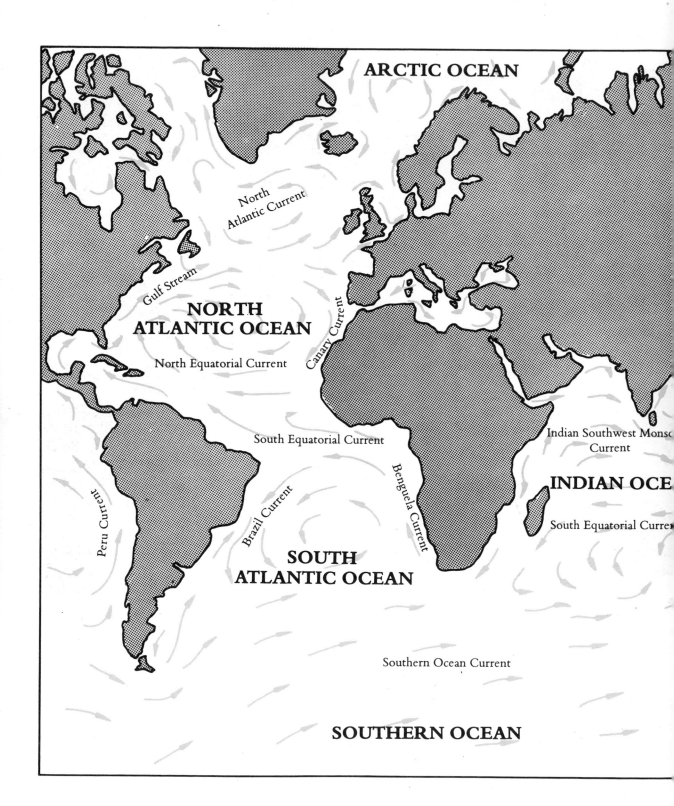

ARCTIC OCEAN

North Atlantic Current

Gulf Stream

**NORTH ATLANTIC OCEAN**

North Equatorial Current

Canary Current

Peru Current

Brazil Current

Benguela Current

South Equatorial Current

**SOUTH ATLANTIC OCEAN**

Indian Southwest Monsoon Current

**INDIAN OCE**

South Equatorial Curre

Southern Ocean Current

**SOUTHERN OCEAN**

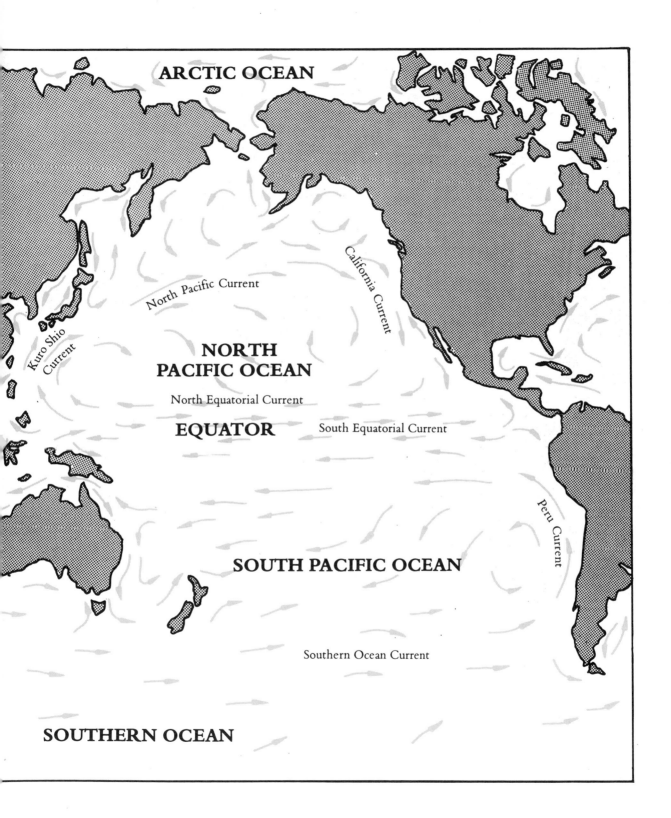

ARCTIC OCEAN

North Pacific Current

California Current

Kuro Shio Current

**NORTH PACIFIC OCEAN**

North Equatorial Current

**EQUATOR**

South Equatorial Current

Peru Current

**SOUTH PACIFIC OCEAN**

Southern Ocean Current

**SOUTHERN OCEAN**

# Wind & Weather

Wind and weather have always occupied the mind of the sailor, particularly in the days of sail, when the strength of the wind provided motive power for his ship and determined its direction, enabling him to set course for his destination or holding him back for days at a time waiting for the wind to change. If the wind was too strong and the sea became rough it could endanger the ship and, depending on the season of the year, it could mean an uncomfortable, overcast, wet time, as with a westerly wind in the approaches to the English Channel. For a collier in the North Sea, a northerly or north-easterly wind in the winter months meant a piercing blast from the Arctic, and the crew clawing at stiff ropes and thrashing canvas with frozen hands. The fear of being caught on a lee shore by an unfavourable wind and being unable to claw off was ever present in a master's mind, and the enormous numbers of ships wrecked along the coasts each year were an awful warning of the perils of going to sea in search of a living.

Seamen were not much interested in the causes of the wind that filled the sails of their ships, or in the causes of the weather that they experienced on their voyages, but over the centuries since the first oceanic voyages of discovery they had been collecting information about the wind systems in different parts of the world and recording it in sailing directions. Trading voyages across the Atlantic made use of the clockwise circulation of the winds around the oceans in the northern hemisphere, so that a voyage to the Caribbean necessitated first sailing south-westerly through the Horse Latitudes to get into the north-east Trade Winds in about 15° N latitude, and then sailing across the South Atlantic until a landfall was made, usually at Barbados. The return journey involved sailing north-eastwards from the Bahamas to get into the latitude of the prevailing westerly winds that blow in about 40° N latitude. Voyages to India and the Far East required a knowledge of the monsoon seasons in the Indian Ocean and China Seas, and voyages to Australia the prevailing westerlies to the south of the Cape of Good Hope and Cape Horn. It was in the halcyon days of the clipper ship in the late nineteenth century that ships' captains deliberately sought the strongest winds in search of a record passage. It was here in the Roaring Forties and Screaming Fifties that sailing ships were able to log over 300 miles in one day, and on one occasion in 1888 that most famous of clipper ships, the *Cutty Sark*, actually overhauled and passed the P. & O. mail steamer in the Australian Bight, and raced her to Sydney Harbour.

Scientists had long pondered the reason why the Earth's winds blow as they do, and with the rekindling of scientific enquiry in England and the founding of the Royal Society in 1662 the answer was eventually found. In 1676 Edmond Halley sailed to St. Helena in the South Atlantic to observe the stars of the southern hemisphere, and during the voyage out and his return in 1678 he was able to study the ocean winds at first hand. This eventually led to a paper presented to the Royal Society in 1686, in which Halley likened wind to 'the Stream or Current of the Air' which is caused, and its direction determined, by the distribution of air masses of differing densities, warm air being relatively lighter than cold air. The westward movement of the Trade Winds he wrongly attributed to the sun's westward passage over the oceans and not to the Earth's rotation, but his basic theory is the one still generally accepted today.

Captain James Cook's well-equipped scientific voyages of discovery between 1768 and 1781 marked a significant change of attitude towards the recording of weather data, and it was at this time that the study of the world's weather systems really began. Later scientific voyages continued the trend, but it was largely through the efforts of Lieutenant Matthew F. Maury, Director of the United States Naval Observatory (established in 1844), who collected information about winds and ocean currents from ships' logs deposited at the observatory, that a series of wind and current charts was published in 1847. In 1853 a conference met in Brussels to co-ordinate international research into marine meteorology, and as a result Britain set up a Meteorological Office under Admiral Robert Fitzroy, of *Beagle* fame, in 1854.

Estimating the strength of the wind was an essential operation in deciding what sails a ship could carry without the risk of their blowing out or of straining the rigging. Until the early nineteenth century, the choice of words to describe the force of the wind was a personal thing influenced by a man's early training. However, with the introduction of standardized log entries in the Royal Navy it became important for all ships to record the wind force in the same manner.

Rear-Admiral Sir Francis Beaufort, when captain of the store-ship HMS *Woolwich* in 1895, devised a scale numbered from 0 to 12. This converted wind force into the speed at which it would drive a 'well conditioned man-of-war' with all sails set, or, as the wind increased in force, with her sails progressively reefed. In 1838 the Beaufort wind-force scale became mandatory for log entries in all ships of the Royal

Navy. This scale is still used today, although the numbers now refer to wind speed in knots estimated from the appearance of the sea. Knowledge of the Earth's wind systems was not much help to the seaman in dealing with freak storms that occasionally blew along the shores of western Europe. In November 1703 one such storm devastated much of southern England, wrecked hundreds of ships and completely destroyed the new Eddystone Rock lighthouse off Plymouth. Indeed, Winstanley, its builder, and the lighthouse crew were never seen again, and all that remained of the structure were two twisted bars attached to the rock. A similar storm in 1858 also caused dreadful loss of life amongst the fishing communities, and led to Admiral Fitzroy equipping all fishing ports with a barometer.

The barometer was invented in 1643 by Torricelli and quickly became a household instrument for predicting the weather, although rarely taken to sea at this time. By the end of the seventeenth century, seamen were taking 'storm glasses' to sea. The storm glass was a type of water barometer which reacted to air pressure but also, unfortunately, to fluctuations in air temperature. High air pressure caused a low level of water in the spout and low pressure a high water level, the last indicating the likelihood of a storm.

Marine mercury barometers were increasingly used at sea in the eighteenth century, slung in gimbals to counteract the motion of the vessel, and with a constriction in the glass tube to stop surging. Only well-found ships would carry such an instrument, and most coasting skippers would rely on age-old jingles to help predict the weather, or on folklore, as recorded by Lecky in his *Wrinkles of Practical Navigation* of 1881, where he states 'By English fishermen an echo at sea is considered a sign of a coming easterly wind, and it is generally thought that much phosphorescence of the water, or a vivid display of the Aurora, is the prelude to a southerly gale in our own latitudes'. Other unpredictable storms with which deep-sea sailors had to contend were tropical revolving storms, which are called by various names in different parts of the world: hurricanes in the West Indies and South Pacific Ocean, cyclones in the Indian Ocean and typhoons in the China Sea. The wind blows with great force around an area of very low pressure, with a spiral movement in towards the centre. The storms can travel at great speed across the oceans and are a great danger to shipping, particularly to sailing ships. In the days of sail, the first indications noted would be a heavy swell not caused by the local wind, a rapidly falling barometer and a threatening sky. Although these storms were not fully understood until as late as the 1880s, there were nevertheless rules laid down for the guidance of seamen, to enable them to avoid being caught in the eye of the storm, where the strongest winds blew and the most confused seas ran, and to at least prepare for the coming tempest. But these rules were of such complexity, that it is little wonder that, before the advent of radio storm warnings and the use of international meteorological observations recorded and transmitted by selected ships all over the world, Lecky could only advise that 'nothing but the hope of better things in the future can save the sailor being disheartened with such little practical result after so many years of investigation. He has, however always been famed for the faculty (possessed by so few) of doing the best with but indifferent means; and it still remains for him to go to sea almost entirely dependent on his own watchfulness and judgment'.

ALAN STIMSON

# The Wind

Many of the terms used at sea to describe wind and weather are self-evident, being the same as those used ashore. The only terms included here are those which are specifically nautical, particularly those that are no longer in use. Furthermore, the terms used in modern meteorology – depressions, anti-cyclones, fronts and so on – are also omitted, not only because they are not specifically nautical, but also because they did not come into use until the First World War.

**Wind.** Air in motion. Winds may be *warm* or *cold*, *moist* or *dry*.

## Wind Direction

**North wind, south wind** and so on. Point of the compass from which the wind blows.

**Wind veering,** or **wind hauling.** Altering direction clockwise, for instance SW to NW.

**Wind backing.** Altering direction anti-clockwise, for instance SW to S.

**True wind.** Point of compass from which the wind is coming, regardless of ship movement.

**Relative wind.** Wind direction as felt in a moving ship, and shown by a mast-head pennant. Expressed in points or degrees from the ship's head.

**Variable wind,** or **erratic wind.** Converse of steady wind. Light variable winds are termed *fluky*.

**Head wind,** or **dead wind,** or **dead on end,** or **wind in the teeth.** Wind blowing from right ahead.

**Beam wind.** Wind coming from the beam.

**Quarter wind.** Wind blowing from the quarter.

**Following wind.** Wind coming from astern.

**Foul wind,** or **contrary wind.** Wind blowing from the direction in which the vessel wishes to sail, or which may set her into danger. A vessel in port unable to sail because of a foul wind is said to be *wind-bound*.

**Fair wind.** Contrary to FOUL WIND.

**Slant of the wind.** Air of which advantage may be taken.

**Slant wind.** Unfavourable but not foul wind.

**Leading wind.** Abeam or quartering wind; free or fair.

**Soldier's wind.** One which serves either way; allowing a passage to be made without much nautical ability. (Mariners never had a very high opinion of the soldiery.)

**Round wind.** One which changes direction 180° during daylight hours.

**Prevailing wind,** or **reigning wind.** The average or characteristic wind at any place.

**Sea breeze.** Onshore wind which occurs in daytime on a coast in settled weather, between about 10 am and sunset. Caused by the land heating up under the sun's rays.

**Land breeze.** Offshore wind occurring after a day of SEA BREEZES, during the night when the land cools and cold air flows out to sea under the influence of gravity. Usually weaker than the sea breeze.

**Young wind.** Commencement of land and sea breezes.

---

## THE BEAUFORT SCALE

| Beaufort Number | Limits of wind velocity in knots | Description of wind | Sails worn by a Man-of-war for each wind strength |
|---|---|---|---|
| 0 | Less than 1 | Calm | Full sail |
| 1 | 1–3 | Light air | Full sail will just give steerage way |
| 2 | 4–6 | Light breeze | Full sail and clear full gives speed of 1–2 knots |
| 3 | 7–10 | Gentle breeze | Full sail and clear full gives speed of 3–4 knots |
| 4 | 11–16 | Moderate breeze | Full sail and clear full gives speed of 4–5 knots |
| 5 | 17–21 | Fresh breeze | Close-hauled the ship could carry: Royals etc. Single reefs and topgallant sails. Double reefs, jib, etc. Triple reefs, courses, etc. Close reefs and courses. |
| 6 | 22–27 | Strong breeze | As for Beaufort number 5 |
| 7 | 28–33 | Moderate gale | As for Beaufort number 5 |
| 8 | 34–40 | Fresh gale | As for Beaufort number 5 |
| 9 | 41–47 | Strong gale | As for Beaufort number 5 |
| 10 | 48–55 | Whole gale | The ship could only just bear close-reefed main topsail and reefed foresail. |
| 11 | 56–63 | Violent storm | Storm staysails |
| 12 | 64 and over | Hurricane | No canvas |

## Wind Strength

**Beaufort scale of wind and weather.** Scale devised in 1806 by Captain (later Admiral Sir) Francis Beaufort for describing wind strength and weather in ship's logs. The first published version was in 1832. It came into general use in the Royal Navy in 1838 and was accepted for international use in 1854. Modified to bring it out of the sailing ship era, it is still used by seamen and meteorologists today.

**Breath of wind.** All but flat calm.

**Capful of wind.** An intermittent breath of wind.

**Fanning breeze.** Wind so gentle that the sail alternately swells and collapses.

**Gust,** or **gush,** or **fall wind.** Increase of wind of very short duration.

**Squall.** High wind arriving suddenly and ceasing suddenly. When this happens with a clear sky, it is a *white squall*; with clouds, a *black squall*.

**Blunk.** Sudden squall.

**Freshening,** or **breezing up,** or **blowing up,** or **frisking.** Wind increasing in strength.

**Spanking.** Brisk, lively.

**Fresh.** Strong but not violent.

**Feeding gale.** A storm on the increase.

**Blowing great guns and small arms.** Blowing hard.

**Lull.** Brief interval of moderate weather during a gale.

**Dropping,** or **easing.** Reducing in strength.

## Ocean Winds

**Doldrums.** Area of low pressure near the equator between the TRADE WINDS, having calms and light variable winds alternating with squalls, heavy rains and thunder storms.

**Sailing ship routes.** Seamen's knowledge of the above very constant winds – largely empirical – gave rise to the sailing ships' regular routes.

**Trade winds.** Winds blowing with great steadiness and persistence (except when modified by seasonal monsoons and occasional tropical revolving storms) in an area between the oceanic anti-cyclones and the DOLDRUMS. In the northern hemisphere, the winds are *north-east trades*; in the southern, they are *south-east trades*. Their average force is 3–4.

**Variables.** Area covered by oceanic anti-cyclones, between the TRADE WINDS and WESTERLIES. Generally fair or fine. In the North Atlantic, it is known as the *Horse Latitudes*.

**Westerlies.** Area where the prevailing winds are westerly, though they are not permanent in the same way as the TRADE WINDS. The constant passage of depressions from west to east causes winds to vary greatly in direction and strength, with frequent gales, especially in the Southern Ocean, which has the *Roaring Forties*.

**Monsoon,** or **anniversary wind.** Seasonal wind. From the Persian *mounsum*, meaning a season.

**South-west monsoon** (or, in India, 'The Rains'). Seasonal south-west winds which blow in India and in the Indian Ocean, Arabian Sea, Bay of Bengal, China Sea and western North Pacific during the summer from May to September. Frequently gale force at the height of the season, they are very constant, displacing the north-east trades in the Indian Ocean.

**North-east monsoon.** North-east wind felt in the Arabian Sea, Bay of Bengal, China Sea and western North Pacific from October to March; fresh or strong in the China Sea and western North Pacific; moderate to light elsewhere.

**North-west monsoon,** or **cross monsoon.** South of the equator, the north-east monsoon is deflected and blows from the north-west or west from November to March.

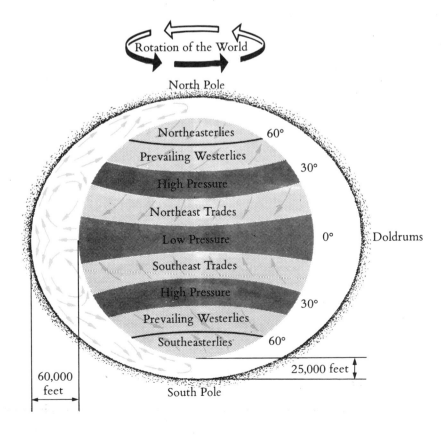

# Seasonal wind patterns of the world

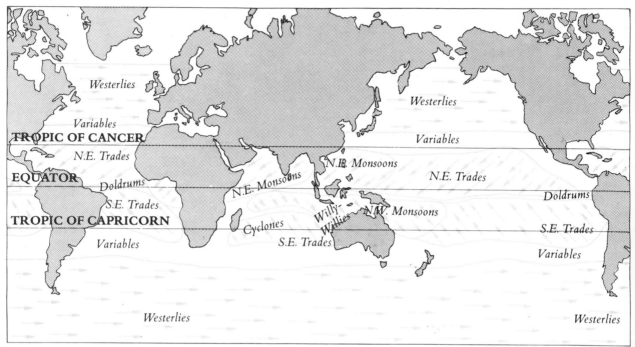

January–March

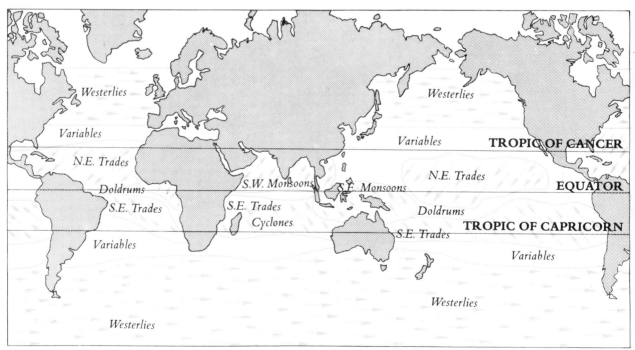

April–June

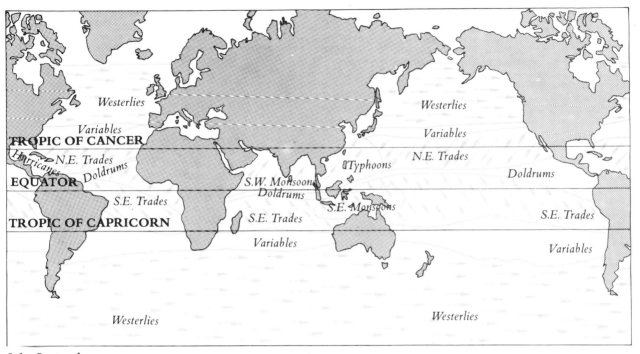

**July–September**

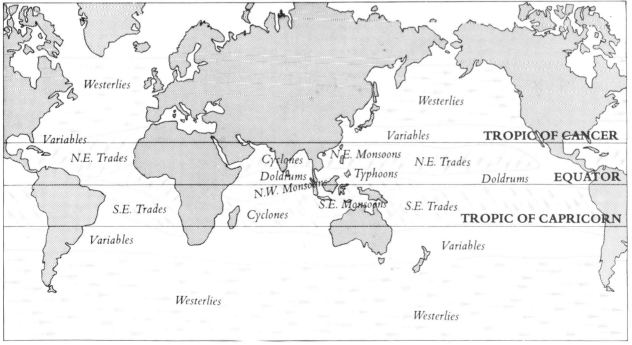

**October–December**

# Local winds table

| Mediterranean Sea and Southern Europe | | | | |
|---|---|---|---|---|
| Levanter | Straits of Gibraltar | — | E | Moist |
| Vendavales | Straits of Gibraltar | Spring; autumn | SW | Strong |
| Levache | SW Spain | — | SE-SW | Dry, sand laden |
| Llevantades | E Spain | Spring; autumn | NNE-EWE | Gales |
| Levante | E Spain | — | NE | |
| Bize | S France | Winter | NW-NE | Cold, dry, cloudy |
| Mistral | Gulf of Lions | — | N | Cold, gales, fine weather |
| Leste | N Africa | — | S | Hot, dry |
| Bora | NE Adriatic | — | NE | Gales |
| Scirocco | Entire Mediterranean | — | S | Hot, dry, dust-laden |
| Gregale | Central and W Mediterranean, Malta | Winter | NE | Strong |
| Solano | SE Spain | — | E-SE | Rain |
| Marin | Gulf of Lions | — | SE | Warm, moist, cloudy |
| Libeccio | N Corsica | — | W-SW | Squalls |
| Maestro | Adriatic | Summer | NW | Fresh, fine |
| Tremontana | W Italy; N Corsica | Winter | NE-N | Mistral type |
| Khamsin | Egypt; Red Sea | — | Southerly | Hot, dry, dust laden |
| Meltemi (Etesians) | Aegean Sea | Summer | NE-NW | Cool, fine weather |

| Red Sea, Persian Gulf and Arabian Sea | | | | |
|---|---|---|---|---|
| Kharif | Near Berbera | Summer | SW | Blows 22.00–noon |
| Simoom | Persian Gulf | April–June September–November | SE-E | Hot, dry, dust-laden |
| Belat | S Arabia | Winter; early spring | NW | Strong |
| Shamal | Persian Gulf | Summer | NW | Cloudless, very hot and dry |
| Seistan | E Persia | Summer | N | 'Wind of 120 days'; strong to gale force |
| Kaus | Persian Gulf | Winter | SE | |
| Suahili | Persian Gulf | Immediately after Kaus | SW | Strong |
| Sharqui | Persian Gulf | — | SE | |

**Indian Coast**

| | | | | |
|---|---|---|---|---|
| Elephanta | Malabar Coast | September–October; end of SW Monsoon | S–SE | Strong |
| NE Monsoon | India | October–March | NE | Cool, dry |
| SW Monsoon | India | June–October | SW | Moist; 'The Rains' |

**Malacca Straits**

| | | | | |
|---|---|---|---|---|
| Sumatra | Malacca Straits | June–October | Any direction | Line squalls, thunder storms |

**Australia**

| | | | | |
|---|---|---|---|---|
| Brickfielder | S Australia; Victoria; NSW | — | N | Hot, dry, dust-laden |
| Southerly buster | NSW | Spring; summer; immediately following a Brickfielder | S | Line squall, cold, violent rain |

**West Africa**

| | | | | |
|---|---|---|---|---|
| Tornadoes | Congo and Guinea coasts | Late spring and autumn at beginning and end of rains | Any direction | Violent storms with rain and lightning; not to be confused with US tornadoes, which are more violent |
| Harmattan | Cape Verde Island; Guinea Coast | November–March | N–E | Dry and relatively cool; dust-laden; 'The Doctor' |

**South Africa**

| | | | | |
|---|---|---|---|---|
| Black South-easter | Cape of Good Hope | — | SE | Produces the 'Tablecloth' |

**South America**

| | | | | |
|---|---|---|---|---|
| Williwaw | Strait of Magellan | Chiefly winter | Any direction | Very violent squalls |
| Pampero | Argentine and Uruguay | — | S–SW | Line squalls, cool |
| Zonda | Argentine and Uruguay | Immediately before Pampero | N | |
| Brisas or Briza | NE coasts | — | NE | NE Trades |

**Central and North America**

| | | | | |
|---|---|---|---|---|
| Norther | Gulf of Mexico; Central Pacific | Northern winter | N | Cool, dry, strong |
| Santa Ana | S California | Chiefly winter | Easterly | Hot, dry, dust-laden |
| Tornadoes or Twisters or Travado | US | Summer | Whirling anti-clockwise | Funnel-shaped cloud; very violent within small radius |

# Weather

## Weather Features

**Sea fret.** Sea fog blown over the land.

**Frost smoke.** Arctic sea smoke.

**Wind gall.** Luminous halo on the edge of a distant cloud, indicating rain to windward.

**Water spout.** Vertical revolving column of water.

**Blustrous.** Stormy.

**Blizzard.** Snow squall.

**Boldering weather.** Cloudy and thundery.

**Fair weather.** Good, favourable weather.

**Foul weather.** Bad, unfavourable weather.

## Weather Systems

**Gale.** A strong wind. *It's blowing a gale!* Winds of *gale force*. When beginning to improve, a gale is said to be *blowing itself out!*; that is, it is at the *breaking of the gale*.

**Storm.** A strong gale.

**Loom gale.** An easy gale.

**Equinoctial gales.** Gales of unusual strength which tend to occur in March and September near the equinoxes.

**Tropical revolving storms.** Vigorous low-pressure systems originating in certain tropical oceanic areas, called by different names according to the locality:

| | |
|---|---|
| *Hurricanes* | Western North Atlantic<br>West Indies<br>Eastern North Pacific<br>South Pacific |
| *Typhoons* | China Seas<br>Western North Pacific |
| *Baguio* | Philippine Islands |
| *Cyclones* | Indian Ocean<br>Arabian Sea<br>Bay of Bengal |

*Willy-willies* NW Australia

Though less extensive than the depressions of temperate latitudes, tropical revolving storms are far more vigorous, with winds of over 70 knots, gusting to 150 knots, and mountainous seas within 75 miles of the centre – known as the *eye of the storm*.

After forming in the tropics, a northern hemisphere storm moves along a north-westerly track until it reaches latitude 25°N or so, when it usually re-curves onto a north-easterly track and reaches various speeds to 25 knots or so, sometimes even 40 knots. But sometimes the storm continues in its original track and, when it reaches the mainland, it quickly fills. If it re-curves, intensity decreases above latitude 35°N, and it may turn into an ordinary depression. In the southern hemisphere circulation is clockwise and tracks are south-westerly until re-curving in latitudes 15°S to 20°S to a south-easterly track.

**Navigable semi-circle.** Area on the side of the path of a tropical revolving storm farthest from the normal direction of re-curvature, in which a sailing ship will tend to be blown away from the storm centre. If the storm re-curves the ship will be blown even farther off.

**Dangerous semi-circle.** Area on the side of the path of a tropical revolving storm towards the normal direction of re-curvature. If caught here, a ship may be blown towards the path of the storm.

**Dangerous quadrant.** The most dangerous storm area in which a ship can find herself.

**Storm signals.** Visual storm signals from coastguard stations and so on, showing the direction of an expected gale. The *north cone* (point upwards) is used for gales from a northerly point; the *south cone* (point downwards) for gales from a southerly point.

*The loss of the* Magnificent *during a storm*

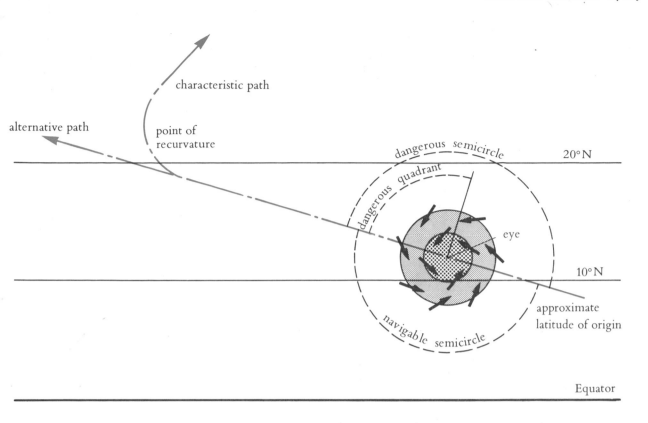

characteristic path

alternative path

point of
recurvature

dangerous semicircle 20° N

dangerous quadrant

eye

10° N

approximate
latitude of origin

navigable semicircle

Equator

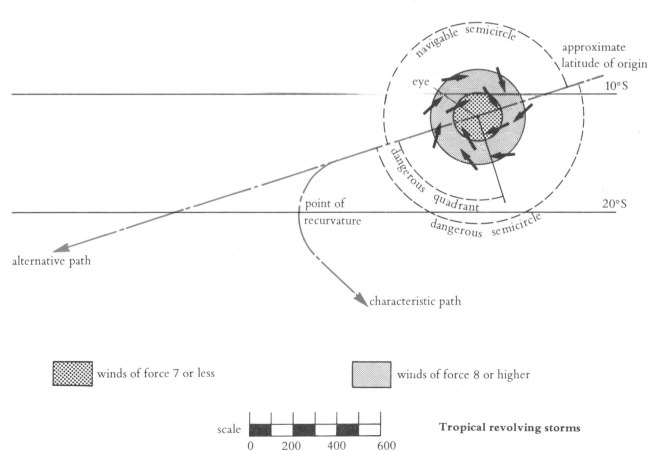

navigable semicircle

approximate
latitude of origin

eye

10° S

dangerous quadrant

20° S

dangerous semicircle

point of
recurvature

alternative path

characteristic path

winds of force 7 or less

winds of force 8 or higher

scale

0   200   400   600

**Tropical revolving storms**

# Clouds and Sea

*Cumulus*

**Mares' tails,** or **curl cloud.** Cirrus.

**Mackerel sky.** Cirro-cumulus.

**Wane cloud.** Cirro-stratus.

**Lamb's wool sky.** A collection of white orbicular masses of cloud. Probably strato-cumulus or alto-cumulus.

**Stacken cloud.** Cumulus.

**Rain cloud.** Cumulonimbus.

**Scud.** Cumulus fractus.

**Brewing.** Storm clouds seen to be developing.

**Overcast.** Generally stratus.

## WAVES

**Cat's paw.** Disturbance on a calm surface due to a passing light air. Also, the wind itself; a *puff*.

**Poppling sea,** or **rippling sea.** Ruffling of the water surface.

**Broken water.** Disturbed sea surface due to something other than wind, for instance currents meeting or shoal water.

**White horses,** or **white caps,** or **sea caps.** Waves with breaking crests due to wind of force 4 or more.

**Breakers.** Waves with breaking crests due to shoal water. 'Breakers ahead!' is the look-out's warning indicating shoal water ahead.

**Surf.** Breaking waves in the area between shore-line and outer limit of breakers.

**Spume.** Froth of sea foam.

**Spray.** Water blown, or thrown, into the air in particles.

**Spindrift,** or **spoondrift.** Fine spray blown off the crests of waves in very high winds, filling the air as with vapour.

**Green sea.** Sea that sweeps over a vessel without breaking.

## SEA AND SWELL

**Sea.** In this context, waves that are generated by wind blowing at the place and time of observation.

**Swell,** or **sea gait.** Waves caused either by a wind at a distance or by winds in the locality previous to the time of observation. Larger and more regular than SEA, swell reaching shoal water becomes higher and shorter and is then termed *ground swell*.

**Rollers.** SWELL in shoal water which does not break.

**Fetch.** Area of sea surface over which the sea or swell is generated. The larger the fetch, the longer the period of the wave.

**Short sea,** or **cockling sea,** or **choppy sea,** or **chopping sea.** Short, abrupt, breaking waves dashing against each other.

**Lop.** Small but quick-running seas. Hence *loppy*.

**Cross sea,** or **counter sea.** Series of waves or swell crossing another wave system at an angle. Generally a *confused sea*, it often happens after a gale and may be hazardous.

**Head sea, beam sea, quartering sea** and **following sea.** Sea from the direction indicated.

## WEATHER JINGLES

**Of gales and the barometer**

Long foretold, long last;
Short notice, soon past.

First rise after low
Foretells a stronger blow.

**Of wind (in or near Britain)**

A veering wind, fair weather,
A backing wind, foul weather.

If the wind is north-east, three days without rain.
Eight days will pass before south wind again.

When the rain's before the wind,
Topsail halyards you must mind;
When the wind's before the rain,
Hoist your topsails up again.

*Cirrus*

*Spume and spray*

# Pilotage & Charts

Pilotage is the oldest of all navigational skills and was defined by John Seller in 1669 as 'the Domestick or more common navigation', that is, 'the coasting or sailing along the shore'. It was not to be confused with the art of navigation, 'which guides the ship on her course through the Immense Ocean to any port of the Known World'.

Every coastal navigator is involved in pilotage, although the term 'pilot' was eventually to be applied to a specialist skilled in the dangers of a particular area through which he was licensed to conduct ships. Originally, a pilot used only a compass and sounding lead, and his ability was measured by the skill with which he steered his ship from headland to headland, avoiding rocks and shoals, and by his knowledge of the sea-bed. He was also skilled in recognizing features of the coastline, sea-marks and buoys, and could predict the times of high and low water for all the ports he visited. Generally, his knowledge was local or confined to a particular trade, so that a man engaged in the carriage of coal from the Tyne to London might have an encyclopedic knowledge of the North Sea and its coasts but be completely lost elsewhere.

This information was at first handed down from master to apprentice, but as trade increased around the shores of north-west Europe and ships traded further afield it became necessary to gather information from other sources. Manuscript sailing directions in medieval times were exchanged and copied, until a ship's master might eventually collect a complete set of instructions for the coasts of England and Wales, and along the shores of Europe to the Straits of Gibraltar. In about 1510 one such collection of sailing directions was printed in France complete with repetitions and mistakes, and an expanded version, *Le Routier de la Mer,* was published in English as *The Rutter of the See* in 1528. The 'rutters', as English seamen called them, were illustrated with crude woodcut elevations of important landmarks and headlands, and enabled a coastal navigator for the first time to sail into areas outside his own experience.

By the middle of the sixteenth century, charts were beginning to be used by north European seamen. The vellum portolan chart of the Mediterranean area, based on magnetic compass courses and estimated distances, had existed since the twelfth century, and gradually this kind of chart began to be more widely used. At first used only to record the oceanic discoveries of the Portuguese and Spanish, it was eventually used to depict northern European areas. It was brightly coloured and covered in a maze of rhumb lines springing from the many compass roses on its surface. A latitude scale was added in the early sixteenth century and charts with soundings on them are recorded as early as 1560, this last being a most important improvement for seamen in the shallow waters of the English Channel and North Sea.

In 1569, the Flemish cartographer Gerhard Mercator published a world map in sixteen sheets, constructed on a projection which compensated for the errors inherent in drawing the world's round surface on a flat piece of paper or vellum. It also enabled accurate true courses to be laid off for the first time, as the spiral rhumb lines of the globe were now straight lines on Mercator's chart. Mercator did not explain exactly how he constructed his chart but an Englishman, Edward Wright, in his *Certaine Errors of Navigation* published in 1599, calculated a mathematical solution to the problem and advised its use in the strongest terms. Despite the obvious advantages of these new charts, it was to be many years before seamen could be persuaded to give up their old plane charts. As late as 1700 about half the published charts in sea atlases were still of the plane type.

A significant step forward in pilotage was achieved by the publication of a combined sailing directory and sea atlas by Lucas Janszoon Waghenaer, entitled *Spieghel der Zeervaert,* in 1584. It was quickly translated into English, and appeared in 1588 as *The Mariner's Mirror,* running into several editions. 'Waggoners', as English seamen called them, combined for the first time printed sailing directions with large-scale plane charts of the coast, drawn to emphasize the harbours and navigational dangers. Elevations of the shore, with conspicuous towers, windmills and hilltops, were provided with each chart, and for the first time a system of symbols to depict buoys and beacons was included. The Dutch had a virtual monopoly of printed charts and atlases at this time, which was not broken until John Seller published his *English Pilot* in 1671, although many of the plates used for this work were obtained secondhand from Dutch printers and revised.

In 1681 Captain Greenville Collins was authorized to survey the whole of the British Isles, and the result of this enormous task appeared seven years later as *Great Britain's Coasting Pilot*. Although much criticized at the time and compared unfavourably with *Le Neptune François* published in 1693, it did fulfil a need, and ran into many editions in the eighteenth century. *Le Neptune François* itself set new standards, because many of the charts were constructed on the Mercator principle and based on the elder Cassini's astronomical fixing of the longitude of the French coast following the Jupiter's satellite method carried out by 1681. In France, Le Depot des Cartes et Plans de la Marine was established in 1720, and it was from about this time that French charts superseded the Dutch as the best available.

In 1795 the Admiralty finally decided to establish a Hydrographer of the Navy, whose task it was to collate and publish charts based on the many excellent British charts surveyed since the time of Cook. Cook had set new standards for maritime surveys, and his methods were passed on through Bligh, Vancouver and Flinders, who all helped to establish a tradition of surveying excellence which was the hallmark of British Admiralty charts during the nineteenth century.

One major difference in the charts of different nations during the eighteenth century was the position of the meridian from which longitude was calculated. It was generally based on the national observatory or capital city of each country, so it was not uncommon to find some charts, particularly the French, with three or four longitude scales engraved upon them. However, in 1884 an international conference agreed that the Greenwich meridian should be the zero meridian from which all time, and consequently longitude, should be calculated.

Published sailing directions developed as merchant companies traded further afield in areas that had formerly been the province of one nation. By the mid-eighteenth century, William Herbert's *New Directory for the East Indies* had been published. Herbert's work was followed in 1816 by James Horsburgh's *Directions for sailing to and from the East Indies, China, New Holland, Cape of Good Hope and the Interadjacent Ports.* During the nineteenth century, Admiralty surveys of many ports of the world enabled the Hydrographic Office to publish its own pilot books to supplement the charts, the first of the series being the Channel Pilots, of 1856. These eventually superseded all the earlier commercial directories.

As these developments in surveying and charting were taking place, there were parallel developments in shore aids to pilots. Lighthouses to guide ships into harbour were first built in classical times. In the fifteenth and sixteenth centuries, many light-towers were built in the Mediterranean, but northern seamen still relied on daylight aids, such as church towers, windmills and any prominent land features, to find their way along the coast. In low-lying estuaries with few easily recognizable features and many shoals, buoys and beacons began to be laid in about 1520 to assist the navigator.

Four societies of mariners, known as Trinity Houses, flourished in England in the Middle Ages, and there were a further two at Leith and Dundee in Scotland. Originally, they were founded as charities for old and disabled seamen, and to protect seamen's rights. Early in the sixteenth century, they became chartered in order to improve the skills of mariners and to regulate pilotage and maritime law in their areas of jurisdiction. Trinity House, Deptford, was given powers for the safety and progress of shipping in the Thames River and estuary in 1514, and in 1604 James I conferred on it the right to enforce pilotage of shipping and the exclusive right to license pilots in the river. (Trinity House's responsibility for sea-marks had begun in the reign of Elizabeth I.)

During the seventeenth century it became the practice for the Crown to issue licences to individuals to erect lighthouses around the coast. Ship owners were charged 'light dues', partly for the upkeep of the lighthouse but mostly for the profit of the lighthouse owner. A Northern Lighthouse Board was established in 1786 with responsibility for Scottish coastal lights, and the lights along the Irish coast were placed in the charge of the Dublin Port Authority in 1810. However, it was not until 1836 that Trinity House was empowered to control all English lighthouses. These three lighting authorities still control and maintain the lights, buoys and beacons around the British Isles and share the light dues charged on each ship entering their waters.

Lighthouses were at first illuminated with coal fires. Candles and then oil lamps were used, but when in 1782 Aimé Argand invented an oil lamp with a circular wick and surrounding glass chimney, a really satisfactory bright flame was produced. At about the same time, it was found that a parabolic reflector placed behind the lamp was able to direct the beam of light and increase candle power many hundreds of times. The first flashing light was installed by Robert Stevenson at Walney in 1820. Other important improvements were Augustin Fresnel's dioptric lense of 1822 and the introduction of gas lighting in 1865.

Light buoys were established from about 1880, after a reliable method of gas lighting had been evolved, making night pilotage a much safer operation. The introduction of lighthouse fog signals is of comparatively recent date, with explosions of one form or another preceding bells and later the use of compressed-air diaphones, horns and sirens.

ALAN STIMSON

# Piloting and pilotage

**Pilot** (vb). To navigate a vessel on or near a sea-coast, through intricate channels, or in or out of harbour.

**Coasting.** Navigating along a coast.

**Pilotage.** The act of piloting a vessel. The term came into use in the nineteenth century in place of the sixteenth-century *navigation common* to describe coastal and harbour navigation (as distinct from *navigation proper*, which was ocean navigation). Also, the fees and charges paid for the services of a pilot.

**Pilot.** Person properly qualified and licensed to pilot ships, having an intimate knowledge of his own area – the appearance of the land from sea-ward, navigational aids, time and direction of tides, reigning winds, roads and havens, different depths of water, quality of ground, and so on. In the eighteenth century, the *coast pilot* took charge of the ship while coasting, the *branch pilot* when entering or leaving rivers or harbours. Today there are *channel pilots*, *river pilots*, *harbour pilots* and others.

**Pilotage authority.** Official body responsible for licensing and organizing pilots in a particular *pilotage district*. For example, in the eighteenth century, Trinity House of Deptford Strand, and the Society of Pilots at Dover.

**Pilotage waters,** or **pilots' water,** or **pilot-water.** Any area where pilotage is compulsory.

**Pilot cutter,** or **pilot vessel.** Sea-going vessel which cruises in a specific *pilot station* for the purpose of putting pilots on board inward-bound ships recovering them from outward-bound ships.

**Pilot boat.** Small craft used for embarking and disembarking pilots in sheltered waters.

## PILOTING

**Transit,** or **range** (US). When two objects appear directly in line, one behind the other, they are said to be *in transit*, or *in range*, and together constitute a *transit*, or *range*. For

accurately charted objects, this provides the most accurate line of position obtainable, and one of the easiest to observe, demanding no compass or other instrument.

**Leading line.** Transit line chosen to lead safely down a particular track. The marks used are called *leading marks* and may be natural or artificial, sometimes being erected specially for the purpose. They may also be *leading lights*. When the two marks are seen to be in transit (and thus the ship must be on the desired line), the transit is said to be *on*, and the marks are *in one*. When the rear mark is obscured by the front one or by the land, it is said to be *shut in*.

*Pilot and Helmsman aboard the* Penag

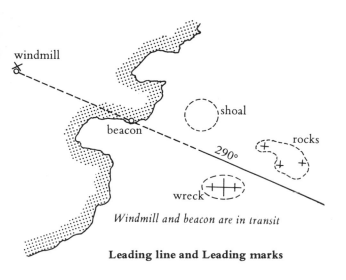

*Windmill and beacon are in transit*

**Leading line and Leading marks**

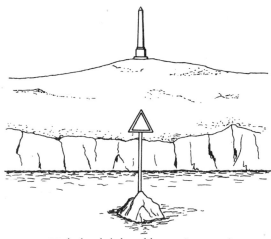

*With the obelisk and beacon **in transit**, the transit is **on** and the two marks are **in one**.*

**Clearing line and Clearing marks**

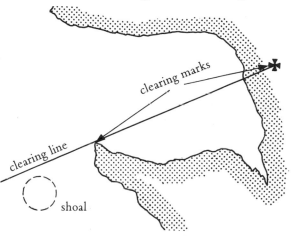

*As long as the church is **open** of the headland, the shoal can be cleared.*

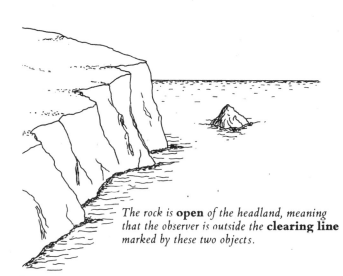

*The rock is **open** of the headland, meaning that the observer is outside the **clearing line** marked by these two objects.*

**Clearing line.** Transit line chosen to mark the limit of a danger area. Care must be taken not to go inside the transit line of the *clearing marks*: so long as these are kept *open*, the ship must be clear of danger.

The following extracts from the chapter 'Examination of a young sea officer' from Norie's *Epitome* (3rd ed. 1810), pp. 301–3, give an idea of how these terms were used in the days of sail:

'Q What are the marks for going between the Race and the Shambles in the night?

'A The two lights on Portland, bearing N.N.W½W. I would run in until the land shuts in the new light-house, then steer N.N.E.

'Q How would you sail through the middle channel into Plymouth Sound?'

'A Bring Plymouth Old Church, which has 4 spires on it, bearing N.N.E. on with the white or middle Obelisk; and to turn between the Knap and Panther, Tinker and Shovel, I would bring the Old Church just to touch the east side of the west, or black Obelisk; and the west side of the east, or red Obelisk.

(Spithead)
'Q What is the mark for the South-east buoy of the Dean?'

'A Ashey Down mark on with the southernmost of the two clumps of trees at the Priory House, on the Isle of Wight, and the Spire of Portsmouth Church, a sail's breadth open to the eastward of South Sea Castle.

'Q What is the mark for going into Spithead?

'A The Spire of Portsmouth Church, North a little westerly, or Kicker Gill and Fort Monkton in one.'

# Aids to navigation

**Landmark.** Conspicuous object, natural or artificial, visible from seaward.

**Beacon.** Mark, such as a post or stake erected on a rock or shoal or ashore, used as an aid to navigation. May be fitted with a light, TOPMARK or fog signal. Assumed to be fixed, unless specifically described as a *floating beacon*. Beacons include *leading marks*, *perches* (which have topmarks), *Jack in the baskets* (basket topmark) and *daymarks* (specifically for use in daytime, or a shape hoisted by a light-vessel for identification in daytime).

**Lighthouse.** Structure exhibiting a major light, designed to serve as an aid to navigation. Until the nineteenth century, lighthouses were generally fixed lights (though by 1800 St. Agnes, Scilly Isles, had a flashing light to distinguish it from the fixed light in the Longships lighthouse).

*The Skerryvore Lighthouse*

**Light-vessel,** or **lightship,** or **floating light.** Vessel moored in a particular position to mark a danger. Before the days of flashing lights, several fixed lights were often exhibited together, for example, in 1800, Galloper had two lights one above the other; North Sand Head (Goodwins) had three in a triangular form; Owers had one; Caskets had three in a triangular form.

**Topmark.** Characteristic shape secured to the top of a buoy or beacon to aid identification; for instance, a globe, cage, diamond, triangle, cross, cone, can, T, sphere or flag.

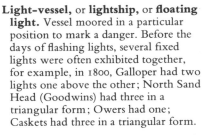

*The Eddystone Lighthouse. This illustration shows the third Eddystone Lighthouse built in 1756–1759 by John Smeaton. The original lighthouse, begun by Henry Winstanley in 1696 and built of wood, was swept away along with Winstanley in 1703. The second lighthouse, also built of wood in 1706, burned down in 1755. The third, though built of more durable materials, was eventually undermined by the sea and a fourth was erected by Sir James Douglass from 1878–1882.*

*Bell buoy*

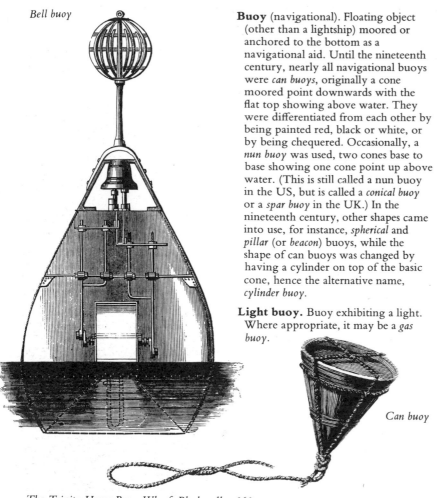

**Buoy** (navigational). Floating object (other than a lightship) moored or anchored to the bottom as a navigational aid. Until the nineteenth century, nearly all navigational buoys were *can buoys*, originally a cone moored point downwards with the flat top showing above water. They were differentiated from each other by being painted red, black or white, or by being chequered. Occasionally, a *nun buoy* was used, two cones base to base showing one cone point up above water. (This is still called a nun buoy in the US, but is called a *conical buoy* or a *spar buoy* in the UK.) In the nineteenth century, other shapes came into use, for instance, *spherical* and *pillar* (or *beacon*) buoys, while the shape of can buoys was changed by having a cylinder on top of the basic cone, hence the alternative name, *cylinder buoy*.

**Light buoy.** Buoy exhibiting a light. Where appropriate, it may be a *gas buoy*.

*Can buoy*

**Whistle buoy, bell buoy** and **gong buoy.** Buoys fitted with sound-producing apparatus to aid identification in fog.

**Dan buoy.** Light spar-buoy, generally fitted with a flag, used by fishermen and surveyors as a temporary mark.

**Port–hand buoy** and **starboard–hand buoy.** Buoys to be left to port or starboard respectively when entering harbour or going with the main flood-stream. Originally differentiated solely by colour but, since 1889, port-hand buoys have generally been can-shaped, starboard-hand conical (nun).

**Middle-ground buoy.** Buoy marking a shoal in a fairway, having a channel on either side. Since 1889, middle-ground buoys have been spherical.

**Channel buoy,** or **mid-channel buoy.** Buoy marking the centre of a channel. Often a pillar buoy.

**Fairway buoy.** Buoy marking a fairway, with safe water on both sides.

**Farewell buoy,** or **sea buoy.** Buoy at the seaward end of a channel, sometimes acting as a *landfall buoy*.

**Bar buoy.** Buoy marking a harbour bar.

**Watch buoy,** or **station buoy** (US). Buoy moored close to a light-vessel to give warnings should she drag her moorings.

*The Trinity House Buoy Wharf, Blackwall, 1868*

**Wreck buoy,** or **wreck-marking buoy.** Buoy that marks the location of a wreck.

**Buoyage.** System of buoys.

*Nun buoy used as an anchor buoy*

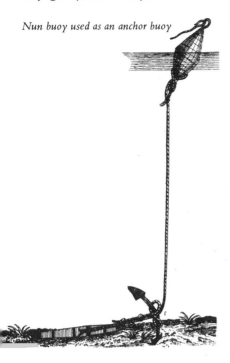

**Anchor buoy.** Buoy attached to an anchor and used to indicate the anchor's position when it is on the bottom.

**Fixed light** (F.). A constant light.

**Flashing light** (Fl.). One or more flashes at regular intervals, the duration of the light being less than that of each interval.

**Occulting light** (Occ.). Light totally eclipsed at intervals, the duration of the light being equal to or greater than that of each interval.

**Group flashing** (Gp. Fl.) and **group occulting** (Gp. Occ.) **lights.** Flashes or occultations of light occurring regularly in groups of two or more; for example, Gp. Occ. (3).

**Alternating light** (Alt.). Light showing periodical colour variations; for example, flashing alternately red and white (Alt. Fl. R.W.).

**Light sector.** Sector in which a navigational light is (a) either visible or obscured, or (b) has a distinctive colour differing from that in adjoining sectors.

**Period of a light.** Interval needed to complete a cycle.

**Characteristics of a light.** Sequence, lengths of light and dark, and colour.

| Characteristics with their abbreviations | Time in n seconds |
|---|---|
| fixed light<br><br>F. | |
| flashing light:<br>flash every 5 seconds.<br><br>Fl. 5 Sec. | |
| group flashing light:<br>group of 3 flashes every 11 seconds.<br><br>Gp. Fl. (3). 11 Sec. | |
| quick flashing light:<br>more than 60 flashes a minute.<br><br>Qk. Fl. | |
| occulting light:<br>eclipsed every 5 seconds.<br><br>Occ. 5 Sec. | |
| occulting group light:<br>group of 3 eclipses every 10 seconds.<br><br>Occ. Gp. (3), 10 Sec. | |
| interrupted quick flashing light:<br>4 quick flashes at intervals of 10 seconds.<br><br>Int. Qk. Fl. (4), 10 Sec. | |
| fixed and flashing light:<br>one brighter flash every 5 seconds.<br><br>F. Fl. 5 Sec. | |
| fixed and group flashing light:<br>group of 3 bright flashes every 11 seconds.<br><br>F. Gp. Fl. (3), 11 Sec. | |
| alternating light:<br>colour changing from white to red over a period of 5 seconds.<br><br>Alt. W.R. 5 Sec. | |

# Charts and sailing directions

**Sea-chart,** or **nautical chart,** or **plat,** or **sea-card.** Map designed for use at **sea.**

**Draught.** Drawing or plan.

**Sea-atlas,** or **waggoner.** Sea-charts bound into a book. ('Waggoner' comes from the Dutch Lucas Waghenaer who published the earliest printed sea-atlas in 1584. The term was used in England until the end of the seventeenth century.)

**Marine surveying.** The art of properly representing an accurate view of a coast or harbour on a map or chart.

**Hydrography.** The science and practice of surveying the seas and oceans, charting their coasts, collecting navigational data, studying tides, and supplying navigators and others with information on the facts so determined.

**Hydrographer.** One who practices HYDROGRAPHY.

**Plane chart.** Chart constructed on the supposition that the Earth is flat, resulting in the distortion of all but the smallest areas.

**Mercator chart.** Chart constructed on the so-called *Mercator projection* in which (a) all meridians are made parallel, and (b) the latitude scale increases in the same ratio as the longitude scale in a particular latitude; (c) RHUMB LINES (15.06) are then represented by straight lines but (d) distance must be measured on the part of the varying latitude scale opposite the area concerned. This has been the principal projection used for sea-charts since about 1750.

**Gnomonic chart.** Chart constructed on the *gnomonic projection*, the principal properties of which are (a) GREAT CIRCLES (15.07) form straight lines; and there is (b) little distortion of small areas and (c) little distortion of polar areas, Used today for large-scale plans, for polar charts and, in small scales, for the planning of GREAT-CIRCLE (15.07) sailing.

**Portulan chart,** or (erroneously) **portulan.** Nineteenth-century term for an early Mediterranean PLANE CHART, hand-drawn on vellum with a LOXODROME (15.06) network and strict conventions for placing of names, colours used and features shown.

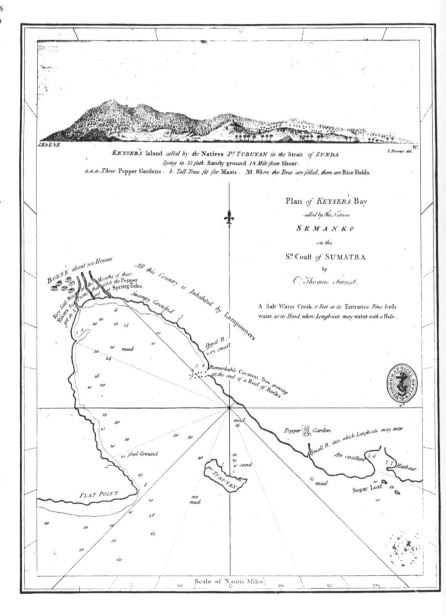

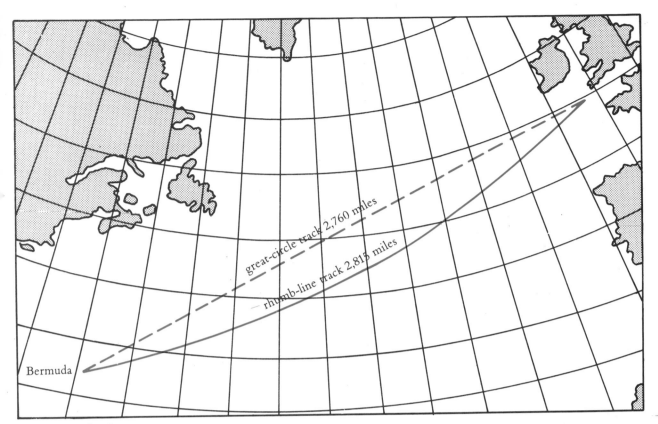

**Mercator projection**

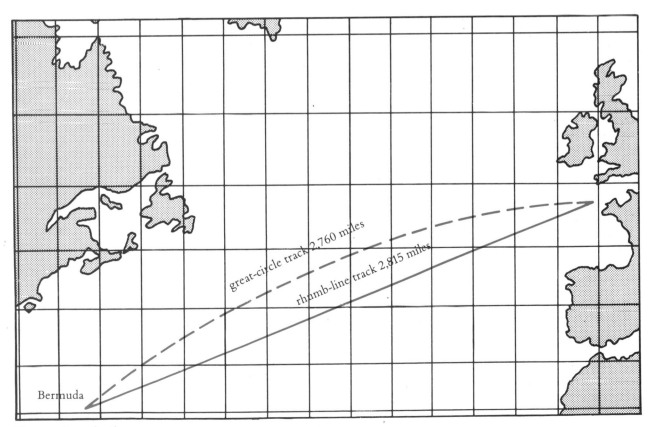

**Gnomonic projection**

**Bluebacks.** Charts privately published in England by various firms since about 1760, so called because of the stiff blue backing paper. Frequently of very large dimensions, they were generally kept rolled rather than folded flat as were the smaller Admiralty charts.

**Admiralty charts.** Official charts published by the British Admiralty since 1801, under the superintendence of the *Hydrographer of the Navy*.

**Loxodromes,** or **rhumbs,** or **winds.** Network of lines placed on the sea areas of nearly all charts until the end of the eighteenth century, from which courses and bearings could be measured.

**Compass rose,** or **flower of the winds.** Graduated circle on charts which, from the early nineteenth century, superseded the LOXODROME network for measuring courses and bearings.

**Graduation,** on charts. Scales of latitude and longitude around the chart borders.

**Soundings.** Figures on charts indicating depths of water, reduced to CHART DATUM (16.02). Added letters may indicate *nature of the bottom* or *quality of the sea-bed*; for instance, M = mud; S = sand; Sh = shells.

**Fathom lines,** or **depth contours,** or **fathom curves** (US). Contour lines in the sea areas of charts following certain depths such as 1, 3, 6, 10, 30 and 100 fathoms.

**Drying height.** Height above CHART DATUM (16.02) of a feature which dries at low water.

**Elevation,** on charts. Height of land features above datum plane.

**Vigia.** Supposed navigational danger, reported but not verified by survey.

**Portolan,** or **portulan.** Early Mediterranean sailing directions or pilot book. From the Italian *portolano*, a port-book. Often wrongly used to describe a PORTULAN CHART (18.04).

**Rutter.** Early north-west European sailing directions. From the French *routier*, a route-book.

**Pilot,** or **pilot book,** or **sailing directions.** Book describing winds, weather, currents, coasts and harbours in a specific area; for example, *North Sea Pilot*.

**Notice to mariners.** Bulletin issued periodically by a competent authority to give information about changes in navigational aids and new dangers discovered, and to promulgate changes to be made to published charts.

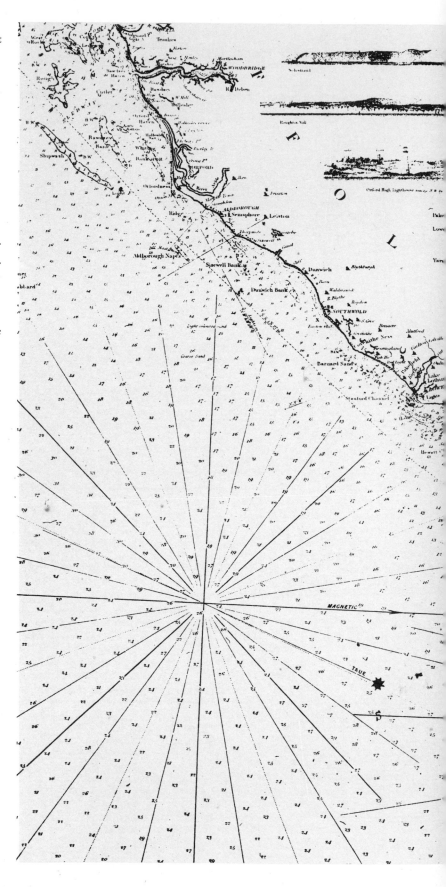

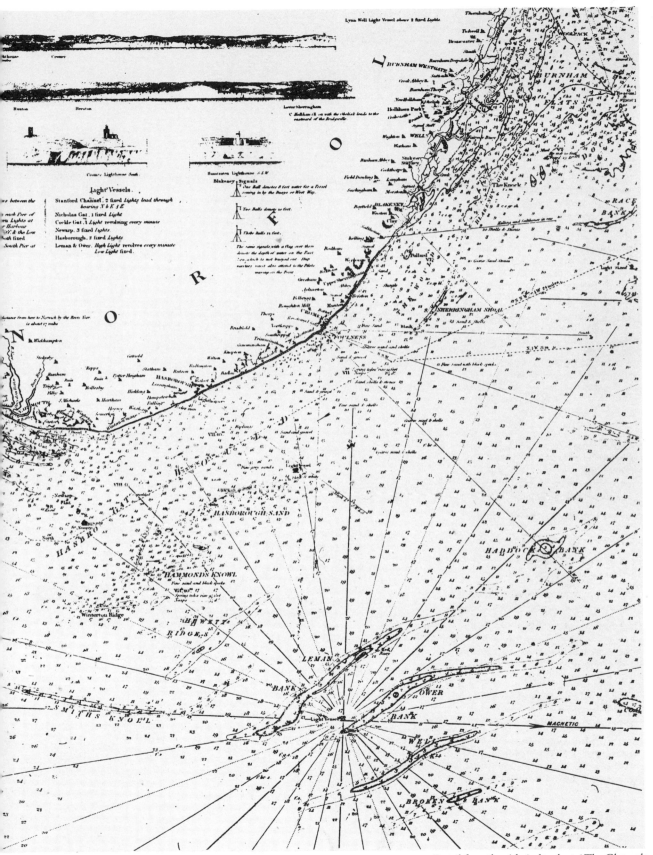

*Detail from the Admiralty chart 'The Channels Between Ushant and the Mainland', 1818*

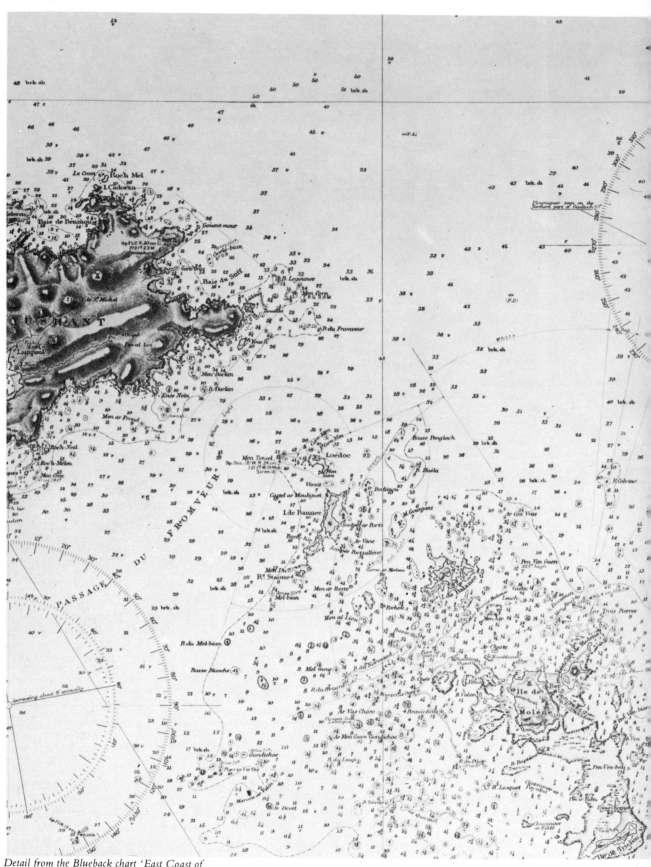

*Detail from the Blueback chart 'East Coast of
England from Harwich to Kingston-upon-Hull,' 1857*

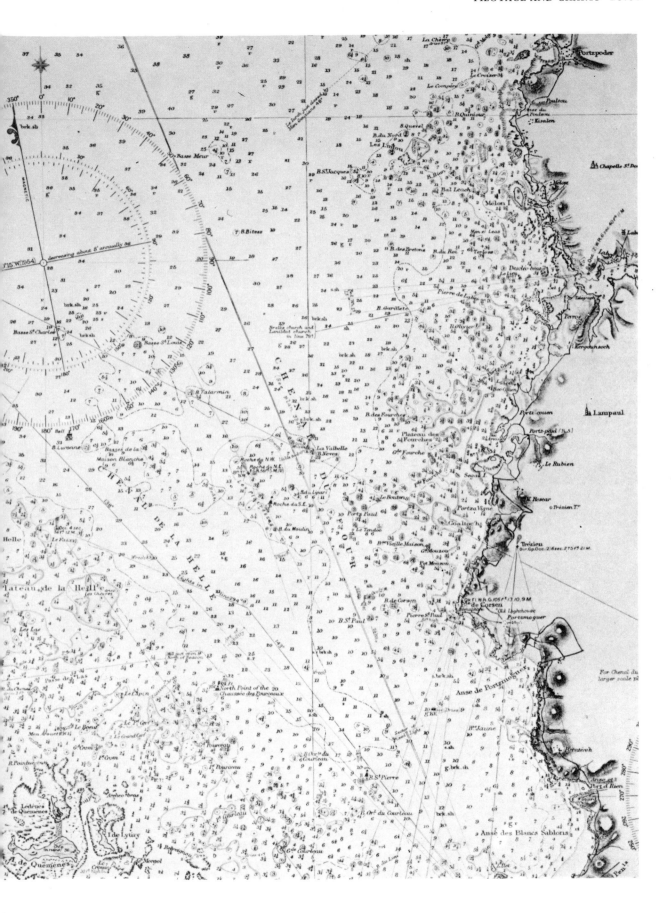

# Navigational Instruments

Seamen have had remarkably little to say about the tools of their trade over the centuries, and this is particularly true of navigators. A conservative approach to their calling has ensured that what changes have taken place have usually been because of a fundamental alteration in navigational technique rather than a desire to improve existing instruments. The result was that in the earlier part of the eighteenth century many seamen were using instruments and methods little changed from those in use a hundred years earlier.

It is easiest to think of navigational instruments used in the eighteenth and nineteenth centuries in two groups: those supplied by the shipowners and those supplied by the navigator himself. The former were those items of ship's equipment with which dead reckoning was made and soundings taken – that is to say, the compass for direction, the log for estimating speed and the lead and line for sounding depth of water. These were the instruments with which a daily account of the ship's offshore or shallow-water progress could be made by estimation, coupled with years of accumulated experience.

Perhaps the oldest of all navigational aids, the sounding lead and line in its deep-sea and shallow-water forms, was widely used throughout the period. The traditional markings of leather or of coloured cloth introduced in about 1600 are still in use today. Samples of the sea-bed brought up in the tallow arming plugged into the base of the lead, coupled with the depth of water, could be an indication of position when compared with the chart or pilot book. It was said that some coastal seamen could navigate by the smell of the sample on the base of the lead alone.

Probably the most important instrument in the ship was the steering compass, yet it was often the most primitive. It was crudely made, usually with a turned wooden bowl, the card pivoted on a brass pin driven through the base of the bowl and balanced with sealing wax. The soft-iron wire needle required constant re-magnetizing, and so ignorant were most seafarers about magnetism that it was not uncommon for iron objects to be stowed in the binnacle. After the wreck of Sir Clowdisley Shovel's ships in 1707, the Admiralty examined a number of compasses in the fleet, and found that out of 145 inspected only three were serviceable. Later, in the 1750s, Dr Gowin Knight developed a method of permanently magnetizing steel needles and designed an improved compass which was tried by Captain James Cook on his voyages of discovery between 1768 and 1780.

However, its performance in rough seas was not entirely satisfactory.

Further attempts were made to improve the compass, notably by Ralph Walker in 1793 and Captain Phillips in 1825, but it was not until the Admiralty Compass Committees of the 1830s and 1840s and the Liverpool Compass Committee of 1861 established a more scientific approach to compass construction and theory that matters improved. By 1876 Sir William Thomson, late Lord Kelvin, had patented his dry-card compass and binnacle which was used in the Merchant Service, although many sailing ships still mounted their standard compass high on a wooden pole above the upper deck in an attempt to escape the effect of the ship's magnetism.

Distance sailed was still estimated with the English log, first used at the end of the sixteenth century. It is described by John Hamilton Moore in 1782 in his *Practical Navigator* as 'a flat piece of wood rather like a flounder . . . having its circular side loaded with lead sufficient to make it swim upright in water. To this log is fastened a long line of about 150 fathoms, called the log line, which is divided into certain equal spaces. . . .' The main problem was the considerable difference of opinion among sea captains as to how far apart the 'certain equal spaces' should be. Although Richard Norwood in 1637 had recommended spacing the knots correctly at intervals of 51 feet, Hamilton Moore goes on to say that '. . . experienced commanders find that the allowing of 50 feet a knot generally makes the ship ahead of the reckoning; and to avoid Danger, mostly divide the log-line in knots of 7 or $7\frac{1}{2}$ fathoms, of 6 feet each, to correspond with a Glass that runs 28 seconds'.

This difficulty was eventually overcome when Edward Massey patented his mechanical towed log in 1801, for this relied on a rotator connected to a geared counter showing nautical miles. It proved to be the first commercially successful mechanical log, despite having to be heaved in and read each watch, and eventually developed into the taffrail log which was in common use until modern times. The ship-owners also supplied such things as sand-glasses for regulating time on board, until the 1820s and 1830s, when the carriage of chronometers and deck watches became general in large ships. In the second half of the nineteenth century, marine barometers were increasingly carried.

The navigator's contribution was in the newer art of astronomical navigation, and consisted of various instruments, which he had to provide at his own expense. As the standard of navigational expertise varied enormously, so did the quality and number of instruments taken to sea. Basically, the navigator would have with him a wooden backstaff and a cross-staff for altitude observations of the sun and stars, and perhaps a boxwood nocturnal for telling the time at night from the constellations of the Great and Little Bears. He would also have a Gunter's scale and dividers, or a sector, for manual working of mathematical problems, as well as the necessary almanacs and nautical tables. These instruments equipped him for latitude navigation.

In the Merchant Service, the ship's master also bought his own charts, usually bound as an atlas and protected by canvas covers, and each navigator would own a pair of dividers for pricking the ship's position on the chart, which was normally done at noon each day on an ocean passage. After 1714, when the British government offered a prize of £20,000 for a practicable means of finding longitude and set up a Board of Longitude to examine submissions, much time and thought was devoted to the problem by scientists and instrument makers.

The first useful consequence of the prize was John Hadley's octant, described to the Royal Society in 1731 as an instrument designed to measure the exacting angles required in the lunar-distance method of finding longitude. It was also a tremendous improvement on all existing instruments in use at sea for taking meridian altitudes. Despite this obvious superiority, Edward Hauxley could write about the backstaff in his *Navigation Unveiled* of 1743, 'a great many Seafaring Men are bigotted to this instrument for its ease I suppose, yet I could wish that it were intirely laid aside and Mr Hadley's . . . substituted in its place. . .'. Perhaps the complexity and price of the new instrument discouraged seamen from adopting it in large numbers before the 1750s and prolonged the backstaff's use into the 1770s.

With the solving of the longitude problem by John Harrison's prize-winning watch of 1759 and the publication of the lunar tables in the *Nautical Almanac* for 1767, a need for a more accurate version of Hadley's octant became apparent. In fact, experiments at sea by Captain John Campbell in 1757 and 1758 had led to the development of the sextant by the London instrument maker John Bird. Demand for the sextant increased rapidly after Captain Cook's voyages proved the efficacy of the new navigational methods. Initially of 20-inch radius and cumbersome, the sextant was drastically reduced in size and weight, with increased accuracy, by the use of Jesse Ramsden's scale-dividing machine, invented and perfected between 1768 and 1773.

Chronometers were at first prohibitively expensive, but by the 1770s John Arnold and Thomas Earnshaw had simplified chronometer production and made it commercially successful, and the instruments were increasingly used. At first, only Admiralty expeditions and East India Company ships were able to afford them, but by 1850 recognition of the benefits they conferred had resulted in most ocean-going ships carrying them. The nineteenth century continued to to be a period of refinement for all navigational instruments, with the British government instituting higher standards for navigators and their equipment – an example being the Kew Observatory certificates of accuracy for sextants.

In the eighteenth century the makers of British seamen's instruments were mostly concentrated in London, in the city and in the riverside areas of Wapping, Limehouse and Rotherhithe, although there were some in other large ports. A few had international reputations as makers of astronomical and scientific instruments of the highest quality, but most turned out vast numbers of mediocre wooden octants, backstaffs and scales in little dockstreet shops with the sign of Hadley's quadrant above the door. One such shop is brilliantly described by Charles Dickens in *Dombey and Son*: 'Anywhere in the immediate vicinity there might be seen pictures of ships speeding away full sail to all ports of the world . . . and little timber midshipmen in obsolete naval uniforms eternally employed outside the doors of nautical instrument makers in taking observations of the hackney coaches. . . . The stock in trade . . . comprised chronometers, barometers, telescopes, compasses, charts, maps, sextants, quadrants and specimens of every kind of instrument used in the working of a ship's course or the keeping of a ship's reckoning, or the prosecuting of a ship's discoveries. . . .'

By the 1850s, the type of instrument maker described by Dickens went out of business as the production of scientific instruments was concentrated in the hands of fewer and fewer firms. However, there were still many varied outlets for their products, and many second-hand octants and sextants available. Lecky, in his *Wrinkles in Practical Navigation* of 1881, warned against rushing wildly into buying a sextant. 'A good Quintant or sextant costs money – *and is worth it* . . . it is easy to be deceived in purchasing as in buying a horse. The market is glutted with sextants *made for sale*. Every pawnbroker's window in every seaport town is half full of them.' There follows much careful advice on what to look for in a good instrument, but it must be admitted that many seamen bought their instruments second-hand, without much thought as to their condition.

ALAN STIMSON

# Depth measurement

**Sound** (vb). Originally, to measure the depth of the water, and the quality of the ground, by means of a plummet sunk from a ship to the bottom. Today, this includes any method – by hand, by machine or by echo.

**Sounding.** Depth of water at a particular cast of the lead at a particular moment. On a chart, the depth of the water (reduced to CHART DATUM, 16.02) and the nature of the bottom in a particular position. Also, a specimen of the ground brought up adhering to tallow in the base of the lead, including sand, shells, ooze and so on.

**Lead and line.** Instrument for discovering the depth of the water and the nature of the bottom; probably the most ancient of navigational aids. It comprises a tapered cylinder of lead attached by a strop to the *lead-line*. The lead has a recess in its base which, when *arming the lead*, is filled with tallow so that specimens can be brought up from the bottom when taking SOUNDINGS.

**Hand–lead and line.** For use in channels and harbours from a ship with way upon her. The lead weighs 7–10 lb, and the line measures about 25 fathoms,

marked up to 20 fathoms. The system of marking has been in use with minor modifications since 1600.

**Deep-sea lead and line.** For use up to 200 fathoms or more, with the ship stopped. The lead weighs 25–30 lb. The line is marked with knots every 10 fathoms, sometimes every 5. It has been superseded by mechanical sounders.

**Boat's lead and line.** The lead weighs about 7 lb; the line measures 14 fathoms, marked like a hand-lead but with additional markings every foot below 3 fathoms.

**Heave the lead.** The act of taking a SOUNDING from a ship with way upon her by swinging the lead to and fro, usually whirling it around above the head several times, and then letting it go so that it enters the water as far ahead as possible. In this way, the sounding line will be more or less vertical by the time the lead reaches the bottom.

**Cast of the lead.** The taking of a single SOUNDING.

**Leadsman.** One who heaves the lead. In a sailing ship, he did this from the windward main CHANNELS (01.01).

**Lazy leadsman.** The leadsman's mate, who helps to haul in the line after each cast.

**Calling the soundings.**

*Marks* – Fathoms marked: 2, 3, 5, 7, 10, 13, 15, 17, 20.

*Deeps* – Fathoms not marked.

| Sounding | Call |
|---|---|
| 5 fathoms | By the mark, five! |
| $5\frac{1}{4}$ ,, | And a quarter, five! |
| $5\frac{1}{2}$ ,, | And a half, five! |
| $5\frac{3}{4}$ ,, | A quarter less, six! |
| 6 ,, | Deep, six! |

No bottom. No bottom at 20 fathoms!

**Deep-sea sounding.** With the ship stopped, men were stationed at intervals along the ship's side, each with a coil of the deep-sea line, and with the lead right forward. After the lead was dropped, each man let his coil go as he felt the strain coming on, warning the next man with the cry 'watch, there, watch!'.

**Mechanical sounding.** Any method not using a conventional lead and line or echo sounding. Several basic principles have been used;
(a) measuring the amount of wire or rope out when the lead hits bottom, using a *feeler* (Burt, Kelvin);
(b) measuring the amount of water which enters a tube closed at one end attached near the lead (self-acting sounder, Ericsson, Kelvin);
(c) attaching a *rotator* similar to a TOWED LOG (19.01) near the lead, and counting the number of revolutions from casting until the lead hits bottom (Massey, Walker).

**Kelvin sounding machine.** The most successful mechanical device, using both principles (a) and (b) above, with a wire line and, later, an electric motor to rewind the wire.

*Hand–lead and line*

# Measurement of speed and distance run

**Log.** Instrument for measuring distance run through the water, and hence the ship's speed. With pressure logs (Pitot), the speed is measured directly.

**Common log,** or **English log.** Type of LOG comprising:
*Log chip,* or log ship. A piece of wood about six inches across.
*Log line.* Line about 150 fathoms long marked with knots between 42 and 50 feet apart. (The variation was due to past uncertainty about the length of a degree of the meridian.)
*Log reel.* Reel on which the line was wound.
*Log glass,* or half-minute glass. Sand glass used for timing the running out of the line, sometimes running only 28 seconds to compensate for erroneous distances between knots.

**Stream the log,** or **heave the log.** To operate the LOG.

'In heaving the log, one Man holds the Reel upon which the Log-line is wound, and another holds the Half-minute Glass; an Officer of the Watch heaves the Log over the Stern on the Lee-side, and when he observes the stray Line is run off the Reel (to denote which there is fixed a Red Rag) he cries *turn!* the Glass-holder answers *done!* who, watching the Glass the Moment it is run out, cries *stop!* the Reel being immediately stopt, the

Knots, or Knots and Fathoms run, shew the Ship's Rate of Sailing per hour, if the Wind is constant.

'... In King's Ship's, India Ships, and some others, the Log is hove every Hour, but in Coasters, and those using short Voyages, every two Hours.'
(J. H. Moore, *Practical Navigation,* 3rd ed. 1976).

**Dutchman's log.** Piece of wood thrown overboard well forward and used for determining the speed of a ship by timing the log's passage between two marks of known distance apart on the ship's side.

**Towed log,** or **patent log.** LOG consisting of a *rotator* towed behind the ship by a *log-line.* A count of the revolutions shows distance run on a *register* which, in early models, was attached to the rotator itself while streamed astern, but was later fixed inboard. The log was sometimes towed from a boom abeam, but more often from the stern, as a *taffrail log.* The principal types are the Massey and the Walker logs.

**Bottom log.** Type of LOG in which the speed-measuring device protrudes through the ship's bottom. Seldom used in sailing ships.

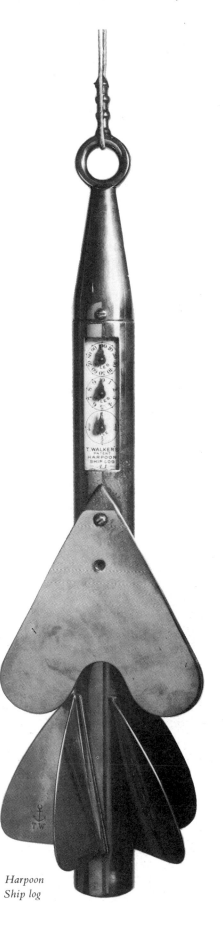

*Running the log*

*Harpoon Ship log*

# Angle measurement

**Cross-staff,** or **arbalest,** or **Jacob's staff,** or **fore-staff.** Instrument of great antiquity for measuring the altitudes of celestial bodies, consisting of a *cross* (or *transversary*) with a square hole in its middle, sliding on a square-section *staff* graduated in degrees of altitude. It was generally made of boxwood. To cover different ranges of angles, several crosses of different lengths were supplied, each face on the staff being graduated for use with a different cross. It continued in use until the invention of HADLEY'S QUADRANT (19.03).

**Backstaff,** or **Davis's quadrant,** or **sea quadrant,** or **English quadrant.** Instrument invented by the English Captain John Davis (c.1550–1605) for measuring the sun's altitude. The user (a) stood with his back to the sun; (b) placed the *shade vane* on the *sixty arch* at a convenient exact number of degrees *less* than the expected altitude of the sun; (c) looked through the *sight vane* and aligned the aperture in the *horizon vane* with the horizon; (d) keeping the horizon in the *horizon-vane* aperture, moved the sight vane up and down on the *thirty arch* until the sun's shadow, cast by the *shade vane,* was precisely in line with the horizon in the aperture; and (e) read off the sun's altitude by adding the position of the shade vane on the sixty arch to that of the sight vane on the *diagonal scale* on the thirty arch.

*Cross-staff. Made by Thomas Tuttell (London) c.1700*

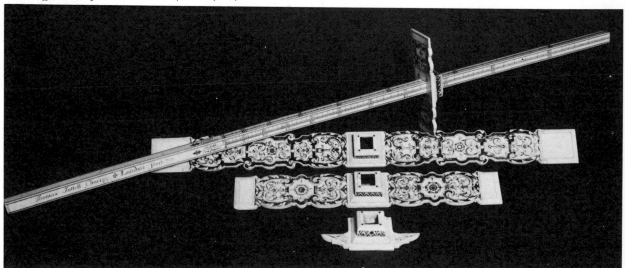

*Backstaff*

*Octant. Made by G. Adams (London), 1753*

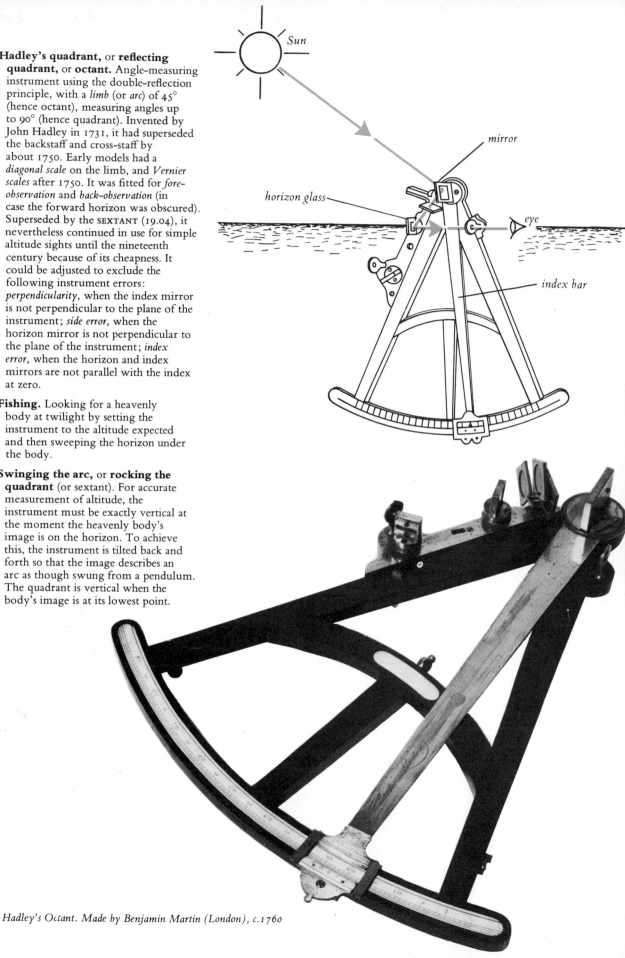

**Hadley's quadrant,** or **reflecting quadrant,** or **octant.** Angle-measuring instrument using the double-reflection principle, with a *limb* (or *arc*) of 45° (hence octant), measuring angles up to 90° (hence quadrant). Invented by John Hadley in 1731, it had superseded the backstaff and cross-staff by about 1750. Early models had a *diagonal scale* on the limb, and *Vernier scales* after 1750. It was fitted for *fore-observation* and *back-observation* (in case the forward horizon was obscured). Superseded by the SEXTANT (19.04), it nevertheless continued in use for simple altitude sights until the nineteenth century because of its cheapness. It could be adjusted to exclude the following instrument errors: *perpendicularity*, when the index mirror is not perpendicular to the plane of the instrument; *side error*, when the horizon mirror is not perpendicular to the plane of the instrument; *index error*, when the horizon and index mirrors are not parallel with the index at zero.

**Fishing.** Looking for a heavenly body at twilight by setting the instrument to the altitude expected and then sweeping the horizon under the body.

**Swinging the arc,** or **rocking the quadrant** (or sextant). For accurate measurement of altitude, the instrument must be exactly vertical at the moment the heavenly body's image is on the horizon. To achieve this, the instrument is tilted back and forth so that the image describes an arc as though swung from a pendulum. The quadrant is vertical when the body's image is at its lowest point.

*Sun*

*mirror*

*horizon glass*

*eye*

*index bar*

*Hadley's Octant. Made by Benjamin Martin (London), c.1760*

*Octant. Made by Jan Corneelyz, 1775*

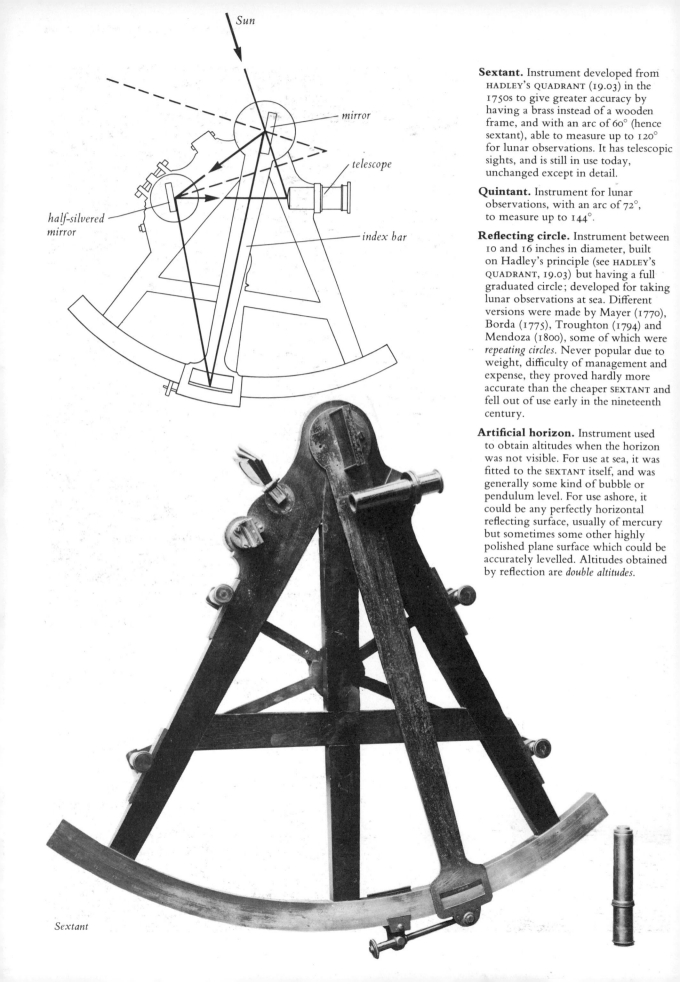

Sun

mirror

telescope

half-silvered
mirror

index bar

Sextant

**Sextant.** Instrument developed from
HADLEY'S QUADRANT (19.03) in the
1750s to give greater accuracy by
having a brass instead of a wooden
frame, and with an arc of 60° (hence
sextant), able to measure up to 120°
for lunar observations. It has telescopic
sights, and is still in use today,
unchanged except in detail.

**Quintant.** Instrument for lunar
observations, with an arc of 72°,
to measure up to 144°.

**Reflecting circle.** Instrument between
10 and 16 inches in diameter, built
on Hadley's principle (see HADLEY'S
QUADRANT, 19.03) but having a full
graduated circle; developed for taking
lunar observations at sea. Different
versions were made by Mayer (1770),
Borda (1775), Troughton (1794) and
Mendoza (1800), some of which were
*repeating circles*. Never popular due to
weight, difficulty of management and
expense, they proved hardly more
accurate than the cheaper SEXTANT and
fell out of use early in the nineteenth
century.

**Artificial horizon.** Instrument used
to obtain altitudes when the horizon
was not visible. For use at sea, it was
fitted to the SEXTANT itself, and was
generally some kind of bubble or
pendulum level. For use ashore, it
could be any perfectly horizontal
reflecting surface, usually of mercury
but sometimes some other highly
polished plane surface which could be
accurately levelled. Altitudes obtained
by reflection are *double altitudes*.

# Time measurement

**Marine chronometer,** or **marine timekeeper.** Timekeeper specifically designed for navigational use at sea; either a *box chronometer* or a *pocket chronometer*. It first proved a practical possibility in the 1770s, and began to come into general use about 1810. Larger ships generally carried at least three chronometers, so that bad timekeeping could be detected by comparing one against the other, the results being recorded in the *chronometer comparison book*.

**Deck watch,** or **hack watch,** or **job watch.** Timekeeper used for timing astronomical sights, to save taking the chronometer itself on deck or ashore.

**Chronometer error.** Number of seconds fast or slow on mean time, found by comparison with a standard clock or a time signal, or by astronomical observations ashore.

**Daily rate,** or **rate of going.** Number of seconds or parts of seconds gained or lost daily.

**Accumulated rate.** Total number of seconds gained or lost over a specified period somewhat illogically called the *epoch*.

**Rate a chronometer.** To determine a chronomerter's daily rate of going over a period. $\dfrac{\text{Accumulated rate}}{\text{Epoch}} = \text{daily rate.}$

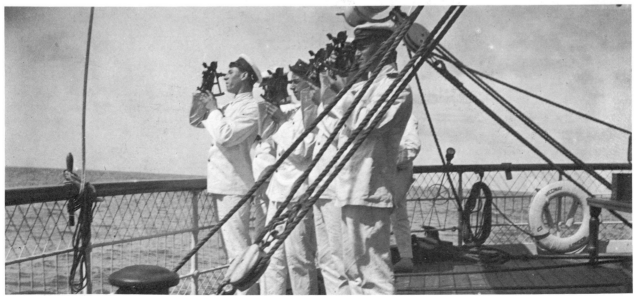

# Instruments for drawing and calculating

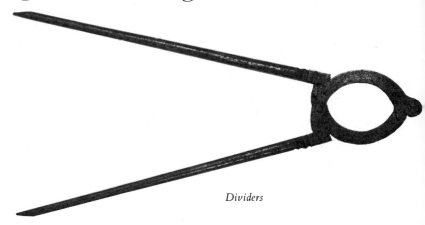

**Dividers,** or **pair of dividers.** Instrument used for measuring and transferring distances by *pricking the chart. One-handed dividers* are peculiarly nautical.

**Parallel ruler.** Instrument for transferring a line parallel to itself, particularly for transferring a line to a compass rose (or a printed LOXODROME, 15.06) and vice versa. It can be either a *sliding parallel ruler* or a *rolling parallel ruler.*

**Protractor.** Some protractors were specifically designed for use at sea, including *Hart's goniometer* (c.1800) and the *Douglas protractor* (c.1925).

**Station pointer,** or **three-arm protractor.** Instrument for plotting a position obtained by horizontal sextant angles.

**Gunter's scale,** or **Gunter.** Flat wooden rule either 12 or 24 inches in

*Dividers*

length and $1\frac{1}{2}$ inches broad, with various lines and scales engraved upon it to assist in calculations. For example, using the logarithmic line of numbers and a pair of dividers, multiplication and division can be done as with a modern slide rule.

**Gunter's sector,** or **compass of proportion.** Two hinged rulers or legs of box, ivory or brass, particularly useful for solving trigonometrical problems without tables.

**Sliding Gunter.** Ancestor of the modern slide rule.

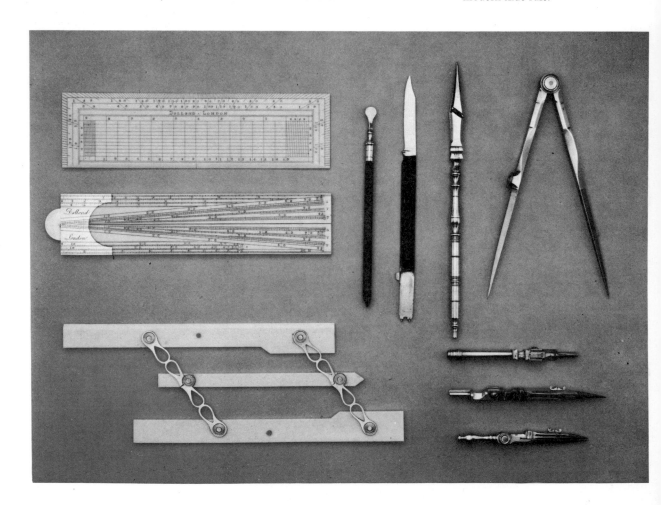

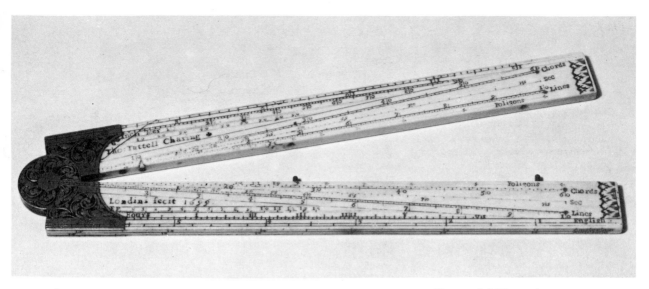

*Gunter's sector*

*Gunter's scale*

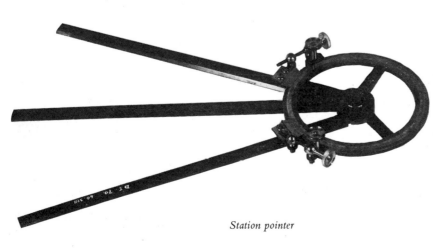

*Station pointer*

## Terrestrial Magnetism

**Red and blue magnetic poles.** By convention, the two ends of a magnetic bar are known as the *red* and *blue* poles. A fundamental law of magnetism is: unlike poles attract, like poles repel.

**Terrestrial magnetism.** The Earth's magnetic field is similar to that which would be produced by a short magnet near the Earth's centre, its axis passing through the neighbourhood of Hudson's Bay in the north and South Victoria Land in the south, known as the *North Magnetic Pole* (Blue) and *South Magnetic Pole* (Red) respectively. These magnetic poles do not coincide with the north and south geographical poles and are constantly moving, although comparatively slowly.

**Magnetic equator.** Line approximately half-way between the magnetic poles, where the angle of DIP is zero.

**Dip,** or **magnetic inclination.** A magnetic needle freely suspended at any point will line itself up with the Earth's magnetic lines of force at that point. The vertical angle between the needle and the horizontal is called the *angle of dip*, being zero at the magnetic equator and 90° at the poles. The needle lies in the *magnetic meridian*. (See also MERIDIAN, 15.01.)

**Variation,** or **magnetic declination.** Horizontal angle between the magnetic and true meridians. (See also MERIDIAN, 15.01.)

**Variation chart.** Chart showing lines of equal magnetic variation, or *isogonic lines*.

# The magnetic compass

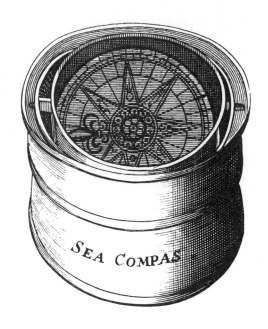

**Compass.** Instrument for indicating direction relative to the MERIDIAN (15.01).

**Magnetic compass.** Compass whose directional property is due to its needles seeking the magnetic meridian (see DIP, 19.05).

**Mariner's compass,** or **sea compass.** Compass comprising *needles, card* or *fly, pivot,* and *bowl* or *box.*

**Lubber's line,** or **lubber's point.** Line in the direction of the ship's head marked inside the compass bowl.

**Binnacle,** or **bittacle.** Stand of wood or metal, in which the MARINER'S COMPASS is suspended, generally in gimbals (two rings pivoted at right angles to each other so as to keep the compass horizontal regardless of ship movement).

**Steering compass.** The compass used by the HELMSMAN (10.02).

**Azimuth compass.** Compass specially fitted with vertical sight vanes, used for finding magnetic VARIATION (19.05) by the observation of bodies up to about 15° above the horizon.

**Variation compass.** Compass used for the same purpose as the AZIMUTH COMPASS, but ashore.

**Tell-tale compass,** or **overhead compass,** or **hanging compass.** Compass hanging face downwards from the beams in the cabin, to show the direction of the ship's head without the need to go on deck. From its shape, sometimes called a *crown compass.*

**Dry-card compass,** or **dry compass.** One having no liquid in the bowl.

**Liquid compass,** or **wet compass,** or **fluid compass.** Bowl filled with liquid with a low freezing point. It contains a *float* attached to a card, so that the weight on the pivots is reduced. The card is steadier in a seaway. The liquid compass was a nineteenth-century innovation.

**Standard compass.** Magnetic compass placed in a selected position and used as the principal compass for navigational purposes.

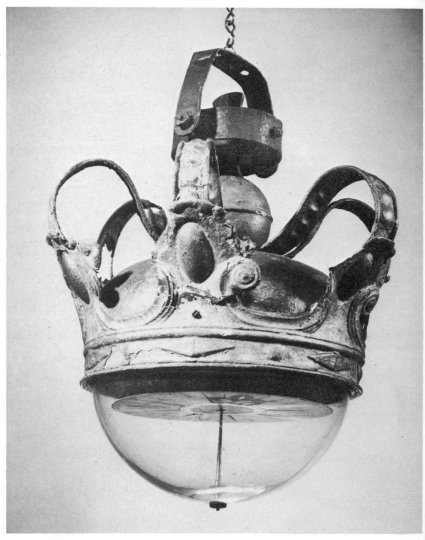

*Tell-tale or hanging compass*

**Boat's compass.** Small compass designed for boats.

**Deviation of the compass.** The angle the compass needle makes with the magnetic meridian (see DIP, 19.05) due to attracting forces from the iron and steel within the ship herself. First recognized as a problem in about 1800.

**Correcting magnets, Flinders' bar** and **soft-iron spheres.** Devices used in *compass correction*, to reduce the effects of the DEVIATION OF THE COMPASS. Today, generally part of the BINNACLE, or attached to it.

**Swinging ship.** Putting the ship's head through all the points of the compass to determine DEVIATION OF THE COMPASS on different headings, often recorded on a *deviation table* or *deviation card*.

**Bearing plate.** Plate used for taking relative bearings.

**Pelorus.** Dumb compass dial set by hand, which can be shipped on an appropriate mounting to observe the bearings of objects obscured at the compass position.

**Dipping needle,** or **dip circle,** or **inclinatory needle.** Instrument for measuring the angle of DIP (19.05).

### Other Instruments

**Traverse board.** Wooden board marked with compass points and having holes radiating from its centre in which pegs were inserted at the appropriate distance to indicate direction and distance sailed on various TACKS (12.08) during the watch. The information was transferred to the LOG BOARD (15.04) after each watch.

**Star globe.** Globe about six inches in diameter, showing the principal navigational stars. It can be rectified to show star positions at any moment, to help discovery and identification of stars at twilight.

**Spy glass,** or **marine telescope,** or **kenning glass.** Short telescope used at sea.

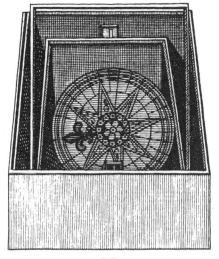

*Traverse board*

# Inshore & Ashore

It is perhaps not generally realized that a large proportion of a sailing ship's time was spent 'inshore and ashore'. In addition to the time spent in unloading at the quayside, moored offshore or while beached on occasion, all major maintenance and repairs had to be undertaken in suitable and safe surroundings and conditions.

The Howland Great Wet Dock at Rotherhithe, on the Thames, was probably the first dock to be constructed in Britain, being in use by 1703. About 10 acres in extent, it was 44 feet wide and 150 feet long. At spring tides there was 17 feet of water over the sill and its proprietors boasted that:
*It would commodiously receive His Majesty's third rate ships; upwards of 120 sail of the largest merchant ships can be accommodated at one time. There is a mast crain for taking out and setting in masts in ships in the Wet Dock which answers the end of a hulk with proper pits and crab for careening three or four ships at once.*
The value of the dock was tested in the great storm of November 1703. On that occasion all the ships in the river which rode at chains or at their moorings were forced adrift, many being driven ashore and damaged. Within the new dock only one vessel was slightly damaged, despite the fact that the trees planted around the dock as windbreaks were as yet small. The dock also served to protect ships from the ice which came down river during a hard winter. There was safety from fire, as cooking-places for crews were provided ashore. It was claimed that ships could be kept in the dock at low cost since they did not wear their cables or chains, nor did they need to shift their moorings frequently, as was necessary in the river.

With the expansion of trade in the eighteenth century and with the consequent need for world-wide naval forces to protect the trade routes, it was essential for the Royal Navy and for the East India Company to have dockyards in foreign ports capable of repairing damaged fighting ships. Admiral Sir Edward Hughes wrote, in 1784, on the importance of Bombay:
*At Bombay, as the only place of refit (in the area), are deposited all the masts and other stores for the ships, and it not only furnished a great number of expert native artificers, but its docks are of the utmost consequence. . . . I instance the nine sail of His Majesty's line of battleships which arrived in this harbour on the 17th of December 1782 and after four severe conflicts with the French squadron had suffered greatly in their hulls, not a serviceable lower mast on board any of them, nor a fish for a mast or a spar for a top mast to be found but at Bombay, five ships of the number uncoppered and fouled by being two years off the*
*ground and of course heavy clog to the operations of the other ships of the squadron that were coppered. At the same time the ships' companies reduced to half their complements by sickness. Under all these circumstances of distress and difficulty, you gentlemen, saw, with mixed pleasure and surprise, that very squadron in less than three months put to sea to seek the enemy, completely refitted and the health of the ships' company in great manner restored.*

By the nineteenth century, there was an established practice for completing the complex arrangements necessary to make a sailing ship ready for a commission or voyage. When the officers had been selected and the crew mustered there was plenty to occupy them while the ship rode at anchor in her home port. Apart from ensuring that she was supplied with spare cordage, canvas and timber, the vessel had to be provisioned for a voyage that might last many months. The Naval Cadets Manual, published in 1864, gives instructions on how the young officer should go about seeing to this:
*In completing provisions and stores when plenty crewmen are available the more lighters that can be had the better, though care is necessary to ensure that the lighters bring the articles out according to the order in which they are to be stowed. . . . Each cask has its contents and date of package marked on it; and the provisions are stowed in such a way that one days allowance of every kind can be got out without breaking bulk. The newest sort are placed lowest and all casks are stowed bung up. Billets of wood (dunnage) are packed under the chines so that not only is the whole stowage made secure from the danger of shifting, but a sufficiency of fuel for the ovens is daily forthcoming. A press of work such as this unavoidably affords opportunity for trickery; and as in the early history of a ship there are always some who are more skilful with a gimlet and piece of straw than with a marlingspike and piece of rope, spirit casks should be struck down and secured in the spirits room without a minutes delay.*
Provisions for the inner man formed only part of the intake; clothing, fodder for livestock and religious books were all taken on in stipulated quantities.

Finally, all is ready: the passengers have come on board and stowed their belongings away, the ship has been cleaned down and all gear made tidy and readied to hand as needed. However, it was not uncommon for sailing to be delayed by contrary winds. The absence of wind, too, made departure difficult. Captain Kellet had trouble getting out of Petropavlovsk in HMS *Herald* in 1849:
*We weighed on 25th June in a calm and towed out from the anchorage. We got a light wind from the southward, bringing with it a fog, though still not so thick but that both sides of the entrance could be seen. In beating out, and in*

making a stretch over to the eastern shore from Babouski Island, the fog closed down over the rocks and deceived us as to their distance; we hove the ship in stays but the whirls of the tide made her slack, and shot her onto the rocks before we had time to bring up with an anchor. The stream-anchor and cable were laid out and hove taut and at 2.10 pm the ship was hove off into deep water having been nearly three hours on shore; fortunately the water at the time was glassy smooth. The ship lay perfectly quiet until a short time before getting off, when she lifted and struck heavily by the bow two or three times, bringing away on each occasion small pieces of her false keel. We remained at anchor during the night, and the next morning weighed with a light southeast wind, but, it being a calm, and a current setting directly on shore, we were obliged to anchor again in a very exposed position.

Some harbours were regular ports of call for all types of vessels. Pilots were to be had, docking and repair facilities were available, there was the possibility of replenishing provisions, and a chance for officers and men to go ashore for relief and entertainment. Captain Cook, arriving at Cape Town in HMS *Resolution* in 1772, described the formalities and facilities of this major port:

*Saturday 30th, Fresh gales and rain in the night. At 2 pm saw the land of the Cape of Good Hope, the Table Mountain which is over the Cape Town bore ESE distant 12 or 13 leagues. At 7 am anchored in Table Bay (the Adventure in company) in 5 fathom Water Green Point NWBW and the Church SWBS. Distant from shore 1 mile. Sent an officer to notify our arrival to the Governor and on his return saluted the Garrison with Eleven Guns which was returned. Moored NE and SW a cable each way, hoisted out of the long boat and prepared to heel and water the Sloop. . . . My next care was to procure the necessary provisions and stores wanting, to get the Sloops caulked and to prepare the Casks for the Brandy Wine and other provisions all of which was set about without delay. But as the Bread we wanted was as yet unbaked and all the Spirits to be brought out of the country it was the 18 of the following month before everything was put on board and the 22 before we could put to sea. During this stay the seamen on board were employed in overhauling the rigging, and the Carpenters in caulking the Sloops' sides and decks, also painting these. The crews of both Sloops were served every day with new baked bread, fresh Beef or Mutton and as much fresh vegetables as they could eat, they also had leave to go ashore 10 or 12 at a time to refresh themselves.*

In less populous parts of the world, ships would anchor offshore and send in a boat to get water and collect firewood. On these occasions the native population came out in small boats offering to barter chickens and fresh fruit and vegetables in exchange for whatever trade goods the captain might be able to offer. After a long period at sea, both the ship and her crew could be in poor condition. Lack of fresh vegetables led to scurvy and general sickness among the men, while in warm tropical seas growth of weed on the ship's bottom slowed down her speed and teredo worms bored their way into and through the hull. Philip Carteret, sailing round the world in the *Swallow*, took advantage of a stopover on a Pacific island in August 1767:

*We were now all hands employed in Clearing & lightning the Ship, to come at the leak, & clean her bottom, which we did by heeling the ship, and paid her bottom over as far down as we could get at it, and with hot Pitch, & Tarr boild together, the Carpenter did what he could to the Leak, for he was the only man of that Crew that was able to work, We found the sheathing much decayed, & the bottom much eaten by the worms. The Scorbutick people went on shore every day, with a guard of Armed men, who were put sentrys for fear of surprise, to guard them and the other people which were at work wooding, watering &c.*

Finally the journey is over; the vessel approaches her home port and makes land. Preparations begin well beforehand, as Brady's *The Kedge Anchor, or Young Sailors' Assistant*, describes in 'Preparations for going into harbour':

*The paintwork outside should be scrubbed and, if the weather permit, freshened up where most wanted, for instance under the bows. The masts should be scraped and properly stayed, the tips of studding sails painted, and the rigging slightly touched with blacking, where brown or worn. The good order of the ratlines should be attended to, swinging-boom ladders and pendants got ready, and all the chafing gear taken off. The boats' sails and awnings should be clean and ready for use, the masts and oars scraped, scrubbed or painted as required; the smokesail clean, also the windsails. Clean hammocks may be slung and neatly stowed. The cables should be bent in plenty of time, the ship's company clean and in uniform. The accommodation got ready and in good order for shipping when at anchor.*

And so the vessel again lies at anchor in her home port. Officers and men have been discharged, and the ship will undergo repairs and perhaps alterations to make her ready for the next voyage.

ANITA McCONNELL

# Ashore

**Aground.** Said of a vessel when she has come to rest on solid ground other than a dry dock. A vessel left aground by the tide is said to 'take the ground'.

*A vessel beached, 1819*

**Anchorage.** Area where holding ground is good and where depths are suitable for ships to anchor. Where there is little or no shelter, it is said to be an *open anchorage*; or it may be sheltered from one direction but *open to the north-east*, for example.

**Bank.** Shoal which rises significantly above the surrounding ground. Also, the right or left bank of a river, viewed from its source.

**Beach.** To run a ship ashore in order to prevent her foundering in deeper waters or repair her underwater hull and bottom.

**Beneaped.** Said of a vessel left aground by the spring tide, too high for the neaping tide that follows to refloat her. As the spring tide is the highest high water, a vessel so grounded must await the next spring tide.

**Berth.** Any secure mooring point for a vessel in port. Also, safety margin of distance to be kept by a vessel from another vessel or from an obstruction, hence the phrase 'to give a wide berth'.

**Bluff.** Large, high, steep cliff that projects into the sea.

**Bold shore.** Steep, abrupt.

**Bream** (vb). To burn off accumulated weeds and barnacles from a vessel's underwater hull and bottom by means of kindled furze, oil-soaked OAKUM (03.02) or reeds (see GRAVING).

**Careen** (vb). To haul a ship over to one side by means of tackles leading from the masts to the shore, in order to carry out caulking, repairing and cleaning work on the underwater part of her hull and on her bottom.

**Channel.** Navigable passage.

**Chops,** or **chapp.** Entrance to a channel, hence *chops of the* [*English*] *channel.*

**Culage.** Term used to describe the laying up of a ship in a dry dock for repairs, refitting and so on.

**Departure.** Position on losing sight of land, on which DEAD RECKONING (15.01) will at first be based.

**Docking.** Act of bringing a vessel into a dock. Also, charge levied on a vessel for use of a dock.

**Embayed.** Said of a vessel unable, due to bad weather, currents or heavy seas, to pass safely through the entrance to a bay or basin.

**Fetch away.** To break away from shore or mooring ground and drift with the wind or tide.

**Fitting out.** Installation of masts, rigging, anchors, cables, boats, derricks and other gear required to make a newly built ship seaworthy.

**Foul berth.** Anchorage where there is no room to swing on the change of tide.

**Foul ground.** Sea bottom on which wrecks or other obstructions may cause the anchor to foul.

**Graving.** Cleaning a vessel's bottom by burning off weeds and barnacles before re-tarring, a process necessarily performed in dry dock or while the ship is CAREENED.

**Ground** (vb). To bring the vessel's keel in touch with the bottom, usually by accident rather than intent.

**Gut.** Narrow strait. The Straits of Gibraltar have been known as 'The Gut' by the Royal Navy since the eighteenth century.

**Half sea.** Old term for mid-channel.

**Half-tide rock.** Rock awash at half tide, therefore covered at high tide and showing at low tide.

**Heaving down.** Act of hauling on the tackles which connect the ship's masts to the shore in CAREENING.

**High and dry.** Condition of a ship run aground so that the tide, falling away, brings her keel above water. Origin of the familiar phrase referring to someone left stranded and helpless.

**Holding ground.** State of the bottom in relation to the security it affords a vessel at anchor. Clay or mud are 'good' holding grounds. Soft mud, sand or rocky bottoms are 'poor' or 'foul' holding grounds.

**Lie alongside.** To be secured to a pier, quay or jetty, or to another vessel.

**Middle ground.** Shallow water between navigable channels.

**Nipped.** Situation of a vessel when she is beset by ice on both sides.

**Outfit** (vb). To install the gear and equipment necessary to make a newly launched vessel completely seaworthy.

**Parliament heel.** List put on a ship so that part of her bottom is above water, for cleaning and repairing purposes. (See also CAREEN.)

**Pile up.** To run a vessel ashore or aground on a shoal or rock.

**Reach.** Straight stretch of water between two bends in a channel or river.

**Refit** (vb). To replace defective equipment – rigging, spars and other gear – on a vessel lying in dock or on a vessel that has been careened.

**Repair** (vb). To undertake the general overhaul of a vessel, usually in DRY DOCK (20.02).

**Right** (vb). To return to her proper upright position a vessel that has LISTED (02.03) or has been CAREENED.

**Roader.** Vessel riding at anchor in a ROADSTEAD (20.03), bay or river.

**Sallying.** Rolling a vessel to refloat her when she is lightly grounded. Also, breaking light surface ice around a vessel.

**Sand warped.** Said of a vessel stranded on a sandbank at ebb tide, or on the flood tide before the water is deep enough to float her.

The Christiania *embayed in the ice, 1894–5*

**Sea reach.** Reach between the last bend of a river and its point of discharge into the sea.

**Sew,** or **sue** (vb). To require a greater depth of water in order to float. Said of a vessel AGROUND, signifying the difference between the water-level and the vessel's flotation-mark, as in 'she sews eight feet'.

**Shoal** (vb). To become shallower.

**Shoal,** or **shoal water.** Shallow water.

**Sighting the bottom.** Examination of a vessel's bottom in dry dock or while CAREENED, in order to determine the nature and scope of the cleaning and repairing work to be carried out.

**Smelling the ground.** Said of the behaviour of a vessel when she runs into shallow water and is more difficult to steer. Also said of a vessel sailing close to a sandbank or shoal and caught by a backsurge of water which causes her to sheer suddenly.

**Sound.** Narrow expanse of water between two land masses.

**Stranded.** Description of a vessel that has run AGROUND by accident and remains so for a substantial period of time. In legal terminology, a vessel whose voyage has been brought to a premature end by grounding.

**Strike** (vb). To touch the bottom with the vessel's keel; to run AGROUND.

**Strip** (vb). To remove all the running rigging and other gear from the masts.

**Swashway,** or **swash.** Channel across a bank or between shoals as, for example, between the Goodwin Sands.

**Tideway.** That part of the channel through which the tide runs strongest.

**Touch and go.** To run a vessel AGROUND but refloat her almost immediately.

**Touch at.** To stop briefly at a port or harbour, for example in order to take on or discharge passengers.

**Touch the ground.** To graze the bottom very lightly, in such a way as not to cause any serious damage or even check the vessel's way.

**Track** (vb). To take a vessel, usually a small craft, in tow from a position on shore.

**Voluntary stranding.** Deliberate grounding of a vessel in an emergency in order to save the vessel, its crew and cargo.

**Water** (vb). To take in supplies of fresh water in port or harbour, in suitable casks or by pumping.

**Wind-taut.** Said of a vessel when the strength of the wind is such as to make her strain at the cable and LIST (02.03).

# Coming inshore

**Close the land.** Draw near to the land.

**Club** (vb). To drift down with the current or tide, with the anchor out.

**Coast** (vb). To sail along the line of the coast.

**Doubling.** Sailing round a point of land.

**Hug** (vb). To keep as close as possible to the shore.

**Ice lead.** Any navigable passage through sea ice.

**Keep the land aboard.** To keep the vessel in sight of the shore.

**Landfall.** Land first sighted or approached when coming in from the sea.

**Lee shore.** A ship is on a lee shore when she is near it with the wind blowing on to it.

**Lie along the land.** To sail very close to the coast, or on a course roughly parallel to the coastline.

**Lie off.** To stop well clear of the land or of another vessel.

**Make the land.** Of a vessel, to come within sight of land.

**Off and on,** or **stand off and on.** To sail alternately towards the land and then away from it. This was done by a vessel at night when waiting for her pilot or for daylight, before entering an unfamiliar harbour.

**Raise a light.** To cause a light to appear above the horizon.

**Raise the land.** To steer towards the land so that its height appears to increase, or so that it comes into sight.

**Range** (vb). To sail along a coast.

**Set the land.** Take compass bearings of the land.

**Stand in.** To sail towards the land.

**Stand out.** To sail away from the land.

**Stemming.** Steering directly into the tide or current with sufficient way to maintain the vessel's position in relation to the ground, keeping her more or less stationary.

*Dutch ship careened and being graved*

# Harbours and docks

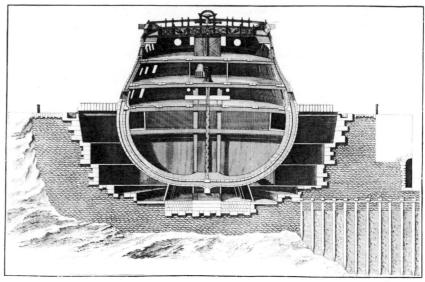

*Vessel in dry dock*

**Apron.** Underwater masonry platform or ledge at the entrance to a dock. In enclosed docks, the part over which the gates close.

**Bar.** Barrier of sand or mud across the mouth of a river or harbour, formed by the action of currents or tide, which obstructs the passage of ships other than those of reduced draught.

**Basin.** Enclosed area of water provided with facilities, such as quays, wharves and jetties, to load, unload and repair ships.

**Bilge blocks.** Short timbers used to support the bilges of a ship in DRY DOCK after the water has been pumped out. They are brought in contact with the hull by means of bilge-block chains as the ship settles in the dock.

**Bollard.** Short thick post of wood or iron (often mounted in pairs) used for securing mooring ropes, SPRINGS (20.03) or hawsers.

**Boom.** Floating barrier, often of logs, designed to prevent enemy ships from entering a river or harbour.

**Breakwater.** Structure built across part of the mouth of a harbour in order to break the force of the waves and protect vessels lying within.

**Breast off.** To hold a vessel a short distance away from a wharf or quay, for instance by means of long timbers called *breasting-off spars*, in order to provide space for lighters to pass be between the vessel and the quay walls.

**Brow.** Gangway between ship and shore equipped with rollers at its shore end to allow for the rise and fall of the ship.

**Cane fender.** Bundle of canes lashed together and placed against the ship's side to protect it from friction, for instance against the side of a wharf or quay.

**Dock.** Artificial basin equipped with installations and facilities for loading, unloading and repairing vessels. See DRY DOCK; FLOATING DOCK; WET DOCK (20.03).

**Dockyard.** Location comprising wharves, jetties and other facilities necessary for servicing vessels and handling their cargo.

**Dry dock.** Dock fitted with watertight gates which, when closed, enable it to be pumped dry so that work can be done on a vessel's underwater hull and bottom.

**Floating dock.** Form of DRY DOCK consisting of a submersible bottom pontoon on which the ship rests and two side walls or pontoons to assist its stability. The bottom pontoon is sunk by filling its water tanks, and then raised, with the ship in place, by pumping out the tanks, thus lifting the ship clear of the water.

**Gang-board.** Plank with several rungs or steps mounted on to it, used for access to a boat when the boat cannot be brought close up to the landing place.

*Eighteenth-century dry dock*

**Graving dock.** Dock in which GRAVING (20.01) is performed. Came to mean more generally any DRY DOCK.

**Gridiron.** Framework of cross-beams supporting a vessel in a dock, allowing repairs to be carried out on the vessel's bottom. At low water, the vessel is left high and dry, kept upright by the gridiron.

**Harbour.** Sheltered area of calm water providing ships with a safe anchorage protected from wind and heavy seas.

**Harbourage.** Any area of water where ships may find shelter from winds and heavy seas.

**Hard.** Stony or gravelly section of foreshore providing vessels with a firm landing place.

**Hazel rod fender.** Bundle of hazel rods lashed together and used to protect the ship's side while in dock.

**Heaving alongside.** Bringing a vessel to berth alongside a dock, pier or jetty.

**Icebound.** Said of harbours, bays or inlets frozen over and inaccessible to vessels except with the aid of an ice-breaker.

**Jetty.** Structure such as a pier or embankment, constructed of stone, timber or other material and projecting outward into the water.

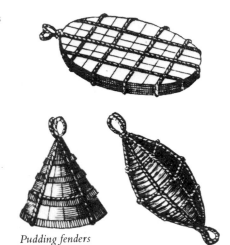

*Pudding fenders*

**Keel blocks.** Short timbers used to support the keel of a vessel in a DRY DOCK or shipyard. They are $3\frac{1}{2}$ to 4 feet high and spaced about four feet apart, allowing easy access for men working on the vessel's bottom.

**Landlocked.** Harbour where the sea cannot be seen from inside except over intervening land.

**Landmark.** Any distinctive feature ashore, such as a lighthouse, beacon or unusual contour of the land, that can serve as an aid to navigation or to locating a harbour.

**Lock.** Enclosed basin connecting a higher to a lower stretch of water, and through which vessels can transfer from one level to another.

**Lock gates.** Gates placed at the upper and lower ends of a LOCK. In transit to a higher level of water, the upper gate is closed while the vessel sails through the open lower gate. The latter is then closed and the former opened, to flood the lock to the higher level. In transit to a lower level the process is reversed.

**Mole.** Structure, usually of stone, acting as a breakwater on one side and providing facilities for the loading and unloading of ships on its inshore side. Moles can also have a military function as part of the defences of a port or harbour.

**Moor** (vb). To anchor a ship, or otherwise secure her to some fixed point provided for the purpose.

**Open roadstead.** Location some distance to seaward of a port or harbour, with good HOLDING GROUND (20.01) for a vessel, though not protected against wind and seas.

**Pier.** Structure extending into the water from the shore, built to provide vessels with mooring and loading facilities.

**Port.** Location, under the supervision of suitable authorities, providing facilities for the loading and unloading of ships, landing and boarding of passengers and ancillary commercial activities. The term may include a city or town where such facilities are provided.

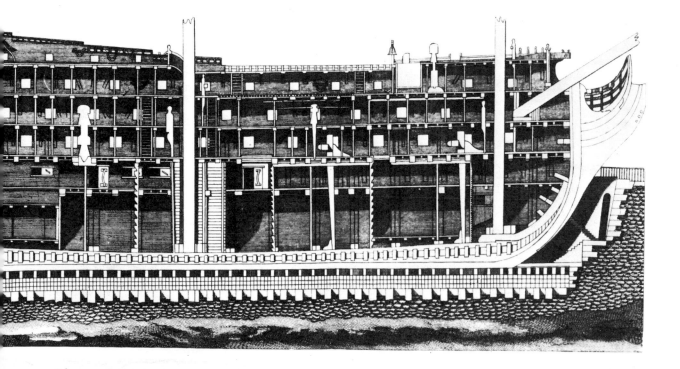

*Timber ships icebound in the Thames, c.1900*

**Port of refuge.** Port, harbour or any location which serves as a temporary anchorage for a vessel endangered by storms or heavy seas.

**Pudding fender.** Small cylinder-shaped canvas bag filled with cork, placed against the ship's side to protect it from chafing against the wall of a quay or wharf.

**Quay.** Harbour structure, usually of stone, projecting into the water and equipped with facilities for loading and unloading ships.

**Roadstead.** A good anchorage where a vessel may hope to ride safely in all but heavy weather.

**Slip.** Inclined masonry plane leading from a shipyard to the water, providing a foundation for the construction and repair of ships. Also, a stretch of water lying between two wharves or piers.

**Staith.** Elevated quayside structure, provided with rails or tracks to enable cargoes such as coal to be pitched directly into a vessel's hold.

**Stem fender.** Heavy manila mat placed against the stem as a protection against contact with a quay or wharf wall. Also placed on the stem of tugs when they are carrying out pushing operations.

**Tier.** Row of mooring buoys at which several vessels lie alongside or close to each other, all pointing in the same direction.

**Trinity House.** Association established by Henry VIII to oversee the construction of Royal Navy ships, its later duties being the maintenance of navigational aids. such as lighthouses, and the supervision of pilots. Its managing board, known as the Elder Brethren, are elected, two from the Navy and eleven from the merchant service, and act as advisers and assessors in Admiralty courts. Other members of the House are known as the Younger Brethren.

**Wet dock.** Enclosed dock equipped with gates which are closed when the tide begins to fall, ensuring that the vessels within are kept permanently afloat. Generally, any dock, with or without gates, in which ships are berthed afloat.

**Wharf.** Alternative term for QUAY. Originally, a wharf was built of timber or stone, whereas a quay was built only of stone. The terms are nowadays interchangeable.

**Wharfinger.** Owner or person in charge of a wharf. Also, a shipowner's representative who oversees the loading and unloading of cargo in dock.

**Winding.** Manoeuvring a vessel in dock between two piers or buoys, so that she turns 180° and is brought round end to end.

# Moorings

**Backspring.** Mooring line attached to the forward part of a vessel and led aft to a buoy or other mooring point, in order to prevent the vessel moving ahead or heave her astern.

**Bow-fast.** Mooring rope or line led out from the bow of a vessel and made fast to a fixture on a quay or dock.

**Breast-fast,** or **breast rope.** Mooring rope at right angles to a vessel's fore-and-aft line.

**Bridle.** Any length of rope or chain secured at each end.

**Bridle cable.** Cable leading from a ship to a span of rope or chain which is secured at both ends, securing the ship when she lies to moorings.

**Casting off.** Letting go the mooring lines, and releasing the ropes and wires securing a vessel to a dock, quay or buoy, so that she can move away and proceed to sea.

**Catching-up rope,** or **picking-up rope.** Small rope or line which acts as a vessel's temporary mooring to a buoy or dock until stronger moorings can be secured.

**Double up.** To double the number of mooring ropes holding the ship to dock or quay; for instance, when a strong gale is anticipated.

**Fast.** Rope or chain securing a vessel to a dock or quay, named according to the part of the ship from which it leads: bow-fast, breast-fast, head-fast, stern-fast and so on.

**Guess warp.** Rope with one end secured ashore and the other inboard, enabling the crew to move their ship by hauling on the inboard end (see WARP).

**Head-fast.** Mooring rope leading directly forward from the stem of a vessel to the shore.

**Head rope.** Steel wire or fibre rope leading forward from the bows of a ship, used for WARPING or MOORING (20.02) purposes.

**Quarter-fast.** Rope or cable leading from the quarter of a vessel to the shore or to a buoy.

**Run out.** To lead out the end of any cable, warp or rope in order to secure it to a buoy or to a position on shore.

**Singling up.** Taking in some of the lines securing a ship to a dock or pier so that only a minimum number will need to be let go when the ship has to get under way.

**Slip** (vb). To release the inboard ends of mooring lines securing a ship to the mooring cleats on shore.

**Slip rope.** Rope whose end is passed through the ring of a mooring buoy and brought back on board. By letting go one end of the rope and hauling in on the other the ship can be easily freed from her mooring.

**Snubbing line.** Rope used as a safety constraint to check a vessel's way while she is being WARPED in a dock or harbour.

**Spring.** Rope run from a vessel to a wharf or jetty, in order to turn or move her.

**Springing.** Moving a vessel ahead by heaving on a SPRING.

**Stern-fast.** Mooring line leading aft at an angle of less than 45° with the vessel's fore-and-aft line.

**Transporting line.** Rope used for warping (see WARP).

**Unmoor.** To free a vessel from her moorings. Also, when a vessel has two anchors down, to weigh one of them.

**Warp** (vb). To move a vessel from one mooring to another by heaving on a rope, called a *warp* or *transporting line*, secured to some fixed point – an anchor, buoy or mooring position on shore.

**Warping chock.** Secured block or wedge of wood on shore to which a WARP, or transporting line, can be fastened.

# Further Reading List

## General

H.I. Chapelle, **The History of American Sailing Ships,** New York, 1936.

**(Falconer's Marine Dictionary:)**
William Falconer, **An Universal Dictionary of the Marine,** London, 1780; facsimile by David & Charles Reprints, Newton Abbot, 1970.

William Falconer, **A New Universal Dictionary of the Marine,** modernized and enlarged by William Burney, London, 1815; Library Editions, New York, 1970.

Peter Kemp (ed.), **The Oxford Companion to Ships & the Sea,** London, 1976.

C.W.T. Layton, **Dictionary of Nautical Words and Terms,** Glasgow, 1973.

**The Lore of Ships,** Gothenburg & New York, 1975.

**The Mariner's Mirror** Volumes 1–, (1911–).

A. Moore, **The Last Days of Mast and Sail,** Oxford, 1925.

J.R. Stevens, **Old Time Ships,** Toronto, 1949.

H.A. Underhill, **Deep-Water Sail,** Glasgow, 1952.

Alan Villiers, **The Way of a Ship,** New York, 1970.

## Building a Ship

A.R. Bugler, HMS VICTORY, **Building, Restoration and Repair,** London (HMSO), 1966.

**Falconer's Marine Dictionary** (see above)

C.N. Longridge, **The Anatomy of Nelson's Ships,** 1955.

Capt. Paasch, **Dictionnaire de Marine,** Paris, 1924.

**Rees' Naval Architecture,** 1819.

## Mast, Spars, Sails and Rigging

Robert Kipping, **Rudimentary Treatise on Masting, Mastmaking and Rigging of Ships,** 1928.

Robert Kipping, **Sails and Sailmaking,** London, 1936.

Darcy Lever, **The Young Sea Officer's Sheet Anchor,** London, 1819; facsimile, New York, 1955.

H.A. Underhill, **Masting and Rigging: The Clipper Ship and Ocean Carrier,** Glasgow, 1946.

H.A. Underhill, **Sailing Ship Rigs and Rigging,** Glasgow, 1938.

## Reeving and Bousing

Clifford W. Ashley, **The Ashley Book of Knots,** London, 1977.

Jarman and Beavis, **Modern Rope Seamanship,** 1976.

Captain Jutsum, **Brown's Knots and Splices,** Glasgow, 1973.

Commander T.P. Walker, **Alston's Seamanship,** Portsmouth, 1893.

## Anchor, Capstan and Windlass

**The History of the Anchor,** The Mariner's Mirror, Volume 13, 1927.

**Anchors and Accessories,** The Mariner's Mirror, Volume 31, 1945.

**The Anchor,** The Mariner's Mirror, Volume 37, 1951.

**From Rope to Chain,** The Mariner's Mirror, Volume 49, 1963.

## Ballast, Stowage and Cargo

**Falconer's Marine Dictionary** (see above)

William Hutchinson, **A Treatise on Naval Architecture,** Liverpool, 1794; new impression, London, 1969.

Robert W. Stevens, **The Stowage of Ships,** London, 1867.

## Ship-Types

R.C. Anderson, **The Sailing Ship,** London, 1926.

R. Budd (ed.), **Sailing Boats of the World,** London, 1974.

H.I. Chapelle, **The National Watercraft Collection,** Washington DC, 1960.

Björn Landström, **The Ship,** London, 1967.

D. MacGregor, **Fast Sailing Ships,** Lymington, 1970.

Sam Svensson, **Sails through the Centuries,** London, 1965.

H.A. Underhill, **Deep-water Sail,** Glasgow, 1952

H.A. Underhill, **Sailing Ship Rigs and Rigging,** Glasgow, 1942.

G.R.G. Worcester, **Sail and Sweep in China,** London, 1966.

## Boats and Boatwork

W.E. May, **The Boats of Men of War,** London (HMSO), 1974.

**Man of War Boats,** The Mariner's Mirror, Volume 1, 1911.

**The Newquay Pilot Gigs,** The Mariner's Mirror, Volume 41, 1955.

**The Pilot Gigs of Cornwall and the Isles of Scilly,** The Mariner's Mirror, Volume 55, 1969.

## Sailors' Life, Customs and Tools

Dudley Jarrett, **British Naval Dress,** 1960.

Peter Kemp, **The British Sailor, A Social History of the Lower Deck,** 1970.

Christopher Lloyd, **The British Seaman,** 1968.

C.N. Robinson, **The British Tar in Fact and Fiction,** 1909.

## The Language of Flags

E.M.C. Barraclough, **Flags of the World,** London/New York, 1969.

J.S. Corbett, **Fighting Instructions 1530-1816,** Navy Records Society, London, Volume XXIX, 1905.

J.S. Corbett, **Signals and Instructions 1776-1794,** Navy Records Society, London, Volume XXXV, 1908.

I.O. Evans, **Flags,** London, 1970.

P. Kannik, **A Handbook of Flags,** London, 1958.

Commdr. H.P. Mead, **Sea Flags – Their General Use,** Glasgow, 1938.

W.G. Perrin, **British Flags,** Cambridge, 1922.

A.A. Purves, **Flags for Ship Modellers & Marine Artists,** London, 1950.

Vice-Admiral R. Siegel, **Die Flagge,** Berlin, 1912.

## Fishing and Whaling

C.W. Ashley, **The Yankee Whaler,** London, 1938.

F.M. Davies, **An Account of the Fishing Gear of England and Wales,** London, 1958.

G.F. Dow, **Whale Ships and Whaling,** Salem, Mass., 1925.

W.C. Hodgson, **The Herring and its Fisheries,** London, 1957.

F.W.H. Holdsworth, **Deep-Sea Fishing and Fishing Boats,** London, 1874.

J.T. Jenkins, **The Sea Fisheries,** London, 1920.

B. Lubbock, **The Arctic Whalers,** Glasgow, 1937.

E. March, **Sailing Drifters,** London, 1952.

E. March, **Sailing Trawlers,** London, 1953.

## Navigation

C.H. Cotter, **A History of Nautical Astronomy,** London, 1968.

C.H. Cotter, **The Complete Nautical Astronomer,** London, 1969.

E. Forbes, **The Birth of Navigational Science,** National Maritime Museum Monograph no. 10, 1974.

J.B. Hewson, **A History of the Practice of Navigation,** Glasgow, 1951.

W.E. May, **A History of Marine Navigation,** London, 1973.

D.H. Sadler, **Man Is Not Lost,** London (HMSO), 1968.

E.G.R. Taylor, **The Haven Finding Arts: A History of Navigation from Odysseus to Captain Cook,** London, 1971.

D.W. Waters, **The Art of Navigation in England in Elizabethan and Early Stuart Times,** London, 1958.

## Tides and Currents

C.H. Cotter, **The Physical Geography of the Oceans,** London, 1965.

M. Deacon, **Scientists and the Sea: A Study of Marine Science,** London, 1971.

C.P. Idyll, **The Science of the Sea: A History of Oceanography,** London, 1970.

M.F. Maury, **The Physical Geography of the Sea,** Cambridge, Mass., 1963.

## Wind and Weather

C.R. Burgess, **Meteorology for Seamen,** Glasgow, 1963.

M. Deacon, **Scientists and the Sea; A study of Marine Science,** London, 1971.

G.E. Earl and N. Peter, **Maritime Meteorology,** London, 1961.

## Pilotage and Charts

L.A. Brown, **The Story of Maps,** Boston, 1949.

L.S. Dawson, **Memoirs of Hydrography,** London, 1969.

Vice-Admiral Sir A. Day, **The Admiralty Hydrographic Service 1795-1919,** London (HMSO), 1967.

D. Howse and M. Sanderson, **The Sea Chart: An Historical Survey based on the collections of the National Maritime Museum,** London, 1973.

C. Koeman, **The Sea on Paper: The Story of the Van Keulers and their 'Sea Torch',** Amsterdam, 1972.

G.S. Ritchie, **The Admiralty Chart: British Naval Hydrography in the Nineteenth Century,** London, 1967.

A.H.W. Robinson, **Marine Cartography in Britain: A History of the Sea Chart to 1885,** Leicester, 1962.

R.A. Skelton, **Explorer's Maps: Chapters in the Cartographic Record of Geographical Discovery,** London, 1960.

D.W. Waters, **The Rutters of the Sea: The Sailing Directions of Pierre Garcie,** New Haven, Conn., 1967.

## Navigational Instruments

S. Bedini, **Thinkers and Tinkers: Early American Men of Science,** New York, 1975.

H.R. Calvert, **Scientific Trade Cards in the Science Museum,** London (HMSO), 1971.

M. Daumas, **Scientific Instruments of the 17th and 18th Centuries and their Makers,** London, 1972.

R.T. Gould, **The Marine Chronometer,** London, 1960.

W.E. May and H.L. Hitchins, **From Lodestone to Gyro-compass,** London, 1952.

H. Quill, **John Harrison, The Man who found Longitude,** 1966.

E.G.R. Taylor and M.W. Ritchie, **The Geometrical Seaman: A Look at Early Nautical Instruments,** London, 1962.

E.G.R. Taylor, **The Mathematical Practitioners of Tudor and Stuart England 1485-1714,** Cambridge, 1970.

E.G.R. Taylor, **The Mathematical Practitioners of Hanoverian England 1714-1840,** Cambridge, 1966.

H. Wynter and A. Turner, **Scientific Instruments,** London, 1975.

## Inshore and Ashore

William Brady, **The Kedge-Anchor, or, Young Sailor's Assistant,** New York, 1857.

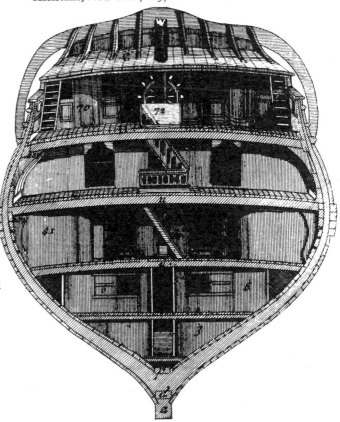

# Index